Religion in America

ADVISORY EDITOR

Edwin S. Gaustad

JOURNAL

OF THE

LIFE AND

RELIGIOUS LABOURS

OF

ELIAS HICKS

ARNO PRESS & THE NEW YORK TIMES
New York 1969

Reprint edition 1969 by Arno Press, Inc.

*

Library of Congress Catalog Card No. 78-83424

*

Reprinted from a copy in the
Library of the Union Theological Seminary

*

Manufactured in the United States of America

JOURNAL

OF THE

LIFE AND RELIGIOUS LABOURS

OF

ELIAS HICKS.

WRITTEN BY HIMSELF.

FIFTH EDITION.

NEW–YORK;

PUBLISHED BY ISAAC T. HOPPER.

1832.

PUBLISHED FOR THE PROPRIETORS.

NEW-YORK:

STEREOTYPED BY REES & REDFIELD.

No 216 William-street.

PREFACE

 AMONG the papers which were left by Elias Hicks, there were several manuscripts, written by himself, containing many particulars respecting his life and religious engagements. His connexions have collected these Memoirs, and now present them to the notice of the public. In performing this office, they believe that they will be rendering an acceptable and useful service to his survivors. To those who were personally acquainted with him, it will be interesting to review this brief record of his long and useful life; and to all, it may be animating and instructive to contemplate the feelings and experience of an individual, who, it will be seen, was, in his retired moments, as fervent in his aspirations for purity and humility of heart, as he was faithful and diligent in his public labours for the promotion of truth and righteousness in the earth.

CONTENTS.

CHAPTER I.

JOURNAL OF ELIAS HICKS.

CHAPTER I.

Birth, 1748.—Early visitations of Divine grace.—Apprenticeship.—Trials and temptations.—Marriage, 1771.—Renewed visitations of Divine love.—Appearance in the Ministry.—Situation of Friends during the war.—Journey to Philadelphia, 1779.—Visit to Friends on the Main, 1781.—Illness, 1781.—Visit on Long Island, 1782.—Visit to the Meetings on the Main, 1782.

HAVING experienced many mercies and preservations, both spiritual and temporal, in passing through this probationary state, I am induced to record some little account of them, under a sense of humble gratitude to my gracious and merciful Creator and Preserver.

I was born on the 19th day of the third month, 1748, in the township of Hempstead, in Queens county, on Long Island. My parents, John and Martha Hicks, were descended from reputable families, and sustained a good character among their friends and those who knew them. My father was a grandson of Thomas Hicks, of whom our worthy friend Samuel Bownas makes honourable mention in his journal, and by whom he was much comforted and strengthened, when imprisoned through the envy of George Keith, at Jamaica, on Long Island. Neither of my parents were members in strict fellowship with any religious society, until some little time before my birth. My father was at that period united in membership with Friends; but as his residence was mostly at some distance from meeting, and in a neighbourhood where very few Friends lived, my associates, when young, were chiefly among those of other religious persuasions, or, what was still worse for me, among those who made no profession of religion at all. This exposed me to much temptation; and though I early felt the operation of divine grace, checking and reproving me for my lightness and vanity, yet being of a lively active spirit, and ambitious of excelling in my play and diversions, I sometimes exceeded the bounds of true moderation, for which I often felt close conviction and fears on my pillow in the night season.

When I was about eight years old, my father removed his habitation and settled on a farm which his father had left him, on the south side of the island, near the sea shore. This introduced a new scene of diversion to my active mind, which was prone to pleasure and self-gratification. The shore abounded with fish and wild fowl, and I soon began to occupy myself with angling for the former, and shooting the latter. These amusements gained an ascendency in my mind, and although they were diversions for which I felt condemnation at later periods, yet I am led to believe that they were, at this time, profitable to me in my exposed condition, as they had a tendency to keep me more at and about home, and often prevented my joining with loose company, which I had frequent opportunities of doing without my father's knowledge. My mother was removed by death when I was about eleven years of age, and my father was left with the care of six children, three older, and two younger, than myself; and although he endeavoured to keep his children within the limits of truth, yet opportunities sometimes occurred to join with vain companions. But the Lord was graciously near to my poor soul in my tender years; and he followed me with his reproofs, and his dread made me afraid.

When I was about thirteen years of age, I was placed with one of my elder brothers who was married, and lived at some distance from my father's residence. I was here without any parental restraint; and mixing with gay associates, I lost much of my youthful innocence, and was led wide from the salutary path of true religion, learning to sing vain songs, and to take delight in running horses. Yet I did not give way to any thing which was commonly accounted disreputable, having always a regard to strict honesty, and to such a line of conduct as comported with politeness and good breeding. Nevertheless, I became considerably hardened in vanity, and on several occasions in riding races was exposed to great danger; and had it not been for the providential care of my heavenly father, my life would have fallen a sacrifice to my folly and indiscretion. O my soul, what wilt, or canst thou render unto the Lord for all his benefits, for his mercies are new every morning!

About the seventeenth year of my age, I was put an apprentice to learn the trade of a house carpenter and joiner, and this by no means placed me in a more favourable situation than before; for my master, although considered an orderly man, and one who frequently attended Friends' meetings, was yet in an eager pursuit after temporal riches, and was of but little use to me in my religious improvement. We had to go from place to place, as our business called, to attend to our work, and I was thereby introduced into hurtful company, and learned to dance and to pursue other frivolous and vain amusements. During my apprenticeship I passed through many trials and much exposure; and I have often thought, that had it not been for the interposition of divine mercy and goodness, I should have fallen a prey to the varied temptations which surrounded me; for although I was overtaken in many faults, in which my poor soul was deeply wounded, and for which I afterwards felt the just indignation of an offended God, yet when I have looked back on this scene of my life, and recounted the many snares that I escaped, all that is truly sensible within me has been bowed in humble admiration of the Lord's mercies and deliverance; and in reverent gratitude, I was made to praise and magnify his great and adorable name, "who is over all, God blessed for ever." In the midst of my vanity and exposure, the Lord, as a gracious father, was often near; and when I was alone, he inclined my mind to solid meditations.— Some of my leisure hours were occupied in reading the Scriptures, in which I took considerable delight, and it tended to my real profit and religious improvement.

My youthful companions would often endeavour to persuade me and each other, that the amusements, in which we spent much of our precious time, were innocent; yet being very early

2

convinced by the divine light that its teachings were truth, it had, in my calmer moments, an ascendency in my mind over all the reasonings and persuasions of men. Nevertheless, I had such a proneness to levity and self-gratification, that I often ran counter to clear conviction, and went on for a considerable time, sinning and repenting ; for the Lord in great mercy had regard to me in my tried condition, and often opened a door of reconciliation to my poor soul. But I was too weak to keep my covenants in the midst of so many temptations, until by his righteous judgments, mixed with adorable mercy, he opened to my mind, in a very clear manner, the danger I was in of falling into eternal ruin.

Under the weight of this impression, my heart, in the midst of merriment, was often made very sad ; and while engaged in the dance my soul was deeply sensible of its evil and folly : even my reasoning powers, when thus enlightened by the clear evidence of divine light, were made to loathe it as a senseless and insipid pursuit, and utterly unworthy of a rational being. But although I formed resolutions to refrain from this evil and others of a like nature, yet it was difficult to resist the importunities of my companions ; and I found by experience, that if I would altogether cease from them, I must wholly withdraw from the company of those who were inclined to such pursuits. On the last occasion that I was present at a dance. and in which I was pressed to take a part, I was brought under great concern of mind, and was struck with a belief, that if I now gave way after forming so many resolutions, and should again rebel against the light, I might be left in an obdurate situation, and never have another offer of pardon. I also clearly saw that this would be just, and that my blood would be upon my own head ; and feeling the dread of the Almighty to cover me, and a cry raised in my soul towards him, when I was called to participate in the dance, it seemed as though all my limbs were fettered, and I sat down and informed the company that I was now resolved to go no further. I was deeply tried, but the Lord was graciously near ; and as my cry was secretly to him for strength, he enabled me to covenant with him, that if he would be pleased in mercy to empower me, I would for ever cease from this vain and sinful amusement; and he instructed me, that if I would escape the danger of another trial, I must keep myself separate from such companions; and blessed for ever be his right worthy name, in that he hath enabled me to keep this my covenant with him from that time inviolate.

In looking back to this season of deep probation, my soul has been deeply humbled; for I had cause to believe that if I had withstood at this time the merciful interposition of divine love, and had rebelled against this clear manifestation of the Lord's will, he would have withdrawn his light from me, and my portion would have been among the wicked, cast out for ever from the favourable presence of my judge. I should also for ever have been obliged to acknowledge his mercy and justice, and acquit the Lord my redeemer, who had done so much for me; for with long-suffering and much abused mercy he had waited patiently for my return, and would have gathered me before that time, as I well knew, as a hen gathereth her chickens under her wings, but I would not. Therefore it is the earnest desire of my spirit, that the youth, and others whom it may concern, may wisely ponder their ways, and not think that the frivolous excuses which those make, who endeavour to justify themselves in such vain and wicked diversions, by saying that their parents judge it innocent, or their teachers have instructed them so to believe, or that under the law it was deemed admissible, will stand them in any stead in the day of solemn inquisition: for what are all these carnal reasonings worth, when weighed in the balance of the sanctuary, against one single conviction of the divine light in the secret of the heart. The last is clear and self-evident; the others are mere evasive excuses: and I often reflect with surprise on the conduct of those parents, who are spending their substance in hiring idle dancingmasters to teach their children this unnatural and unchristian practice, and who plead for excuse the example of righteous David. But how unlike is their dancing to his, who did it only in worship and honour to his God, and in conformity with the outward dispensation under which he lived. We have, however, a better and higher example than David, the Lord Jesus Christ, who is the mediator of a better covenant; this covenant is *inward*, even the law written upon the heart, which no outward example of others can ever abrogate or disannul ; nor do his doctrines or self-denying example in any wise approbate or justify this foolish and idle practice, but, in all parts thereof, condemn and disapprove it : for if none can be his disciples, except those who deny themselves, and take up their cross daily, as assuredly no others can, how can those be acceptable to him who are living in the daily gratification ot their own licentious wills, and spending their precious time and talents in such fruitless and vain sports.

His self-denying apostles also have left us neither example nor precept in justification of such wanton and evil amusements ; but we are exhorted by them to redeem the time, because the days are evil, and to use diligence to make our calling and election sure, and to follow them as they followed Christ : there is not a word of learning to dance, or of dancingmasters, but an exhortation to abstain from all idle and vain sports, and foolish talking and jesting, which are contrary to Christian gravity, and to the self-denying example of the blessed Jesus, who, when personally on earth, was a man of sorrows and acquainted with grief; and, therefore, the house of mourning is recommended to all who are wise in heart, for it is the fool's heart only that is captivated in the house of mirth.

My apprenticeship being now expired, I gradually withdrew from the company of my former associates, became more acquainted with Friends, and was more frequent in my attendance of meetings ; and although this was in some degree profitable to me, yet I made but slow progress in my religious improvement, until several years after I had entered into a married state. The occupation of part of my time in fishing and fowling had frequently tended to preserve me from falling into hurtful associations; but through the rising intimations and reproofs of divine grace in my heart, I now began to feel that the manner in which I sometimes amused myself with my gun was not without sin; for although I mostly preferred going alone, and while waiting in stillness for the coming of the fowl, my mind was at times so taken up in divine meditations, that the opportunities were seasons of instruction and comfort to me; yet, on other occasions, when accompanied by some of my acquaintances, and when no fowls appeared which would be useful to us after being obtained, we sometimes, from wantonness or for mere diversion, would destroy the small birds which could be of no service to us. This cruel procedure affects my heart while penning these lines; but my gracious Redeemer was drawing my mind from such low amusements, and I was led to consider conduct like this to be a great breach of trust, and an infringement of the divine prerogative. It therefore became a settled principle with me, not to take the life of any creature, except it was really useful and necessary when dead, or very noxious and hurtful when living. And, in exercising this privilege, we ought to be careful to do it in the most mild and tender manner in our power; for I think every candid mind must be convinced, that the liberty we have for taking the lives of other creatures, and using their bodies to support our own, is certainly an unmerited favour, and ought to be received by us as the bounty of our great benefactor, and be acknowledged with great humility and gratitude.

I have likewise from reflection, founded on observation, and from the nature and reason of things, been led to believe, that we frequently err by the liberty we take in destroying what we esteem noxious creatures; and not only abuse the power given us over them by our great Creator, but likewise act very contrary to our own true interest. For, as all in the beginning was pronounced good that the good God had made, we ought not to destroy any thing that has life, for mere gratification. It is our indispensable duty, as reasonable accountable beings, wisely to ponder our ways, and consider the consequent effect of all our conduct; for if we are to give an account of every idle word, how much more so of every presumptuous act.

In the twenty-second year of my age, apprehending it right to change my situation from a single to a married state, and having gained an intimate acquaintance with Jemima Seaman, daughter of Jonathan and Elizabeth Seaman, of Jericho, and my affection being drawn towards her in that relation, I communicated my views to her, and received from her a corresponding expression of affection; and having the full unity and concurrence of our parents and friends, we, after some time, accomplished our marriage at a solemn meeting of Friends, at Westbury, on the 2d of 1st month, 1771. On this important occasion, we felt the clear and consoling evidence of divine truth, and it remained with us as a seal upon our spirits, strengthening us mutually to bear, with becoming fortitude, the vicissitudes and trials which fell to our lot, and of which we had a large share in passing through this probationary state. My wife, although not of a very strong constitution, lived to be the mother of eleven children, four sons and seven daughters. Our second daughter, a very lovely promising child, died when young with the small pox, and the youngest was not living at its birth. The rest all arrived to years of discretion, and afforded us considerable comfort, as they proved to be in a good degree dutiful children. All our sons, however, were of weak constitutions, and were not able to take care of themselves, being so enfeebled as not to be able to walk after the ninth or tenth year of their age. The two eldest died in the fifteenth year of their age, the third in his seventeenth year, and the youngest was nearly nineteen when he died. But, although thus helpless, the innocency of their lives, and the resigned cheerfulness of their dispositions to their allotments, made the labour and toil of taking care of them agreeable and pleasant; and I trust we were preserved from murmuring or repining, believing the dispensation to be in wisdom, and according to the will and gracious disposing of an all-wise providence, for purposes best known to himself. And when I have observed the great anxiety and affliction, which many parents have with undutiful children who are favoured with health, especially their sons, I could perceive very few whose troubles and exercises, on that account, did not far exceed ours. The weakness and bodily infirmity of our sons tended to keep them much out of the way of the troubles and temptations of the world; and we believed that in their death they were happy, and admitted into the realms of peace and joy: a reflection, the most comfortable and joyous that parents can have in regard to their tender offspring.

In the spring after our marriage, my wife's relations gave me an invitation to come and live with them, and carry on the business of their farm, they having no other child than her. I accepted this proposal, and continued with them during their lives, and the place afterwards became my settled residence. My advantages, in a religious point of view, were greater than before; as I had the benefit of the company of several worthy Friends, who were my neighbours, and by whose example I was frequently incited to seriousness and piety; yet, having entered pretty closely into business, I was thereby much diverted from my religious improvement for several years. But, about the twenty-sixth year of my age, I was again brought, by the operative influence of divine grace, under deep concern of mind; and was led, through adorable mercy, to see, that although I had ceased from many sins and vanities of my youth, yet there were many remaining that I was still guilty of, which were not yet atoned for, and for which I now felt the judgments of God to rest upon me. This caused me to cry earnestly to the Most High for pardon and redemption, and he graciously condescended to hear my cry, and to open a way before me, wherein I must walk, in order to experience reconciliation with him; and as I abode in watchfulness and deep humiliation before him, light broke forth out of obscurity, and my darkness became as the noon-day. I had many deep openings in the visions of light, greatly strengthening and establishing to my exercised mind. My spirit was brought under a close and weighty labour in meetings for discipline, and my understanding much enlarged therein; and I felt a concern to speak to some of the subjects engaging the meeting's attention, which often brought unspeakable comfort to my mind. About this time, I began to have openings leading to the ministry, which brought me under close exercise and deep travail of spirit; for although I had for some time spoken on subjects of business in monthly and preparative meetings, yet the prospect of opening my mouth in public meetings was a close trial; but I endeavoured to keep my mind quiet and resigned to the heavenly call, if it should be made clear to me to be my duty. Nevertheless, as I was, soon after, sitting in a meeting, in much weightiness of spirit, a secret, though clear, intimation accompanied me to speak a few words, which were then given to me to utter, yet fear so prevailed, that I did not yield to the intimation. For this omission, I felt close rebuke, and judgment seemed, for some time, to cover my mind; but as I humbled myself under the Lord's mighty hand, he again lifted up the light of his countenance upon me, and enabled me to renew covenant with him, that if he would pass by this my offence, I would, in future, be faithful, if he should again require such a service of me. And it was not long before I felt an impressive concern to utter a few words, which I yielded to in great fear and dread; but O the joy and sweet consolation that my soul experienced, as a reward for this act of faithfulness; and as I continued persevering in duty and watchfulness, I witnessed an increase in divine knowledge, and an enlargement in my gift. I was also deeply engaged for the right administration of discipline and order in the Church, and that all might be kept sweet and clean, consistent with the nature and purity of the holy profession we were making; so that all stumbling blocks might be removed out of the way of honest inquirers, and that truth's testimony might be exalted, and the Lord's name magnified, "who is over all, God blessed for ever."

A war, with all its cruel and destructive effects, having raged for several years between the British Colonies in North America and the mother country, Friends, as well as others, were exposed to many severe trials and sufferings; yet, in the colony of New-York, Friends, who stood faithful to their principles, and did not meddle in the controversy, had, after a short period at first, considerable favour allowed them. The yearly meeting was held steadily, during the war, on Long Island, where the king's party had the rule; yet Friends from the Main, where the American army ruled, had free passage through both armies to attend it, and any other meetings they were desirous of attending, except in a few instances. This was a favour which the parties would not grant to their best friends, who were of a warlike disposition; which shows what great advantages would redound to mankind, were they all of this pacific spirit. I passed myself through the lines of both armies six times during the war, without molestation, both parties generally receiving me with openness and civility; and although I had to pass over a tract of country, between the two armies, sometimes more than thirty miles in extent, and which was much frequented by robbers, a set, in general, of cruel unprincipled banditti, issuing out from both parties, yet, excepting once, I met with no interruption even from them. But although Friends in general experienced many favours and deliverances, yet those scenes of war and confusion occasioned many trials and provings in various ways to the faithful. One circumstance I am willing to mention, as it caused me considerable exercise and concern. There was a large cellar under the new meeting-house belonging to Friends in New-York, which was generally let as a store. When the king's troops entered the city, they took possession of it for the purpose of depositing their warlike stores; and ascertaining what Friends had the care of letting it, their commissary came forward and offered to pay the rent; and those Friends, for want of due consideration, accepted it. This caused great uneasiness to the concerned part of the Society, who apprehended it not consistent with our peaceable principles to receive payment for the depositing of military stores in our houses. The subject was brought before the yearly meeting in 1779, and engaged its careful attention; but those Friends, who had been active in the reception of the money, and some few others, were not willing to acknowledge their proceedings to be inconsistent, nor to return the money to those from whom it was received; and in order to justify themselves therein, they referred to the conduct of Friends in Philadelphia in similar cases. Matters thus appearing very difficult and embarrassing, it was unitedly concluded to refer the final determination thereof to the yearly meeting of Pennsylvania; and several Friends were appointed to attend that meeting in relation thereto, among whom I was one of the number. We accordingly set out on the 9th day of the 9th month, 1779, and I was accompanied from home by my beloved friend John Willis, who was likewise on the appointment. We took a solemn leave of our families, they feeling much anxiety at parting with us,

3

on account of the dangers we were exposed to, having to pass not only the lines of the two armies, but the deserted and almost uninhabited country that lay between them, in many places the grass being grown up in the streets, and many houses desolate and empty. Believing it, however, my duty to proceed in the service, my mind was so settled and tiust-fixed in the divine arm of power, that faith seemed to banish all fear, and cheerfulness and quiet resignation were, I believe, my constant companions during the journey. We got permission, with but little difficulty, to pass the outguards of the king's army at Kingsbridge, and proceeded to Westchester. We afterwards attended meetings at Harrison's Purchase, and Oblong, having the concurrence of our monthly meeting to take some meetings in our way, a concern leading thereto having for some time previously attended my mind. We passed from thence to Nine Partners, and attended their monthly meeting, and then turned our faces towards Philadelphia, being joined by several others of the Committee. We attended New Marlborough, Hardwick, and Kingwood meetings on our journey, and arrived at Philadelphia on the 7th day of the week, and 25th of 9th month, on which day we attended the yearly meeting of Ministers and Elders, which began at the eleventh hour. I also attended all the sittings of the yearly meeting until the 4th day of the next week, and was then so indisposed with a fever, which had been increasing on me for several days, that I was not able to attend after that time. I was therefore not present when the subject was discussed, which came from our yearly meeting ; but I was informed by my companion, that it was a very solemn opportunity, and the matter was resulted in advising that the money should be returned into the office from whence it was received, accompanied with our reasons for so doing : and this was accordingly done by the direction of our yearly meeting the next year.

The yearly meeting closed on the 2d day of the following week ; and feeling my health a little restored, though still very weak, I left the city, and was taken by my kind friend John Shoemaker to his house. The next morning being rainy, and being still unwell, I rested here during the day, but my companion proceeded to attend the monthly meeting at the Falls. The next day I went to Byberry meeting, after which I rode with our valuable friend James Thornton to John Watson's, at Middletown, where I was again joined by my companion. We attended their monthly meeting, and found things in but poor order, and discipline at a low ebb, for want of faithful standard bearers. We then attended meetings, to some satisfaction, at Wright's Town, Plumbstead, and Buckingham. From thence we proceeded to the monthly meeting at Hardwick, where things appeared very low as to the right exercise of discipline ; but feeling our minds engaged, we laboured, in the ability received, for their assistance and encouragement. After this we passed on to the Drowned Lands, and attended a meeting with the few Friends of that place, and some others who came in ; but things, pertaining to religion, seemed at a very low ebb with them, which makes hard work for the poor traveller. From thence we went pretty directly to Nine Partners, and after having two meetings there, we proceeded to Oswego and Appoquague, and then to the monthly meeting at Oblong, in all which meetings truth was exalted, and I left them with peace of mind. We then turned our faces homeward, and after going a few miles on our way, we were overtaken by a constable, with a warrant from a magistrate to bring my companion before him, who, after examination, committed him to a board of commissioners, as a dangerous person to travel at such a time. We were led to believe, on inquiry, that this interruption was merely the fruit of envy, and occasioned by two acquaintances of my companion, who had fled from the Island for refuge. However, after a short detention, which gave me an opportunity of visiting a few families of my relations, and of attending a small meeting which I had passed from in some heaviness before, he was set at liberty, and we attended the quarterly meeting at Oblong. After this we passed on, taking meetings at Peachpond, Amawalk, and the monthly meeting at Purchase, and from thence proceeded home. I found my family well, which, together with the preservations and favours experienced in our journey, impressed my mind with thankfulness and gratitude to the great and blessed author of all our mercies. I was from home in this journey about nine weeks, and rode about eight hundred and sixty miles.

After the close of the aforesaid journey, I felt my mind engaged to make a general visit to Friends on the Main belonging to our yearly meeting; and with the concurrence of Friends, and in company with William Valentine, who, under a like concern, had agreed to be my companion, I left home on the 1st of the week, and 4th of 3d month, 1781, in order to accomplish the same. We sat with Friends in our own meeting, and then proceeded to Flushing; and the next day, the commanding officer of the king's troops at this place permitting us, we crossed the Sound to Frog's Neck, and lodged with our friend Joseph Caustin. On the following day we attended an appointed meeting at Westchester, and then went forward, taking meetings as they came in course for fifteen days successively, the last at Little Nine Partners: and although in many places meetings appeared in a low state, as to the life of religion, yet, through divine favour, help was afforded, insomuch that I generally left them with the satisfactory evidence, that my way had been rightly directed among them.

After the last mentioned meeting we set forward towards Saratoga, and lodged that night at an inn. The innkeeper's wife, in the course of some conversation, discovered that my companion and I were from Long Island, where the king's party bore rule , and she, being a friend to their cause, seemed to wonder much, that we should leave them, and come out among the Americans, signifying that if she was there, she should not be willing to come away ; and when I informed her that I expected we should shortly return thither again, her admiration was still more excited, and she was surprised how we should dare to act so : whereupon I took occasion to acquaint her how we stood in regard to the contending parties ; informing her that as we took no part in the controversy, but were friends to them and to all mankind, and were principled against all wars and fightings, the contending powers had such confidence in us, and favour towards us, that they let us pass freely on religious accounts, through both their armies without interruption ; a privilege, which they would not grant to their own people. This account made her marvel greatly, having never heard of the like before. She acknowledged it was very good, and wished for herself that she could come into the same situation, but said she could not, unless she first had retaliation for the wrongs she had received, after which, she said she should be willing to forgive them ; not considering, that there was nothing to be forgiven, where full pay or satisfaction had been received. Nevertheless, this is the natural condition and disposition of all wordly-minded men and women, who have not known, through the powerful influence of the gospel of Christ, the work of regeneration and the new birth, whereby they might experience redemption from such a malicious and revengeful spirit.

On the next day we proceeded to Coeman's Patent, on the west side of Hudson river, which we crossed at a place called Claverack landing. We reached there on 7th day evening, and the following day had a meeting with the few Friends, who had lately settled at that place, and some of their neighbours, who were mostly Baptists. It was the first Friends' meeting ever held there, and was a satisfactory season. We then rode that afternoon about twelve miles towards Albany, and lodged at an inn ; and the next day we reached Saratoga, since called Easton, and lodged with our friend Daniel Cornell. It was late in the night before we arrived, and the evening snowy ; and the country being newly settled, Friends' houses were generally but poor, so that several times, while in these parts, I felt the snow fall on my face when in bed. This affected me with a heavy cold when I first came here, but afterwards I was much favoured during the journey, having in good measure become inured to the hardships we had to go through. We attended the meetings belonging to this monthly meeting, being four in number ; viz. Saratoga alias Easton, Danby about forty miles further to the north east, White Creek, and Hoosack. The monthly meeting was held alternately at this latter place and Saratoga. We also visited nearly all the families belonging to this monthly meeting, and had good satisfaction, and a peaceful reward of our labours. From thence we went to New Britain and visited three families, in each of which there was but one member of our Society. We then returned to Nine Partners, and attended their monthly meeting, also several other meetings in that neighbourhood which we were not at in our way up. After this we attended Oblong quarterly meeting, and next the monthly meeting of Shapaqua; and then taking meetings at Purchase, Mamaroneck and Westchester, we passed the Sound again, and got safe home the 15th day of 5th month. I was gladly received by my family and friends, having been absent on this journey about ten weeks, and rode about eight hundred and fifty miles. We attended thirty-two meetings, six of which were monthly meetings, and one quarterly meeting, and visited about ninety families.

It was in the latter part of this journey, between Mamaroneck and Westchester, that we met with the interruption, which I before alluded to, from some of those robbers, who frequented the country between the two armies. I was a little ahead of my companion and some other Friends, and was met, and accosted by two of those persons in a very rough manner. I did not see them until they spoke, and one of them demanded very rudely to know where we were going. I looked calmly upon him, and informed him, without the least interruption of mind, where we were intending to go. He then interrogated me further, as to where we had been, what our business was, and where we were from, to all of which I gave true and suitable answers in a mild and pleasant tone. They seemed thereby to be entirely disarmed of their rage and violence, although they had just before robbed and beat a man; and the one, who had hitherto stood silent, being the most overcome, said to his fellow, "Come, let us go, the Quakers go where they please;" and, then turning away, they left us to pursue our journey without further interruption. I considered this as a merciful preservation through the interference of divine providence, who, by his power, not only sets bounds to the sea, and saith, "Hitherto shalt thou come, but no further; and here shall thy proud waves be stayed," but also limits the rage and will of wicked men, and turns them from their purpose; and thereby delivers, from their power and cruelty, those that put their trust in him.

In the fall of the year 1781, I was taken sick with a fever, which lasted for several months, in the course of which my strength became very much exhausted, and some of my friends were ready to conclude, that I should not continue long with them; yet, through the whole of my indisposition, I had to believe that I should recover. But through the exercise and distress both of body and mind which I experienced, it proved a very humbling dispensation to me. One circumstance in particular made it peculiarly exercising to my mind, although it was that on which I principally grounded my belief of recovery. When I was reduced nearly to the lowest state of bodily weakness, a prospect opened on my mind to pay a religious visit to some parts of our island where no Friends lived, and among a people, who, from the acquaintance I had with them, were more likely to mock, than to receive me, seeing that I considered myself but a child in such a service. But when the prospect first presented, it was very impressive on my mind, and an injunction seemed to attend requiring my assent thereto; and although I pleaded as an excuse my weakness and inability of body, as well as my unfitness, even if I was well, for such a service, yet with all my reasonings and pleadings I could feel no excuse granted me, and the requisition lay heavy upon me both day and night. By my thus standing out, I was brought very low both in body and mind; and finding that I could get no peace in this state of refusal, and that if I did not yield, my life must be taken for my stubbornness without any prospect of peace hereafter, I at length yielded to the heavenly call, which brought immediate peace and comfort to my afflicted soul; and the Lord was very gracious, opening many things for my encouragement. In the forepart of the next summer, having fully recovered my health, and apprehending the right time had arrived to perform this service, I opened it to the monthly meeting, and obtained its unity and concurrence, and two Friends agreed to bear me company. We set out about the middle of the 8th month, 1782, and had a very favoured meeting at Jamaica, with a considerable number of the inhabitants. After this we had a meeting at Samuel Doughty's, on the south side of the island, and then passed on to a Dutch settlement called Flatlands, where we had some difficulty to obtain a meeting, in consequence of the priest of the place being opposed thereto. The people seemed generally afraid to offend him, but said that if he would consent, they should be very willing to attend. However his assent could not be obtained, for he appeared very jealous lest his interest in the people should be affected. But there was one man, who seemed so much master of his own house, that he said we were welcome to have a meeting in it, let others say what they might. A meeting was accordingly appointed, which, although small, was a satisfactory opportunity. The master of the house and his wife, in an especial manner, seemed much affected therewith, and pressed us to come and see them again. From thence we passed on, and had meetings at Gravesend, New-Utrecht, and Springfield, all to good satisfaction. From the latter we proceeded home, feeling the comfortable reward of peace for this service, and very thankful to the Lord, my gracious helper, for his countenance and support therein. May his name be praised for ever.

In the latter part of 1782, I attended, with a committee of the yearly meeting, the quarterly meeting on the Main, and the monthly meetings thereunto belonging, on a proposition from the said quarterly meeting for a division thereof. We were absent about seven weeks, and rode about six hundred and sixty miles.

CHAPTER II.

In the fall of the year 1783, I attended the quarterly meeting at Nine Partners, also the meeting for sufferings, which was held there at this time; and, on my return, I was at the meetings held at Oswego and Perquage. I was from home about eleven days, and rode about one hundred and seventy miles. The reward of peace which I felt for this little service, and finding my family well on my return, excited gratitude and thankfulness of heart to the author of all our mercies and blessings; who richly rewardeth every labour of his dependent and devoted children.

A concern having for some time impressed my mind to pay a religious visit to the inhabitants of some of the adjacent towns, who were not in profession with us, and having obtained the unity and concurrence of my friends therein, I left home on the 1st day of the week, and 13th of 6th month, 1784, in order to perform that service. I attended our own meeting in the forenoon; and, in the afternoon, one appointed at Hempstead Harbour, to good satisfaction. Our next appointment was on 2d day, at a village called Herricks, where there was but little profession as to religion; nevertheless, we had a refreshing season among them. The power and presence of the Lord were witnessed to preside amongst us in an eminent manner. Many hearts were tendered; and the peaceable kingdom and government of the Messiah was exalted: to Zion's king may all the praise be ascribed, who only is worthy for ever.

4

From thence we went to the widow Cornell's at Success, where we lodged, and had a satisfactory meeting there the next day; many present were affected by the power of truth, which ran freely over all, to the comfort and refreshment of the sincere-hearted. After this we rode to Benjamin Doughty's and lodged; and the next day we had a meeting at the Little Plains, about a mile from our lodgings, among a loose airy people. The Lord's power was manifest for our help, bringing things close home to their several conditions. The day following, we attended two meetings, one at Jamaica, and the other at a place called the Fresh Meadows, near Flushing. Although the people were too generally at ease, and in an unconcerned state, with regard to their religious improvement, yet, through the interposition of divine goodness and mercy, some hearts were tendered by the convicting power of truth, and ourselves comforted in the faithful discharge of duty. After these opportunities, we rode to our friend Isaac Underhill's at Flushing, and lodged; and the next day attended a meeting appointed in Friends' meeting-house in that town, wherein the Master's presence was witnessed, to the comfort and satisfaction of the upright in heart.

From thence we went to Newtown, and lodged with a man not in profession with us. We had a meeting at his house the following day, wherein the spirit of truth favoured with gospel communication, suited to the states of those present, and relieving to my own mind. The four following days we attended meetings at the Kilns in Newtown, Bushwick, Brooklyn, Flatbush, Flatlands, and Gravesend. After the last, we turned our faces homeward, having a meeting at Samuel Doughty's, and another at a wigwam, among the black people and Indians; both satisfactory seasons. The next meeting was at Springfield, among a people, who appeared to be in a state of great darkness; but the Lord was pleased, by his own power, to command the light to shine in many hearts; insomuch that the meeting ended under divine favour. To Him alone may all the praise be ascribed, who is worthy for ever. The day following, attended two meetings; one at Foster's Meadow, the other at the widow Keziah Mott's.

After this we rode to my father's at Rockaway, on the south side of the Island ; and the next day attended a meeting there. The day following attended two meetings at Hempstead South, the latter at the house of our friend John Smith ; all, I trust, in a good degree, profitable and instructive seasons. Our next and last appointment, at this time, was in the town of Hempstead, the following day. It was a large satisfactory opportunity ; wherein divine help was afforded to minister suitably to the states of those present, and to the comfort and edification of many minds. To the Master of our assemblies, be the praise. Nothing is due to man. From hence I returned home, and found my family well ; having rode, whilst out, about one hundred miles.

A few weeks after my return from the aforesaid visit to the inhabitants of some of the adjacent towns, not feeling my mind relieved from the service, I again left home on the 4th of the 8th month following, in order to finish the visit. The first meeting I attended was again at Hempstead; and from thence proceeded along the south side of the island, having meetings at Thomas Seaman's near Jerusalem, and Thomas Sands' at Huntington South. The next was at Islip, on 7th day; but not feeling clear, I appointed another the following day, being the 1st of the week. This proved a satisfactory season. The same afternoon, I attended another meeting about thirteen miles farther east, at a place called Blue Point. Thence passing on along the south side of the island, I attended meetings at Patchogue, the Fire Place, South Hampton, North Sea, Amaganset and Montauk at the east end of the island, among the Indian natives. In all of them, strength was afforded to preach the gospel in a good degree of divine authority, and to the general satisfaction of those assembled, and the solid peace of my own mind.

After the meeting at Montauk among the natives, we returned that afternoon to a meeting at East Hampton, which we had appointed in our way down, and was held at the fifth hour. The priest of the town, and a considerable number of his hearers, attended, and all passed away quiet. We went from thence to the north part of the island, having meetings at Sagharbour, Shelter Island, Southold, Oyster Pond Point, and Stephen

Vail's, a little back from the Point; thence back by Riverhead to St. George's Manor, where we had a meeting, and all satisfactory seasons. We passed from thence by Wading River to Setauket, and Stonybrook, holding meetings at the two last places to good satisfaction. The meeting at Setauket, especially, was a solemn time; the Lord's presence was witnessed, to the tendering many hearts. After this we took meetings at Jonah Wood's, and James Oakley's, and from thence returned home, and found my family well; for which favour, with the peace and satisfaction I felt in the performance of this tour of duty, my mind was inspired with gratitude and humble acknowledgments to the Lord, my gracious helper.

In the 12th month following, feeling my mind drawn to a few places eastward, on the north part of the island, I again left home on the 2d of said month, and took meetings at Huntington, Cowharbour, Crab Meadow, Smithtown, Setauket, Wading River, Quoram, Joshua Smith's near the branch; and from thence home. In all those meetings, truth favoured me with ability to discharge myself faithfully, to the peace of my own mind; and, I trust, to the edification and instruction of the honest-minded in the several meetings.

Having felt drawings on my mind to pay a religious visit to some, not in profession with us, on the western part of our island, New-York, and Staten Island, and obtaining the concurrence of our monthly meeting, I proceeded therein, the 28th of 3d month, 1790, Fry Willis kindly bearing me company. Our first appointment was at Newtown, at the widow Smith's, who received us, and opened her house for a meeting, which was held to good satisfaction. The next day we had two meetings; the first, at Friends' meeting-house at the Kilns, the other, in the evening, at a neighbouring village, called Juniper Swamp; both favoured seasons, many hearts being tendered by the prevalence of the spirit of truth, which, through heavenly help, was exalted over all. The day following, way opening therefor, we had a meeting at Hurlgate in the afternoon, to the general satisfaction of those present, and to my own comfort; having been enabled to discharge myself faithfully, in a plain way among them. After this we proceeded to New-York, and the evening of the next day, we had a large, and, I trust, profitable meeting, in a public building called the City Tavern. Our next appointment was in Friends' meeting-house, the evening following; it was a very large collection, and, through the gracious extendings of divine mercy, the power of truth was exalted over all, to the comfort and strength of my own mind. and the solid satisfaction and rejoicing of many present.

The day following we passed to Staten Island, and the next day, being the 1st of the week, we had two meetings : the first, at the house of Peter Prawl, who was favourably inclined towards Friends. It was a favoured season, wherein the Master's presence was witnessed eminently to preside, and in the precious influence thereof, the gospel was preached in demonstration of the Spirit, and with power, to the awakening and tendering the hearts of many present : to the Lord only wise, be the praise and glory of his own work; for he only is worthy for ever. The meeting in the afternoon, held at the house of the widow of our friend Thomas Ridgway, proved a trying season, but I trust ended well. We had two more meetings on the island the next day, and the solemnity attending gave encouragement to hope, that they were of some use to those assembled. After this we returned to New-York with peace of mind, accompanied with the good wishes of many of those we had visited.

The day after our arrival in the city, Friends' monthly meeting was held, which we attended; and the evening of the next day, we had a large satisfactory meeting in the suburbs of the town, in a large building called the Hospital. The next day, at the tenth hour, visited the poor in the poor house. The visit was comfortable and satisfactory. At the third hour we had a pretty full meeting, in a house belonging to the Methodists, which they offered us for that purpose; and in the evening we had another large meeting in Friends' meeting house; both satisfactory seasons, and, I trust, comfortable and edifying to many who attended. The next day we visited a few families of Friends, as way opened, which closed our visit for this time to the city. The day after, being the first of the week, and the 11th of 4th month, we had a satisfactory meeting at Brooklyn. The two following days we attended two meetings on our way home, the first at Samuel Doughty's, at Jamaica South, the latter in Jamaica town; both favoured seasons, although many who attended were light and airy; yet the power of truth rising into dominion, a comfortable solemnity was spread over the assemblies. I left them in the enjoyment of true peace of mind, and returned to my family the evening following, and found all well; which, with other unmerited favours, witnessed in the course of this little engagement, filled my mind with thankful acknowledgments to the Shepherd of Israel, who is over all, worthy for ever.

In the latter part of the summer of this year, I performed a visit, in company with James Parsons of New-York, to some people favourably disposed towards Friends, who resided in the towns of Strafford and Sharon, in the State of Vermont, about fifteen miles west of Connecticut river. I left home the 28th of 7th month, and attended Purchase quarterly meeting, and a meeting on first day, at Cornwall in Connecticut, on our way, and then passed on to Northampton on Connecticut river; from thence up the east side of the river, through Massachusetts and part of New Hampshire, as far as Hanover; then crossing the river, we rode about fifteen miles westerly, to the town of Strafford, to the house of Timothy Blake, who was principally instrumental in collecting those people. Their first meeting was at his house. He appeared convinced of the principle of the inward light, as held by us; and had gathered a number into the same belief, in a good degree. They held two meetings when we came among them, one at his house, and the other at the adjacent town of Sharon; but, for want of keeping inward enough to the principle of divine light and grace, they became weak; and those, who apprehended it their duty to teach, had got too much out into words and speculative preaching and doctrine, which soon produced discord and a schism among them. They appeared to have been at times much favoured, and several of them had their understandings considerably illumined; insomuch that they were joined, at their request, in membership with Friends, and their meetings came under Friends' notice; but being far distant from any other meeting of the society, and not keeping low and little enough, they mostly became bewildered and scattered, and their meetings dropped. Yet a few kept, or regained, their first love; several of whom afterwards removed nearer to Friends. We passed several days among them; and then, taking leave, returned homeward by Danby, Saratoga alias Easton, and Hudson, to Nine Partners, attending meetings as they fell in our way, and reached Nine Partners in time for their quarterly meeting. After this we passed pretty directly home, attending a meeting at Shapaqua on first day. I was from home, on this journey, about three weeks and five days, attended two quarterly meetings, and seven particular meetings, and travelled about five hundred and ninety-one miles.

In the latter part of the winter, and spring of the ensuing year, in the drawings of gospel love, and with the unity of my friends, I performed a visit to a number of the adjacent towns and villages on our island, among those not in profession with us. I was from home about two weeks, and attended fifteen meetings, and rode about one hundred and fifteen miles.

A prospect having for some time impressed my mind to make a general visit to Friends of our yearly meeting, and to have some meetings among those not in profession with us, in parts adjacent, with the concurrence of my brethren at home, I set out on this service, the 23d of 10th month, 1791, and had meetings at Flushing, Newtown and Brooklyn, on my way to New-York. Our quarterly meeting was held there at this time; it ended on the sixth day of the week, and was a solemn season, and graciously owned by the Master's presence; many weighty subjects were opened through well qualified instruments, to the satisfaction and encouragement of the living. We were favoured with the company of our beloved friend Mary Ridgway, and her companion, from Ireland. The 29th, I proceeded on my journey, with Andrew Underhill, who had kindly given up to bear me company. We went by water to Staten Island, and the next day, being the first of the week, we attended two appointed meetings, the first at the house of a man inclined to Friends, whose wife was convinced of our principles; the latter at the house of a professor among the Methodists. Both were favoured seasons, many hearts being tendered through gospel communication, which flowed freely to the people. The 31st, we had another meeting on the island, at the house of the widow Ridgway; after this, in the evening, we had a favoured and instructive season with the widow's family. The next day we passed over to Rahway, in East Jersey. And on fourth day, the 2d of 11th month, we attended Friends' meeting at Plainfield, and an appointed meeting in the evening at Elijah Pound's, near Brunswick; both, I trust, profitable seasons to some present.— We returned next morning to Rahway, and attended Friends' meeting in that place; and one in the evening at Woodbridge, and returned to Rahway to lodge. The next day we passed over again to Staten Island, and had two meetings in the south-western part, wherein help was afforded to discharge myself faithfully, in a plain way, suited, as I believe, to the states of those who attended; they were of different professions, being Episcopalians, Presbyterians, Baptists, and Methodists. We returned again on seventh day evening to our lodgings at Rahway, to the house of our kind friend Joseph Shotwell; and the next day, being the first of the week, and 6th of the 11th month, we attended their forenoon and afternoon meetings; both, I trust, instructive edifying seasons, worthy of remembrance. To the Lord only wise, be the praise and glory of his own work, for to him it is due.

The following day we attended an appointed meeting at the eleventh hour in Elizabethtown, at the house of our friend Joseph Stackhouse; and, although small, yet it proved a satisfactory season; and in the evening, one at Newark, held in their court-house, which was large and much crowded. I was drawn forth among them in a large doctrinal testimony, I believe to general satisfaction, and greatly to the peace and relief of my own mind. Our next appointment was on the evening following, at a place called the English Neighbourhood, on the east side of Hackensack river, at the house of Thomas Frost, a physician. Although it was the first meeting appointed by Friends, ever held at that place, and the people mostly unacquainted with us and our principles, yet they came freely together, and generally behaved in an orderly and commendable manner. The meeting was much favoured, being evidently owned by the Head of the Church ; and ability was received to communicate divers things, relative to the true ground of real religion and spiritual worship, which appeared to obtain the general assent of those present. The next day, in the evening, we had a meeting at the house of our friend Daniel Lawrence, at Tappan, which, although small, was in the main a satisfactory season. On the three following days, we had two meetings, by appointment, on our way to Cornwall ; one at Kakiat, at the house of the widow Seaman, the other at William Thorne's, at Smith's Clove. In going to the latter place, we rode over the western part of the mountains, called the Highlands. We got to the house of our friend William Titus, at Cornwall, on seventh day evening. The next day attended Friends' meeting there, and one, by appointment, in the evening at New Windsor ; and lodged with our friend James Thorne. The next day crossed the Hudson river, and had a meeting at Fishkill, in our way to Nine Partners ; where we arrived on 3d day, and attended the quarterly meeting of Ministers and Elders, which opened at the eleventh hour. The two following days, the meeting for discipline and a parting meeting for public worship, were held. They were all favoured seasons, in which the faithful had cause to bless the name of the Lord, for his mercy in manifesting his gracious presence for the strength and help of his people and servants ; in a sense whereof, we parted from each other with mutual rejoicing.

On sixth day, we rode to Sharon in Connecticut, and the day following held a meeting for the town's people in a large upper room in their school-house. A considerable number attended ; and, through heavenly goodness, it proved a memorable time ; the testimony of truth went freely forth among them, powerfully reaching and tendering many hearts. To the Lord alone, be the praise.

After this meeting, we rode to the house of Simeon Prague, about three miles north of the town, and attended a meeting there that evening. Next day, being the first of the week, we rode to Goshen, and attended the meeting held there, at the

5

house of Charles Richards; notice having gone before of our coming, it was a pretty full meeting, and ended to satisfaction. We passed from thence to Tyringham, in the state of Massachusetts; and, on third day, attended a meeting in that neighbourhood. Then travelling on that afternoon and the next day, we got to Westfield, and lodged at an inn; and the following day, held a meeting at our lodgings, for the neighbourhood. After this we rode to Norwich, and attended a meeting that evening at the house of Phineas Mixer, which proved, through heavenly help, a comfortable edifying season, although the general part of those who attended were strangers to us and our principles. The three following days, we passed on through the towns of Northampton, Hadley, Sunderland, Montague, Northfield and Walpole, to John Cook's, in Claremont, where we appointed a meeting to be held the next day. Our landlord undertook to give the notice to his neighbours; and having heard that Friends sometimes sit their meetings in silence, he was afraid, as he afterwards informed me, to notify any of the meeting, except two or three of his particular friends; lest, if it should prove silent, they might laugh him to scorn. In consequence thereof, the meeting was very small. But such was the kindness of divine Providence, that he did not fail to manifest his presence powerfully among, as it were, the two or three, to the conviction and reproof of our unfaithful landlord; insomuch that he informed me, when I came that way again, that his folly and blindness had given him much trouble and distress; and he was now very pressing and desirous I would appoint another meeting, that he might give all the neighbourhood general notice. But we let him know, that we were not at our own disposal; and, as no way appeared open in our minds for such an appointment at present, we could not comply with his desire.

After the last mentioned meeting, we passed the next day to Windsor, the most south-easterly town in the state of Vermont, on the west side of Connecticut river. Here we had a meeting in their court-house, which was very commodiously fitted up for the purpose, and proved a solid satisfactory opportunity. After this we rode to James Willard's, in the town of Hartland; who, although brought up without any particular knowledge of Friends, was yet so far one in principle with us, that he had maintained, by himself alone, a testimony against a hireling ministry, against fighting, and oaths, and the superstitious observance of days; and had, by sound reasoning, so far defeated all his opponents, that he was permitted to remain quiet; although his residence had mostly been among those rigid in the Presbyterian profession. We had a meeting in his house, which appeared always to be open to Friends, after his gaining an acquaintance with them; but it being on the day set apart by those in authority as a day of thanksgiving, the meeting was small.

We took leave of our kind landlord, and journeyed forward; and got to the town of Sharon the next day, to the house of Jared Bassett, who, with some of his neighbours, who were likewise measurably convinced of our principles, held meetings together, after our manner. Here we continued some days, visiting those people, and attended their meeting on first day, the 4th of 12th month; which, through favour, was, I trust, a profitable, edifying season.

On third day we rode over to Hanover, a town on the east side of Connecticut river. And the day following had a meeting in the east part of said town, among a people mostly of the Baptist profession; it was, I trust, an instructive season; things, relating to true religion and spiritual worship, being largely opened. And after the meeting, we had some free conversation on several material points; viz. election, falling from grace, water baptism and the right use of the scriptures, all of which were opened apparently to the satisfaction of most present. The evening of the next day, we had an appointed meeting near Dartmouth College, which proved a very disturbed opportunity, by reason of the attendance of the young students, whose behaviour was very rude and unbecoming; nevertheless, I hope the season was profitable to some present.

We returned the next day to Jared Bassett's, at Sharon, and the following day attended two meetings, one at Strafford, and the other in the evening at a place called the Hollow. After this we returned again to Jared Bassett's, and the next day, being the first of the week, and the 11th of 12th month, we attended the meeting at his house; which, with the two last, were, to myself at least, satisfactory seasons; feeling conscious of having discharged my duty faithfully among them, and having the answer of peace therein. The next day we set out for Danby, the nearest meeting of Friends to this place; but by reason of a great fall of snow, and the way being mountainous, we did not arrive there until the third day after we set out. The next day after our arrival, their monthly meeting began, which continued two days. It was a low time, wherein I felt my mind much oppressed with the apparent careless indifferent way in which Friends there conducted the weighty affairs of the Church; many of them appearing to act in their own will, in as light a manner, as they would in their own trivial outward business. Much labour was bestowed in a plain way, in order to impress their minds with the necessity of being more weighty in their spirits, when they presumed to be active in the affairs of truth; and, I hope, to the encouragement of the honest hearted. We stayed their first day meeting, which was large, and proved a trying season; but I was favoured to relieve my mind among them, although they appeared too generally insensible of the operation of truth.

After meeting, we rode that afternoon, on our way towards Lake Champlain, about twelve miles, and attended a meeting at the house of our friend Joseph Button, that evening, among a people mostly of the Baptist profession. It was a favoured season, and ability was received to open many things, in a plain way, relating to the Christian religion. The strange doctrine of absolute personal election and reprobation was exposed, also that of the impossibility of falling from grace; and the true baptism explained, in opposition to that of water. The next day we pursued our journey towards Lake Champlain, where we arrived on second day, and were in the neighbourhood of the lake, in different towns, for about fifteen days, and attended eleven meetings among Friends and others, to general satisfaction, and the peace of my mind.

After this we returned to Danby, and from thence we passed on, through Queensborough, to Saratoga and Easton; in which neighbourhood we had divers comfortable and edifying meetings, among Friends and others. Then we went on through Pittstown, Williamstown, East Hoosack, New Britain, Kline-kiln, Coeman's Patent, crossing the Hudson river on the ice to the last mentioned place, and from thence to Hudson; most of the way upon the ice on the river. We had a meeting at each of those places to good satisfaction, also one at Hudson the next day after our arrival there. After this we passed on, attending meetings at Little Nine Partners, and one at the house of our friend Tideman Hull; thence to the Creek, where we had a precious opportunity on the first day of the week, in a large meeting of Friends and others. Then having meetings at Crum-elbow and Oswego, we got in time to Nine Partners, to attend their preparative meeting the fifth day following, which proved a comfortable season; and the next day attended a profitable meeting, appointed at a place called Chesnut Ridge. The two following days we attended two meetings, one at the Branch, and the other on the hill at Oblong; and the day after, their monthly meeting; and returned to Nine Partners to attend the quarterly meeting, which began the next day.

The quiet and comfort of this meeting seemed much interrupted by the forwardness and inexperience of some in the ministry, which was cause of much affliction to my mind. Oh what great need there is for those, who apprehend themselves called to that great and solemn office, to know self wholly reduced; for, otherwise, there is danger of their endeavouring to clothe themselves with the Lord's jewels, which, nevertheless, will turn to their own shame and confusion. I had some close exercise in the meeting of Ministers and Elders on that account. On sixth day we were at the monthly meeting at the Creek, which was attended with a degree of divine power, but not without suffering some hurt, by the forward unskilful workmen before mentioned.

From this meeting we crossed the Hudson again, and had meetings at Little Esopus, Marlborough, and Newburg Valley; and then returned to Nine Partners, and attended their monthly meeting. After this, taking leave of Friends there, we turned our faces homewards, having meetings at Amawalk, Joseph

Weeks' near Salem, Purchase, Mamaroneck, and Westchester; all favoured seasons, especially the last, which was mostly composed of those not in membership with Friends. I was enabled through divine aid, to open much doctrine to them, suitable to the occasion, and to the states of those present, to their general satisfaction; and I felt great peace in my labour, not only for the service of this meeting, but for all my past labour in this journey; wherein I had been graciously favoured, to my humbling admiration. To the Lord only wise, be all the glory.

The next day we rode to New-York, where I lodged with my kind companion, and was cordially received by his beloved wife, and many other near and dear friends. We had been from the city four months and three days. The next day being the first of the week, I attended their forenoon and afternoon meetings, which were large; and the day following rode to my own home, and, with a mind full of peace and solid satisfaction, the sure reward of obedience, found my dear wife and children all well: for which favour, also for the manifold unmerited mercies and preservations I have from time to time received, my spirit bows in humble adoration before thee, O Lord God of our health and salvation, and desires to ascribe unto thee greatness, with glory, thanksgiving, and high renown; for thou art worthy to receive it, throughout all ages and generations, world without end. Amen.

I was from home on this journey four months and eleven days; rode about one thousand five hundred miles, and attended forty-nine particular meetings among Friends, three quarterly meetings, six monthly meetings, and forty meetings among other people.

In the latter end of the 7th month, 1792, I left home, in company with some other Friends, by appointment from the yearly meeting of Ministers and Elders, to visit the subordinate meetings throughout the yearly meeting. I was from home nearly a month, in which time we visited most of the meetings of Ministers and Elders, and attended many other meetings; and, I believe, the visit was truly useful. We had many seasonable and comfortable opportunities among Friends, and, I trust, the labour was blessed to some, and I felt peace of mind for this little service.

A concern having for some time rested on my mind, in the feelings of gospel love, to pay a religious visit to Friends in New England, in the spring of 1793, I opened it to my friends, and obtained their certificate for that purpose. But I did not proceed therein till after our yearly meeting. I left home the 2d of 6th month, being the first of the week, and after attending our own meeting, I crossed the Sound that afternoon, and got to the house of our friends Daniel and Samuel Titus at Horseneck, that evening. Here I met my companion James Mott from Mamaroneck, who had kindly given up to be my companion in this journey. We set forward next morning through the state of Connecticut, which took near three days, and arrived on fourth day evening at the house of our friend Amos Collins in Stonington, and the next day attended Friends' meeting at Hopkinton, in the state of Rhode Island. From thence we proceeded on towards Newport, attending meetings in our way, at Westerly, Richmond, South Kingston, Upper and Lower House, and Canonnicut Island; all satisfactory opportunities. After this we crossed the ferry to Newport, and lodged at the house of our kind and very hospitable friend, the widow Mary Rodman, who, with her two worthy daughters, Sarah and Hannah, treated us with great kindness and affection; and where we continued to lodge, during our stay in that town. The meeting of Ministers and Elders opened the next day at Portsmouth. After this we lodged that night at our friend Jacob Mott's, and the next day attended a meeting for worship at that place, which was very large; although things appeared very low, as to the life and virtue of truth, both among Friends and others, and lukewarmness and indifference seemed to prevail, which made it a laborious time for the honest travellers, yet ability was afforded to discharge myself among them to a good degree of satisfaction, and peace to my own mind; and we returned that evening to Newport.

The yearly meeting closed on the third day following; and although strength was afforded me to discharge myself in the several sittings thereof, both for worship and discipline, in a manner productive of that true peace, which is the sure reward of a faithful discharge of duty, yet it was, for the most part, a dull time, and the spring of life seemed very low; occasioned, in part, as I apprehended, by a very small number taking upon them the whole management of the business, and thereby shutting up the way to others, and preventing the free circulation and spreading of the concern, in a proper manner, on the minds of Friends; which I have often found to be of very hurtful tendency.

On fourth day morning we left Newport, and rode to Portsmouth, and attended their preparative meeting. The forepart of the meeting for worship was a heavy season, in which it was my lot to be baptized for the dead; but, as I patiently abode under suffering with the pure seed, the Lord was pleased to arise, and give ability to come forth, and sound an alarm to the lifeless; whereby his power and presence were experienced, in good measure, to cover the meeting, to the comfort and encouragement of the living travellers; to the Lord alone be the praise, who is worthy for ever.

The next day we passed the ferry, and rode to Tiverton, on the Main, and attended a meeting, by appointment, which was chiefly made up of people not of our society. Through the prevalence of divine love, after a season of close labour, strength was afforded me, largely to open the truths of the gospel, in a clear manner, greatly to my own satisfaction, and apparently so to most or all present; for which my spirit was truly thankful. The next day we attended a meeting at Little Compton, which was large, and mostly composed of people of other persuasions. It was a comfortable edifying season; the Lord was graciously pleased to be near, and to afford wisdom and utterance; many things were opened in a doctrinal way, suitable to the states of those present, in the clear demonstration of the spirit, and with power; in a sense whereof, the living were made to rejoice, and return thankful acknowledgments for such unmerited mercy.

The day after, we attended the monthly meeting of Friends of Acoakset, held at Westport; the meeting for worship was very large, and like the former, mostly composed of people of other persuasions. Ability was afforded me largely to open the nature of true worship, and to show the fruitlessness of mere outward performances in religion, without the animating, quickening virtue of the word of eternal life, influencing and assisting the soul in that solemn act. The meeting for discipline was small, and very few of those present appeared to be under right qualifications to be active in the affairs of the Church ; consequently their business was conducted in great weakness, and in a way far short of maintaining the proper dignity of a monthly meeting. No way seemed to open to afford relief; as the disorder and weakness appeared to be much in those, who assumed the place of leaders and heads in the meeting, and great and uncommon rawness in most of the youth. Under the consideration thereof, my mind was deeply affected with concern for their own, and the testimony's, sake.

Our next appointment was at Centre, on first day ; and previous notice having been given of our coming, the meeting was very large ; there were many more than the house could hold, and it was a precious edifying season. We then rode to Newtown, taking some refreshment on our way ; and attended a meeting at the fourth hour in the afternoon, which was large, and proved a satisfactory opportunity, and I felt sweet peace in this day's labour.

The next day we attended the monthly meeting of Aponegansett, alias Dartmouth, which proved a hard, painful season, things being much out of order with Friends there. Most of the young people, and some of those that were older, were very raw and ungoverned ; insomuch that the meeting was much interrupted by an almost continual going in and out, although frequently reproved for it. It rendered the prospect very afflicting, to see the professors of truth so regardless of their own reputation and real good, as well as of the good and reputation of society. I left this place with a degree of sadness, on account of the prevailing darkness and ignorance ; yet I felt peace to attend my mind, having faithfully discharged myself among them.

We rode after meeting to New Bedford, in company with our

6

beloved friend Thomas Rotch, who met us at this place; and we lodged at his house, where we found a cordial reception, and kind entertainment from him and his beloved wife, who appeared to be hopeful young Friends. The next day we attended their monthly meeting, which proved a very comfortable, edifying season. This monthly meeting was but newly settled, and Friends appeared desirous of improvement. There were a number of promising young Friends in this place, to whom my spirit was nearly united, and a sympathetic travail experienced for their growth and preservation. My mind was covered with much sweetness in the course of this meeting, and it proved a time of revival to my spirit; having experienced much depression and discouragement in the two foregoing monthly meetings.

The next day we rode to Long Plain, and attended a meeting at the eleventh hour, which proved, through heavenly help, a comfortable, edifying season. After this we rode back to Accushnet, and attended a meeting at the fourth hour that afternoon, in which I found it my business to set the people an example of silence; and returned that evening to our lodgings at New Bedford. The next day we embarked for Nantucket, and arrived there before night, having sailed about sixty miles in our way thither. We took our lodgings at the house of our kind friend Samuel Rodman, and stayed on the island several days, in which time we attended their monthly meeting, and a meeting of Ministers and Elders belonging thereto; and two meetings on the first day of the week. After this, on second and third day, their quarterly meeting was held, and on fourth day I was at their meeting held in the middle of the week, in the north meeting-house. Although things in general were much out of order with many of the professors of truth in this island, and the pure seed of the kingdom much oppressed, and gloominess seemed to spread over the camp, yet the Lord Almighty, in the riches of his love, was pleased to furnish ability to sound an alarm to the dead, and to press upon the lukewarm and careless professors, the necessity of using all diligence to make their calling and election sure, while time and opportunity were yet graciously afforded : and also to administer Gilead's balm, to bind up the broken-hearted, and to encourage the faithful labourers in the family, to a perseverance in faith and patience. To a remnant of these, my spirit was nearly united in the real bond of Christian fellowship, and our hearts were filled with gratitude to the God and Father of all our sure mercies, that he was graciously pleased to distil the heavenly dew for refreshing the weary travellers, and crowning the several meetings with the glorious diadem of his holy presence; to him alone be the praise, for he is worthy for ever.

On fifth day, the 4th of 7th month, we left the island, and crossed over to Falmouth, about forty miles, by water; after landing, we travelled about four miles to the house of our friend Richard Lake, and lodged. The next day we attended their monthly meeting, which proved a time of deep exercise to my spirit; occasioned, as I believed, by the dead and lifeless state of the professors of truth in that meeting. I sat through the meeting for worship in silence, under a great weight of death and suffering, and saw no way of relief until near the close of the meeting for discipline, when a prospect opened in my mind, with a degree of light, to propose to Friends, that the men and women should sit together again at the close of their business. This proposition was agreed to by Friends, and way was made to clear my mind, in a good degree, amongst them, of the burden I had sat under, in a close searching communication of my prospect respecting their state, as it opened in the view of my mind. This appeared to have considerable effect on the minds of some, yet some others appeared too much in that state, of all others the most to be dreaded, of self-justification, and of being righteous in their own eyes, which rendered them indisposed to improvement.

I left that place the day following, with some weight on my spirit, under a sense of the low state of things among them, and rode to Yarmouth, and attended a meeting there the next day, which proved a satisfactory season. The three following days we passed on through Sandwich, Pembroke, and Boston, to Salem; having meetings at Sandwich and Pembroke, both, I trust, profitable edifying seasons to some present. We reached Salem on fifth day, the 11th of 7th month, just in time to attend their

monthly meeting, having rode diligently the morning and afternoon before to accomplish it; and had a pretty satisfactory time
with Friends at this meeting. After this we rode back to Lynn,
and the next day attended an appointed meeting there, which
proved a large, favoured, and I trust, profitable meeting to many,
not soon to be forgotten; there were a considerable number of
hopeful young people in this place. In the afternoon, we had a
precious opportunity at a Friend's house, where there were a
number of young people and others collected; it was a heart-
tendering season. For this, with other favours conferred from
time to time, my heart was made truly thankful to the Father of
mercies, and God of all comfort, who is over all, blessed for ever.

We proceeded the next day to Almsbury, and lodged with our
friend Ezekiel Jones, and the next morning rode back to Newbury, and attended Friends' meeting at the eleventh hour. Although the meeting was small, Friends being much reduced
there, yet some of the neighbouring people coming in we had a
precious opportunity together, to our mutual comfort; the way
of life and salvation being clearly opened to them, in the demonstration of the spirit, and with power; for which my spirit was
reverently thankful. We rode back and attended a meeting at
Almsbury that afternoon, at the fourth hour; a large number of
those, who were not members of our society, assembled with the
few Friends of that place, insomuch that the house could not contain them. It proved a painful season, by reason of the prevailing
death and darkness that seemed to spread, not only over Friends,
but the assembly in general. My spirit was brought into a state
of deep suffering and baptism, but as I patiently endured the
conflict, way was made, and ability afforded, to open to them
their states and conditions, with the necessity of being redeemed
therefrom, and the way whereby it must be effected. The people were generally solid, and I trust it was a profitable season to
many minds present.

We returned that evening to the house of our friend Ezekiel
Jones, and the next day proceeded to Newtown, where we had a
meeting, which proved, I trust, an instructive edifying season to
some present; although the life of religion appeared very low in

that place. We lodged here, and the day following we went to Halestown alias Wear, and took our lodgings at the house of our friend Ebenezer Breed. We attended their monthly meeting next day; things in general appeared in a low state with Friends here, much of which weakness I apprehended arose from these two causes. First, from a forward spirit, which appeared very predominant in some members, who were not under a right qualification to be active in meetings for discipline, not having their spirits sanctified: and their unseasoned offerings and forward activity were a great burden to the living concerned members, being often opposed to the right exercise of discipline, which caused divisions and parties in the meeting: Secondly, those Friends who seemed to have the cause of truth at heart, for want of dwelling enough in the root, and in that perfect love that casts out all fear, were led from an apprehension of necessity, in order to keep down those forward spirits, to make use of some undue methods in the exercise of discipline. This, originating in fear, and being the result of human contrivance, instead of subjecting, had a tendency to strengthen them, in their opposition : for nothing can promote the Lord's work but his own peaceable spirit and wisdom, and this stands out of all human consultation and contrivance, which, when given way to, although ever so well intended, always mar his work. I was much exercised, both in the meeting for worship, and that for discipline ; and I was helped to administer much counsel and advice for Friends' improvement in general, and particularly that those before mentioned difficulties might be removed ; and felt much peace in my labour.

The next day, being the 5th of the week, and 19th of 7th month, we rode to Epping, about forty-two miles, and lodged with our friend Joshua Fulsome, an approved minister, and attended Friends' meeting there the following day. In the forepart of this meeting, my mind was reduced into such a state of great weakness and depression, that my faith was almost ready to fail, which produced great searchings of heart, so that I was led to call in question all that I had ever before experienced. In this state of doubting, I was ready to wish myself at home, from an apprehension that I should only expose myself to reproach, and wound the cause I was embarked in ; for the heavens seemed like brass, and the earth as iron ; such coldness and hardness, I thought could scarcely have ever been experienced before by any creature, so great was the depth of my baptism at this time ; nevertheless, as I endeavoured to quiet my mind, in this conflicting dispensation, and be resigned to my allotment, however distressing, towards the latter part of the meeting a ray of light broke through the surrounding darkness, in which the Shepherd of Israel was pleased to arise, and by the light of his glorious countenance, to scatter those clouds of opposition. Then ability was received, and utterance given, to speak of his marvellous works in the redemption of souls, and to open the way of life and salvation, and the mysteries of his glorious kingdom, which are hid from the wise and prudent of this world, and revealed only unto those, who are reduced into the state of little children and babes in Christ. It proved a time of renewed strength and consolation to myself, and I trust it was so to many present. Renowned for ever be the name of the Lord, who hath his way in the cloud, and in the thick darkness, and who can cause the light to shine out of obscurity, when he pleaseth, for the comfort and help of his devoted children, and cause their darkness to become as the noonday.

We passed on from thence through Dover to Berwick, where the monthly meeting for Dover was held the next day. It proved a very exercising season, great weakness attending the meeting, on account of the same rending, dividing spirit getting in among Friends there, mentioned at the foregoing monthly meeting at Wear. It had made great havoc among them ; a great number of members had been separated, and others were about to be separated, by minutes of denial from the monthly meeting. I had some close labour with them, not only by endeavouring to stir up and warn the careless and refractory members ; but I also found it necessary to caution and warn those, who had the chief management of discipline. I believed they had too much departed from the meek spirit of Jesus, in ordering the affairs of truth ; and instead of giving the right portion of meat in due season to their fellow members, had given way to a spirit of impatience, and therefore did not stand wholly clear of beating and abusing their fellow servants. O how necessary it is for all those, who think themselves called to be active in the discipline of the Church, to know their own spirits fully subjected, that nothing of the unmortified will of the creature may be found acting in the work of the Lord; or mixing its own forward unsanctified zeal, with that true and holy fervour of soul, which animates, quickens, and constrains, by the mere force and influence of the pure love of Christ, our holy head, and heavenly high priest, from whence it derives all its power and authority, in putting right discipline in practice, and laying true judgment on the head of transgressors, and refractory members. We tarried here the next day, it being the first of the week. The meeting was pretty large, and was composed of Friends and others, and favoured with the reachings forth of heavenly regard, consoling many hearts, and refreshing the weary travellers; of these, there appeared to be a small remnant preserved in almost every place. The meeting ended with humble supplication, and praise to the great Author of every blessing, who is over all, worthy for ever.

The next day, the 22d of 7th month, we proceeded on towards Falmouth, at Casco Bay, attending a meeting at Portland, in our way thither. On fourth day we attended the monthly meeting of Falmouth, and, on sixth day, the monthly meeting of Durham; they were in general satisfactory seasons. The next day we rode to Georgetown, and attended a meeting appointed there at the eleventh hour. After this we proceeded on to the widow Gardner's, in a town called Bordingham; in getting to this place, we had to cross the great river Kennebeck twice. The next day, being the first of the week, and the 28th of 7th month, a large meeting was held there by our appointment, there being no meeting in that place. It was a time of hard labour for a season, by reason of the indifference and ignorance of many present; nevertheless, ability was afforded to discharge myself among them, to pretty good satisfaction, and, I believe, generally so to those present; and, I trust, by some, the season will not soon be forgotten.

We went by water that afternoon up the aforesaid river, about seven miles, to the house of our friend George Ramsdale, having sent our horses there the night before. The next day we passed on to Vassalborough, and the day following rode up the river to Fairfield, and attended a meeting, and returned to Vassalborough that afternoon. The next day we attended Friends' meeting there, which proved a heavy dull season, till near the close, when ability was afforded me to clear myself among them, in a close searching communication, which appeared to have a good effect, and the meeting ended well.

We passed on that afternoon twenty miles to Winthrop, and the next day had a meeting there. After this we rode to Greene, and from thence to Lewistown, having a meeting at each place; both precious heart-tendering seasons, especially the latter, which was attended by a large number of young people, many of whom were greatly affected by the power of truth. We left them in a tender loving frame of mind, and rode that afternoon to Durham. The next day, being the first of the week, and 4th of 8th month, we attended Friends' meeting there, in which I was favoured to open many things in a doctrinal way, there being many present, who were not in membership with Friends. I was likewise led to speak largely of the good effects of pure love.

We passed on from thence through Falmouth to Portland, where we had a meeting appointed for the town's people; it was held in their court-house, and was, through heavenly help, an instructive season. Many doctrines of the gospel were clearly opened; and the unsound doctrines of original sin and predestination, also the schemes of the Universalists, Atheists, and Deists, were confuted from scripture and reason. And a pressing exhortation was extended to all present, to attend to the leadings of the spirit of Christ in their own hearts, so as to be sensible of their fallen condition, and to become acquainted with the neces-sity, means, and manner of their salvation. Truth was over all, and I had great peace in my labour.

We returned that evening to Falmouth, and the next day went to Windham, and attended a meeting, wherein I was led to be an example of silence. After this we rode to the house of our friend John Robinson, and lodged; and a prospect opening for paying another visit to Friends at Wear, we accordingly proceeded, attending meetings in our way, at Gorham, Lymington, New Sandwich, and Gilmantown, all satisfactory seasons; and reached Wear in time to attend their monthly meeting. Although the same dividing spirit was still discernible among them, which produced much weakness, yet we had pretty good satisfaction in our visit. We proceeded from thence through Pittsfield, and Lee, in our way to Dover, having a meeting at each place, and reached Dover in time to attend their monthly meeting, held on seventh day, the 17th of 8th month. Although discipline is at a low ebb with Friends here, yet, through divine condescension, I hope the season was profitable and instructive to many present. We were at their first day meeting in the forenoon; and, in the afternoon, had a satisfactory meeting at Kittery; and, on second day, we attended meetings at Madersborough, and Rochester, both, I trust, profitable seasons. On third day we rode to Hampton, and the next day had a comfortable meeting with Friends of that place; and from thence we returned to Salem, and attended a meeting. Then we proceeded to Lynn, and attended their forenoon and afternoon meetings on first day. On second day we rode to Boston, and attended a meeting at the eleventh hour; although the meeting was but small, there being but very few Friends in that place, and only a small number of the town's people came in, yet we had pretty good satisfaction in giving them this opportunity, and way opened to clear ourselves among them. After this we passed on, having a meeting at Taunton, and then attended Providence monthly meeting, held at Smithfield; things appeared but low with Friends of this monthly meeting, their attention being too much turned to worldly concerns. We next attended the monthly meeting held in the upper part of Smithfield, being about nine miles from the latter; this was in general a satisfactory season; and the following day we attended Uxbridge monthly meeting, to good satisfaction.

7

Our next appointment was at Freetown, the first of the week, and the 1st of 9th month, and was a satisfactory opportunity; and, on second day, we attended the monthly meeting at Swansey; here things appeared much out of order, and in a low state; but, through divine favour, ability was given me, to clear my mind among them, in a way, that I hope, will tend to their profit. From thence we passed on to Providence, where we had a satisfactory meeting. The four following days we had meetings at Cranston, Greenwich, Foster and Scituate; all satisfactory meetings, particularly the last; it was an open edifying season, many hearts being comforted by the power of truth, which prevailed over all, and was cause of deep thankfulness to my mind. Our next meeting was at Wankeg, on first day, the 8th of 9th month; it was a profitable edifying season. Then passing on, we had meetings as they were laid out for us, on second day at Gloucester, on third day at Douglass, and on fourth day at Smithfield. The last was a large meeting, and many things were opened in a clear manner; confuting that dark belief in election and reprobation, and the impossibility of falling from grace. Also showing the necessity of regeneration, through the operation of the one essential baptism of the Holy Ghost; and that all were the objects of universal, and saving grace, and how all might be saved by it, if they did not reject it to their own destruction.

The next day we attended a meeting at Mendham; it was a comfortable season to myself, and I believe, to most or all present, and was cause of thankful remembrance. From thence we passed on, having meetings at Northbridge, Bolton and Leicester; at this place we also attended a burial, and had a favoured opportunity with the people. Then we went to Richmond, and attended their monthly meeting, where things were much out of order, and the meeting was small, and in a weak situation. I cleared my mind in a plain way among them, and found peace therein.

This was the last meeting we attended in the compass of Rhode Island yearly meeting. Then we passed on into the state of Vermont, in order to visit Friends of our own yearly meeting, who resided in that state. We reached Sharon, in time to attend their meeting on first day, the 22d of 9th month; and the next day attended a meeting at Strafford, which was a dull heavy time, in which I found it my place to be silent. The next day we crossed Connecticut river to the town of Hanover, and attended a meeting in a school-house, no Friends living in those parts. It was a satisfactory season. We lodged with a man attached to Friends, of the name of John Williams, who, with his wife, were convinced of the principles of truth; yet found it a great trial, faithfully to take up the cross, as they lived among a people much opposed to them in that respect. We left them the next day in a tender frame of mind, and I have a hope they will improve. We returned over the river and attended a meeting in the town of Norwich, at the fourth hour of the afternoon, which was a small, but favoured meeting. We lodged that night with a person who had requested to be joined to Friends, of the name of Zebulon Huntington. The next morning we returned to Sharon, and attended a meeting at the eleventh hour, it being their usual meeting day, which was a favoured season. The next day we attended a meeting in the northeast part of the town of Strafford, among those not of our society. After this we set forward for Lake Champlain, and got to Ferrisburg just in time to attend their meeting on first day, the 29th of 9th month, which I sat in silence; and returned after meeting to the house of our friend Nicholas Holmes and lodged. The next day we rode to our friend Cornelius Halbert's, and attended a meeting at the fourth hour, which proved a comfortable season; it was mostly composed of those not in membership with us.

From thence we proceeded to Grand Isle, which is situated nearly in the middle of Lake Champlain, having a meeting at Wiltston, in our way thither. We had a comfortable meeting at our lodgings at this place, and then crossed over by water to the west side of the lake, to the river Sable. We walked on foot about six miles near this river, to the house of our friend Richard Keese, where we had a satisfactory opportunity, in a meeting appointed in his house. It was a newly settled place, and no meeting of Friends within forty miles. We returned then to Grand Isle, and the next day, the first of the week, and the 6th of 10th month, we attended another meeting there, and then returned to Monkton, to the house of our kind friend Nicholas Iolmes, who had accompanied us in this little tour to the north-ward. We rested the next day, and the day following had an appointed meeting at the house of my kinsman Stephen Haight. On fifth day we had a comfortable opportunity with Friends here, at their preparative meeting. After this we took leave of our friends of this place, and rode to Vergennes, and lodged at our friend Thomas Robinson's ; and the next day proceeded on our way to Queensbury, where we arrived on seventh day evening. The day after, the first of the week, and the 13th of 10th month, we attended two meetings ; the first, at Friends' meeting-house, at the usual time ; and the latter, at a Friend's house, where a considerable number of people, who were not in profession with us, assembled.

On second day we rode to Easton, and lodged at our friend William Coffin's ; on third day, it being rainy weather, we rested ; and on fourth day, we attended the preparative meeting of Ministers and Elders for Easton monthly meeting. On fifth day their monthly meeting began, which held three days, and, in general, was conducted to good satisfaction. I felt near sympathy with Friends of this place, as their monthly meeting was bordering on an extensive newly settled country, to which Friends were moving from various parts. It made the bounds of their meeting very wide, and the members much scattered from one another ; and caused much labour and exercise to the concerned part of the meeting, in attending to, and conducting the affairs of truth. It likewise occasioned them to have, almost continually, a great load of business before the monthly meeting. The day after, being the first of the week, we attended a meeting at Saratoga. It was a large comfortable edifying meeting, and very refreshing to my spirit, which had been much exhausted by the exercise and labour of the three foregoing days.

In the course of this week we attended meetings at Greenfield, Ballstown, Troy, Albany, and Coeman's Patent; and reached Hudson on seventh day evening. The next day, the first of the week, and 27th of 10th month, we attended their morning meeting, and then proceeded on, being desirous of reaching the quarterly meeting at Oblong, which began on third day. We arrived there on second day evening, where we met with several beloved friends from near our own homes, to our mutual comfort. After the close of this meeting, we proceeded directly home; where I arrived the 2d of 11th month, and found my dear wife and family in a pretty good state of health, to our mutual rejoicing. I had renewed cause to bless the name of the Lord for his preserving providence and mercy, who is over all, worthy for ever.

I was from home in this journey about five months, and travelled by land and water about two thousand two hundred and eighty-three miles; having visited all the meetings of Friends in the New England states, and many meetings amongst those of other professions; and also visited many meetings, among Friends and others, in the upper part of our own yearly meeting; and found real peace in my labours.

CHAPTER III.

Visit to the Meetings of Ministers and Elders, 1795.—Visit to Friends in Pennsylvania, New-Jersey, Delaware, Maryland, and Virginia, 1798.

On the 26th of 7th month, 1795, I left home in order to join a committee of Friends, appointed by the yearly meeting of Ministers and Elders this year, to visit the quarterly and preparative meetings, and Friends individually, in those stations, throughout the yearly meeting. A concern having arisen in that meeting, occasioned by the many obvious deficiences and departures amongst us as a people, from the purity and simplicity of our holy profession, a minute was issued and recommended to the inferior meetings, setting forth the ground of this concern, and for the purpose of stirring up and encouraging Friends to a diligent search and labour, that the many hurtful disorders might be removed, and a right reformation, from those prevailing weaknesses, effectually take place.

This being the first day of the week, I sat with Friends in their meeting at Westbury; and although it was a dull time in the forepart, yet, through the comforting assistance of heavenly help, it was made, I believe, an edifying season to many minds. I crossed the Sound that afternoon to New Rochelle, and the next morning met some of the committee at the house of our friend Hugh Judge. We had an opportunity with his family, which proved a refreshing season, it being evident that he, and his wife, joined heartily with the concern. We visited several other families that day, and had the satisfaction to believe, that the concern and labour were owned by the Head of the Church, and, we believe, will be blessed to many.

The next day the quarterly meeting at Purchase began, and through the several sittings was made, I trust, a profitable season ; it ended on fifth day. The next day we had opportunities with two families, which, through the fresh extendings of holy help, proved very instructive and encouraging. After this we set out for Nine Partners, their quarterly meeting coming in the ensuing week. I reached there on first day morning, the 2d of 8th month, and attended their meeting, which proved a heart searching season, it being too manifest that many professors had suffered their minds to be captivated by a worldly spirit, which had introduced great death and darkness into our meetings, to the grief and trouble of the honest-hearted. But help was graciously afforded me to set forth, in a plain manner, the danger attending such a departure from the life and power of religion ; and to stir up also the lukewarm from their supineness and ease, and enforce the necessity of a more full dedication of their hearts, and their all, to the Lord's service.

The next day we attended the preparative meeting of Ministers and Elders at the Creek, in which much weakness was apparent. The three following days we attended the quarterly meeting at Nine Partners ; on the last of which, I was favoured to relieve my mind among them, in a season of close searching labour, by way of communication. After this we proceeded towards Easton, to attend the quarterly meeting there, and to visit the families of Ministers and Elders within the compass of that meeting, which we performed in about a week. Although weakness seemed to abound with Friends there, yet we were comforted in believing, that the visit had a profitable effect, and afforded encouragement, and a renewal of strength, to the sincere-hearted.

On seventh day, the 15th of 8th month, we rode to East Hoosac, and the next day attended Friends' meeting there, which was large, many people of other societies attending. It proved an open satisfactory time, and ended under a renewed sense of the merciful extendings of holy condescending love ; for which, I trust, many minds were made humbly thankful. The afternoon and next morning were passed in visiting the families of

Ministers and Elders; and although things were not all well among them, yet we had satisfaction and peace in our own minds, by a faithful discharge of the trust committed to us. The next day we rode to New Britain, and visited a Friend in the ministry there, he being the only select member in that meeting. From thence we passed on to Kline-Kiln, where there was likewise but one member of the select meeting, an Elder, whom we visited. We then went to Coeman's Patent, where there were three select members, to whom we paid a satisfactory visit, and then proceeded to the city of Hudson. The evening after our arrival, and the next day, we had opportunities with the Ministers and Elders of that place. They proved seasons of heart-searching labour, things appearing much out of order with some of them; and, among these, there was a disposition apparent, to lay waste good order in the Church. O the great want of honest, faithful labourers in the vineyard.

After our services were finished here, we left them with the answer of peace, and rode that afternoon to Nine Partners. The next day we attended Friends' meeting at Stanford, which proved a season of hard labour. There was a great want of solid weight, and a living travail, in order to experience the renewals of strength; the power of truth went forth freely, for the stirring up, and arousing the careless and supine from their beds of ease. After this we visited two families of Friends, and, the two following days, finished our visit to the rest of the families of Ministers and Elders in Creek monthly meeting. The rest of the week was taken up in visiting those under the notice of our appointment, in the monthly meeting of Nine Partners; and I may truly say, it was, in general, a sorrowful affecting time, in beholding the great departure of many of the Ministers and Elders, in their families, from that faithful discharge of duty, which their stations require; for want of this, their children had almost all gone out from plainness. We endeavoured to lay before them, in sincerity and simplicity of heart, the great danger attending such a conduct, and the necessity of a reform in those things; and felt peace of mind in our labour.

On seventh day afternoon we rode to Marlborough, and

attended Friends' meeting there the next day; it was an exercising season, on account of the great rawness and inexperience of the members of the meeting too generally, and the great lightness manifest, in most of those of other societies, a number of whom were present. My mind, after a time of hard labour, and suffering with the seed, was engaged in some service addressed to the latter class. Afterwards way opened to have Friends select, to whom my mind was led to communicate some things in a plain way, with the view of stirring them up to more diligence and circumspection in their families, the better ordering and disciplining of their children and household, and keeping things sweet and clean, agreeably to the simplicity of our holy profession; and I had peace in my labour. That afternoon, and the two following days, we visited all the families of Ministers and Elders in that monthly meeting, except one. After this I returned home, and found my family as well as usual; which I esteemed as a favour from my great and good Master. For this, with all his other mercies and preservations dispensed from time to time, I felt a return of thankfulness and grateful acknowledgment to Him, who is the author and giver of every good and perfect gift, and " who is over all, God blessed for ever."

Having for several years felt my mind drawn, at times, in gospel love, to visit Friends of the yearly meeting of Pennsylvania, New-Jersey, Delaware, Maryland and some parts of Virginia, in the fall of the year 1797, apprehending the time to be nigh for the performance of the visit, I laid my concern before Friends of the monthly and quarterly meetings of which I was a member; and received certificates of their unity and concurrence. I left home the 12th of 12th month, accompanied by Joseph Cooper, a member of our meeting, in the station of an Elder; taking leave of my family and friends, we rode to New-York, and the meeting for sufferings sitting there the next day, I attended it; and the day following being the meeting day for Friends of that city, I felt most easy to stay and attend it, which proved a comfortable strengthening season. After this I took leave of my friends there, parting from them in near unity and brotherly affection, and passed the next morning by water to

Staten Island. The day following we had two meetings there, and though small by reason of rain, were, nevertheless, both attended with a comfortable degree of divine favour. The next day we left the island and rode to Shrewsbury; and the day after, being first day, we sat with Friends there, and, I trust, it was a profitable season to some present, and relieving to my own mind; strength and utterance being furnished to open divers truths of the gospel, in the demonstration of the spirit, accompanied with a good degree of the divine power; to God only wise be the praise, who is over all, worthy for ever.

On second day we attended a meeting at a Friend's house about seven miles from Shrewsbury, on our way to Squan. On third and fourth days we were at Squan and Squancum, both small meetings, as there are but few of our society in those parts; yet they were, for the most part, satisfactory seasons. We also sat with Friends in their preparative meeting in the latter place, which appeared in a state of great weakness; but as way opened, I was led to make some remarks, in order to stir Friends up to more diligence and circumspection; and to show the necessity of an inward travail for the arising of truth, which can only qualify for the right ordering of the affairs of society. The next day we rode to Barnegat, and after an opportunity with Friends there the following day, we passed on to Little Eggharbour, where we remained till first day, the 24th of the month. Notice being spread of our intention of attending Friends' meeting there, many of the neighbouring inhabitants came in, and sat with Friends, and were very attentive; divers truths of the gospel were opened in the clear demonstration of the spirit, and I was helped to leave them with a peaceful mind. On the 25th we rode to Great Eggharbour, and the three following days attended meetings at the upper and lower meeting-houses of Friends there, also an appointed meeting near the head of Great Eggharbour river, at a place called Stephens' Creek; they were generally small, yet attended with a good degree of favour; for which my spirit was made humbly thankful. On sixth day we attended a meeting at Cape May, which, through the gracious condescension of the Shepherd of Israel, was made a truly comfortable season,

and His great name magnified and praised, who is worthy for ever.

From thence we rode to Morris' river, and attended a meeting appointed at the house of Isaac Buzby, a man inclining to Friends. The spirit of truth favoured me with wisdom and utterance, to divide the word suitably to the states of those present; and apparently to their and to my own satisfaction and comfort. We rode that afternoon to the house of a Friend of the name of Henry Rulon, where we had an appointed meeting the next day. After this we passed on to Greenwich, and the two following days attended a meeting there, and one at the head ot Cohansy Creek. Then we rode to the house of our kind friend Mark Miller, at Salem, and rested the next day. The day following, being the first of the week, and 7th of 1st month, we attended the meeting there, which was very large, many coming in that were not members; the power of truth was exalted over all, to the comfort of many hearts, and to the praise and glory of Him, who is the strength and help of his dependent children. On second day we attended a meeting at Woodstown; I was closely engaged among them in a searching testimony, pointing out the great danger, and hurtful tendency of the want of unity, and joining in with the spirit of the world, and neglecting a right conformity to the wholesome order, established among us, as a religious society; whereby many disorders had crept in, wounding to many: strength was afforded me, and utterance given, and truth exalted over all opposition and disorderly spirits. The four following days we attended meetings at Penn's Neck, Mullica Hill, Upper Greenwich, and Woodbury; they were all seasons of favour, especially the last, where truth was eminently exalted, and the doctrines of the gospel held forth in the demonstration of the spirit; and the hearts of the faithful were made to rejoice in a sense of the Lord's goodness, to whom belongs the praise of his own work for ever.

On seventh day we rested with our esteemed friend Joshua Evens; and on first day attended Newtown meeting, and the day following, that at Haddonfield, both of which were profitable edifying meetings. In the afternoon, after the latter meeting, we crossed the river Delaware to Philadelphia, and the three following days attended the three meetings in that city; they were all opportunities of favour, and I had much satisfaction in this short visit to Friends of this place. I was comforted in the experience of an open door among them, both in meetings and in families where my lot was cast; and I felt my spirit nearly united to a living remnant, especially a number of the beloved youth, who are under the forming hand, preparing for service; some of whom, I trust and believe, will be as valiants in their day, for the promotion of the cause of truth and righteousness in the earth. May the Lord bless, and keep them faithful to himself, and cover their heads in the day of battle.

On sixth day, the 19th of 1st month, we left the city in order to attend a meeting at Darby, notice having gone before of our intention; it proved an open time, but the meeting was hurt by an indiscreet appearance towards the end, which clothed my spirit with sorrow, not only on the Friends' account, but especially on account of the people, for whose information and religious instruction, my mind had been closely engaged. We rode that afternoon to Chester, and the next day attended a meeting there, which was owned with manifestations of divine favour; and I was instructed to hand out doctrine, suitable to the states of the people present. After this we rode to Wilmington; and the next day, being the first of the week, and the 21st of 1st month, we attended their forenoon and afternoon meetings. I was silent in the first; but, through the merciful assistance of the Shepherd of Israel, the latter proved a comfortable strengthening season; after a time of close exercise in silent labour, and deep baptism into death and suffering with the seed, the power of truth went forth with authority against many things that opened to view, as the cause of that deep oppression of the seed of life among them; the meeting ended under a sense of the Lord' goodness, and many hearts were made to rejoice.

The six following days we attended meetings at Whiteclay Creek, Appoquinamink, Duck Creek, Little Creek, Motherkill, and Camden, which is a village where no meeting of Friends is held; things appeared low in most of them, as to the life of religion. But, through the condescending goodness of the Shepherd of Israel, I had an open door among them, and many gospel truths were held forth, in the clear demonstration of the spirit, and with power; the last, especially, was a time thankfully to be remembered by me, and, I believe, by many others present; thanks be to God for his unspeakable gift, that he is not leaving himself without a witness in the hearts of the people. The next day, first of the week, we attended Millford meeting; things appeared very low, and but few of our society in that part, and those appeared very indifferent, and several of them were absent. On second day we attended a meeting at Cool Spring, and the next day attended an appointed meeting on our way towards Third Haven; it was held in a Friend's house, who had lately been received a member, and who before was a professor with the people called Nicholites; he appeared to be a pretty solid man. The meeting was in a good degree favoured; the way of preparation, as held forth in John's dispensation, for the more full manifestation of the gospel state, was set forth, with the nature of true Christian or spiritual baptism; and that John's baptism was only a figure thereof, and, therefore, was no part of Christ's baptism, and, consequently, had no place in, nor could be of any use under, the dispensation of the gospel. The people appeared generally satisfied, and I parted with them in peace of mind.

The six following days we attended meetings at North West Fork, Marshy Creek, Centre, Greensborough, Tuckahoe Neck, and Tuckahoe; and, although these meetings were attended by but few of those who were joined in fellowship with us, yet they were mostly crowded full meetings, many of the neighbouring inhabitants coming in, divers of whom were holders of slaves, and others very raw and ignorant. My spirit was much exercised in travail among them, being baptised into their low and uncultivated states; nevertheless, through the merciful interference of the Shepherd of Israel, their lost and undone condition, without a Saviour, was clearly laid open before them; also the way of return, reconciliation, and salvation. Many present were aroused and reached by the power of truth, which was graciously prevalent in most of these meetings; their spirits greatly tendered, and the few faithful among them were made to rejoice; and my spirit was humbly thankful, in a sense of the Lord's goodness; to him alone be the praise; nothing due to man.

Three of the above meetings were held in meeting-houses belonging to a people under the denomination of Nicholites; many of them were led into great self-denial, particularly in regard to dress and household furniture. They appeared one in principle with us, their faith and doctrine being founded on the manifestation and influence of the divine light, inwardly revealed. Most of them, of late, have requested to be joined in membership with Friends, and have been received. Many of them appear to be a worthy people; yet, I fear, some were a little hurt by being too tenacious in their dress, particularly in making it a point to have all parts of their clothing white. Yet, in general, they appeared to be a plain innocent upright-hearted people; and I felt a concern lest they should be hurt by the great and prevailing deficiencies manifest amongst us, by many turning away from the purity and simplicity of our holy self-denying profession. This, I believe, is a subject worthy of the deep consideration of those delinquent brethren. For if it be a truth, as most certainly it is, that whosoever offendeth one of the least of those who believe in Christ, it were better for him that a millstone were hanged about his neck, and he cast into the sea; what will become of those, who live in the daily practice of those things, which give continual offence to their brethren, and are stumbling blocks in the way of honest inquirers.

After attending the aforesaid meetings, we passed on, having meetings at Choptank, Third Haven and Bayside, on the eastern shore of Maryland. The two first were attended by many of other societies, a number of whom were Methodists, and at each was one of their ministers; both of whom were very solid, and paid great attention; one of them was much affected, and wept freely for a considerable time; and, with divers others, manifested their full satisfaction. My spirit was much humbled, and made to rejoice in the Lord, that he was graciously near, and made bare his arm for our help, and carried us through the exercise of those meetings, to the honour of his own name, who is over all, worthy, for ever.

After leaving Bayside, we attended a meeting which we had appointed the day before, on our way thither, at a village called St. Michael's, among the Methodists; the people were nearly all of that profession in this place. It was held in their meeting-house, and was the first meeting appointed by any Friend in that place, except a small one by some women Friends some years before. There was, at this time, a general collection; and, considering their unacquaintance with us, and our manner of sitting in silence, they behaved pretty well. A comfortable degree of the divine presence was witnessed, and many minds tendered and comforted, and divers gospel truths clearly opened to the apparent satisfaction of most present.

We left them with peace of mind, and the next day attended a meeting at Easton, alias Third Haven, among the black people, which we had appointed some days before. It proved a favoured opportunity, and to the edification, comfort, and encouragement of this poor, injured, and too much despised people; many of whom, I believe, have good desires begotten in their minds after the knowledge of the truth.

The next day, the first of the week, and the 11th of 2d month, we attended Friends' meeting at this place, and information of our intention of being here having been given before, the neighbouring inhabitants generally came in, so that the house was much crowded. The gospel was largely and freely preached among them, to the apparent satisfaction of all present. How marvellous is thy loving kindness, O Lord, to the workmanship of thy holy hand; how art thou graciously holding out, from season to season, offers of reconciliation to thy revolting and rebellious children, and art calling to them, by thy servants, now, as formerly, return, return, repent and live; for why will ye die, O house of Israel, saith your God. We continued here and attended their meeting of Ministers and Elders; and, on fifth day, their monthly meeting, which was in some degree favoured; divers things were opened for the improvement and encouragement of Friends in well ordering the affairs of truth.

The day following we rode to Chester, and the next day attended Friends' monthly meeting at Cecil, which was small; but truth favoured me with ability to labour, to stir up Friends to more vigilance, and careful waiting for the arising of the spring of life; as nothing short of the divine power, and renewed quickenings of the holy spirit, can qualify for the promotion of good order and discipline in the Church. The next day, the first of the week, we attended the meeting here. Notice having been given to the neighbouring inhabitants, many came in, most of whom appeared very raw and light; nevertheless, as Friends kept down to their exercise, towards the close of the meeting, truth came into dominion; and all that opposed it was made to bow and acknowledge its power; for which my spirit was made thankful to the Author of every blessing. On second and third days following, we attended two meetings; the first, in Friends' meeting-house at Chester, and the latter at Chestertown in their court-house; both pretty large meetings, and overshadowed with the wing of divine power; although, in the latter meeting, we had to arrive at it through deep baptism, and suffering with the seed; for those that reign with Christ, must be willing likewise to suffer. The people, in the forepart, were very light, often whispering one to the other; a spirit of licentiousness appeared to be prevalent with many of them; but as truth arose, they were gradually subjected, until a becoming solemnity appeared in almost every countenance. I trust some good was effected in some minds; but we must leave the event to the Lord, to whom alone belongs all the praise; nothing due to man, but blushing and confusion of face.

The next day we attended a meeting at the head of Chester; it was somewhat hurt, in the forepart, for want of room. The house was not sufficient to contain all who came, and the weather too cold to stand without; yet, as it settled into quiet, it proved a precious baptizing season, and many hearts were melted into deep contrition. I had cause to hope that if the few Friends in that place show forth a good example, there will be some gathered. The day following we attended the meeting at Sassafras, to pretty good satisfaction. The next day we rode to East

Nottingham, and attended their monthly meeting the day after; it proved a very exercising meeting, things being much out of order among them. I was led forth in a line of close searching labour, both in testimony in the first part of the meeting, and likewise in that for discipline ; but I got little relief, except from a consciousness, in myself, of having discharged my duty faithfully among them. The next day, the first of the week, and 25th of 2d month, we attended their particular meeting ; in which I had to expose, in a close, arousing testimony, that spirit among Friends, which pleads for joining with those active in civil government, and taking part therein, and adopting the maxims and spirit of the world. Truth reigned triumphantly in this meeting over all opposition and disorderly spirits. The 26th we rested. The 27th we attended West Nottingham meeting to good satisfaction, and were made to rejoice in truth's victory over death and darkness, for which the honest-hearted were made thankful. The 28th we attended a meeting, lately established, about five miles distant from the former, which I sat mostly in silence, feeling no clear commission for preaching the gospel among them.

The 1st of 3d month, we attended Little Britain meeting, wherein I was opened and led into a large doctrinal communication, suited to the states of many present. The meeting was large and solid, and, I trust, edifying and instructive to a number present. But too many, who have ears to hear, and are led to acknowledge the truth of testimonies delivered, neglect the practical part, which is the most essential ; and are, therefore, in a situation like those, who, seeing their natural faces in a glass, turn away, and forget what manner of persons they are. The 2d, we passed over the river Susquehannah, and lodged at Richard Webb's, at Fawn, and attended their meeting next day. It was a solid, and, I believe to many, a profitable season. The 4th, and first of the week, we attended Deer Creek meeting, which was large, and favoured with the overshadowing wing of heavenly regard. The condescending goodness and mercy of a gracious God to his sinful creatures were marvellously displayed. The meeting was composed, in part, of a number of

9

dark undisciplined spirits, many of whom, it was thought, had not been at any meeting for several years, and some of them never at any of ours before. The meeting appeared to be generally brought under a becoming solemnity, and concluded to our solid comfort. The 5th, we attended Bush River meeting, and although it was composed generally of a loose careless-minded people, yet truth favoured me; and, through divine help, the gospel was preached in the demonstration of the spirit, and with power. Many present were made sensible of its baptizing influence; and all contrary spirits appeared subjected, and brought down, and truth reigned triumphant.

The 6th and 7th of 3d month, we attended the meetings at Little Falls, and Gunpowder, both seasons of favour. The 8th we attended Friends' monthly meeting at Baltimore. It was, I trust, a profitable season, both in the meeting for worship, and that for the discipline of the Church. In the meeting for worship, I was led, in a close searching testimony, to set forth the great danger, and hurtful effects, of Friends joining in with the spirit of the world, and taking any part in the fluctuating governments, customs, and manners thereof. Things opened clearly to show, that, in days past, the apostacy took place through that medium, both among the primitive Christians, and also in our own society; and that the only way, for us as a people to regain the primitive state, was to return back into ancient simplicity, to separate from the world, its spirit, governments, manners, and maxims; and to make no league with those actuated thereby. Truth rose into dominion, and the faithful among them were strengthened. May praises for ever be ascribed to the Shepherd of Israel, who is indeed a God near at hand, and a present helper in every needful time.

The 9th we rested, and I wrote to my family and friends at home. The 10th, we visited several families in the morning, and in the afternoon, at the third hour, attended a meeting among the poor, at the alms-house belonging to this city. It proved a comfortable season, and I was glad I gave up to the service. The 11th being the first of the week, we attended Friends' meeting in the forenoon, and some notice being given among the town's people of our being there, it was large; and after sitting a considerable time in silent labour, wherein my mind was baptized into the states of those present, I stood up with a prospect of the hurtful tendency of pride, both in religious and civil society. Truth opened the way, and gradually rose into a good degree of dominion, and, I trust, it was a profitable season to many present. In the afternoon, at the third hour, we had a meeting with the black people; and, except the hurt received by their long and untimely gathering, I think it was, in general, a comfortable season; and many among them appeared to be brought into a becoming solemnity, and we parted under the savour of truth.

On the 12th, we attended a meeting at Elk Ridge; it proved, in general, a heavy season, yet, I trust, a time of profit and favour to some. We rode that afternoon thirteen miles towards Indian Spring meeting, which we attended the next day. In this meeting, I was led, in a plain and full manner, to expose the enormous sin of oppression, and of holding our fellow creatures in bondage, with the pernicious fruits and effects of it, to those who are guilty thereof, especially to their children; who, being supported by the labour and toil of those held in slavery, and thereby brought up in idleness, were led into pride, and a very false, and dark idea respecting God, and his superintending providence, and into many other evils, fatal to their present and eternal well being, and tending to disqualify them from being useful in almost any respect, either to themselves or society, and thereby rendering them unworthy of the respect of wise and good men. Truth rose into dominion, and some present, who were slave holders, were made sensible of their conditions, and were much affected. I felt a hope to arise that the opportunity would prove profitable to some, and I left them with peace of mind. Since then, I have been informed, that a woman, present at that season, who possessed a number of slaves, was so fully convinced, as to set them free, and, not long after, joined in membership with Friends: which is indeed cause of gratitude and thankfulness of heart, to the great and blessed Author of every mercy vouchsafed to the children of men.

On the 14th we were at Sandy Spring meeting, to satisfaction. The 15th, we attended Friends' preparative meeting at Alexandria. It was a small weak meeting, very few manifesting any real concern for the support of our Christian testimonies. They gathered there from different parts of the country, mostly for the advancement of their temporal interest; and this being uppermost with them, they were disqualified for improvement in religious experience. O that we, as a people, were more weaned from the world and its fading enjoyments, and our affections placed on celestial treasure; then would the light of the Church break forth out of obscurity, and her darkness become as the noonday; thousands would then be gathered from the highways and hedges, and flock to the brightness of her arising, with everlasting joy upon their heads.

The 16th we rode to Fairfax, about forty-six miles. The 17th we attended their select quarterly meeting. The 18th, the first of the week, we attended the meeting at this place, which was large, composed of Friends and others. I was led to open the great advantages attendant on a life of righteousness, from that scripture passage, "Righteousness exalteth a nation; but sin is a reproach to any people;" and showing the difference between a righteousness, founded on the laws, maxims, and precepts of men, and the righteousness that is witnessed by faith in the Son of God, as revealed to the hearts and souls of the children of men through the holy spirit. Although there were many raw, and uncultivated persons present, yet truth came into a good degree of dominion and victory, and, I trust, it was a profitable season to some.

The 19th we attended the quarterly meeting for discipline, in which I had some service, in opening the nature and end of discipline, and encouraging Friends to an improvement therein, to the solid satisfaction of the honest in heart. The next day was the youth's meeting for the last time; the quarterly meeting, the day before, having concluded to discontinue the same thereafter, from a belief that its usefulness was over; and that it had become more hurtful than beneficial. A great concourse of idle people came together at that time, not so much for the sake of the meeting, as to see and be seen, and to make it a place of diversion. I had considerable to say among them, but got but little relief; by reason, as I apprehended, of a spirit of infidelity and licentiousness, too generally prevailing among the people. I was satisfied the quarterly meeting had done right in discontinuing that meeting; believing, if continued, it would have been very prejudicial to the youth, for whose good, in the first institution thereof, it was intended.

The 21st we attended the preparative meeting of South Fork, which is a branch of Goose Creek monthly meeting. I was silent in the meeting for worship, but had some close labour with Friends in their preparative meeting. I felt my spirit much oppressed with a sense of the great lukewarmness, and love of the world, which appeared to prevail in such a manner, that the business of the preparative meeting was conducted in a very weak vague manner, and void of a right sense of the dignity of such a meeting, or a due concern for the preservation of right order. I felt peace of mind in a faithful discharge of my duty among them.

The 22d we were at Goose Creek preparative meeting, which was large in the first sitting, many of other societies coming in. After a considerable time of silent labour, in deep baptism with the suffering seed, my mouth was opened in a clear full testimony, directed to the states of those present. And many were brought under the influence of that power which "cut Rahab, and wounded the dragon." Truth came into dominion, and a good degree of victory over all was witnessed. Nevertheless, such is the deadness and indifference of some who go under our name, that, at the close of this very solemn meeting for worship, they withdrew with those who were not members, and continued out until the preparative meeting had proceeded considerably in its business; and then came in one after another, in a very careless unthinking manner. My heart was grieved, and I have often been affected with similar conduct in many places in those parts, as also in some others; a conduct, which appears to me to carry in it great indignity to our high and holy profession; and, I believe, is greatly offensive to the great Head of the Church, for the promotion of whose righteous cause, these meetings for discipline are established. I believe one great cause of this sorrowful weakness and declension is owing to a want of due administration of discipline, by those who are called thereto. By overlooking one little thing after another, custom establishes those bad habits; and great loss is sustained by the Church in general, and by some of its members in particular. It is very observable that meetings, where those things are apparent, are generally in a declining state. I was exercised in a plain way of dealing with those delinquents, showing them the hurtful tendency of such conduct. Truth prevailed, and many hearts were much tendered, and the hands of the faithful strengthened; to the Lord only wise be the praise of his own work, who is over all, worthy for ever.

The 23d we attended a meeting at a place called the Gap, where there was a small meeting of Friends. It was, however, a large collection, many of other societies attending, more than the house could hold. Many of them appeared to be a raw insensible people, void of any right idea or knowledge of true religion, which made the meeting very trying and painful; yet not without some degree of favour towards the conclusion, by truth's obtaining the victory over death and darkness.

Whilst in this neighbourhood, my mind was brought into a state of deep exercise and travail, from a sense of the great turning away of many among us, from the law and the testimony, and the prevailing of a spirit of great infidelity and deism among the people, and darkness spreading over the minds of many as a thick veil. It was a time in which Thomas Paine's *Age of Reason* (falsely so called) was much attended to in those parts; and some, who were members in our society, as I was informed, were captivated by his dark insinuating address, and were ready almost to make shipwreck of faith and a good conscience. Under a sense thereof, my spirit was deeply humbled before the majesty of heaven, and in the anguish of my soul, I said, "spare thy people, O Lord, and give not thy heritage to reproach," and suffer not thy truth to fall in the streets.

The 24th we attended the monthly meeting at Fairfax, which

was an exercising season, things being much out of order, for want of more faithfulness among the members, and a due attention to discipline. I laboured among them in the ability received, for their encouragement, and incitement to their respective duties; but alas for us, most men mind their own things, and not the things that are Jesus Christ's. A worldly spirit too much prevails among the professors of truth, to their great hurt, and to the great grief of the honest-hearted, who are in travail for Zion's prosperity, and Jerusalem's peace.

The 25th, we attended their first day meeting, which was large, and in it strength was graciously afforded to minister to the people in truth's authority, which came into dominion over all. This afternoon we passed over the great river Potomac, in our way to Bush Creek, in Maryland; this, by reason of rains, was very full, and difficult to pass. After we had passed over the river Potomac, we had much difficulty in crossing a creek not far from it. There was a floating bridge over it; but the water was so high, that we could not approach the bridge by the road commonly used; and we only succeeded in reaching it, by proceeding ourselves on the top of a high fence, and leading our horses by our sides. Mine fell into a deep part of the creek; but he soon rose, and swam to the shore. A Friend was in company with us, with a one horse carriage; and there appeared to be no way of getting his conveyance over, but by the horse swimming with it over the creek. This we knew would be attended with considerable risk, as the creek was deep in the middle, and the carriage a heavy one. But as there were no inhabitants on this neck of land, nor near to it, and as night was coming on, we pursued that course, and led the horse with the carriage into the creek; and after violent exertions, being at one time drawn under water by the weight of the carriage, he took it safe over. We were thus favoured to surmount this great difficulty, without any hurt to ourselves, or our horses; which was cause of thankfulness and gratitude to the great Author of every mercy and blessing.

We proceeded to a Friend's house by the name of Richard Richardson, where we had a meeting the next day, with his family, and a number of the neighbouring people, who were not Friends. It proved a favoured season, and I trust will not soon be forgotten by some present; may it fasten as a nail in a sure place; and to some I have a hope it may be as bread cast upon the waters, to return after many days.

The day following we attended Bush Creek meeting, notice having gone forward some days before, of our intention of being there at this time; it was large, and greatly favoured with the prevalence of truth, by way of testimony. Many things, relative to true gospel worship, were clearly opened, and the fallacy and fruitlessness of all-will worship, and mere bodily exercise, in matters of religion, manifested to the view of all present, who had eyes to see, and hearts to understand, what the spirit saith to the Churches. It was a very solemn time, worthy of grateful remembrance.

The 28th we attended Pipe Creek meeting, wherein I was greatly afflicted with evil thoughts, which would keep arising in my mind, that I was almost at times taken off from my proper exercise. This very much grieved my spirit; but, as I endeavoured to keep up the warfare, I was led to believe it was the case with too many present; and that by giving way to such thoughts, some had become captivated by their own lusts, wounding one another; and divers disorders, and a want of unity, had got in among them, and many hurt thereby. I was led into the necessity of bearing testimony against these things, as way opened, and calling the attention of all present, to the light, spirit, grace, and truth of our Lord Jesus Christ, our holy pattern, as the only place of refuge and preservation from these, and all other hurtful things. After this meeting, the Friend, where we lodged, informed me the next morning, that himself and his wife were uneasy that no Friends had come in to see us after the meeting, and were afraid they would judge them of having informed me of their condition, the states of many had been so exactly described in the meeting; but I told him they need not be troubled, as they knew themselves to be clear.

The two following days we attended meetings at Monallen and Huntington; they were both exercising seasons; nevertheless, truth favoured me with ability and understanding to communicate in a close searching manner, suited to the states of those present; and a crumb of consolation was handed forth to the few honest-hearted, who were in travail for Zion's arising, and who went mourning on their way, and bowed in spirit, from a sense of the great turning away from the law and testimony, and the prevalence of a spirit of ease and great indifference, whereby many wrong things had entered.

From thence we passed on to Warrington and Newberry, in each of which meetings truth favoured with victory; and the hidden things of Esau, or the first nature, which are earthly, were brought to light, searched out, detected, and condemned. The manner and way in which the new or second birth, which is spiritual, and which has the promise, is brought forth and effected, was clearly shown and pointed out; with the blessing attendant thereon, to the comfort of the faithful, and the few willing minded among them, and to the stirring up and arousing the lukewarm, careless, and indifferent professors, from their beds of ease and carnal security. The latter meeting especially was a time to be remembered; many hearts were greatly affected, and, I trust, the season will not soon be forgotten by some. I was very thankful for the relief I felt to my own mind, after many days of deep baptism with the suffering seed. Religion appeared to be at a very low ebb in those parts, by the prevalence of a worldly spirit, which makes hard work for the poor travellers, who have to go up and down among them, as with their hands upon their loins for very pain. Did those lukewarm careless professors rightly consider the great distress and exercise they bring upon their concerned brethren, who are in travail for their redemption and salvation; and who are going up and down as with their lives in their hands, through difficulties and dangers, in jeopardy by sea and by land, and among false brethren, we might reasonably suppose it would be a means to stir them up to more diligence and circumspection, that they might thereby comfort them in their exercises, and relieve them in their tribulations; then they that sow, and they that reap, might rejoice together, and joy in the God of their salvation.

Our next meeting was at Yorktown, where we tarried two days, and were at their monthly meeting, wherein things appeared distressingly low, as to the right conducting of discipline in truth's authority: indeed the meeting seemed sunk so below any proper sight and sense of right order, that no way opened to administer much or any help; and we left them without obtaining much relief of mind. We passed on, having a meeting near Wright's ferry; and then crossed the great river Susquehannah, and had meetings at Lancaster and Lampeter. On first day, the 8th of 4th month, we attended a meeting at Sadsbury, which, through hard labour, proved a season of enlargement, in a line of close doctrine, suited to the varied states of those present; some minds appeared to be much humbled; may it not be in vain, but as seed sown on good ground.

The 10th of 4th month we attended West Caln meeting, the 11th Fallowfield, both favoured meetings. The 12th we attended London Grove meeting, wherein I was led to open the duty and obligation incumbent on ministers, elders, overseers, and heads of families. I began with this query of the prophet Isaiah, " Watchman, what of the night;" showing that for want of keeping up a strict watch, with an eye single to that inward holy monitor, or spirit of pure unerring wisdom, many hurtful and destructive things had got in among us. Especially for want of a godly care in parents and heads of families, over their children and those under their charge, many pollutions had got in, and spread among them; particularly the youth, not only in regard to a departure from the simplicity and purity of our holy, self-denying profession, in dress and address, but also in many other unseemly and reproachful practices; which is but the natural consequence of parents indulging undue liberties in their children. It was a solemn time, worthy of grateful remembrance. The 13th we were at West Grove meeting, in which I had to go through a similar exercise; from a sense of the great want of faithfulness among the members, whereby many deficiencies were apparent, wounding the faithful. Truth favoured me with ability to clear myself among them, with plainness of speech; which was cause of thankfulness to the honest-hearted.

The 14th we attended New Garden meeting, mostly in silence, in which I had peace. The 15th, and first of the week, we attended Hockesson meeting; and, at the fourth hour in the afternoon were at Center; the 16th at Kennet; these were, for the most part, suffering seasons. Although there is a small remnant preserved, who are in travail for truth's arising, yet the greater part are too much captivated by a worldly spirit; which leads into a neglect of attending meetings, and great carelessness in respect to the right ordering their families; by reason whereof, many undue liberties have got in among them, wounding the faithful and honest-hearted.

The 17th we attended Chichester meeting; it was a time thankfully to be remembered; the everlasting gospel of peace and salvation was preached in truth's authority; and all contrary spirits were subjected and brought down. Truth reigned triumphantly over all; magnified for ever be the name of the Lord, who made bare his arm for our help, and the strengthening and refreshing of my poor soul. I had been at times, for days and nights past, ready to sink into discouragement and dismay, by reason of the deep baptisms I had to pass through, unknown to man, but in fellowship with the suffering seed, which lies smothered and pressed down in the hearts of many careless and lukewarm professors, as a cart under sheaves. Oh how does darkness and death spread itself, as a curtain, in this once highly favoured land! Alas for the people, for the professors of truth; what will become of them, unless they repent and turn to the Lord. Parents and children, in some places, are so estranged from the law and testimony, that many seem plunged into the condition of Jerusalem formerly, when this pathetic lamentation was taken up by the dear Master; "O Jerusalem, Jerusalem, thou that killest the prophets, and stonest them which are sent unto thee, how often would I have gathered thy children even as a hen gathereth her chickens under her wings, and ye would not. Behold your house is left unto you desolate." Oh how is this verified; what great desolations, in a religious sense, are apparent with many professors; and how are the poor servants, that are sent forth among them for their recovery, as with their lives in their hands, as it were stoned, and often so plunged into death and sufferings, as almost to despair of life! Oh the pangs that my poor soul has endured of late, in many places; so that I had often to say in secret, with the holy apostle; "why stand we in jeopardy every hour?" No tongue can tell, nor is it in the power of language to communicate, the distress and anguish, which is sometimes endured by the poor travellers, in filling up their measure of the afflictions of Christ, for his body's sake, the Church. But, in this also, we are sometimes strengthened to rejoice, that we are accounted worthy to suffer with Him, that when he is pleased to arise in his own strength, as the light of the morning, we may be permitted to reign with Him; and rejoice with joy unspeakable and full of glory.

The three following days, we were at Concord, Birmingham, and Bradford, all favoured meetings, through fervent labour, and the prevalence of truth; may the Lord make it effectual, and fasten it as a nail in a sure place. The 21st we were at East Caln, mostly silent. The 22d, and first of the week, we were at Uwchlan; the meeting was large, wherein I had to expose the danger of self-righteousness, or a trust in natural religion, or mere morality; showing that it was no more than the religion of Atheists, and was generally the product of pride and self-will; and, however good it may appear to the natural unregenerate man, is as offensive in the divine sight, as those more open evils, which appear so very reproachful to the eyes of men. I was favoured by the spirit of truth, in a large searching testimony, to the convicting and humbling many hearts, and comfort of the faithful.

The 23d we attended the meeting at Nantmill, mostly in silence. The three following days, we were at Pikeland, Valley, and Willistown meetings; all in a good degree favoured. The 27th we were at Goshen; the meeting was large. I had to caution Friends against mixing with the people in their human policies, and outward forms of government; showing that, in all ages, those, who were called to be the Lord's people, had been ruined, or suffered great loss, by such associations; and manifesting clearly by scripture testimony, and other records, that our strength and preservation consisted in standing alone, and not to be counted among the people or nations ; who were setting up party, and partial interests, one against another, which is the ground of war and bloodshed : these are actuated by the spirit of pride, and wrath, which is always opposed to the true Christian spirit, which breathes "peace on earth, and good will to all men." Those, therefore, who are in the true Christian spirit, cannot use any coercive force or compulsion by any means whatever ; not being overcome with evil, but overcoming evil with good. Although there were many opposing spirits present, who, in their creaturely wisdom and human policy, are pleading for those kinds of associations, and taking part in those political governments, yet truth favoured, and came into a good degree of dominion over all, strengthening and encouraging the true travellers for Zion's prosperity.

The 29th, and first of the week, we attended Middletown meeting ; and, at the fourth hour in the afternoon, were at Providence ; both large crowded meetings, more than the houses could contain. I was favoured by the power of truth, in an eminent manner, especially in the former meeting ; where many hearts were deeply bowed, from the sensible evidence of the prevalence of divine power, which was in dominion over all, tendering the hearts of most present. It was a precious season, worthy of thankful remembrance, and humble gratitude to the blessed Author of all our rich mercies and blessings, "who is over all, God blessed for ever."

The 30th we attended the monthly meeting at Providence, consisting of the particular meetings of Providence, Middletown, Springfield, and Chester. Things in this meeting appeared in a low state, as to the right ordering of the affairs of the Church. Numerous, and great, were the apparent deviations among them ; many of their youth were gone out into the foolish fashions and vain customs of the world to such a degree, as not to retain any marks of true primitive plainness. " O how is the gold become dim ; how is the most fine gold changed !" Many parents, who retain a good degree of outward plainness themselves, for want of dwelling enough in the pure spring of divine life, have suffered the eye of their minds to be so far blinded by the god of this world, as not only to suffer these improper indulgences in their families, and among their children, but, in some instances, are ready to plead for them. The sense of this much affected my mind, and under this exercise I was led forth in a line of close searching labour among them, to stir up Friends to more diligence, and honest care in those respects; which, I trust, afforded a degree of comfort and strength to the honest-hearted, and procured peace to my own mind, which is a treasure I prefer to all this world's glory and honour.

The 1st of 5th month we attended the meetings of Springfield, and Haverford; both favoured, profitable seasons. The 2d we were at Newtown, where, in a line of close searching labour, I was led to show the danger of trusting the salvation of our souls to any thing short of a full surrender of our wills, and an entire dedication of our hearts to the Lord, in an humble circumspect walking before Him ; and separating ourselves from the world, its spirit, manners, maxims, governments, honours and customs; all of which are polluted, and arising from the lusts of the flesh, the lusts of the eye and the pride of life. Truth rose into victory, softening many hearts, and comforting and strengthening the faithful. Surely God is good to Israel, although in a state of great revolting ; yet he delighteth in showing himself merciful; praised and magnified be his great and adorable name, over all for ever.

The 3d and 4th we attended meetings at Radnor and Merion; and then passed on to Philadelphia, to attend their quarterly meeting, which opened on the 5th, with a meeting for Ministers and Elders, and closed on third day the 8th of the month, with a meeting for the youth, and one for the black people, in the afternoon. I think, in general, it was a time of favour, through much hard labour in the several sittings. Indeed we have no reason to expect to come at the spring any other way, than by faithfully digging, as with our staves, while there remains so much rubbish on the well's mouth.

The 9th we attended the select quarterly meeting at Abington; and the day following the quarterly meeting for discipline. I was engaged among them, in each meeting, and the favour extended was cause of thankfulness to the honest-hearted. The 11th we returned to Philadelphia; and, in the afternoon, passed over the river Delaware to Haddonfield in West Jersey. The 12th we attended a monthly meeting at Upper Evesham; it was a low time, with not much of that divine life and power, which only can qualify for the right conducting of discipline, to be felt among them; and left them without much relief of mind.

The 13th of the month, and first of the week, we attended meetings at Evesham, and Cropwell; in the former, I was helped to labour pretty largely in testimony, to the comfort of a few honest-hearted, and a number of youth with tender minds; but the greater part of the meeting appeared to be in a state of great insensibility and ease; a situation which is generally callous to all the tender invitations, and entreaty of their friends, who are in travail for their redemption and salvation; and too much like the deaf adder, which will not listen to the voice of the charmer, although he charm ever so wisely. In the latter meeting, I was silent as to ministry.

The 14th we attended the monthly meeting at Haddonfield, in which I laboured, in the ability received, for their help and improvement. But alas, some meetings are so lost to the life of true religion, and so many, who go under our profession, are sunk into such a state of indifference and lukewarmness, that the affairs of the Church are too much conducted in a kind of rotation, and creaturely wisdom, void of that true weight, and feeling sensibility, which only gives right qualification for service in the Church; hence great weakness ensues, and the way of right reformation is closed, and truth prevented from arising in its primitive splendour and beauty.

The 15th we were at Moore's Town and Rancocus; in the former meeting, the power that "cut Rahab, and wounded the dragon," manifestly prevailed to the tendering many hearts. Truth came into victory over all; praised for ever be the right worthy name of Israel's King, who, in holy condescending love, was pleased to make bare his arm for our help; and once more redeemed my poor soul out of adversity, and the deep depressing baptisms, which for some days past it had been plunged into, by suffering with the seed, which lies pressed down in the hearts of many lukewarm worldly minded professors, as a cart with sheaves. From thence we passed on, having meetings at Mansfield Neck, Burlington, Mansfield, and Bordentown; which were all favoured meetings, truth being near for our help.

The 20th, and first of the week, we were at Trenton; the meeting was large, many of the town's people, of other professions, came in. Strength was made manifest in the midst of weakness, and, as truth arose, the gospel was preached in the clear demonstration of the spirit; many hearts were tendered and comforted, and the few faithful made to rejoice, in a grateful sense of the Lord's mercies.

The 22d we were at Stony Brook meeting, wherein my heart was made glad through holy help, and I was enabled to labour among them in truth's authority, to the comfort of the willing-hearted, and the solid peace of my own mind. The two following days we were at Plainfield, and Rahway; in the latter meeting I was wholly silent; but the former was a time of close labour, in a clear plain way, to stir up the minds of the people to more diligence, and an inward humble walking with the Lord; which appeared to be too much wanting among them.

The 25th we attended an appointed meeting at Newark, a town wherein no Friends reside. The meeting was small, and those gathered appeared mostly in a loose uncultivated state of mind; yet, I believe, there were some thoughtful persons present; and, I trust, the meeting was in some degree profitable. I left them with peace of mind, and proceeded that evening to New-York to attend the yearly meeting, which was to be opened there on the next day, with a meeting for Ministers and Elders. After the first sitting of the meeting, I rode home, not only to see my dear wife and family, from whom I had been absent more than five months, but also to assist them in getting out to the yearly meeting. Our rejoicing was precious, and mutual, in and under a sense of the Lord's mercy and goodness, for whose gracious preservation and help, in this arduous journey, my spirit was made to bow in humble adoration and praise, beyond the expression of language. Oh my soul, what canst thou render unto the Lord for all his benefits! Nothing can be more acceptable, than an entire surrender of thine all to his holy disposing; and to endeavour, as at the present time, to continue humbly to worship at the footstool of his holy throne of grace. Amen.

I was absent from home in this journey about five months and two weeks, and rode about sixteen hundred miles, and attended about one hundred and forty-three meetings.

11

CHAPTER IV.

Visit to Connecticut, 1799.—Visit to Oblong and Nine Partners, 1800.—Visit on Long Island, 1800.—Visit to Friends in New-Jersey, and Pennsylvania, 1801.

HAVING felt a concern, for some time, to pay a religious visit to some towns and places in Connecticut, and, in my way, to be with the few Friends at West Hartford, I laid my prospect before my friends in the fall of the year 1799, and received a minute of concurrence and unity from our monthly meeting. I left home the 26th of 10th month, and proceeded to Oblong, in order to meet a committee of our yearly meeting, appointed this year, to visit the quarterly meetings of Nine Partners and Oblong, and the monthly meetings belonging thereto ; a proposition having been made for a new arrangement of those meetings, so as to establish another quarterly meeting. I accompanied the committee in the attendance of both quarterly meetings.

After this, we proceeded into Connecticut, attending meetings in our way to West Hartford, in the following manner, viz : three in the town of Sharon, one at Cornwall, one at Goshen, and one at Litchfield. They were all favoured meetings. Four of them were held in meeting-houses belonging to the Presbyterians. The latter meeting was but small, considering the largeness of the town, and the great openness manifested by their leading members ; there were three of their ministers, and some other leading men present. Truth was prevalently manifest in this meeting, tendering and comforting the honest-hearted, a number of whom, I believe, were at the meeting, whose words and conduct clearly manifested a hearty thankfulness for, and satisfaction with, the opportunity. Although the great opposition those meet with, in coming out of their old traditions, may prevent any open and manifest effects for the present, yet, I believe, it will be as bread cast upon the waters, which will return after many days; so that his word which goeth forth, may not return void, but will accomplish the purpose for which it was sent, to the praise and glory of his own worthy name, "who is over all, God blessed for ever."

After this meeting, we passed directly to West Hartford, and lodged with our friend Ebenezer Crosby, whose daughter Abigail had come in company with us from Nine Partners. She was a discreet religious young woman, whose mind, I apprehended, was under the operation of the forming hand, for her good; may she be preserved in faith and patience, under the varied turnings thereof upon her; and then, I have no doubt, she will become a useful member in the Church.

The next day we rode to Springfield, about twenty-six miles north of this place; and attended a meeting there the following day. Although the people appeared generally raw and ignorant, as to the internal work of true religion on the heart, being mostly of those persuasions, whose doctrines lead them to place too much trust and dependence on the external works of a *Saviour without them*, and an *imputative righteousness;* and not experiencing the *internal work of sanctification*, wrought by the spirit and power of a *Saviour within them;* which is a very dangerous errour; nevertheless, I was favoured by the Lord's power to relieve my mind, and divers appeared to be tenderly affected, and manifested much satisfaction with the opportunity, as did the auditory in general.

We rode back that afternoon to West Hartford, and the day following, the first of the week, and 17th of 11th month, we attended Friends' meeting; and another at the house of our friend Ebenezer Crosby, in the evening. They were full meetings, many of other societies attending, mostly Presbyterians. Truth favoured, in an eminent degree, in both opportunities, but especially in the latter, wherein it rose into great dominion, breaking down, and apparently reducing every contrary spirit. A remarkable calm, and general solemnity was felt to spread over the assembly, to the solid rejoicing and comfort of many hearts, and the exaltation of the cause and testimony of our God ; who, for this, and his multiplied favours and blessings, vouchsafed from time to time, is worthy of all honour, dominion and glory, both now and for ever.

The next day, feeling my mind drawn to some of the adjacent towns, we rode about ten miles, to a place called Perquanock, a thickly settled village in the west part of the township of West Windsor. We had a precious opportunity there that evening, in a large school-house. Although the notice was very short, it being late in the afternoon when we came there, yet, when we reached the meeting, which began at the sixth hour, the house was nearly full, and soon after taking our seats was crowded with as many as it could well contain. A commendable stillness was maintained during the silent part of the meeting, which we thought a little uncommon, as the people were generally strangers to us, and our ways. After a time of solemn waiting, my mouth was opened in a clear full testimony ; wherein the doctrines of the gospel were largely and plainly held forth, in the demonstration of the spirit, and with power, tendering many hearts, and to the apparent satisfaction of the people in general ; many expressing their thankfulness for the favour. We left them with the answer of peace in our own minds, and in a full persuasion, that the Lord is secretly at work in the minds of many of the people in these parts, in order to deliver them from the power of their dark and blind leaders, who, for a long time, by their carnal and lifeless teachings and doctrines, and many *vain traditions*, have formed almost a total eclipse between God and their souls. May the Lord hasten this good work in his own time, that those merchants of Babylon, who are trafficking in the souls of the people, those blind guides may be so discovered, that no man may buy their merchandize any more.

The day after, we attended a meeting in Windsor town ; the people here seemed to be more under the dark power of their teachers, being much blinded with the prejudice of education, so that the meeting was but small. Nevertheless, truth favoured me with ability to preach the gospel, with a good degree of divine authority, to the comfort and edification of some seeking minds present. The two following days we attended Friends' meeting at Hartford, the latter of which was appointed by our friend Jervis Johnson, from Ireland. Both were comfortable seasons.

The sixth of the week, and 22d of the month, we rode to the city of Hartford; and way opening for an opportunity with the people, a meeting was accordingly appointed at the sixth hour in the evening, to be held in a large meeting-house belonging to the Presbyterians. A great number of the citizens assembled, supposed to be near a thousand, among whom were most of the principal inhabitants. The Lord, in whom was our trust, was graciously near, and furnished us with ability to conduct the meeting to the satisfaction and peace of our own minds; and to the edification of many present, and general satisfaction of the assembly.

We rested on seventh day, and, on first day, we were again at Friends' meeting at West Hartford; and notice that we were to be there having spread, a considerable number of the neighbouring inhabitants and some from the city came in. It was a season of high favour; many weighty truths of the gospel were clearly opened, and the way of life and salvation placed before the minds of the people; and a general solemnity appeared to reign, which was manifest in almost every countenance, silencing every opposite spirit. The hearts of Friends, with my own spirit, were bowed in humble acknowledgment and gratitude to the Lord our helper, for granting us so great a mercy; and under a solemn sense thereof we parted, and took leave of each other in great nearness of spirit.

On second day we turned our faces homeward, attending meetings in our way at Cambridge and Woodbury; at the latter place we had two meetings; we also had meetings at Middlesex, and Stamford, and again at Middlesex on first day; these were generally seasons of divine favour, edifying and instructive. After this we passed on into the state of New-York, and had meetings the six following days, at Rye, White Plains, North Castle, Shapaqua, Amawalk, and Croton. As my mind was led, in faith and patience, to close in with the baptismal influence of the spirit of truth, it was reduced into a state of suffering with the precious seed in the hearts of the people, and their divers states were felt, and way made to divide the word aright to those assembled; who were a mixed number of Friends and others. Truth was exalted, and set over every contrary spirit, and the honest-hearted comforted and encouraged to persevere in the "work of righteousness," which "shall be peace; and the effect of righteousness, quietness and assurance for ever."

The following first day we attended Friends' meeting at West Chester; and in the afternoon we had an appointed meeting at East Chester, principally among those not of our society. We had cause, in both these meetings, to magnify and adore the name of the Lord, who deigned to be near with his saving help, and furnished with ability to preach the gospel of life and salvation, in the clear demonstration of the spirit; the power attending, convicting and tendering many hearts. The few Friends, who dwell in that place, were strengthened and encouraged, and my spirit refreshed and made to rejoice, in those closing opportunities. After this I returned home, and found my dear wife and tender children all well, to our mutual rejoicing. I was out about six weeks, and attended about thirty meetings, and two quarterly meetings.

On my return from my late visit in Connecticut, I felt my mind not fully clear of a prospect I then had of a few other places; and the way opening with greater clearness, and feeling a motion of love to draw towards again attending the ensuing quarterly meetings of Oblong and Nine Partners, after attending our quarterly meeting at Westbury, in 1st month, 1800, I set out with Amos Whitson as my companion. We attended Purchase meeting on first day, which I sat in silence, and passed from thence to Oblong, and attended their quarterly meeting. After this we had a meeting at Kent, in our way to Nine Partners. The people of this place are mostly of the Presbyterian society, and a considerable number assembled, and behaved in an orderly manner. I trust the opportunity was a season of profit, and that the labour bestowed may be, to some of those present, as bread cast upon the waters. After attending the quarterly meeting of Nine Partners, we had two meetings in our way to Cornwall and Goshen, among those not of our society, though nothing very remarkable occurred in either. We had a comfortable meeting at Cornwall, and visited Charles Richards and some others, who appeared to be going into a separation from Friends, having already set up a separate meeting, for which they were not long after disowned. They had given way to some very inconsistent notions, in which they became so hardened as not to take the tender counsel and advice of their friends, who laboured much with them for their recovery. From thence we returned home, having a few meetings in our way, mostly among people of other persuasions. We got well home on first day evening, the 16th of 2d month, after attending the morning meeting at New-York. As I took this little journey in part to fill up what seemed lacking in the other, I now felt clear, and my mind was accompanied with true peace, which raised in me humble acknowledgments and gratitude to the great and blessed Author of all our mercies.

Soon after my return from the above little journey, I felt my mind drawn, in the renewed feelings of gospel love, to pay a religious visit to some of the inhabitants of our island, not of our profession. After having opened my prospect to Friends and obtained the unity and concurrence of our monthly meeting, I performed that service, in the latter part of the fall, and beginning of the winter following. I was out from home twenty-seven days, rode about one hundred and ninety miles, and attended thirty-five meetings ; only two of which were held in our meeting-houses. They were generally seasons of great favour, in which my mind was deeply bowed, under a humiliating sense of the Lord's mercy, extended from day to day, not only in opening the hearts of the people to receive us and our testimony with manifestation of much love and good will ; but also in furnishing matter suitably adapted to the states of those assembled. Truth was raised into victory, in a remarkable manner, in almost every meeting ; and in several, to a very eminent degree, even beyond, as I thought, what I had ever before experienced.   It ran over like oil.   All appeared broken down by its precious and embalming influence, in which the Lord was worshipped, and his great and glorious name praised and exalted over all, who is worthy for ever.

In the spring of 1801, feeling my mind engaged, in the love of the gospel, to proceed in a visit to Friends, in some parts of Jersey and Pennsylvania, and some places adjacent thereto, I left home the 11th of 4th month, with the concurrence and unity of my friends; and with Edmund Willis as a companion.   We rode to New-York, and attended Friends' forenoon and afternoon meetings there, on first day.   Although the life of religion appeared at a low ebb with Friends of that city, in too general a manner; yet a number of the younger class, and some more advanced in life, gave some hope of improvement.   My mind was deeply engaged among them.   And, through the condescending goodness of the Shepherd of Israel, strength was witnessed to preach the gospel in the demonstration of the spirit, and with power; insomuch that a fresh visitation was extended to many present. May it rest, and be fastened by the Master of assemblies, as a nail in a sure place, to the honour of his great and glorious name, who is the blessed Author and finisher of every good word and work.

On second day we left the city, and passed to Elizabethtown Point, Woodbridge and upper Freehold.   And on fourth day, we attended a meeting in the neighbourhood, called Robbins' meeting, at the usual time; and in the afternoon attended Upper Freehold meeting.   The former was usually a small, weak meeting; but information of our intention to be there, being generally spread, many came in who were not members; and it proved a profitable edifying season, worthy of grateful remembrance.   The latter was rather a season of suffering with the seed.   I was mostly shut up as to any ministerial communication.   The next day we attended the meetings of Crosswicks, and Upper Springfield; at both of which strength was afforded to communicate what opened in the line of duty, in such a manner as to find relief of mind, which I account a great favour.

We rode to Philadelphia on sixth day, and the next day the

yearly meeting of Ministers and Elders opened; and on the ensuing second day, the yearly meeting for discipline, which was very large, and continued, by adjournments, through the week, and closed on seventh day. Many weighty subjects were opened for deliberation. But through the prevalence and mixture of unsubjected spirits, who were too forward and active in their own unmortified wills, much weakness was apparent. This greatly increased the burden of the living, and truly baptized members, of which class there were a very considerable number, who were deeply engaged for the promotion of the cause of truth, and that the family at large might be kept in decent and commendable order, consistent with the gospel of Christ; and become established on the ancient foundation of our holy profession. These were nearly united in spirit and in travail for Zion's arising, and the Lord was graciously pleased to water them together, at seasons, with the descendings of heavenly dew; by which, encouragement was witnessed, to persevere in patience, and in thankful acknowledgment, for his continued mercy; and they were favoured to return from their annual solemnity with rejoicing, for all the good the Lord had been pleased to favour them with.

We remained in the city over first day, and attended the forenoon meeting at Market-street, which was very large. My spirit was set at liberty, and ability afforded to divide the word among them, according to their varied conditions, in a large searching and effectual testimony; whereby a holy solemnity was witnessed to spread over the meeting, to the great rejoicing of the honest-hearted. But alas, how oft are those seasons of comfort interrupted and hurt, by the indiscreet forwardness of some who have been called to publish the gospel; but, for want of dwelling enough in the root, have branched out in the fertility of their own natural abilities, and become too active in their own spirits; and are thereby not only in danger of losing their gifts, and falling into a bewildered state, but often hurt the service, and take off the savour of many of our most favoured solemnities. This was affectingly the case at this time, by the addition of a long, but very lifeless testimony; and although delivered in sound words, yet being destitute of the life and power, tended greatly to burden the living, and grieve the upright in heart. Great advantage would redound to the Church in general, and to this class of its members in particular, if those, who stand in the station of Elders, were more deeply centered in their minds to the well-spring of eternal life; waiting for, and feeling after a spirit of right discernment, that so they might be enabled to judge righteous judgment, and distinguish rightly between the living and the dead. Then would the hand be seasonably laid upon the head of this *transforming spirit*, and those, in danger of being deceived thereby, witness preservation.

On second day, the 27th of 4th month, we left the city, and passed over into West Jersey, in order to take some meetings which I had not been at. We were at five in the course of the week; and although the life and virtue of true religion appeared to be at a low ebb, among those professing with us, in too general a manner, in those meetings; yet as public notice was given of our attendance, many of the neighbouring inhabitants came in. There were, I believe, some seeking minds among them, and these generally add life to meetings, and draw down the compassion, and tender regard of the heavenly parent, who, in his condescending goodness, made way for the gospel to be preached among them, in those several meetings, in a good degree of divine authority. Many minds were tenderly affected, and the assemblies solemnized; the lukewarm aroused, and the hypocritical, worldly-minded professors forewarned of the danger their situations exposed them to. My spirit was made thankful for the relief I obtained, although through a line of deep inward travail and baptism with the oppressed seed; but the Lord's power rose in victory over all, to the honour of his right worthy name, who will be glorified in his saints, and sanctified in all those who come near him.

We returned to the city on seventh day, and attended the quarterly meeting of Ministers and Elders; in which I was led, in a short, but relieving testimony, to call Friends' attention back to primitive simplicity and integrity; the great need there is of being more separated from the world, its spirit, manners, maxims, and customs; and to live daily under an exercise and travail, for the arising of that life and power, which only can enable us to separate from those things, that have a tendency to hurt and defile; and through which life and power, Ministers and Elders can only be rightly qualified to lead and feed the flock, over which the Holy Ghost hath made them overseers, consistent with divine appointment. For want of this fervent labour and travail, great weakness is apparent amongst us as a people, in many places; and the great and worthy name by which we are called, ofttimes dishonoured, to the grief of the upright in heart, who are exercised for Israel's prosperity, and Jerusalem's peace; and who go almost daily, as with their hands on their loins for very pain.

On first day, we attended the north meeting, in the morning, and that in Market-street in the afternoon. They were both instructive edifying seasons; wherein I had full opportunity to relieve my mind, being, through gracious assistance, led in the clear openings of the divine light, to set forth the great danger of mixing in with the spirit of the world, which leads to strife and contention, and the promotion of parties and party animosities in civil governments: all of which have a direct tendency to engender war and bloodshed, and are therefore inconsistent for us, as a people, to touch or take part with, or to suffer our minds to be agitated thereby; as it always has led, and always will lead those, who are leavened therewith, out of the meek spirit of the gospel, which breathes " peace on earth, and good will to all men." This was the Lord's doing and marvellous in our eyes. Friends were much comforted and united in this day's exercise, and my spirit made joyful in the saving help, and continued mercy of Israel's true Shepherd, who is over all, worthy, and blessed for ever

The quarterly meeting was held on second day, which was likewise a time of favour. Divers communications were made, tending to unite Friends in an exercise for the advancement of the testimony, that the numerous causes of weakness, which brought pain, and many deep baptisms on the living part of the body, might be done away, and the camp cleansed.

I left the city on third day morning, with a peaceful mind, and rode to Frankford; and attended a meeting there in the forenoon, and one at Germantown in the afternoon, in both of which I laboured in the ability received. The first was a very searching season; things were laid open in such a manner, that the dead, in some instances, seemed to be raised, and that power felt, which opened the graves formerly; and some of those, who were settled down in their polluted rests, had their heavens shaken, and their rocks made to melt, by the fervent heat of the *divine word*, which was as a fire and a hammer. Truth prevailed, and was eminently in dominion over all.

On fourth and fifth days, we attended the quarterly meeting of Abington; in which I was exercised in a line of close fervent labour, both in the meeting for Ministers and Elders, and the quarterly meeting at large. It was a season which gave hope of some improvement in many, but others appeared too much in a state of *self-sufficiency*, a most deplorable condition, sickly and wounded, and which refuses to be healed. For these, my mind felt pained. O, that they might, ere the day of their visitation pass over, witness their eyes anointed with the eye-salve of the gospel, that so they might be brought to see the precipice on which they stand, and be thereby reduced into the valley of humiliation; where alone true honour and right exaltation are known, and where they might experience a being washed from all their pollutions, and healed of all their wounds.

We attended a meeting at Byberry on sixth day, and, through the Lord's presiding presence, it proved a day of signal favour. The doctrines of full and complete redemption from sin and death were clearly opened, and truth exalted over all the dark tenets, and carnal reasonings of men, which lead to unbelief and infidelity.

On seventh day we returned to Abington, where we had another large favoured meeting, wherein many things were opened in a plain way, tending to gather the minds of the people out of the spirit of the world, which leads to strife and contention, from whence party animosities arise, often a prelude to war; and calling their attention home to the great gospel privilege, the holy *unction* and *anointing within:* so that they need not that any man teach them, but as the same anointing teacheth;

which, as they come to believe in and obey, would qualify them to judge of all ministry, and from whence it had its rise and spring; and thereby be delivered from all false glosses and mixtures in religion, and become established in that which never fell, the immoveable rock Christ Jesus, against which the gates of hell will never be able to prevail.

On first day, the 10th of 5th month, we attended Horsham meeting, and in the afternoon, the meeting at North Wales. It was a day of high favour, the Lord's arm was graciously made bare for our help; and the meetings were very large, many not of our society attended. The gospel was freely preached among them, in the clear demonstration of the spirit. They were truly humbling seasons, especially the former, wherein a great number were much contrited, and wept freely. The rocks seemed to melt at the presence of the mighty God of Jacob, whose power was prevalently witnessed in that large assembly, to the praise and exaltation of his great and glorious name.

We attended the meeting at Plymouth on second day. Although there was an evident want, affectingly manifest, of that primitive zeal and integrity which distinguished our worthy predecessors, with too many of those, who fill up their places in outward profession; yet it was comforting to find, that the Shepherd of Israel was still graciously pleased to continue his merciful visitations, and renew his gracious calls to these, to return, and renew covenant with him. This was the substance of this day's testimony and labour; may the Master of assemblies make it effectual, to all that were present of this description, is my sincere prayer. On third day we were at Providence meeting, which was small; nevertheless, through gracious regard, it proved an edifying, heart-tendering season. The states of the people were opened and spoken to, in the authority of truth, to their great humiliation; many hearts were much broken and reduced, and the Lord's power exalted over all.

After this meeting, my mind was turned towards the quarterly meeting of Caln, to be held this time at Sadsbury, a newly established quarterly meeting, in the county of Chester. Finding it necessary to comply with the motion, believing my peace consisted in it, we set out immediately after dinner, having thirty miles, or upwards, to ride to it. The journey proved very wearisome to my infirm body, being much troubled at this time with a painful complaint, with which I was greatly afflicted during the time of this quarterly meeting, especially in the forepart of the public meeting, preceding the meeting for discipline. I was ready to conclude that I should be obliged to leave the meeting, my distress of body was so great; but feeling my mind drawn to the people, there being a large congregation present, I continued, and way opening, I was enlarged in clear, pertinent doctrine. Truth rose into dominion, in an eminent manner, and ran over all as oil, comforting and breaking many hearts, and reducing, and silencing every opposite spirit. A very precious solemnity was spread over the meeting, rejoicing the upright in heart, relieving to my own mind, and alleviating my bodily affliction. These are high favours; may an humbling and grateful sense thereof rest continually upon thee, O my soul, and mayest thou never forget how much thou owest to thy Lord, how deep and solemn are thy obligations to the God of thy salvation; how hath he often taken thee out of the horrible pit, and out of the miry clay, and set thee upon a rock, and put a new song into thy mouth, even praises, high praises to him.

From this meeting we returned to Caln, and attended their monthly meeting, held the sixth of the week. I was enabled to labour among them in much plainness, both in the meeting for worship, and for discipline; and left them with a peaceful mind. The three following days we attended meetings at Robinson, Exeter, and Reading. The number of members which constituted these meetings was small, but a considerable number of the neighbouring inhabitants attended. Ability was graciously afforded to preach the gospel freely in each, and the power attending broke and tendered many hearts, and an excellent savour and solemnity was felt to spread over the meetings, in an eminent manner; for which I was made humbly thankful to the bountiful Author of all our blessings. These favours were more than an adequate reward for all my toil and exercise; although I had been, for some days past, under the pressure of much bodily infirmity, accompanied with seasons of great uneasiness and pain; but the Lord's power was over all, and kept my mind in patience, and sweet peace from day to day; blessed for ever, be his right worthy name.

The fourth of the week, and the 20th of 5th month, we attended the meeting at Maiden Creek. The same afternoon, and the next day, we crossed the Blue Mountains to Roaring Creek; and the day after, attended a meeting there. Both of these meetings were crowned with the Lord's presence, and were edifying and instructive seasons. The morning following we rode to Catawissa, and attended their monthly meeting; and continued there until after their first day meeting. I was enabled, through the Lord's good presence attending, to labour among them, both in the meeting for discipline, and those for worship, in much plainness; divers matters relative to the well-ordering of the affairs of truth were opened, which proved instructive and edifying.

After the latter meeting, we passed on that afternoon fifteen miles to Berwick, crossing the river Susquehannah in our way. The day following, the 25th of 5th month, although my bodily indisposition still continued, we had a meeting there, among the town's people, and the few Friends of that place. It was a comfortable season, edifying and strengthening to Friends; and confirming to a number who were looking towards us with desires for further information. After this meeting, we rode to Fishing Creek, about eighteen miles; and the day following had a very satisfactory meeting at that place. Although in this journey, for a considerable time past, I have experienced much bodily infirmity; yet the Lord, in his abundant mercy, hath been graciously pleased to keep my mind stayed upon him. My trust and confidence have not at any time failed, not even when I have been reduced into a state of great distress and suffering; and my poor soul plunged into the mighty abyss of surrounding darkness, and sunk, as it were, to the bottom of the mountains: for as I patiently abode under those trying baptisms, and was made willing to endure my portion thereof, my spirit was raised out of this horrible pit; wherein I had been a partaker with the suffering seed in the hearts of those, who, through supineness, ease, forgetfulness, unbelief and a worldly spirit, had become like a bottomless abyss of corruption, darkness and errour : and I was enabled, through a real feeling of their deplorable states, to administer to their several wants, and open to them their condition. Many were reached in heart, and convinced of the errour of their ways, and were led to give God the glory of his own work. And, O, saith my soul, may all those who are sent out on this solemn embassy and most important service, dwell low in their minds, and keep a single eye to the Lord's honour, that so self may be thoroughly abased : otherwise, there is great danger, in those trying and most afflictive dispensations, of the mind getting into a state of impatience, and therein be led to judge the people of hardness, and a spirit of opposition. This will not fail, if given way to, of centering the minds of such, either into a state of silent sadness and discouragement, that, like the disciples formerly, they will be for sending the people away fasting, and empty ; or else raise in them a hot fiery zeal, in which they will throw out some hard censures, or harsh reproof, untempered with that charity, requisite and necessary always to attend every gospel communication : for want of which, both speaker and hearers will be wounded, much hurt done, and many opportunities, I believe, have been entirely lost by these means, which might have been crowned with the Lord's presence, and his truth exalted. Nay I have no doubt, but some meetings have been held to the dishonour of truth, and wounding many tender minds. And I have sometimes been afraid, that some, who are rightly called, and sent on this greatest of errands, have so far missed their way, while under some of those excruciating baptisms, which they have been led into, in order to qualify them rightly to administer to the states of the people, as to suffer an impatient spirit to rise up ; and have thus brought a gloom of darkness over their minds, which has continued with them from day to day, greatly to their distress. Although they have continued to attend meetings, they have been so shut up in total darkness, as not to see any way of relief, except in uttering their complaints, similar to the murmurings of Israel in the wilderness. Where I have found such things left on record, I have thought they always tended to discouragement and dismay, when coming from the leaders of the people. Although the Lord was graciously pleased to condescend to the weakness of Israel, and deliver them out of the distress which their impatience had brought upon them ; yet he very clearly manifested his displeasure thereat. And if only one instance of impatience and improper zeal in Moses drew upon him such severe censure, as we read it did, how ought all those, who are now called forth as leaders of the people, to stand always on their guard against every motion of impatience, and impure zeal, lest they also fall under the displeasure of the Captain of their salvation.

Although, after those gloomy dispensations, we may be again favoured, in renewed mercy, and helped out of this horrible pit, and witness the lifting up of the light of the Lord's glorious countenance upon us ; yet this is no proof of the rectitude of our conduct, any more than his showing mercy to Israel, after their murmurings, was a justification thereof. Yet I have been afraid, that some have considered those renewed favours, as a consequence of their own sufferings ; which, to me, carries too much of selfishness, and savours of a desire of clothing ourselves with the Lord's jewels, instead of rendering to him, with heart-felt gratitude, the glory of all his works ; and receiving this act of unmerited redemption from the gloom, our own impatience, and the want of a thorough reduction of self, had cast us into, as flowing purely from his forbearing mercy, condescending goodness and free love.

After the aforesaid meeting, we rode to Muncy, and lodged with our kind friend William Ellis. The next day, the fourth of the week, and the 27th of 5th month, their meeting was held; and notice being spread that we were there, it was large. Although I had to sit some time in the forepart of the meeting, in much weakness and depression, both of body and mind ; yet as I abode in patience and resignation to my allotment, willing to be any thing, or nothing, and to do, or to suffer, according to the Master's will ; after a time of solemn waiting, a little opening presented, attended with some glimmering of light ; and as my

13

eye was kept steadily to it, I felt a necessity to stand up; and as I proceeded in guarded care, it opened to a large field of doctrine, suitably adapted, I believe, to the states of those present. A very comfortable solemnity was felt to spread over the meeting, rejoicing the hearts of the faithful.

We rested for a day or two after this meeting, with our aforesaid friend, in order to recruit, feeling myself very unwell with a cold, which had attended me for some time; and being much worn down by constant travelling under such bodily infirmities. The 30th of the month, and seventh day of the week, we attended a meeting at a place called Pine Grove; a small meeting of Friends being held there. On first day we had a large meeting, by appointment, at a town called Williamsport, which was held in their court-house; but the room was not large enough to contain the people, and although very much crowded, and many standing, they behaved soberly, and a blessed meeting we had. I was led forth among them, in a large affecting testimony, wherein the truths of the gospel were clearly opened and explained to the weakest capacities, and the Lord's power was in dominion, in a very eminent manner. It was a season thankfully to be remembered, and greatly refreshing to my drooping spirit, making up every deficiency for the want of bodily health. I could with heart-felt gratitude cheerfully acknowledge, it was the Lord's doing.

After this meeting we set forward on our journey towards Redstone, having meetings in our way, at Job Packers, Milesburgh, Half-moon Valley, and Downing's Creek. Then we passed directly over the Alleghany mountains, into the compass of Redstone quarterly meeting. On fourth day, the 10th of 6th month, we attended a meeting at Sewickly, on the western side of the mountains, a branch of Redstone monthly meeting. After this, we were at Providence on fifth day, Center on sixth, and Fallowfield on seventh day. Although these were seasons of close exercise, accompanied with some painful labour, and deep baptisms, in suffering with the seed; yet my mind was favoured in the openings of gospel light, so to discharge myself in those meetings, as to leave them with solid peace of mind. I believe they were seasons of renewed visitation to many who attended, that will not soon be forgotten by them.

On first day we attended the meeting at Pike Run, and the two following days were at Westland, and Redstone meetings. My mind was under a very great pressure of distress, in passing along through those six last mentioned meetings; both from an inward sense, and an outward discovery, of great weakness prevailing among them; occasioned by an unwarrantable credulity, and letting out their minds to listen to, and believe in, the vulgar, and shamefully ridiculous notion of witchcraft. Some of their leading members openly acknowledged, they believed that a family of their near kindred, several of whom were troubled with a kind of periodical fits, were actually thus affected by one of their neighbours. My spirit was exceedingly grieved by their asserting their belief in those abominable reports, and by discovering how their minds were led away thereby; and my grief was also much increased by their confidence in a certain boy in the neighbourhood, who pretended to tell secrets, saying, that he could see persons whom any should inquire after, although in a very distant part of the world, and would tell those who came to see him, notwithstanding they lived on the other side of the Atlantic, that he could see the very place of their residence, and of what materials their houses were made, as if he was present at the place; and would pretend to tell the conditions and dispositions of persons, whom he had never before seen, and what they were guilty of, as to their private sins, and who was a witch, and who not; and he had so far got the ascendency in the minds of those who had given way to the absurd notion of witchcraft, that whatever he said, in these respects, obtained their implicit belief. And if he impeached the most unblemished character of being a witch, or charged such with being guilty of any baneful sin, they were ready to believe it; by which means great hurt was done. I was exceedingly burthened therewith, and had conversation with divers- on the subject; but they were so carried away with these notions, that reasoning seemed to have no weight with them. While any man or woman can give way to believe in such things, and go to dark, undisciplined, and irreligious men, to be healed of those infirmities, which they are told are the effect of witchcraft, it is certainly denying the God that made them, who only hath all power in heaven and in earth, and can wound and heal, kill and make alive at his pleasure. God forbid, saith my soul, that any, professing the name of a Friend, should ever thus desert the God of his salvation; for if he doth, it will no doubt tend to his confusion, and in which state, he will be given over to strange delusions, even to believe a lie; a most wretched state for any poor soul to be in. I was enabled, through condescending goodness, to clear my mind among them, by divers large full testimonies to the truth, and the excellency of its power, to deliver from every thing that tends to hurt or defile.

I left them with peace of mind, and proceeded to Connelstown, where we had a very comfortable heart-tendering season, among a few Friends, and the town's people. Next we attended Sandy Hill meeting; and the day following were at Sandy Creek Glades, both comfortable seasons. These closed our visit to Redstone quarterly meeting. We then returned across the Alleghany mountains, with a view to attend the meetings belonging to Hopewell, in the compass of Fairfax Quarterly meeting. We reached Bear Garden particular meeting on first day, having rode diligently the day before, for that purpose; not having much prospect thereof when we left Sandy Creek. The distance between the two places was about ninety-two miles, and the way very mountainous, and having had but little more than a day and a half to ride it. This meeting, in the forepart, was heavy, but ended well; and we left them with solid satisfaction, and passed on to Back Creek meeting that afternoon; held near a small town, or village, called Penn's Town. Many of the neighbouring people came in, so that the meeting was pretty large, and I had considerable to communicate among them, but without obtaining much relief of mind.

In the course of this week we attended meetings at the Ridge, Centre, Crooked Run, Mount Pleasant, Hopewell, and Lower Ridge; and on the first and second days, of the following week, we were at Middle Creek, and Berkly meetings. These were, most of them, favoured seasons, particularly that at Middle

Creek, wherein the Lord's presence was powerfully manifest. Truth rose into great dominion, preciously uniting and edifying the honest-hearted, and breaking down all opposition, affecting and mollifying the hearts of, almost, the whole assembly. It was indeed a precious solemnity, not soon to be forgotten, but to be held in grateful remembrance.

After those meetings, we turned our faces homewards, attending meetings in our way, at Little York, Columbia, Pottstown, and the Great Swamp, alias Richland; these were through divine favour, instructive seasons. The next meeting was at Plumbstead, in the compass of Buck's quarterly meeting, which we attended on third day, the 7th of 7th month : and on the two following days, we were at Buckingham, and Wright's Town meetings. My mind, in those meetings, was brought under a close exercise, from a prospect of Friends being too much leavened into the spirit of the world, its customs and maxims ; by which, many appeared to be greatly wounded, and had become as dwarfs in our Israel. And I believe, nothing contributed more to this, than their becoming parties in the civil government, and taking offices therein ; for here, the spirit of contention gets in, and a striving to be uppermost, and fill the principal seats : then party animosities take place, from whence are derived envy and jealousy, one against another ; and then reviling, and neighbours speaking evil of each other ; hence wars and fightings arise, as from their natural ground. As any give way to these things, it leavens their minds into the spirit of the world, which is a spirit of darkness, that blinds the understanding and hardens the heart, and draws into many hurtful and pernicious practices, such as dealing in ardent spirits, drinking strong drink, and handing it out in their fields to their workmen, to stimulate them to an excess of labour ; hence an excess of drinking strong drink is gradually introduced among the poor labourers, by means of which many families are ruined.

My spirit was deeply exercised on those accounts, but as I patiently endured the baptisms I had to go through, and submitted to communicate what appeared clearly to open ; I was enlarged in setting forth the dangerous and hurtful tendency of such conduct, and its great inconsistency with our holy profession, and to exhort Friends to a more frequent recurrence to the first principle of our profession, the light within; whereby deliverance and preservation could only be experienced. The Lord was graciously with us in those meetings, and the faithful were encouraged and edified, and many hearts greatly tendered, under a sense of the Lord's mercy and goodness extended to us in these seasons.

On sixth day we attended a meeting at Makefield, and in the afternoon, had a large meeting at Newtown. It was held in their court-house, and mostly composed of those not professing with us. I felt in this meeting, the pressure and prevalence of a spirit of darkness and unbelief; and was led to open the ground thereof, and to show its inconsistency with the self-evident experience of every rational mind. For although men in the ignorance and darkness of their own hearts, may strive to settle themselves in unbelief, in order to live quietly in the gratification of their own wills and creaturely appetites, without any controul; yet, they never can fully come to this; for that just witness, placed in every bosom as a reprover for sin, will continue to disturb all those false rests, and shake every heaven of man's making. For although men, through the hardness of their hearts, may not submit to the guidance of this just principle, so as to have a saving belief therein; yet they will thereby be compelled into a belief, similar to that of the devils, and which they will never be able fully to divest themselves of by all their carnal reasonings and fleshly wisdom; but it will continue, at times, to make them fear and tremble, and by its tremendous power will cause the very top of their Sinai to shake, and blast all their false hopes. For it is the determinate counsel of unerring wisdom, that the hope of the hypocrite shall perish: therefore let all prize the day of their visitation, while the Lord is graciously striving with them, by the clear, self-evident touches of his light in their hearts; in order that the wicked may turn from his wicked way, and the unrighteous from his unrighteous thoughts, and turn unto the Lord who will have mercy upon him. and unto our God, who will abundantly pardon.

The meeting at Makefield was likewise a precious opportunity. The Lord being mightily with us in our passing along, from season to season, to our humbling admiration, furnishing with strength for every service ; so that we indeed found him to be strength in weakness, and riches in poverty. For I never felt greater weakness and nothingness, as to self, than in this journey ; and could truly say, that our sufficiency was not of ourselves, but of God ; and that the Lord was our strength from day to day, who is over all, blessed for ever.

The three following days we attended meetings at Middletown, Bristol, and the Falls. I was led forth in these meetings to show wherein real Christianity consists ; and although the people of christendom had the name of Christians, yet, so long as they lived in the gratification of their own wills and carnal lusts, from whence discord, animosities, envyings, strife and every evil work originated, they were only heathens in disguise. For true Christianity is nothing else than a real and complete mortification of our own wills, and a full and final annihilation of all self-exaltation : and the contrary is the true antichrist, that sitteth in the seat of God, who opposeth and exalteth himself above all that is called God, or that is worshipped. Therefore, none are any further Christians, than as they come to experience the self-denial, meekness, humility and gentleness of Christ, ruling and reigning in them, so as to become their real life ; and in, and by which, they become partakers of the divine nature, and know the *life of God* raised up in the immortal soul ; which is the new birth, or *Christ formed in us,* and without which, as our Lord told Nicodemus, no man can see the kingdom of God.

After these meetings we crossed the river Delaware into New Jersey, attending meetings on our way, at Kingwood, Hardwick, Mendham, and one near Paulingskiln. From thence we passed to Cornwall, in the state of New-York. We reached there seventh day evening, the 18th of 7th month, and the next day were at their first day meeting. I was much worn down by constant travelling and hard labour, and felt much fatigue when we came here ; and in going to this meeting, I felt a desire to rise in my mind, that I might have a good silent meeting. The prayer of my spirit was answered, for I had not sat long before a perfect, sweet calm ensued, wherein my whole man was swallowed up in divine seraphic enjoyment; so that not only my mind, but also my wearied body forgot all its toil; and my soul was so inflamed with gratitude, to the all-bountiful Author of all our rich mercies and blessings, that praises and thanksgiving ascended as incense from the altar of my heart to his great and glorious name, who remains to be God over all, blessed for ever, world without end. Amen.

In the course of this week we attended meetings at Newburgh Valley, the Paltz, Marlborough, and on fifth day were at Cornwall monthly meeting. The meeting for worship which preceded the business, was large. I was led among them in a line of close searching labour, which, for some time, seemed to have but little entrance among them; mankind being too generally disposed, while in a state of unsoundness, to shut themselves against *that*, which they know, if they are open to receive, would find out all their secret lurking places, where *self-love* and *self-will* lie shrouded under a mask *of doing good*, while it is gratified in the full enjoyment of all its beloveds, and with whom it is daily committing adultery and fornication: but as I continued to persevere in faithfulness to the opening, although the prospect for a time seemed discouraging, truth began to make way by its own power, and gradually spread over the meeting, breaking down all opposition, and tendering and mollifying many hearts. The meeting for discipline appeared to be pretty well conducted, there being, I believe, a remnant honestly engaged for the promotion of the cause of truth ; and these the Lord delights to favour, and furnish with strength to carry on his own work of truth and righteousness in the earth ; and he will continue to reward these with the real enjoyment of his life-giving presence; while those who sit as mere idle spectators, will be sent empty away.

On sixth day we had an appointed meeting at the house of our friend Thomas Jones at Walkiln ; on seventh day, one at Goshen, and on first day, we were at Smith's Clove. All satisfactory seasons, especially the last, wherein truth was powerfully manifest, tendering the hearts of the people in a remarkable manner; so that a very precious solemnity was witnessed to spread over the meeting. After these meetings we turned homewards, attending meetings in our way at Kakiat, Tappan and New-York. We reached home on fourth day evening, the 29th of 7th month. I found my family in usual health, which, together with an endeared and cordial reception in the feelings of mutual love, and flowings of that peace of mind attendant on a faithful discharge of manifested duty, filled my heart with thankful acknowledgments to the great and bountiful Author of every blessing.

I was from home in this journey three months and eighteen days, and travelled about sixteen hundred and thirty miles.

CHAPTER V.

Visit to Friends in Canada, and some of the northern parts of the yearly meeting of New-York, 1803.—Visit on Long Island, Staten Island, and New-York,
  1806.—Visit to Purchase, Nine Partners, and Stanford, and some adjacent
  parts, 1806.—Visit to Nine Partners, 1807.—Visit to Purchase, Nine Partners,
  and Stanford, 1808.—Visit to the subordinate meetings, 1808.—Visit to Purchase, 1809.—Visits on Long Island, 1812 and 1813.—Visit to Purchase in
  1813.

In the fall of the year 1803, I performed a visit to Friends of
Upper Canada, and some other of the northwestern parts of our
yearly meeting.   Daniel Titus was my companion in this journey.   We left home the 20th of 9th month, and proceeded
directly to Canada, in company with two other Friends, who,
with us, were appointed to attend the monthly meeting of Adolphustown on a particular concern relative to that meeting.   We
were at but three meetings in our way thither, two at Hudson
on first day, and one at Black River.   We got well to Adolphustown on third day evening, the 3d of 10th month, having
rode about four hundred and ten miles, and crossed the great
river St. Lawrence, which appeared to be a dangerous passage.
We crossed its two branches, an island lying in the middle.
Each branch was nearly five miles over.   We passed the latter
in the middle of the night, by the light of the moon, in two small
flat-bottomed boats, one of them so small as to carry only one
horse.   This latter passage lay open to Lake Ontario, and the
wind being from that quarter, caused the swell frequently to
wash into our boats, so that we had considerable labour to throw
out the water as fast as it came in ; but my confidence was in

Him, who hath the winds and the waves at his command. This kept out fear, and we got safe over about one o'clock in the morning.

On fourth day we attended Friends' meeting at Adolphustown, as it came in course, which proved an instructive favoured season. On fifth day we rode to Green Point, in the township of Sophiasburgh, to the house of our friend Daniel Way ; and had an appointed meeting there that afternoon, at the third hour. In this meeting I was favoured ; and by the prevalence of the power of truth, attending the communication, many minds were much bowed, and their hearts tendered by its secret mollifying influence. Our next appointment was in the neighbourhood of our friend Robert Hubbs, on seventh day, composed mostly of people not of our society, which was a comfortable, edifying season. After this we proceeded to the township of Hallowell, to the house of our friend Thomas Boorman near West Lake ; and on first day attended Friends' meeting there. On second day, we had an opportunity with the people at the east end of the lake, which was held at the house of a professor among the Methodists. These two last meetings were eminently favoured ; truth rose into dominion, and ran as oil over all opposition, to the instruction and comfort of many minds ; and the Lord was praised for his goodness, and for his merciful, loving kindness to the children of men. We returned that evening to the west end of said lake, to the house of our friend Jacob Cronk, and lodged.

On third day the 11th of 10th month, we returned to the house of Cornelius Blount, where the meeting for Friends of West Lake was held. It was the time of their preparative meeting, and many of the neighbouring inhabitants came in, and sat with Friends, during the time of worship ; the forepart of which, was rather low and depressing ; but as patience was abode in, and right attention given to a small opening which presented, and as I moved therein with care, truth gradually rose into dominion, powerfully breaking down all that stood in its way. Many hearts were comforted and refreshed, and a general solemnity spread over the meeting, so that we could truly say, hitherto hath the Lord helped us.

After the preparative meeting was over, which was held in an orderly manner, we returned that evening to the house of our friend John Dorland, in Adolphustown, he having kindly accompanied us since we left that place. On fourth day we attended the preparative meeting there. The meeting for worship was large, many of those who were not members came in, and manifested great willingness to hear the truths of the gospel declared ; yet too many appeared careless and unconcerned, with regard to the practical part, so that in them was fulfilled the saying of the apostle : " For if any be a hearer of the word, and not a doer, he is like unto a man beholding his natural face in a glass : for he beholdeth himself and goeth his way, and straightway forgetteth what manner of man he was." And this, it is to be feared, is too much the case with many amongst us, as a people, who are pleasing themselves with hearing the truth declared, and rejoice in the privilege of sitting under a free, living, gospel ministry, through the labour and exercise of the faithful ; but suffer the cumbering cares and pleasures of this life, so to divert them from a right improvement of their own gifts, that they, in a religious sense, may justly be compared to idle drones, who live on the labour of the industrious bee, and are contenting themselves in a situation like the foolish virgins, who, although they have lamps, yet, are without oil in their vessels ; but alas, what will these do, when the awful midnight cry is heard, " behold the bridegroom cometh ;" then fear and dismay, with an utter exclusion from the marriage chamber, will be the woful doom of all careless, and lifeless professors. O that all might lay these things to heart, and endeavour, in awful fear, to have their day's work done in the day time ; for behold the night cometh, wherein none can work.

On sixth day we attended Friends' preparative meeting at Kingston ; and on seventh day, we had a meeting in the town of Kingston, in the court-house, the first Friends' meeting ever held in that place. The people appeared much unacquainted with the order of our meetings, and some of the principal men seemed at a loss how to behave themselves in the time of silence ; but during the communication, they were generally quiet and solemn, and truth rose into victory, furnishing doctrine, clothed with divine power, and carrying conviction to the minds of most present.

The next day, the first of the week, we again attended Friends' meeting held at the house of the widow Brewer ; they not having any meeting-house in this place. In the afternoon we had an appointed meeting in the west part of this township, on the bay, which was held at the house of John Everit, a man not in strict profession with any religious society. These were both seasons of heavenly refreshment ; the life ran as oil over all ; many hearts were much broken and contrited, under the precious mollifying influence thereof; praised and magnified for ever, be the name of the Lord, for his mercy and loving kindness to the children of men.

The 17th we returned towards Adolphustown, and attended a meeting appointed at an inn on our way, in the town of Earnest. This also proved, through the condescending mercy and goodness of the Lord our gracious helper, a blessed season ; and through the efficacious power attending the word preached, many hearts were pierced, and the whole assembly solemnized. We parted from each other with thankful hearts, and rode to Adolphustown, and lodged with our friend Daniel Haight. The day following we had an appointed meeting at his house, for the neighbouring inhabitants, who were, many of them, professors among the Methodists. This, through divine goodness, was to me a season of great refreshment, and the assembly were generally broken and contrited by the convicting power of divine love, which was mercifully vouchsafed to us at this season.

We then proceeded again to our friend John Dorland's, and rested the next day, as I was somewhat unwell, and considerably wearied by such constant travelling.

On fifth day, the 20th of the month, we attended Friends' monthly meeting for the lower part of the Province of Upper Canada, held at Adolphustown. This closed our visit in these parts ; and we took leave of our friends in much brotherly affection ; their hearts were contrited, and their cheeks bedewed with tears, when we closed our farewell addresses. After this we rode directly to Kingston about thirty-five miles, and there took boat immediately, and crossed one branch of the river St. Lawrence that evening. We likewise crossed the island, which lies between, before dark, it being about five miles over; but as the wind was unfavourable, we did not cross the other branch till next morning. We lodged in a small house, being the only one on that side of the island. Our accommodations were very poor, having to lie on the floor, and on benches ; but having the best of company, peace of mind, and a firm trust in the divine blessing, it kept us comfortable and pleasant.

The next day, the 22d of the month, we crossed early in the morning, and rode that day, to our friend Samuel Brown's, at Black River. The day after, being the first of the week, we tarried there, and had two meetings with his family, and the neighbours ; divers of whom were sober religious Baptists. They were both favoured seasons ; may the Lord bless his own work, and seal it to the lasting advantage of those who attended.

The 24th and 25th, we rode eighty-five miles to Utica, on the upper part of the Mohawk river. The 26th, 27th and 28th, we rode about one hundred and eighteen miles to Palmyra, in Ontario county, to the house of our friend Abraham Lapham. The 29th we rested. The 30th, being the first of the week, we attended Friends' meeting in that neighbourhood, and one in the evening, appointed at a man's house whose wife was a member, about six miles distant from the former. They were both, I believe, profitable and edifying seasons. The 31st we attended a meeting in the town of Palmyra, appointed principally for those not of our society. It was a large solemn meeting, wherein the truths of the gospel were largely opened, affecting, solemnizing and comforting many hearts.

On the 1st of the 11th month, we rode to Bristol about eighteen miles, and attended a meeting at the third hour in the afternoon. It was held in a Baptist meeting-house, and was a hard exercising season. Those who attended appeared to be mostly, very insensible of any right religious concern and exercise ; nevertheless, through ability received, after a considerable time of hard silent labour, the power of truth was exalted among them, and some hearts were reached and tendered thereby, and I left them with peace of mind.

We then rode back thirty-seven miles to Cayuga Lake, and lodged at an inn. On the 3d, we rode to a town called Scipio, where a few Friends resided, who were indulged with holding a meeting under the care of the monthly meeting of Farmington. Here we had a meeting at the eleventh hour, it being their usual meeting day. It was very small and low in the silent part, but as a right exercise in waiting, was patiently maintained, truth gradually rose into dominion, in a very instruc-ive manner, refreshing and comforting our minds, in the sweet enjoyment of the divine presence, who manifested himself to be graciously near for our help in the needful time.

After dining with our friends we took leave, and turned our faces homeward ; and in four days got to Galloway, to the house of our friend Philip Macomber. The next day we rested. The three following days we attended the meetings of Galloway, Ballstown, and Newtown ; which were all comfortable edifying seasons. The 12th we rode to Troy. The 13th, and first of the week, we attended two meetings, the first, at the eleventh hour, at the house of Zachariah Garnrick, about four miles from Troy, where the few Friends of that place and the adjacent neighbour-hood, hold a little meeting. It was enlarged at this time by others coming in, who were not of our society ; and the Lord rewarded us bountifully, and gave us a heavenly season together, wherein his name was gloriously exalted over all ; and we parted with thankful hearts. The latter meeting was held at Troy, in their court-house. It was a large gathering, but hard and heavy.

The 14th we rode to Pittstown, and attended a meeting at the second hour, which was a satisfactory season, and, I hope, profit-able to some ; although others appeared to be too much at ease. The 15th we rode to Easton, and attended the quarterly meet-ing of Ministers and Elders ; and the two following days we attended the quarterly meeting for discipline, and the parting meeting for worship. The latter was a heavenly baptizing sea-son, wherein truth was raised into dominion in a very eminent manner, the hearts of many were much broken and contrited, and a general solemnity spread over the meeting; and the Lord's name praised, and exalted over all, who is worthy for ever.

After this, we rode that afternoon to Saratoga, crossing the river Hudson in our way ; and the next day went to South Greenfield, and attended a meeting at the second hour in the afternoon. The 19th we rode to Providence, and after a meeting there, went back again that afternoon to North Greenfield. The day following, being the first of the week, we attended a meeting there, which was large and favoured, as were the two former. The 21st, we had an appointed meeting at Saratoga Springs, amongst a people not very unlike those, whom the scribes, among the Jews, called publicans and sinners. It was a profitable edifying season, most of those present appearing to receive the word with readiness, and apparent good will ; so that it might have been said of some of them, as our Lord said concerning some of this description in his day, that they were more likely to enter the kingdom, than many of the high professors of religion, who make a great outward show of godliness, but are void of the power.

The 23d and 24th, we attended the monthly meetings of Saratoga and Easton ; and the day following had an appointed meeting at White Creek, and the next day we rode to East Hoosack. The 27th, and first of the week, we attended Friends' meeting there. It was a very comfortable season ; the Lord was with us, and by his power made way in the hearts of the people, for the reception of the testimony given us to bear among them. We left them with thankful hearts, and rode that evening to our friend David Lapham's, in the township of Hancock; and the next day had a meeting at his house, at the second hour, for the neighbouring inhabitants, who were mostly professors among the Baptists, and who behaved very orderly ; and the Lord, in his never failing mercy, favoured us together with a solemn instructive season.

The next day we passed on to New Britain, and rested the following day. The fifth of the week, and the 1st of 12th month, we attended the meeting there, at its usual time ; which was very large, occasioned, in part, by our being there; and there was likewise a marriage accomplished thereat. I think, for the most part, it was a favoured, comfortable season. On sixth day we attended a meeting at Kline Kiln; and on first day were at Hudson, where we had, with Friends and others, at their meeting, a refreshing opportunity; the Lord was graciously near, furnishing with strength and utterance, and an evidence of the divine power attending, rejoicing the faithful, confirming the weak and wavering, and convicting the indolent, the disobedient, and gainsayers. On second day we rode to Little Nine Partners; and the four following days, we attended meetings at that place, Pine Plains, Stanford, and Creek; these were comfortable meetings, wherein, through the prevalence of truth, many were convicted, their hearts tendered, and the faithful few encouraged, and made to rejoice; and the Lord's name praised and exalted over all. On seventh day evening we had an appointed meeting at the house of Thomas Wilbur, about four miles from the latter; and although hard and low, yet I trust in a good degree profitable and instructive.

On first day we went to Crum-elbow meeting, which was very much crowded, and the house not sufficient to hold the people. The season appeared somewhat to represent the time, when the miracle of the loaves and fishes was performed. For the people's attention appeared to be generally outward, many having come together out of curiosity, to see and hear with their outward senses; which makes hard work for the travellers, who are faithfully engaged in Zion's cause. I sat long in silence in great poverty and want, for the people appeared to be void of any spiritual food, and no offering prepared; but as I abode in patience, and in the faith, the query ran through my mind, is there not a lad present, who may have a few barley loaves and fishes. A young man soon after stood up, who, I believed, had for some time, something on his mind to offer; and by a short but pertinent communication opened my way. Soon after he sat down I stood up, and the Lord made way among the people, while I was led to open, in a very enlarged manner, what the young Friend had dropped; and the Lord's power was extended

15

in a marvellous manner over the whole assembly, so that it might be said indeed, that all did eat and were filled, and many fragments remained to be gathered up. It was the Lord's doing, and marvellous in our eyes.

Our two next appointments were at Pleasant Valley, and the Branch, on second and third days. These were comfortable, and I trust, profitable seasons. The four successive days we attended the monthly meetings of Oswego, Nine Partners, Creek, and Stanford. They were all seasons of great favour, wherein I was largely opened in the line of gospel ministry, in four several searching testimonies, greatly to the comfort of the honest faithful travellers, and to the rebuke and warning of the careless, hypocritical, and worldly-minded professors. On first day we attended the meeting at Nine Partners, and notice having been previously given of our intention of being there, the meeting was very large ; and the Lord's power was present with us, enabling me to discharge myself faithfully among them, and instructingly to divide the word, suited to their several conditions. The season concluded with prayer and thanksgiving, to his great and adorable name, who is over all, God blessed for ever.

After this, apprehending I felt liberty to turn my face homeward, and having for the two successive days meetings, appointed at Chesnut Ridge, and Poquague, we proceeded accordingly. Although I was under considerable infirmity of body, and travelled in much pain, yet through gracious aid, furnished from the adorable fountain of all wisdom and strength, I was enabled to attend them to my own satisfaction, and the comfort and encouragement of my friends. I was led forth in both of these meetings in large affecting testimonies; the minds of many present were baptized and humbled, and the faithful few refreshed, whom the Lord delights to honour.

On fourth day we crossed the Highlands, and rode down to the mouth of Croton River, about forty-two miles. It was wearisome to my afflicted body, but believing it right for us so to proceed, and having faith in the divine sufficiency, I was sustained even beyond rational expectation. The day following being Friends' meeting day in that place, we had a comfortable opportunity with them, together with some of their neighbours; and it was, I believe, an instructive edifying season to many. May it fasten as a nail in a sure place.

After this we passed on to New-York, where we tarried over first day, and attended their forenoon and afternoon meetings; also an appointed meeting in the evening, at their new meeting-house. They were large and very exercising, yet, I trust, in the main, profitable meetings. On second day the 26th of 12th month, we rode home, and I found my family well, which, together with the Lord's mercies and preservations, vouchsafed to me in this arduous journey, caused my heart to be filled with gratitude and thanksgiving to His great and worthy name, to whom belongs all praise, adoration and worship, from the rising of the sun to the going down of the same, throughout all ages, world without end. Amen.

I was out in this journey about three months, and rode about fifteen hundred and seventy-five miles.

In the spring of the year 1806, feeling my mind drawn in gospel love, to pay a religious visit to some of the neighbouring towns and villages on our island, Staten Island and New-York, among those not in profession with us; and opening my concern to our monthly meeting, I received the concurrence and unity of my friends therein. I was from home in this service about twenty days, and had about thirty meetings among those not of our society, generally to good satisfaction, and to the peace of my own mind. Many, in most places, appeared convinced of the truth and propriety of our doctrine and principles, as they were communicated, and divers feelingly expressed their satisfaction therewith, and the heart-felt comfort they witnessed in those opportunities; and I had cause to hope that light was breaking forth in some places, which had long been under the power of great darkness, through the undue force of wrong customs, and a false education, principally propagated by a mercenary, anti-christian ministry. My mind was often affected, in considering the emptiness and fruitless state of many of those professors under different names, who had a form of godliness, and were very zealous in attending to the outside ceremonials, of what they called religion and worship; but in their lives and conduct denied the power thereof, being persuaded by their blind guides, to believe they might be saints, while they were sinners, and stand in a state of justification, without sanctification. But this is a false and very dangerous doctrine. O, saith my spirit, may the light of Israel arise and come forth, and by the brightness of its arising, dispel all those mists and fogs, those works of darkness, which those blind guides have raised up between God and the souls of the people; and deliver the nations out of the hands of all oppressors, that so none, at the awful closing period, may witness verified in themselves, that solemn truth, that " if the blind lead the blind, both shall fall into the ditch."

In the fall of the year 1806, feeling my mind drawn to visit some parts of the quarterly meetings of Purchase, Nine Partners, and Stanford, with some adjacent places, not among Friends, and obtaining the unity and concurrence of our monthly meeting therein, I set forward the 8th of 12th month; Thomas Willis kindly joining me as a companion in this journey. On third day we attended the meeting for sufferings in New-York, and in the evening we had an appointed meeting at Brooklyn, which was a solemn, comfortable season. Fourth day, being the day on which Friends' meeting was held in the city, notice was given of our intention of being there. It was a pretty large meeting, and in a good degree favoured with the spreading of the divine canopy, and strength was afforded to communicate to the various situations of those present; to the honest-hearted and truly exercised travellers, comfort and encouragement, and of this number, I trust, there are a few preserved in this city of great stir and commotion; and to the careless, the unguarded and refractory, caution and rebuke.

After this we passed on to Mamaroneck, and lodged with our kind friend Richard Mott. The three following days of this week, we attended the monthly meetings of Purchase, Shapaqua and Amawalk. We stayed over their first day meeting at Amawalk, which was large, many of other societies coming in; and had an appointed meeting in the evening at Peekskill. These were all seasons of favour, comforting and refreshing to my mind.

On second day, the 15th of the month, we proceeded on our journey, and reached, seasonably in the evening, the house of our kind friend Enoch Dorland, at or near Oswego. On third day we rode to Nine Partners. On fourth day we attended the monthly meeting of Oswego ; both the meeting for worship, and that for discipline, were well conducted, and truth reigned ; which made them comfortable and instructive. On fifth, sixth and seventh days, we attended the monthly meetings of Nine Partners, Creek, and Stanford. Nothing transpired in either of these unusual. We attended Friends' meeting at Northeast, on first day, and also a meeting in the evening at Little Nine Partners ; both seasons of favour. On second day we rode to Hudson, and the next day attended their monthly meeting, and likewise had a large public meeting in the evening with Friends and others. I have cause to acknowledge the goodness and mercy of the Shepherd of Israel, who has been pleased graciously to manifest his presence and power for our help and encouragement, from season to season, enabling us to labour, to the comfort and refreshment of the honest-hearted and faithful among the brethren and sisters, and to impart counsel and caution to the varied states of those amongst whom our lots were cast, and stirring up the pure mind in many. So that in many places it appeared to be a renewed visitation of divine love to the people, for which many hearts with our own were made thankful.

On fourth and fifth days we had meetings with Friends at Kline Kiln, and New Britain ; and on sixth day we had an opportunity with those not in profession with us, at a place called Philipstown. The meeting was held in a meeting-house belonging to the Presbyterians, and a precious season it proved, tendering the hearts of most present ; truth prevailing over all, to the praise and glory of His grace, who hath called us to labour in his vineyard.

We went from this place to Troy and attended Friends' meeting on first day ; and had a large public meeting in the evening with the inhabitants of the town. On second and third day evenings, we had meetings in the towns of Waterford and Lansingburgh ; the former was held in a meeting-house belonging to the Methodist society; and the latter, by their voluntary permission, in the Episcopal meeting-house. These were all seasons of favour, especially the last, in which truth was powerfully manifest, solemnizing the assembly, tendering and melting many hearts into contrition, and raising an acknowledgment to its divine power.

On fourth day we attended Friends' preparative meeting at Troy, and also an appointed meeting for the inhabitants of the town in the evening. The next morning previous to our leaving there, we had a precious opportunity with three or four families of Friends, the heads of which were all brethren and sisters of each other, by blood, or marriage. It was a season wherein the Lord was pleased to magnify his power, and cause every heart to bow and acknowledge to its blessed and mollifying influence, which prevailed over all to our mutual rejoicing.

The visit being over we took leave of our friends, and rode that afternoon to Albany, and attended a pretty large meeting, held that evening in their court-house. It was, I believe, to many, a profitable edifying season. On sixth day morning feeling my mind drawn to have a select opportunity, with the few members of our society resident in this city, they were notified thereof, and came together early in the forenoon. We had a satisfactory season with them, in which I was favoured to clear myself of a burden I felt on their account, in a plain tender manner, comforting the sincere-hearted, and stirring up the careless and lukewarm. After this we took our leave in brotherly affection, with quiet and peaceful minds, and with an evidence of having faithfully discharged our duty, which made our journeying forward pleasant, as we passed on to Duanesburgh, where we arrived that evening. On seventh day we rested. On first day the 4th of 1st month, 1807, we attended the meeting there, and notice being given of our attendance, it was a very large meeting, wherein truth reigned. Many doctrinal truths were opened to the people, and the gospel preached in the clear demonstration of the spirit; to the Lord only wise, gracious and merciful, be the praise, who is the blessed author thereof; nothing due to man.

The next day we had a meeting in our way to Otego, near a village called Charlestown, at the house of a man inclining to Friends, in which I was enabled to communicate, in gospel authority, to the tendering and contriting of many hearts.

We reached Otego on fourth day, a little before meeting time, it being Friends' usual meeting day, which, therefore, afforded but little opportunity of notifying their neighbours; but some hearing thereof, attended. It was a glorious meeting, which richly paid us for all our toil in getting there, yea an hundred fold; magnified for ever be the name of the Lord, who graciously manifested his power for our help, comforting many hearts, and causing the faithful to rejoice together, in the sweet incomes of his love and life. On fifth day, we attended Friends' meeting held at Burlington in the middle of the week. The neighbouring inhabitants having notice of our coming, generally attended, and although the life did not appear to rise so high as in the foregoing meeting, yet, for the most part, I believe, it was a profitable edifying season. We rode to Deruyter on sixth day, and on seventh day rested, and mended our carriage, which was much injured and broken by our journey to this place. On first day, we attended Friends' meeting there, which was much crowded, the house being but small. The Lord was with us, and magnified his power, reaching and tendering many hearts; the gospel was freely preached, and appeared to be freely received by the auditory in general.

On second day, we had a meeting at a town called Woodstock, at the eleventh hour, and one in the evening at Cazenovia. There were no Friends living in either of these places, and the people in general appeared dark and ignorant, yet, they were attentive to what was communicated; and many of them appeared thankful for the opportunities, and desired our longer continuance among them; but we took our leave, and left them with our minds clothed with peace. We then turned our faces homeward, being desirous of getting back in time to attend the ensuing quarterly meeting of Nine Partners, to be held in the forepart of 2d month. We felt our minds drawn to return by Burlington, and had meetings in our way there, at Hamilton, Brookfield,

Bridgewater, and one in the evening between Bridgewater and Burlington, held in a school-house, at a village in the township of Brookfield. These were all favoured meetings, comfortable and instructive, many hearts were reached and affected with the power of truth, which was prevalently manifest for our help.

We were at Burlington on first day, and notice being generally spread that we were there, it proved the largest meeting ever held in that place; and through the Lord's goodness and mercy to us, it was made a season gratefully to be remembered, by, I believe, the greater part of the meeting.

This being over, we had another meeting in the evening, in a neighbouring town called Pittsfield, which was held in a large school-house, there being no member of our society there; this was likewise an edifying opportunity. The next day we proceeded to Otego, and attended a meeting there at the eleventh hour, appointed previously by our request. It was a large meeting, and graciously favoured with the overshadowing wing of divine kindness. On third day we had an appointed meeting in the township of Heartwick.

From this place we returned to Duanesburgh, and attended their monthly meeting held on sixth day. This meeting was composed of the preparative meetings of Duanesburgh, Otego, Burlington, and Deruyter. The latter meeting was near ninety miles from the place where the monthly meeting was held at this time. Friends are much scattered in this new country, by reason of which, but few, in some meetings, have much opportunity of attending their monthly meetings; this is a great loss to many families, especially the children, many of whom are thus deprived of the improving company of experienced Friends in meetings for discipline or otherwise. I have often thought it a very weighty matter for a Friend to move with a family of children so far from meetings, and especially meetings for discipline, which, I have often considered as schools of very profitable instruction to well-minded youth. This is a new monthly meeting, made up of Friends of but small experience, many of them newly received members. The business of the meeting was of course but weakly conducted. We laboured among them in the ability received, for their instruction and help, and there appeared a readiness in some to receive, who, I trust, will become useful members, as they abide in humility, and are faithful to the measure of grace received. On seventh day we rode to Oakhill, and on first day attended Friends' meeting there ; it was a very full meeting, and proved satisfactory and instructive.

The four following days we were at meetings at Scott's Patent, Bern, Rensselaerville, one in a Friend's house between the last mentioned place and Coeman's Patent, and one at Coeman's Patent. They were seasons of general satisfaction, especially the last, which was a very large precious meeting, in which the truths of the gospel were largely declared, in the demonstration of the spirit. Many hearts were tendered and contrited, and the Lord's name praised and magnified, who is over all, worthy for ever.

The sixth, we rode to Hudson, and passed most of the way upon the ice, on the river, the weather having been, for some days past, extremely cold. On seventh day evening we had an appointed meeting at Lunenburgh, which lies on the west side of the river Hudson, and opposite to that city. On first day we attended Friends' meeting at Hudson. Both these meetings were held, I believe, to general satisfaction, and I trust, were profitable and instructive to many who attended.

From hence we passed on to Nine Partners, and reached there seasonably to meet with the committee who have the oversight of the boarding-school, held there by the direction of our yearly meeting, we being members of that committee. By the accounts now rendered, the school appears in a prosperous state ; but a considerable difficulty attends procuring suitable tutors and caretakers in the family. On third day, the select quarterly meeting of this place was held, and on fourth day, that for discipline ; and although there was a degree of favour experienced, yet, in general, it was a trying exercising season. This is a large quarterly meeting; and many who attend are mere birthright members, and having never known the baptizing power of truth, to sanctify and prepare for right and useful membership, are but as dead weights in our religious meetings ; and some others, who have joined the society by convincement, for want of faithfully attending to that which first convinced them, have lost their first love, and suffered their minds too much to centre back again into the world, and the love of it; and have thereby become stumbling blocks in the way of others. These bring much exercise and concern to the living, who are daily engaged for Zion's cause, and that truth may prosper and prevail in the earth.

On fifth day, we had an appointed meeting at Pleasant Valley, which was a comfortable instructive season; and another seasonable opportunity in the evening at Poughkeepsie, composed mostly of those not in membership with us. On sixth day, we were at West Branch meeting, which was pretty full, wherein I had to go down into deep baptism with the dead, being plunged into the feeling of a state of great ignorance and unbelief; but as I patiently sat under the burden, light sprang up, and life came into dominion; and I was led, in a clear manner, to show the ground from whence all this darkness and unbelief proceeded; that it was from a want of due attention to, and right belief in, the *inward manifestation of divine light,* which reveals itself in the heart of man against sin and uncleanness; and at the same time shows what is right, and justifies for right doing. Therefore while men disregard this inward divine principle, of grace and truth, and do not believe in it, as *essential* and *sufficient to salvation;* they are in danger of becoming either Atheists, or Deists—these are also in danger of becoming so blinded as not to believe in that necessary and very essential doctrine of perfection, as contained in that clear, rational, and positive injunction of our dear Lord: "Be ye therefore perfect, even as your Father which is in heaven is perfect." And we cannot rationally suppose they can ever be otherwise, while they continue in this situation; as *nothing but this light* is sufficient to produce the knowledge, on which this belief is founded. My mind was likewise largely opened to communicate, how we all might, by faithful attention and adherence to the aforesaid divine principle, *the light within,* come to know and believe the certainty of those excellent scripture doctrines; of the coming, life, righteous works, sufferings, death, and resurrection of Jesus Christ, our blessed pattern : and that *it is by obedience to this inward light only,* that we are prepared for an admittance into the heavenly kingdom. It was a day of high favour, wherein the Lord's arm was made bare for our help, and the exaltation of his own glorious and holy name, who is over all, blessed for ever.

This favoured opportunity being over, we rode that afternoon to Samuel Dorland's, and attended a meeting there appointed for us that evening ; and lodged with our worthy friend Enoch Dorland. On seventh day we crossed the mountains called the Highlands, in our way homeward, and got well to our friend Abraham Underhill's, at Croton River, that evening. The next day, being the first of the week, we attended Friends' meeting there, and notice being given of our attendance, the meeting was pretty full, and graciously attended with the divine presence, in which strength was received to preach the gospel in the demonstration of the spirit. It was a season thankfully to be remembered.

On second day, the 9th of 2d month, 1807, we rode to New York, where I was gladly received by my beloved daughter Abigail, and her kind companion ; we being mutually glad to see each other. The next day we attended our meeting for sufferings. I then rode home, that evening, and found my dear wife and children well, to our mutual rejoicing ; and we greeted each other with thankful hearts.

I was from home in this journey about two months, and attended forty-five particular meetings, nine monthly meetings, one quarterly, and our meeting for sufferings twice; and travelled upwards of seven hundred miles.

After returning from the aforesaid journey, I continued mostly at and about home, for several months, attending our several meetings as they came in course ; and also at different times, some appointed meetings among those not in profession with us, in some adjacent neighbourhoods, to which I could go and return in a few days. In all these seasons, I have thankfully to acknowledge the Lord was near, and graciously manifested himself to be a present helper in every needful time, furnishing with ability to labour in the work of the gospel, convincing, and comforting many hearts; and to the solid relief and peace of my own mind.

In the ensuing fall, having felt my mind renewedly engaged in gospel love to visit a few of the meetings of Friends, in the three lower quarterly meetings belonging to our yearly meeting; and to have some meetings in divers places in those parts, among those of other professions, I left home, with the unity of my friends, the 31st of 10th month, 1807, and the seventh day of the week, and went to New-York, having my beloved wife with me; who proposed to be my companion in part of this journey. We also took our two youngest daughters with us, in order to place them in the boarding-school at Nine Partners. We remained in New-York over first day, and attended Friends' meetings there; that at Pearl-street in the morning, and at Liberty-street in the afternoon. They were both, I trust, profitable meetings, more especially the former; in which truth prevailed, and came into dominion, solemnizing and comforting many hearts; and was very strengthening to my mind, in the prospect before me.

On second day we set out for Nine Partners, and reached there seasonably to attend the quarterly meeting for discipline, the ensuing fourth day; and the latter part of the week, we spent in attending the quarterly meeting of Stanford. After this we returned to the boarding-school and placed our daughters there; and, as I was one of the committee, who have the superintendence of the institution, I remained there about ten days. Then way opening to proceed, I went as far as Hartford in Connecticut; accompanied by two Friends who reside at Nine Partners. As the weather was cold and unsettled, my wife remained at the school, assisting the managers, until I returned. We had several meetings in our way thither, and one as we returned; and were at several in and about Hartford, mostly among those of other professions. And the Lord, magnified for ever be his right worthy name, was graciously pleased to be with us, and manifested his power for our help; giving wisdom and strength, tongue and utterance, and teaching to divide the word aright, to the states of the people; whereby his righteous cause was exalted in many minds, and his glorious holy truth raised into dominion over all, in divers of those favoured opportunities; to the praise of his grace, " who is over all, God blessed for ever."

On my return to the school, I again spent some days with the family, assisting them in the management thereof; and then, my wife and myself took leave of our children and friends, in much mutual affection; and turned our faces homeward. We attended Oswego monthly meeting in our way, on fourth day, the 16th of 12th month; and the next day had an appointed meeting at Apoquague. On sixth day we rode through the mountains to Peekskill, and lodged with our kind friend Nathaniel Brown. We attended their meeting on first day, and on second day, we had an appointed meeting at a place called Crompond; which was held in a meeting-house belonging to the Presbyterians, by their proposal. On fourth day we were at Amawalk, on fifth day at Shapaqua, and on sixth day we had an appointed meeting at Mount Pleasant; this was likewise held in a place of worship belonging to the Presbyterians. We rode to New-York on seventh day, and on first day attended Friends' meeting there. The third day following we left the city on our way home, but a storm came on soon after we left, and increased to that degree, that when we came to the ferry at Hurlgate, where we intended to cross, we found it impassable. We then turned our course and rode to our friend Joseph Byrd's at Harlem, and lodged. I felt my mind drawn towards having a meeting at that place when passing down to the city, but admitting some doubts to arise, as to the clearness of the prospect, I omitted it; but now, way opening with more clearness, we had one appointed the next day, which proved a favoured season. After this we crossed the ferry that afternoon, and rode to Flushing, and the next day being the fifth of the week, and 31st of 12th month, we attended Friends' meeting there; and then rode home that afternoon, and were gladly received by our friends. My spirit was made humbly joyful, in believing that the Lord Almighty had graciously condescended to be with us, to lead us in the way, manifesting his loving kindness and mercy, in a greater or lesser

degree, in all those opportunities, convicting, convincing, edifying and comforting many hearts ; and encouraging the honest
travellers Zion-ward.   May his right worthy name be praised
and exalted above all for ever.

As our return home at this time was hastened by the inclemency
of the season, we being out with a carriage, and likely to be prevented from travelling by the snow, my mind was not relieved
of the prospect before me.   Therefore, after remaining at and
about home a few weeks, I again set out, with the unity of my
friends, in order to finish what was left behind of my former
concern.   Charles Willets a friend and neighbour accompanied me.
We set out the 24th of 1st month, 1808, and attended the three
quarterly meetings of Purchase, Nine Partners, and Stanford, as
they came in course : and likewise five particular meetings in the
intermediate space, between Purchase and Nine Partners.   We
were from home at this time about five weeks ; and attended three
quarterly meetings, one monthly, and twenty-three particular meetings.   And I have abundant cause, with humble gratitude, to
admire the adorable loving kindness, and condescending goodness,
of a gracious God to me a poor creature; in enabling me to surrender all up to his heavenly disposal, to be any thing or nothing, as he
would have me to be ; leading me from place to place, as a weaned
child, by the guiding of his power, and the influence of his precious
love : and teaching me, not only how to suffer want, but likewise,
how to abound ; and in every situation and dispensation which
he is pleased to lead into, to be therewith content.   Under a renewed sense whereof, my spirit is led to acknowledge, that "great
and marvellous are thy works, Lord God Almighty ; just and
true are thy ways, thou King of saints."   Even so.   Amen.

In the spring of the year 1808, our yearly meeting, from an
exercise in observing the many deficiencies, brought up in the
reports from the several quarterly meetings, issued an epistle, or
minute of advice and caution, to its subordinate meetings.   And
in order to strengthen and enforce the same, and to make it the
more effectual to promote a reformation, appointed a committee
to attend therewith.   And I, being one appointed with divers
other brethren and sisters, willingly engaged therein ; as a con-

cern, of a similar nature, had for some time previous thereto attended my mind.

Accordingly, at the close of the yearly meeting, we agreed to enter upon the service at the succeeding quarterly meeting at Nine Partners; and to attend in succession the quarterly meetings of Stanford and Easton, as they came in course. Two men, and three women Friends, joined me in this northern tour; and several others of the committee attended at the quarterly meetings. After those meetings, we proceeded to attend with the minute, all the monthly meetings constituting them; except the three distant ones, of Adolphustown in Upper Canada, and Farmington and Scipio, in the western part of the state of New-York: also a considerable number of the preparative meetings, as way opened therefor. Although great and many were the apparent deviations and departures of many of our members, in the varied classes of society, from that ancient simplicity and integrity, which marked the conduct of our worthy predecessors, in the dawn of this latter gospel day; and by this declension, those noble testimonies given us to bear, for the prince of peace, and the promotion of the cause of truth and righteousness in the earth, were by many, but weakly supported; and by others, almost wholly neglected; grieving and wounding the hearts of the faithful, and reproaching our Christian profession : nevertheless, we had abundant cause gratefully to acknowledge the condescending goodness and mercy of the great Head of the Church, in uniting us together in the work, and in owning the concern from place to place; giving full evidence thereto in a general manner, by the manifestations of his love and power; and thereby enabling and qualifying his weak and unworthy though devoted servants, who were very sensible they had no might nor ability of their own, to perform the service they were engaged in, to his honour, or the promotion of his righteous cause; and to communicate counsel and encouragement, reproof and caution, as occasion required, and opportunity offered; by which the faithful were strengthened, and made at times to rejoice together, the hearts of Friends being in a very general manner, opened cordially to receive us and the concern, with much unanimity.

We had many precious opportunities as we passed along, in public meetings, (many of which were much crowded, by those coming in who were not in membership with us,) and also in meetings for discipline ; truth being often raised powerfully into dominion over all. So that in many of those favoured seasons, we were strengthened to set up our Ebenezer, and to say, in the heart-felt language of filial and grateful acknowledgments, "hitherto hath the Lord helped us." And, I believe, it was a season of renewed powerful visitation, and manifestation of the Lord's mercy to many ; not only to the members of our society, but also, to others that are without, who were favoured with the privilege of attending the public meetings.

After getting through this part of the service, which took us between nine and ten weeks, in which time we travelled upwards of one thousand miles, and attended three quarterly meetings, seventeen monthly meetings, sixteen preparative meetings, and forty public meetings for worship, including those that preceded the monthly and preparative meetings, we returned home, and remained until the time of the next quarterly meetings' coming on when I again joined some of the committee, and attended the quarterly meetings of Westbury and Purchase, and all the monthly meetings constituting them ; except Purchase monthly meeting. And I may say with gratitude of heart, that the same divine power that attended in the foregoing part of the visit, was again manifested for our help, in going through, and finishing the service, to the humble admiration and solid peace of my own mind, and the praise of his own right worthy name, " who is over all, God blessed for ever." How great and wonderful is his goodness and loving kindness to the children of men; his mercies are present every moment ; and as saith the prophet, " they are new every morning :" therefore saith my soul let all praise and exalt him above all, for his mercy endureth for ever.

In the latter part of the winter, and spring of the year 1809, with the concurrence of our monthly meeting, I made a pretty general visit to the meetings of Friends, within the quarterly meeting of Purchase ; and attended some meetings belonging to Nine Partners quarterly meeting ; and also appointed a considerable number among others, in the adjacent parts. I found great openness generally among the people, to hear the truths of the gospel; and a number, I believe, received them with sincerity of heart; and I was made glad in believing, that the Lord was graciously near, and accompanied the word preached, with his heart-tendering power, comforting and refreshing the broken hearted, reviving the spirit of the contrite ones, and stopping the mouths of gainsayers. For these favours my soul was often bowed, in deep humility and contrition of spirit, accompanied with grateful acknowledgments and thanksgiving, for his wonderful works to the children of men.

The year 1810, I spent mostly at home, except performing a visit to some of the neighbouring inhabitants, not in membership with us. I was from home in this service a few weeks in the spring; and in the summer I performed a visit to the half year's meeting at Canada, by appointment from our yearly meeting.

I passed the year 1811 at and near home, in attending our own and some adjacent meetings; also some meetings in divers neighbourhoods among other societies. I had frequent cause to rejoice in a living hope, that truth was gradually rising, and the true light shining more and more in the hearts of the people; and that in the Lord's time, it would be exalted and become a great mountain, and fill the whole earth.

In the winter and spring of the year 1812, with the concurrence of my friends, I passed about four weeks in visiting the neighbouring inhabitants, not of our society. I had twenty-eight meetings, all held in private houses; many of them were very large and crowded, and the Lord was graciously near, comforting and refreshing the sincere-hearted, and opening counsel to those who wanted information, and sealing his testimony on the minds of the people, to the exaltation of his own righteous cause, and to the glory of his excellent name, " who is over all, God blessed for ever."

In the forepart of the winter of 1813, feeling a renewed concern toward the neighbouring inhabitants of our island, and New-York, not in profession with us; many of whom are as sheep

17

without a shepherd, and appeared to be under exercise and concern, to be rightly instructed in the way of peace and salvation, in gospel love, and with the unity of my friends, I paid them a visit. I had upwards of twenty meetings in the different parts, much to my own satisfaction, and, I trust, to the edification and comfort of many who attended. The Lord, our gracious helper, was near, and covered the assemblies with his solemnizing presence and power; and instructed to divide the word to the several states, in the demonstration of the spirit. For these unmerited favours, I was made at seasons to rejoice, and in deep humiliation and thankfulness of heart, to joy in the God of my salvation, who does wondrous things in mercy, for the children of men, in order to hide pride from man, and turn him from his unrighteous purposes, and save his soul from the pit, that so he may know, and seek after God.

Before I had got fully through this little tour of duty, a further prospect opened, toward a visit to Friends and others in the compass of Purchase quarterly meeting, and some of the neighbouring parts of the state of Connecticut, where none of our society reside: and under the impression of duty I laid the concern before our monthly meeting held in 1st month, 1813, and received its concurrence, in a short minute for that purpose. I left home the 6th of 2d month following, my kind friend Gideon Seaman, an Elder, and member of Westbury monthly meeting, accompanied me in this visit.

We passed to New-York on our way, and on first day attended the forenoon meeting at Pearl-street, and the afternoon meeting at Liberty-street; and had an appointed meeting on second day evening in the northeast part of the town, in a large room in a public house. It was a favoured season, and largely attended; many more came than the room could contain. The two foregoing meetings were also favoured strengthening opportunities, affording encouragement in my first setting out in the weighty and solemn service before me, which I always esteem that of appointing meetings to be, more especially those among strangers; many of whom know but little of us, or of the manner in which we hold our meetings, and therefore are apt to get restless, and sometimes much disquieted at our sitting so long in silence, as we often have to do; that it requires, in Friends, at such seasons, a very deep indwelling with the seed of life, to prevent being jostled, or interrupted in our inward travail and waiting, for the pure motion of life; lest, by their eagerness to hear words, Friends on those occasions, might be led to venture on too small an intimation and without sufficiently turning the fleece again and again, . and to feel clearly, that, "wo is unto me, if I preach not the gospel." For want of this care, there is danger sometimes of our running in vain, and so not profit the people at all, nor procure peace to our own minds.

I was from home in this journey about four weeks, and rode upwards of three hundred miles; and attended twenty-five meetings, and our meeting for sufferings twice. Twelve of these meetings were among people not of our society; and where there are no meetings of Friends. Among these I found great openness to receive us, and our testimony; many expressed their satisfaction with the opportunities, and manifested a desire in most places, that we would stay longer with them, and have more meetings. Indeed truth was so prevalent in those meetings, as not only to silence, at least for the present, all opposition, but in many of them to reign triumphantly over all; whereby many minds were comforted and instructed, and the power of truth exalted; and our hearts made glad in believing, that the Shepherd of Israel is still availingly stretching forth the crook of his love, and will gather many from the highways and hedges; whom, as they attend to his call, and abide faithful to the end, he will clothe with the wedding garment, and admit into the marriage chamber of the Lamb; while many of those, who have been long and often invited, but are nevertheless making excuses, in order to attend to their farms, their merchandize, their oxen, &c., will not be able to enter.

CHAPTER VI.

Engagements at and about home, 1813.—Visit to Friends in the middle and
southern states, 1813.

SIXTH day, 26th of 3d month, 1813.   My worldly concerns
engrossed much of my time to-day.   How true is that saying,
"No man can serve two masters."   O, how hard a master the
world is; and from whose servitude I often feel strong desires to
be fully redeemed; so that all my time may be more fully dedicated
to the service of my heavenly master, whom, I often feel, I sincerely
love.

Seventh day.   Part of this day I spent in repairing a vehicle,
in which I have travelled several thousand miles, in my religious
engagements.   Most of the evening was occupied in reading the
excellent doctrine of our Lord relative to the Comforter, and the
union and communion between himself and his faithful followers, as recorded by John the Evangelist.   If it is sweet and pleasant to read, how much more precious and excellent is it to know
and witness it in our own experience.

First day.   Our meeting this day passed in silent labour.
The cloud rested on the tabernacle: and, although it was a day
of much rain outwardly, yet very little of the dew of Hermon
appeared to distil among us.   Nevertheless, a comfortable calm
was witnessed towards the close; which we must render to the
account of unmerited mercy and love.

Second day.   Most of this day was occupied in a visit to a
sick friend, who appeared comforted therewith.   Spent part of
the evening in reading part of Paul's Epistle to the Romans.

Third day. I was busied most of this day in my common vocations. Spent the evening principally in reading Paul. Found considerable satisfaction in his first epistle to the Corinthians; in which he shows the danger of some in setting too high a value on those who were instrumental in bringing them to the knowledge of the truth, without looking through and beyond the instrument, to the great first cause and Author of every blessing, to whom all the praise and honour are due.

Fifth day, 1st of 4th month. At our meeting to-day found it, as usual, a very close steady exercise to keep the mind centered where it ought to be. What a multitude of intruding thoughts imperceptibly, as it were, steal into the mind, and turn it from its proper object, whenever it relaxes its vigilance in watching against them. Felt a little strength, just at the close, to remind Friends of the necessity of a steady perseverance, by a recapitulation of the parable of the unjust judge, showing how men ought always to pray, and not to faint.

Sixth day. Nothing material occurred, but a fear lest the cares of the world should engross too much of my time.

Seventh day. Had an agreeable visit from two ancient friends, whom I have long loved. The rest of the day I employed in manual labour, mostly in gardening.

First day. Felt my mind drawn to attend to-day a meeting, a few miles from home, held, for the present, by indulgence of Friends. I was led forth in a line of encouragement and caution to a seeking travailing remnant; and in warning to the indolent and self-righteous, endeavouring to show them the danger of resting in such a polluted state; many hearts were contrited, and a comfortable solemnity clothed the meeting, for which we were made thankful to the gracious Author of all our blessings.

Second day. This day spent in manual labour, a less proportion of which would suffice for me, if every other man was disposed to do his part: but the poor and the indolent must and will be helped.

Third and fourth days. Mostly occupied in my temporal concerns, with attendant poverty of spirit, and a longing after spiritual food, free from condemnation.

Fifth day. Attended our preparative meeting, at which our queries were read, and answers prepared to be sent to the yearly meeting; but too much, I fear, in a formal way, and may, if not well guarded against, become a snare to us, as the brazen serpent was to Israel.

Sixth day. I can say little more than that I wearied myself with hard labour in assisting my workmen to build stone fences. In the evening read Paul's Epistle to the Galatians, in which I think he has fully shown the final end and abolishment of all outward ordinances and observations in matters of religion.

Seventh day. This day I spent mostly in manual labour. Some little interruption of mind by the improper conduct of one of my labourers. How hard a thing it is to find, in such persons, honesty, industry, and a suitable deportment, united in the same individual; and yet it is no more than ought to be in every man, and it is always their duty and interest to be so.

First day. At our meeting to-day the fire seemed very low on the altar. Dulness, and a spirit of heaviness were too predominant with many; occasioned, no doubt, by a too near attachment to the world, and the things of it, with some, and by too much lightness and vanity with others. Alas, how much good seed is lost by the wayside, in stony places, and on thorny ground. Just at the close, I was engaged to call the attention of the people to the necessity of having always a proper point, or object to aim at, a right centre to all their hopes and desires; and that God was the only proper object for man to set his heart upon, as the doing his will is the whole sum and substance of all true religion and worship.

Second, third and fourth days. Spent in usual labour, with a peaceful mind.

Fifth day. Attended our monthly meeting to day, at which I received a certificate of their unity and concurrence with a prospect, which I had previously opened to them, of performing a religious visit to Friends and others, in some parts of the yearly meetings of Pennsylvania and Baltimore, and the adjacent parts of Virginia. How humbling it is to the natural man to be called to the performance of those duties, for which he feels

himself destitute of every right means and capacity : he is therefore brought under the necessity of trusting in, and depending
upon, that invisible arm of power, which is beyond the reach of
all mortals to command or controul.

Sixth day. Felt much poverty of spirit at our preparative
meeting of Ministers and Elders. How necessary it is for such
as fill those stations in society, to dig faithfully with their staves,
like the princes and nobles of Israel formerly, by the direction of
the lawgiver, saying, " spring up, O well, sing ye unto it ;" that
so they may be favoured both with the upper and the nether
spring : for how otherwise can they be good waymarks and en-
samples to the flock, over whom the Holy Ghost has made all
the rightly qualified of this description overseers, and who will
have to give an account of the flock under their charge.

Seventh day. Spent in my usual vocation as a farmer or
husbandman, in which I need incessantly to watch against the
intrusions of worldly cares.

First day. Had close exercise, through the greatest part of
our meeting to day, in opposing a dull drowsy spirit, which,
through unmerited mercy and help, I vanquished towards the
close : soon after which, I was unexpectedly called upon to
sound an alarm to the youth, and to show them the danger of
suffering the intruding vanities and follies of the world to steal
away their affections from their supreme good, and blessed Author
of their being and well-being, in and on whom they ought to fix
their only best hope and trust, who is the true and only source of
all felicity and blessedness in time and in eternity.

Second day. My temporal concerns necessarily engaged my
attention to day; in pursuing of which, nothing transpired to
interrupt or turn the mind from its proper centre.

The four following days were principally occupied in attending
our quarterly meeting, held, at this time, in New-York. I think
it was, on the whole, a favoured season. The canopy of the
heavenly Father's care was sensibly felt to overshadow the meeting in its several sittings. I spread before the meeting for discipline my prospect of a religious visit to Friends and others in
some of the southern states, with the certificate of concurrence

from our last monthly meeting. The meeting fully united therewith, and I was left at liberty to pursue the journey as way should open therefor. What deep obligations devolve upon us, when thus liberated by our friends, and separated to travel in the service of the gospel, that we are careful, in no case, to make the gospel chargeable to any, nor abuse our power in it; but that, in deep humility and reverential fear, we wait for the putting forth of the Shepherd of Israel, and know him to go before : then will the Lord's cause prosper in our hands, and his people be edified and instructed, and we comforted in our labours of love, to the glory and praise of his right excellent name, who is over all, God blessed for ever.

Seventh day. Was busied to day in my farming business, endeavouring to get all my temporal concerns properly arranged, expecting soon to proceed on the visit already mentioned ; as I consider it my especial duty, as much as in me lies, to leave all in a state of order and quiet, so that nothing may remain on the mind that would tend to interrupt or disturb it, while travelling in this weighty service, nor that any should have cause to complain, whom I leave behind.

First day. Having felt my mind inclined to see Friends in their meeting at Bethpage before I left home, I went there to day, accompanied by my wife, our two youngest daughters, and a sober young woman of our neighbourhood. Their company was pleasant, and, after a time of deep inward travail and suffering, I trust the season was profitable and edifying to a number present. How often are the living baptized for the dead, in order for their arising; for if the dead are not raised, preaching is vain.

Second and third days. Spent in preparing my business, looking for the time of setting out on my intended journey. May I be ready and willing when the time comes, without murmuring or complaining ; for, as I trust and believe a dispensation of the gospel is committed to me, wo is unto me if I preach not the gospel.

Fourth day. Alas, how the cares of the world intrude on the mind and engross its attention, if they are not carefully watched against with fervent prayer !

Fifth day. Attended our usual meeting. Found it necessary to engage against a dull heavy spirit, that seemed very prevalent in the meeting: but, as I maintained the struggle, I was favoured with a good degree of victory towards the close, when a ray of light broke forth, attended with peace and quietude of mind, an ample reward for all my toil.

Sixth day. I endeavoured to spend this day as I ought to do. Met with some interruption from a careless neighbour, by the trespass of his unruly cattle. How much more comfort and satisfaction would neighbourhoods enjoy, if all honestly endeavoured to walk uprightly, agreeably to that excellent rule left us by Jesus Christ: " all things whatsoever ye would that men should do to you, do ye even so to them; for this is the law and the prophets."

Seventh day, 1st of 5th month. Still pressing after a more full release from the world and its cares, endeavouring to redeem the time, because the days are still evil, or attended in many respects, with much evil. The alarm of war is heard in the land, and much contention is among the people. Flee, O my soul, to thy rock, the name of the Lord; for, in it is safety, and a sure refuge from all the storms and tempests, that assail poor mortals in passing through this vale of tears, and state of trial and probation.

First day. Had to suffer through the meeting to-day. Alas, how oft have the poor ministers to be baptized for, and with, the dead!

Second day. Still pressing after a release from my worldly cares; as the time is near at hand, when I shall proceed on my proposed journey to the south and west on my good Master's business, I hope, in the way he is pleased to lead.

Third day. Felt much poverty of spirit to-day, although nothing particular has occurred either on the right hand or the left; therefore I feel, in a good degree, a peaceful mind which is worthy of thanksgiving.

Fourth day. Still pressing after a full settlement of my temporal concerns that I may be in a state of readiness to pursue my journey, as soon as the way opens.

Fifth dáy. Was favoured, towards the close of our meeting to-day, to discharge another debt of love and care to my friends, as it was likely to be the last opportunity I should have with them before I proceeded on my intended journey ; and, through the prevalence of gospel love, it was made a tendering baptizing season to some, and we parted under a degree of the uniting influence of it.

Sixth day. Still aiming at the same mark of readiness and preparation for my journey, expecting to leave home to-morrow, and proceed therein, if the cloud is removed from the tabernacle, and the light should lead the way.

Seventh day, 8th of 5th month, 1813. I commenced the journey on this day, after a precious solemn season with my family, in which I was favoured, in fervent supplication, to recommend them to the divine protection and preserving care of the Shepherd of Israel. Under a thankful sense of his loving kindness we took leave of each other in much affectionate sym pathy and brokenness of spirit, I rode to New-York with a peaceful and quiet mind. My kinsman Isaac Hicks, of Westbury, kindly accompanied me in this journey.

First day. Attended Friends' meetings there, in the morning at Pearl-street, and in the afternoon at Liberty-street. They were both exercising seasons, and I hope profitable to some, as in all right exercise we are encouraged to believe there is profit. After these opportunities, and a favoured season in a family of Friends, the heads of which were Elders, I felt a pretty full release from the city at present.

Second day. Proceeded on our journey to Newark, where we attended a meeting appointed for us at the third hour. It was on the whole, I think, a favoured season ; many truths of the gospel were opened to the people, and appeared to have a good degree of entrance to the minds of some present ; although others appeared to be too much fettered by the prejudice of education to be profited by them. The meeting closed in solemn quiet ; and I left them with a peaceful mind. We then rode to Rahway and lodged.

Third day. This afternoon at the third hour we attended a meeting previously appointed at Elizabethtown. Many of the most respectable inhabitants attended, among whom were the governour of the state of New-Jersey and his wife ; and a very considerable number of young people. The Lord, who is a never-failing helper to those that trust in him, was near, furnishing with ability to preach the gospel of life and salvation to the people, in the clear demonstration of the spirit ; and with a power attending, that produced great brokenness of heart and contrition of spirit among them ; and the power of his divine love was felt to spread over the meeting as a precious canopy. We parted with them in humiliation and deep thankfulness of heart, rejoicing that his loving kindness was still extended to his backsliding and offending creature man.

Fourth and fifth days. We attended Friends' meetings at Plainfield and Rahway.

Sixth day. We had a favoured meeting at New Brunswick among the inhabitants of the town. Many truths of the gospel were opened to their consideration ; and a comfortable solemnity was witnessed to spread over the meeting.

Seventh day. We rode to Upper Freehold, intending to be at Friends' meeting at East Branch in that township on first day. We lodged at the house of our friend George Frost, where I had lodged before in my way through these parts, about twelve years prior to this time. We met a very kind reception from our said friend and his family ; and it seemed like a fresh renewal of friendship and affection between us. How consoling it is for the weary traveller to meet with kind friends ! it is as a brook by the way in a time of drought.

First day. We attended East Branch meeting as proposed The forepart was exercising, for want of a lively travail among the members ; too many of whom seemed in a dead, lifeless state, as to a right religious concern. This makes hard labour for the living exercised members, and is very trying to those who visit them in the service of truth ; yet as we kept up the travail for truth's arising, and patiently abode under suffering, a degree of light broke forth, and led to a seasonable, and I trust, instructive communication; in which I found relief and peace in the labour, which I consider a great favour.

Second day. Were at Upper Freehold meeting. It was a season of deep suffering in the forepart, in which my spirit was deeply baptized with, and for the dead; but as I patiently submitted to the crucifying operation of the present dispensation, a degree of light sprang up, and in it I was led to view the declaration of the apostle Paul, that "death reigned from Adam to Moses," and to show to the people, that all the unregenerate were under the influence and power of the same death. For in Adam, that is, in the transgressing state, all die. And that it is only by and through our attention being turned to the inward divine law, which the apostle calls, " the law of the spirit of life in Christ Jesus," and our yielding full obedience thereunto, that we can be set free and delivered from this law of sin and death, which was typified by Israel's deliverance, from the bondage of Pharaoh, by a full and implicit obedience to the outward commands of God, through his servant Moses. As I attended carefully to the opening, truth rose into victory, and administered cause of thanksgiving, under a grateful sense of the continued mercy and loving kindness of our gracious Creator to his backsliding creature man.

The three following days we attended meetings at Crosswicks, alias Chesterfield, Upper Springfield, and a meeting called the Mount. These were all favoured meetings, wherein the Lord's presence and power were manifested, tendering and contriting many hearts, giving tongue and utterance; and through which the gospel was preached in the demonstration of the spirit, and with a power attending, which carried sharp reproof to the disobedient and unfaithful, strength to the weak and feeble minded, confirmation and encouragement to the honest-hearted, humble traveller; and mutually rejoicing the sincere-hearted. For all these favours my spirit was made humbly thankful to the Shepherd of Israel, to whom all the glory and praise is due, for his mercy endureth for ever.

Sixth day. Attended Friends' meeting at Old Springfield. It was a precious baptizing season, the Lord's presence and power were felt to spread over the meeting, affecting and contriting many present ; and comforting and encouraging the honest travellers Zion-ward. The meeting closed under a thankful sense of divine favour, with prayer and praise.

Seventh day. We were at Mansfield. On first day were at Bordentown in the morning, and at Lower Mansfield in the afternoon. These meetings were well attended and very solemn. The two last, Friends informed me were unusually large. Oh how good is the Lord, and greatly to be praised for his marvellous works, and his never failing loving kindness to the children of men.

Second day. We were at Burlington. In this meeting my mind was opened largely to set forth the nature and design of the gospel dispensation ; and to show, that as none had ever been perfect in it, but the man Jesus Christ, we had not a right, as his professed followers, to take the example of any but his own, for our real perfect rule of life. For all who have gone before us have in a greater or less degree, through the undue force and prejudice of education, fallen short of the perfect rule left us in his example and precepts.

I also showed them that the Christian professors in the varied ages of the Church had very much marred and obstructed the work of reformation, by suffering themselves to be too closely attached to their several particular leaders ; and have therefore justly thrown themselves open to the censure of the apostle ; wherein he blames some of the primitive Christians for setting themselves one against another, by the partiality each had for the minister, by whom he had been brought over to the Christian faith, one crying, I am of Paul, and I of Apollos, and I of Cephas, and some more wise, I of Christ ; to whose example all ought to have looked, and not turned their attention so much to the instruments, by whom they were brought to believe in him. Although many of our worthy predecessors according to their measure of light endeavoured faithfully to do the work of their day, yet few, if any of them, had been so entirely emancipated from the undue force of education, as to see clearly through the cloud of prejudice produced thereby ; and therefore were in the

practice of divers things, not consistent with that perfect justice
which the example and precepts of our Lord call for, and which
are in full unison with the perfect righteousness of the gospel.
The word was preached in a large searching testimony, I trust
through divine assistance, in the demonstration of the spirit, to
the comfort and encouragement of the sincere in heart, and the
peace of my own mind.

Third day. Were at Rancocas. The meeting was solemn, and
the Lord's presence was felt to preside, humbling many minds;
and many truths of the gospel were in an instructive manner
spread before the people.

Fourth and fifth days. We attended meetings at Mount
Holly, Upper Evesham, and were at Easton on fifth day afternoon; these were all favoured meetings. In the two former,
my mind was largely opened in two doctrinal testimonies, wherein
the design and end of all the shadows of the law were clearly
opened; and the necessity of their entire abolishment at the
death and resurrection of Christ clearly shown. I also opened to
them, that, by the primitive Christians retaining many of the
shadows of the law, the apostacy broke in upon the Church, and
that by the retention of some of the same shadows, the reformation had been, and is still greatly retarded: and will never
advance on its right foundation, until those shadows are all dis-
carded and done away. My mind was deeply humbled, under
a sense of the Lord's mercy.

The three following days we were at Lower Evesham, Cropwell, Chester, Westfield, Haddonfield, and at Newtown, attending
two meetings each day. After the latter meeting, on first day
evening, we crossed the river Delaware to Philadelphia. In those
meetings my mind was deeply humbled, under a grateful sense
of the Lord's continued mercy to an unworthy people; rendered
so by the continued disobedience and revolting of great numbers,
who go under our name, not only among the youth, but with
many of riper age, whose experience and daily observation we
might reasonably suppose, had they endeavoured to improve by
it, would, ere now, have taught them better. But how true is
that saying of the great Master: " If therefore the light that is

in thee be darkness, how great is that darkness." This has fallen to the lot of those, by turning their backs upon the true light, and adhering to their own carnal reasonings and fleshly consultations, whereby they have been left like Balaam, through his covetousness, to justify themselves in many things, which the true light in them, had they been obedient to its manifestations, would not have approved. Therefore these are left as a reward of their disobedience to believe a lie to their own confusion.

My mind was largely opened in these meetings, not only to commemorate the Lord's gracious dealings with the children of men; but likewise to set forth and open to the several auditories the subtle workings and varied transformations of that diabolical spirit, which lies in wait to deceive and counteract the gracious designs of heaven among the children of men. And under a renewed sense of the Lord's continued mercy, my spirit was led to exclaim, as did one formerly: " Great and marvellous are thy works, Lord God Almighty; just and true are all thy ways, thou King of saints."

The following week we spent in the city, except on seventh day we rode out and attended two meetings; one in the morning at Frankford, and the other at Germantown, at five in the afternoon. These were both favoured seasons. We then returned in the evening to Philadelphia; and the next day being the first of the week, and the 6th of 6th month, were at Friends' meeting at Arch-street in the morning, and at the North meeting in the afternoon. Some previous notice having been given of my intention of attending them, they were unusually large; and many had to go away for want of room. It was supposed there were three thousand people at the beginning of the meeting, and toward the close many more than the rooms could contain. Through the marvellous condescension and loving kindness of our gracious God, my mind was strengthened and qualified to preach the gospel of peace and salvation to the people, in the demonstration of the spirit, and with a power attending, that brought home the doctrine, to the humbling conviction of many minds. In the first I was engaged to bear testimony to the excellency of a life of strict and impartial justice and righteousness, as the only right foundation of every real religious and moral virtue; and without which no true virtue could possibly exist. The communication comprehended much salutary caution, reproof and encouragement, suited to the varied states present; under a sense of which my mind was deeply humbled, and had gratefully to acknowledge, "this is the Lord's doings, and marvellous in mine eyes." The latter was likewise a favoured season, wherein many truths of the gospel were opened to the people, tending to lead their minds off from all dependence on traditional religion and worship; and to gather them home to the eternal substance in themselves, Christ, the hope of glory and light of the world; by the influence of whose light and spirit, we only can be enabled to obtain victory over the world and its spirit, and become qualified to worship the Father in spirit and in truth.

The 7th we left Philadelphia. In the course of this week and the next first day, we attended eleven meetings in the following order, previous notice having gone forward. On second day at Darby; third day at Haverford in the morning, and at Merion at the fifth hour in the afternoon; fourth day at the Valley; fifth day at Radnor, which was their monthly meeting; sixth day at Newtown in the morning, and at Springfield in the afternoon; seventh day at Middletown in the morning, and at Providence in the afternoon; first day at Chester in the morning, and at Chichester in the afternoon. And although I was taken very unwell on third day afternoon, before the third meeting as above arranged, and continued so through the week, and until the last meeting; insomuch that for several days I could take scarcely any nourishment, my stomach loathing all food; yet to my humbling admiration, I was strengthened to go through the service of these meetings, which in each was arduous and extensive. At the close of some of them my strength was so exhausted, being wet from head to foot with extreme sweating, that it seemed to me after divers of those exercising seasons, almost impossible for me to reach the next; but that which is impossible to man, we often find easy to the great Helper of his people. As my care was wholly cast upon Him, he graciously accompanied, by his holy presence, from meeting to meeting. When I first sat down in many of those meetings, the force of my complaint seemed to absorb all my strength both of body and mind ; yet as I endeavoured to centre in quiet, I seldom sat long before the light sprang up, and dispelled all the darkness, and opened doctrine new and old ; and strengthened to communicate in a way of clear demonstration. The honest-hearted were strengthened and instructed, and conviction and reproof brought home to the delinquent, and a visitation of entreaty and love extended to the beloved young people, whose minds were not yet hardened in vice ; showing them, what great and everlasting benefits and blessings would redound to them, by an early dedication of their hearts to the Lord. My mind at the close of these large solemn meetings, (for many were very large, more than the houses could contain,) was generally centered in perfect peace, wherein I was led to contemplate the Lord's marvellous loving kindness to me a poor unworthy creature, and his wonderful works in mercy to the children of men ; waiting in long forbearance for their return, and continuing his call to them by his spirit, through his servants and messengers, rising up early and sending them, that no means should be left untried for their recovery and reconciliation. O, what shall we render to the Lord for all his benefits !

Having been very unwell, as before observed, most of the last week, I found it necessary to lay by a day or two, which we did at the house of our friend John Talbot. With a little rest I soon found myself better, and being desirous to improve the time, we again proceeded. On fourth day, the 16th of the month, we were at Concord meeting, at Wilmington on fifth day, Centre on sixth day, Hockesson on seventh day, and at Kennet on first day. I was helped to get through the service of these meetings to my own satisfaction and peace of mind ; although some of them were very trying and exercising, by the unfaithfulness and great want of a right concern and zeal, for the support and maintenance of our Christian testimonies, which in some families were very much neglected and let fall. I was led forth generally in those meetings, in close searching testimonies, tending to arouse friends from their bed of ease and carnal security ; brought

19

upon them by an inordinate love of the world, and an increase of temporal blessings; in which their principal enjoyments were too much centered, loving the gifts and forgetting the Giver. I laboured fervently among them, especially in the last meeting, wherein my mind was largely opened to unfold to the audience many of the deep mysteries of the gospel state, making them plain and easy to be understood by the most ignorant, whose minds were in any degree turned to inquire the way to Zion. It was a season in which the Lord's power was manifested in an eminent degree, breaking down and contriting many hearts, and truth appeared to reign triumphantly over all, to the praise of *his* grace who is God, blessed for ever.

The following week we attended meetings at Birmingham, Willistown, Goshen, Westchester, Bradford and Marlborough. These were mostly pretty full meetings, and generally favoured and satisfactory. In some of them, as in many foregoing opportunities, the Lord's power was eminently exalted, and set above, and over, all errour and untruth.

On first day, the 27th of the month, we attended two very large meetings. One in the morning at London Grove, and the other in the afternoon at New Garden. In both of these meetings, my mind, I trust, was opened by that divine key, which, when it opens, none can shut, and when it shuts, none can open. I was strengthened to declare largely of the things of God, and the way to eternal life; to the satisfaction and peace of my own mind; and I trust to the edification and instruction, as well as conviction and reproof, of many present; the spirit assisting to divide the word severally to every one, according to the necessity of their different states. It was a day thankfully to be remembered.

In the course of this week we attended meetings at West Grove, East and West Nottingham, Eastland, and Little Britain. These were all satisfactory seasons; that at East Nottingham particularly, was a heart-searching opportunity, wherein truth was raised powerfully into dominion over all. Many were broken and contrited, and a number wept freely for a considerable time: surely it was the Lord's doing, and marvellous in our eyes. On seventh day we crossed the river Susquehannah, and rode into the neighbourhood of Deer Creek; and attended the meeting there on first day. This also proved a very precious meeting, wherein the Lord's power was eminently manifested; and every mind appeared to be humbled by its blessed influence. The meeting ended with solemn supplication. The two following days, we attended meetings at Little Falls and Gunpowder. After the latter meeting, we rode to Baltimore; and the two following days, attended Friends' meetings there for the Western and Eastern Districts, as they came in course. At the close of each, their monthly meetings were held, which were exercising seasons, but ended to pretty good satisfaction. There appeared to be a concerned remnant in each meeting, through whose care the discipline appeared to be pretty well supported. After the latter, we left the city and rode to Elk Ridge, to attend a meeting appointed for us there the next day, the sixth of the week; which was a satisfactory opportunity. The day after, we attended Indian Spring meeting. It was a solemn, and I trust profitable season to some: may it remain with them as bread cast upon the waters, that may be found after many days.

After this meeting, we rode to the city of Washington; and the next day, being the first of the week, and the 11th of 7th month, we attended a meeting there in the morning; and in the afternoon one at Alexandria. These were both very hard trying meetings ; the people appeared very destitute of real religious engagement, their minds being so swallowed up in their political controversies, and other worldly concerns, that there seemed to be very little room in their thoughts for any thing else. I felt but little satisfaction in these meetings, except a consciousness o having done my duty, in laying before them, in a plain manner divers truths necessary for them to be in the practice of, and without which they could not be real Christians, nor obtain an inheritance in the kingdom of heaven.

The three following days we attended meetings at George-town, Sandy Spring, and Elk Ridge. We had been at the latter place the week before on sixth day. These were seasons of favour : many truths of the gospel were, I trust, clearly opened to the people, accompanied with right authority, humbling many minds, and truth reigned over all. After the last meeting, we rode to Baltimore that afternoon, and attended a meeting previously appointed for us at the fifth hour; and the next day Friends' meeting in the Eastern District was held, and public notice was given of our intention of attending it. These were both full meetings, in which I was led forth in two large doctrinal testimonies, I trust, to the edification and comfort of many minds.

After this I felt easy and clear to leave the city. We proceeded that afternoon about fourteen miles on our way towards Little York, in Pennsylvania; where we arrived the next day a little before evening. On seventh day we had a comfortable instructive meeting there. We then rode to Columbia, crossing the river Susquehannah in our way. The next day being first day, we attended Friends' meeting there. It was large for that place, more came than the house could contain; and was a favoured season; the Lord's power was manifest, and truth reigned over all; and I was made to rejoice, under an humbling sense of his continued mercy and gracious assistance from day to day; wherein we had cause often to set up our Ebenezer, and say, in the language of one formerly, "hitherto hath the Lord helped us."

The three following days, we attended meetings at Lampeter, Sadsbury, and Doe Run. In these, our gracious helper, whom we waited upon, and trusted in, manifested himself to be a God near at hand, and a present helper in every needful time; and was not only mouth and wisdom, tongue and utterance; but likewise sealed the truths communicated by the attendant evidence of his own power, humbling and contriting many hearts and bringing all under subjection to the authority of truth; so that I had often in deep thankfulness of heart, to query like David: "What shall I render unto the Lord for all his benefits towards me."

We then proceeded, attending meetings at Fallowfield, East Caln, Downingstown; and on first day, the 25th of 7th month, were at Uwchlan meeting. It was, I trust, a profitable instructive season, as were also the three foregoing; and I found peace in my labours, which I esteem above all.

On second day we crossed the river Schuylkill, in our way to Plymouth; where, by previous notice, we had a meeting appointed at the fourth hour in the afternoon, which we accordingly attended. The next day we had an appointed meeting at Abington. These were both large meetings, in which the Lord's power was felt to preside. The latter especially was a very comfortable satisfactory meeting, wherein many truths of the gospel were opened to the people's consideration, and they pressed to an engagement of mind to realize them in their own experience; and were shown the great and singular advantage and benefits, that would most certainly result to them and to society, in their so doing. The Lord's power was manifest, and truth reigned over all opposition.

The four following days we were at Byberry, Middletown, Bristol, and the Falls. These were large meetings, wherein, through gracious assistance, my mind was strengthened to labour largely in the gospel; endeavouring, by plain and conclusive arguments, drawn from scripture testimony and their own experience, to gather the minds and attention of the people, from every non-essential and false trust, home to the sure foundation, the elect precious corner stone, which is Christ in them, the hope of glory. These were solemn seasons, wherein the people's minds were generally humbled, the honest-hearted comforted, the youth encouraged and instructed, and the lukewarm and refractory cautioned and reproved. The Lord's power was exalted over all, rejoicing the sincere-hearted, and giving peace to my own mind.

The next day being first day, and 1st of 8th month, we attended Trenton meeting in the morning, and were at Stony Brook at five in the afternoon. The meeting at Trenton was considered to be the largest that had ever been held in that place. It was a favoured precious meeting, wherein the Lord's power was eminently manifest; and my spirit was made to rejoice and joy in the God of my salvation, who had made bare his arm of divine sufficiency; and as I trusted in him, carried me through, and over, every trial and tribulation, that attended in the course of this journey ; enabling me to labour faithfully in the work of the gospel, I trust to the exaltation of his own righteous cause, and to the peace and comfort of my own mind.

These meetings closed my visit in those parts.   We then proceeded directly to New-York, where we arrived on third day ; and as Friends' monthly meeting there was to be held the next day, we concluded to stay and attend it.   I then rode home and found my family well, for which favour, together with the Lord's other multiplied mercies and blessings, conferred in the course of my pilgrimage through this vale of tears, inspire my heart with gratitude and thanksgiving to the great and blessed Author of my being and well-being, " who is over all, God blessed for ever."

Fifth day, 5th of 8th month, 1813.   On this, and the two following days, I made preparations for again entering into the necessary cares of my family.

First day.   After a pretty close exercise in silence in our meeting to-day, I was led to call Friends' attention to more strict watchfulness and circumspection, and to show the necessity of advancing in the work of righteousness, and not to continue any longer at ease in a formal customary way, which is sure to produce dwarfishness and death, not only to individuals, but also languor and dulness in meetings, greatly distressing to the living exercised members.

The following week was spent in my common vocation as a farmer ; except that on seventh day, I went to Setauket, about thirty miles, to visit a sick Friend, who had lately been received a member.   We had a meeting with her and some of her neighbours on first day, after which I returned home that evening.

Second, third, and fourth days, passed, as usual, in a peaceful attention to my ordinary vocations.

Fifth day.   At meeting to day my mind was solemnly humbled in a fresh commemoration of the gracious dealings of our heavenly Father towards the workmanship of his holy hand, especially to his revolting and backsliding creature man ; whom, in great mercy, he is visiting and revisiting in the midst of his iniquities, inviting him in loving kindness to repent and return, that he may bring back his soul from the pit, and be enlightened with the light of the living.

Sixth and seventh days. Was occupied with my temporal concerns, which were trying, through indisposition of body, and much poverty of mind.

First day. I attended our meeting to-day, not so much with an expectation of comfort, as from a sense of real duty, as my bodily indisposition and poverty of spirit still continued ; nevertheless, my mind, soon after I took my seat, was opened into a view of the great hurt man has sustained by suffering himself to be led and governed by his external senses. It is through these avenues that he is principally exposed to temptation in this probationary state. And had he watchfully attended to the internal sense and voice of God to his soul, which his dependent state justly required of him, the tempter would have found no more place in him, than he did in the blessed Jesus. Hence the way of our return lies open before us, through the grace of God or Comforter, by which the internal sense of the soul is again arrested, and strict obedience to its dictates required ; and if yielded to in uprightness and faithful submission, the external senses are thereby subjected and regulated, and every undue desire and passion subdued, and the creature returns a willing subject to the Creator, and primitive harmony is restored. I had largely to communicate on this subject, and to show to the auditory how wonderfully gracious and merciful the Lord is, who in longsuffering and loving kindness is dispensing to every state, according to its necessities, not suffering even a sparrow to fall without his heavenly notice.

The rest of this week was spent in my ordinary vocations. My farming business was very pressing, and it being difficult to procure suitable assistance, my mind was over-burdened with care, which seldom fails of producing leanness of spirit in a lesser or greater degree.

First day, the 29th of 8th month. Attended our meeting in silence. Oh ! what a precious enjoyment to know both soul and body in humble silence, prostrated at the throne of grace.

Second day. Had invitations to attend the funerals of two deceased women Friends on the day following. One of them had been lately, at her request, received into membership by our monthly meeting, but was never able to attend, she living in the town of Setauket, far distant from Friends. We had a meeting at her funeral agreeably to her request. It was a large solemn one. A number of the inhabitants of the town attended, and many, although generally strangers to us, were glad of the opportunity, and appeared well affected therewith. The rest of this week was spent about home in my usual avocations.

First day, the 5th of 9th month. Attended the indulged meeting at Jerusalem, which, in the main, I think was a favoured season, although somewhat hurt in the forepart by an unsavoury appearance in the ministry.

Second, third, and fourth days. Was occupied in attending to my farming business, which, for want of suitable, faithful labourers, is often attended with much care, and too much bodily labour for my time of life, but which cannot well be avoided without my business suffering.

Fifth day. Attended our preparative meeting, at which our overseers brought forward information of one of our members having through unwatchfulness and want of faithful attention to the witness of truth in his own mind, given way repeatedly to use strong drink to excess. This information affected my mind in degree, both with joy and sorrow. I was glad, because from my knowledge of the case, I fully believed it had been too long procrastinated, not only to the hurt and loss of the individual; but also, had brought reproach upon the society, and wounded the noble cause we are engaged to espouse. And it was cause of real sorrow, when I was brought to reflect on the distressed state of the individual, and the great affliction it must necessarily produce to his wife and children, and near connexions. O how necessary to keep up a steady watch and warfare, against this sore evil which destroys so many tens of thousands of the children of men, both in soul and body.

A few following days were spent in much bodily pain from a supposed rheumatic complaint in one of my limbs. O how needful a virtue is patience in seasons of affliction, to keep us from ungrateful murmurings; by which men and women often greatly offend their gracious and beneficent Creator, who designs nothing but good to his creature man in all the varied dispensations of his divine providence.

First day. At our meeting to-day, I was led to show to the people the great harm and loss neighbourhoods, as well as the community at large, sustain for want of a careful submission to the laws, in all points where they do not interfere with conscience; and that those who from their licentious and immoral pursuits, were often transgressing against the moral precepts of the law, were not worthy of living in a free country, while violating the civil policy thereof merely to gratify their own creaturely and selfish inclinations. An honest and faithful attention to the moral law of the country we live in, will, in a certain degree, (as the apostle expressed in allusion to the law of Moses,) be as a schoolmaster to lead to Christ. He only who is faithful in the unrighteous mammon, is likely to make any proficiency in obtaining the true riches.

Fifth day. Attended our monthly meeting; at the first sitting of which, my mind was opened into a clear view of the necessity of our coming to experience a resurrection from a state of spiritual death, to a renewal of spiritual life, through the resurrection of Christ, by his life and power in us; as nothing short of that can give full and satisfactory evidence of his, and our resurrection, from the dead. On this internal testimony our whole salvation depends; and we know and feel, that because he lives we live also; and the life that we now live, is by faith in the Son of God, hence we come to know in our own experience what Paul meant when he thus expressed himself: "my little children, of whom I travail in birth again until Christ be formed in you." *Christ formed in us* is the sum and substance of the gospel state.

Sixth and seventh days. Spent in manual labour, a reasonable portion of which I consider my duty and delight; and the more my delight, because I esteem it my reasonable and Christian service: and as I also abhor idleness and sloth.

20

First day. Sat our meeting in silence under a pretty long testimony of a ministering Friend on a visit to us, who introduced his communication with the following saying of Christ: " Except ye eat my flesh and drink my blood, ye have no life in you; for my flesh is meat indeed, and my blood is drink indeed:" and to show that it was to be spiritually understood and inter nally received, he further added: " The words that I say unto you, they are spirit and they are life." An excellent subject indeed, and while he kept to his text and the subject, it seemed lively; but he after a time departed from it, and the life, I thought, very much departed with it. How very necessary it is for ministers to keep a steady eye to the openings of truth, and not suffer any premature birth to rise up and get in and scatter their attention. For want of this care, I have often thought many good openings have been much lost, and the work thereby marred.

First day, the 10th of 10th month. Alas! how fleeting is time: three weeks have elapsed since my last note; in the course of which I have attended two funerals. Take care, oh my soul! and do not grow careless and forgetful when drawing near to the eve of life; lest the world and its cares get in and choke the bubblings of 'the celestial spring, through the abundant cumber that seems necessarily attendant on my present state in striving to help and comfort others.

First day, the 17th of 10th month. Passed the last week principally in attending to my outward avocations, except attending the funeral of a young man, where we had a solemn opportunity. I was exercised publicly to set forth the necessity and great propriety of an early and timely preparation for death; and to show to the people the way and means by which it only can be effected; founded on the declaration of the apostle Paul, where he asserts that, " not by works of righteousness which we have done, but according to his mercy he saved us, by the washing of regeneration, and renewing of the Holy Ghost." The opportunity closed with comfort and peace of mind, which is the true crown of all.

I sat our meeting to-day in silence, feeling nothing to exercise my mind in a communicative way.

Seventh day. Spent this week mostly in the busy round of outward cares, in my temporal concerns; except attending our monthly meeting on fifth day, and our select meeting for Ministers and Elders on sixth day. In both of these my mind was exercised on account of the apparent languor respecting the right management and want of firmness in the execution of our discipline, even in Ministers and Elders; by which reason the society were very much enveloped in a state of weakness.

First day. Felt my mind clothed with great weakness, and a feeling sense of my own insufficiency, while sitting in our meeting to-day; nevertheless, I was led to view in prospect and contemplation, the great and essential advantages which result to individuals, and society in general, by a strict and steady attendance of religious meetings, from a real sense of duty; as there is scarcely any thing in the outward conduct of men and women, which more fully denotes a mind fixed on God its maker for support and countenance, while passing through the changes and vicissitudes of this mortal life. The subject spread and led to communication, and opened to a large field of doctrine, in which the gospel was preached in the authority of truth, and a very comfortable solemnity covered the meeting.

Third day. Attended the funeral of an acquaintance, a convinced person; it being his request on his death-bed; and also that a meeting might be held at his funeral. It was accordingly so ordered, and proved a very solemn affecting season, particularly so to the near connexions of the deceased. The Lord was graciously near, furnishing ability to bear ample testimony to many truths of the gospel. The people were very attentive, and many hearts were broken and contrited, and the Lord's name and power exalted over all.

Seventh day. The three preceding days I attended our quarterly meeting, which was held at this time at Flushing. The meeting of Ministers and Elders, and the meeting for discipline were very trying heart-searching seasons. The meeting for worship was a quiet favoured meeting. We had great cause to acknowledge the goodness and continued mercy of Israel's Shepherd, who not only furnished wisdom and ability to search out the hidden things of Esau, or the first nature; and to set judgment upon the head of the transgressing nature, in those meetings set apart for the well-ordering of the affairs of the church: but also graciously condescended in the closing meeting held for worship, to gladden our hearts by the effusions of his love, causing the light of his countenance to shine upon us. The minds of the faithful were influenced to return thanksgiving and praise to his ever adorable name, who remains to be " God over all, blessed for ever."

First day. Sat our meeting in silence, and was much interrupted by the intrusion of unprofitable thoughts, against which I had to struggle through most part of the meeting.

Second and third days. Spent in my necessary avocations; but not without considerable fear attending, lest my temporal concerns too much intrude and indispose my mind for heavenly meditations. Nothing material occurred the rest of the week.

First day. Silence as to words sealed my lips through the meeting again to-day; and may they remain shut in all our solemn meetings, unless opened by the key of David.

In the course of this week I attended the funerals of two Friends; at both of which meetings were held. In the first, my mind was largely opened on the subject of religion; wherein I was led to show to the auditory, that a right consideration and frequent remembrance of our latter end, tended to lead into the realities thereof; which consist in nothing but acts of real obedience and humble submission to the manifested will of our heavenly Father, through the inspiration of his grace and light in our own hearts. As we are careful to have this in our daily experience, it qualifies to answer the great end for which we were created, to glorify God and enjoy him; and be thereby prepared to meet death with an even and tranquil mind, having known its sting, which is sin, taken away by the death of the cross. I was also led to expose the doctrine of personal and unconditional predestination and election; and to show the fallacy and inconsistency thereof with the divine character.

In the latter meeting I was concerned to show the dangerous and hurtful tendency of our submitting to be led and governed by the customs and manners of others, without a strict and careful examination thereof; and bringing them to the test of the light in our own conscience. For although the frequency of a thing, and an habitual conformity to that which is not right, often blunts the edge of conviction, and reconciles us to that which is contrary to truth, and derogatory to our true interest; yet the custom of sinning will not lessen its guilt. For in the awful day of final decision, all our fig-leaf coverings will be torn off, and things will then appear as they really are ; and we shall all stand in need of that substantial covering, represented by the coats of skins, which the Lord made for our first parents, and gave them in lieu of their fig-leaves; that is, something of their own inventing, that so their nakedness might no longer be exposed.

My mind was also opened to set forth the design and end of the shadowy or law dispensation ; and that by its consistency and harmony in all its parts, it was a just figure and representation of the gospel state and dispensation. Many of its precepts were not good, nor consistent with the justice and mercy of the all-beneficent and gracious Jehovah ; but were only so, as they stood in relation to the very low, degraded and wicked state of mankind at that time ; and were therefore justly suited to Israel's state, and the states and conditions of the surrounding nations concerned therein, as saith Ezekiel : " Wherefore I gave them also statutes that were not good, and judgments whereby they should not live."

First day, the 14th of 11th month. Attended Cow Neck meeting to satisfaction.

The rest of this week I spent at home, being closely engaged in business, and in making preparation for the more comfortable accommodation of my stock through the inclemency of the approaching winter ; considering that a merciful man is merciful to his beast ; and as I consider it not right to keep in my possession, and under my immediate notice, any more of the animal creation than I can render reasonably comfortable.

Fifth day. Attended our monthly meeting, in which my mind was engaged to show the great benefit that would result to society, and to its members as individuals, by a right exercise and faithful execution of our discipline, without fear or favour; and that some cases of disorder in an individual might turn up, which, with its attendant circumstances, might render it not only necessary to disown the person, but would also prove more to his true interest, and the advancement of the cause and testimonies that we as a people are engaged in, than the reception of any untimely or unseasonable acknowledgment could possibly be. For I have always considered it required, not only deep and solid consideration, but suitable time of waiting, in order rightly to qualify a person to make an acknowledgment for an offence committed against a religious society.

First day.   My mind was closely engaged, and largely opened, to show the inconsistency and unrighteousness of a conformity to the vain and foolish customs of the world; demonstrating from the scriptures, that in all ages since the fall of our first parents, the customs of men and women in their natural estate, were vain, and that there was a certain degree of wickedness attached to every vanity; hence the necessity of our carefully guarding against the conformity to any custom or tradition, until we have first brought it to the test of the light in our own consciences, and the reason of things; and also to its consistency with the precepts and example of our Lord Jesus Christ: and if relating to our duty towards our fellow creatures, examine whether it comports with that most excellent rule given by him as a criterion of conduct: " All things whatsoever ye would that men should do to you, do ye even so to them; for this is the law and the prophets."

Second, third, and fourth days.   Nothing particular occurred. On fifth day I was invited to the funeral of a friend who was a member of Bethpage particular meeting, which I attended. After the interment a solemn meeting was held, in which my mind was largely opened to set forth to the people, the great necessity, as well as wisdom and propriety, of an early preparation for death; and showing them the way whereby it could only be rightly effected.   It was a season of renewed visitation to a remnant, and many hearts were broken and contrited.

CHAPTER VII.

Engagements at and about home, 1813 and 1814.

FIRST day, the 28th of 11th month, 1813. Feeling my mind drawn last evening and this morning to attend Friends' meeting at Martinicock, I submitted thereto and went alone. In the forepart of the meeting, I had to combat a spirit of ease and stupefaction, which is generally prevalent among the worldly-minded, although they may be pretty steady in attending meetings; yet it is to be feared with little or no profit, if it be true what the beloved apostle has affirmed, that: "If any man love the world, the love of the Father is not in him." In the latter part of the meeting I was led to view the excellency of the pacific principles of the gospel, as promulgated by Jesus Christ and his apostles; and to show to the people, the very great and essential benefit and blessing which would result to the professors of Christianity by a strict adherence and submission thereunto; as they stand in direct opposition to the spirit of violence and war, and breathe forth nothing but peace on earth and good will to men. It proved through mercy a season of favour; many hearts were contrited, and the faithful and poor in spirit comforted and strengthened; and my own mind inspired with gratitude and thankfulness for such unmerited mercy.

First day, the 5th of 12th month. The six working days of last week were principally spent in my worldly concerns, except attending our fifth day meeting, and the Charity Society meeting yesterday; an institution of Friends for educating the children of poor black people. Our funds, agreeably to the last report of a settlement with the Treasurer, amount to upwards of thirteen hundred dollars; the interest of which is yearly expended for the above purpose, by a committee of the Society, who superintend the educating of said children. The directors of the Society are limited to thirty members, who meet quarterly for the promotion and oversight of the institution. I attended our fifth day meeting in silence, and sat our meeting in like manner to-day, in poverty of spirit, which terminated in a peaceful close.

First day, the 12th of 12th month. At our meeting to-day, my mind was largely opened to set forth before the people the difference between the law state and that of the gospel. It was, I trust, an instructive edifying season, worthy of grateful remembrance.

Second day afternoon I rode to New-York, in order to attend the meeting for sufferings to be held there the next day. It opened at the ninth hour. We got through the business at two sittings, and closed in the evening. Fourth day afternoon I rode home. Fifth day was our monthly meeting. The meeting for worship was, I think, a favoured comfortable season; and the testimonies communicated instructive and edifying: such repeated favoured seasons make it evident beyond controversy, that we are still a highly favoured people, and shall be accountable according to the manifold mercies and blessings bestowed upon us: and we have great cause often to query, like the psalmist formerly, "What shall I render unto the Lord for all his benefits towards me;" for his mercies are new every morning; great is his faithfulness.

Sixth and seventh days. Spent in my ordinary concerns; yet, I trust, my mind was preserved in a state of watchfulness and care, that what I do, even in my temporal business, may all be done to the glory of God, and be useful to myself and to my fellow creatures.

First day, the 19th of 12th month. While silently musing in our meeting towards the latter part, a subject opened which led to the necessity of communication, wherein that petition in the prayer our Lord taught his disciples, viz: "Thy kingdom come; thy will be done in earth as it is in heaven;" was opened to the audience; and the necessity of our individually witnessing it fulfilled in us, as the only medium through which we can obtain salvation, and a preparation for the kingdom of heaven. This was pressed upon the people, showing from the analogy of things, that as there is nothing but the Lord's will done in heaven, a soul that is not reconciled thereto, cannot enter therein, nor partake of its celestial enjoyment.

The rest of the week was carefully employed in my household concerns, with the attendance of our fifth day meeting, agreeably to my invariable practice when at home, if not prevented by indisposition. It was a quiet comfortable meeting.

Sixth day. Attended the funeral of our honest friend Richard Townsend. There was a large collection of Friends and neighbours, he being generally esteemed. A meeting was held on the occasion, which proved a very solemn season. The people's attention was called to the necessity of a timely preparation for death, in a large arousing testimony; setting forth the great and singular advantages which would redound to the children of men, by their obtaining right ideas and apprehensions of God. The want of these left them to be led away into a belief of many strange and ideal notions concerning him, particularly that of foreordination; the inconsistency of which, my mind was led to unfold to the auditory, by this and other undeniable arguments;—that, as God's ordination, and God's creation, and God's will, are always in perfect unison, and cannot be diverse one from the other; and as all that he wills and creates is immutably good, agreeably to his own declaration in the work of creation; hence, whatever he ordains must likewise be immutably good: therefore, if there is any such thing as sin and iniquity in the world, then God has neither willed it, nor ordained it; as it is impossible for him to will contradictions. And secondly, if he has, previous to man's creation, willed and determined all his actions, then certainly every man stands in the same state of acceptance with him, and a universal salvation must certainly take place; which I conceive the favourers of foreordination would be as unwilling as myself to believe. And moreover, if man was not vested with the power of free agency, and a liberty of determining his own will, in relation to a choice of good or evil, he could not be an accountable creature; neither would it be in his power to commit

21

sin. It was a time of favour, and the Lord's blessing on, the
labours of the day was reverently supplicated. O, saith my, soul,
may they have the desired effect.

First day, the 26th of 12th month. Sat the greater part of
our meeting in much weakness and poverty of spirit, to which I
felt perfectly resigned, believing it to be agreeable to the Lord's
will. But towards the close an honest elderly Friend, though
young and small in such service, expressed a sentence or two
accompanied with a degree of life, which seemed to give spring
to a concern on my mind, which led to communication. The
subject which opened was to show, that plainness and simplicity
were the true marks and badges of the Lord's people and children
in every age of the world, witnessed to by the true nature and
analogy of all things in the universe; and confirmed by the
testimony of the grace and good spirit of God through his servants in all the generations of mankind. The youth were exhorted and tenderly invited to submit to the *cross of Christ*,
with the assurance assented to by the experience of all the faithful; that if they bowed willingly to his yoke, it would become
not only easy but delightful. But alas! how true is that declaration of the prophet: "who hath believed our report, and to
whom is the arm of the Lord revealed?" Certainly to none but
the obedient, which number, if we are to judge by their fruits, is
doubtless very small.

Second, third, and fourth days. Spent mostly in my temporal
business, but not without a watchful care lest it should engage
too much of my attention. The evenings were partly spent in
reading the scriptures, in which I greatly delight. How excellent are those records! although old, yet they seem ever new.
The prophecy of Micah was a part of my present reading; what
a dignified sense and clear view he had of the gospel state and
worship; and how exceedingly it lessened the service and worship
of the law in his view, in the clear sense given him of its full
and complete abolishment, with all its shadowy rituals; when
he was led to set forth its insufficiency, in this exalted language:
"Wherewith shall I come before the Lord, and bow myself
before the high God? Shall I come before him with burnt-

offerings, with calves of a year old? Will the Lord be pleased with thousands of rams, or with ten thousands of rivers of oil? Shall I give my first-born for my transgression, the fruit of my body for the sin of my soul?" No, none, nor all of these were sufficient to give access to the divine presence, or to the divine law under the gospel; they being only shadows, and therefore could only give access to the outward law and outward lawgiver Moses, and the law and ordinances given by him; which were also shadows of the true substance. For Moses, and his outward law and ordinances, stood in the same relation to outward Israel, under the shadowy dispensation, as Christ the spiritual Moses, with his spiritual law written in the heart, does to his spiritual Israel under the gospel; which is a dispensation not of shadow, but of substance; as is clearly shown by the sequel of the testimony of Micah above alluded to, where he goes on as follows: "He hath showed thee, O man, what is good;" then certainly not shadow nor sign, but real substance, "and what doth the Lord require of thee," not only by an outward, but by his inward, divine law, "but to do justly, and to love mercy, and to walk humbly with thy God." This is the sum and substance of all true religion and worship, and needs not the continuance of any outward elementary washings or eatings or drinkings; but opens to the necessity of our drinking at that spiritual river, the streams whereof make glad the whole heritage of God. For those that drink thereof will never thirst again, at least for the water of any other stream.

Fifth day. Sat our meeting to-day in silence. It is not unpleasant to feel ourselves sometimes circumstanced as Mordecai formerly, sitting at the king's gate, and, in its season, is as grateful to the truly humble and submissive mind, as riding on the king's horse, and all bowing before us.

First day, the 2d of 1st month, 1814. Another year is ended. Oh my soul, how hast thou improved it, and what progress hast thou made in thy heavenly journey? As I sat in our meeting to-day, my mind was led to contrast the law and gospel, or shadow and substance. "While I was musing the fire burned," and my heart became warmed within me; "then spake I with my tongue," and endeavoured in a zeal for the Lord's cause, to open to the people, the superiour excellency of the gospel, above and beyond that of the law, as set forth by the precepts, doctrines, example and commands of our great and gracious lawgiver Jesus Christ. The life rose towards the close of the meeting into a good degree of dominion, through hard labour and toil. For many professors lie so securely in their graves, that nothing short of the powerful voice that raised Lazarus formerly, is sufficient to quicken and raise them therefrom.

Second day. This day principally spent in making provision more favourably to meet the inclemency of the ensuing winter.

Third day. Spent as yesterday. In the evening read Thomas Ellwood's relation of his sufferings and cruel usage from his father, because, for conscience' sake, he could not pull off his hat and stand bare before him ; and for using the plain language of thou and thee, instead of the plural you. Alas ! what a spirit of pride, arrogance and cruelty governs the children of men, while living in the lusts of their fallen nature, estranged from God and from his true nature and image. And it is' to be feared that many in this day, who profess to be the successors of those primitive sufferers, our worthy predecessors, who stood faithful, and patiently bore the burden and heat of the day, through many years of cruel persecution, are now turning back like a broken bow; and through the fear or favour of men, are disregarding the testimonies which their forefathers in the truth purchased at so dear a rate ; and are ready to account many of them but small, or as indifferent things, which may, or may not, be attended to at their own pleasure. But alas for these, it is to be feared they will never have a view, much less be permitted to enter the promised land, the heavenly Canaan : but will fall in the wilderness as did the unbelieving and rebellious in former ages. I often mourn and take up a lamentation, when I behold the children of believing parents, turning aside, disobedient to their parents, and disregarding the travail and exercise of their concerned Friends, who are labouring for their return: but those who are faithful to give the watchword in season, will be clear of their blood, and the Lord will be clear. For he will have a people, and, as formerly, will send his servants into the highways and hedges, and gather from thence, that his house may be filled: but those children of the kingdom, who are making excuses, and will not come when they are bidden, will be cast out into outer darkness, where will be weeping and gnashing of teeth.

Fourth day. I was occupied as a carpenter, in making some conveniences for my stock. I felt wearied at evening with the labour of the day, but was comforted with a peaceful mind, feeling myself at peace with all men. A blessed privilege; it is the Lord's doing, and marvellous in mine eyes.

Seventh day. Attended the funeral of an ancient Friend. A meeting was held on the occasion, wherein I was exercised in a large arousing testimony suited to the occasion. May it be to the honest inquirers, as a nail fastened in a sure place; and to those who yet remain unwilling to surrender, as bread cast upon the waters, found after many days.

First day, the 9th of 1st month. At our meeting to-day I was led to reflect on my frequent appearances in the ministry at home, and ready to wonder why I was led so often to communicate to almost the same assembly. But these meditations were soon superseded by a renewed living concern, which opened again to communication, in a deep searching testimony; wherein I was led to show the fallacy and weakness of all man's creaturely and carnal reasoning, that it was all estranged from God, and stood in the ignorance and corruption of his fallen nature; and that man never had, nor could have, consistent with his nature as a dependent being, a right to assume a power to use his reason at his own discretion and will; but only in submission and subservience to the dictates of the light and spirit of his Creator, as paramount both to his reason and animal senses. For his reason is given him as an agent under his Creator, to govern and keep in due order the animal senses; not according to his own discretion and will, but agreeable to the manifestations of the divine spirit, or inward law and will, of his heavenly Father. It was an humbling season, and many hearts with mine own were bowed in reverence, under the sensible impress of the divine power.

The rest of the week I passed in my usual engagements, and in visiting some of my friends.

First day, the 16th of 1st month. Sat our meeting in silence to-day. The three following days I spent in attending to my usual avocations, and in visiting two of my sick neighbours. One of them was a young man, who was convinced of the truth, as held by us, in his young years. He spoke very sensibly of the work of truth on his mind in the early part of his convincement, and of the awe that covered his spirit, through the sensible impressions of the divine power; and recapitulated the precious seasons he had witnessed in the fields, sitting on rocks, and stumps of trees; and that he now felt his love to reach forth and embrace the whole human family. He appeared to be in a sweet and quiet frame of mind, though so weak, as not to be able to speak louder than a whisper. What a precious thing it is when the youth submit willingly to the visitations of divine love in their tender years; how amiable they appear, and how peaceful their close; a pearl to be valued above all temporal enjoyments.

Fifth day. This being the time of our monthly meeting, we had the company of two Friends on a visit to us. One of them appeared largely in the line of the ministry, but a fear attended my mind, lest he had not sufficiently attended to that command, which forbids sowing our ground with mingled seed; or suffering a garment of linen and woollen to come upon us: Oh how necessary it is for all those who apprehend they are called to the work of the ministry, to know self fully reduced; otherwise they may be in danger of endeavouring to cover the harlot, with the Lord's jewels; and with fair words, and fine speeches, deceive the hearts of the simple.

Sixth day. Attended our preparative meeting of Ministers and Elders. I had to drop a caution, founded on the failure of Moses and Aaron at the rock; when instead of speaking to it, as commanded, Moses smote it with his rod, with the addition of, "hear now, ye rebels; must we fetch you water out of this rock?" This act, being the effect of mere creaturely zeal and warmth of natural passions, lost them much; as it prevented their entering into the promised land. Oh how needful it is for those who are called to stand as a medium between God and the people, to be deeply attentive to the word of command, and not add thereto, nor diminish therefrom, under the penalty of his displeasure. For if he spared not Moses who was only guilty of this one fault in his administration, how much less can we expect that he will spare us, if we should add to, or diminish from, the word of prophecy.

Seventh day. Assisted a sick neighbour to settle his outward business by writing his will and seeing it executed. I then endeavoured to stimulate his mind with a concern rightly to improve the few remaining moments which might be permitted him on this side the grave; that so he might be prepared to meet death with a peaceful and trânquil mind.

First day, the 23d of 1st month, 1814. Attended Westbury meeting, at which there was a funeral of a deceased ancient woman Friend. It was a large meeting. Many Friends and neighbours came from a distance to attend the funeral. I had good service among them in the line of the ministry, by way of caution, encouragement and reproof; and was led to press upon the auditory the necessity of a submission of our wills to the divine will, as the only medium through which we could become qualified to answer the great end of our creation; which is to glorify God and enjoy him.

Second day. Attended the funeral of a pious young Friend of our meeting who departed this life by a consumption, after lingering a few months. His corpse was carried into our meeting-house at Jericho. There was a large meeting on the occasion, and through the prevalence of the divine power that presided over the assembly, it proved a very solemn time. Many hearts were broken and contrited by the force of the testimony, which went forth powerfully clothed with the demonstration of the spirit, and the Lord's name was exalted over all.

Seventh day. This being the time of our quarterly meeting, I was mostly employed through the week in attention thereto. It was, I think, through the several sittings a solemn searching time. My mind was closely engaged on several subjects appertaining to our Christian testimonies ; but more particularly that against war, which was now in the land. Friends, with others, were called upon for supplies by way of taxes to carry it on, which were levied various ways on the inhabitants. I felt my mind deeply engaged to lay before Friends the inconsistency of our actively complying with any such military requisitions, believing that if we did, we should not only become accessaries in the war, but should have to bear a part of the guilt of shedding the blood of our fellow creatures. The Lord's power was felt to preside, and the testimonies borne on the occasion were evidently clothed with divine authority, keeping down all opposition. The minds of the faithful were inspired with humble gratitude and thanksgiving to the Lord our gracious helper, under a renewed sense of his continued mercy to us as a people ; and to all the workmanship of his holy hand.

First day, the 30th of 1st month, 1814. As I was sitting in our meeting my mind became exercised in contemplating the danger that some of my fellow professors of the Christian name are exposed to, by placing their dependence for justification and salvation on the *imputative righteousness of Christ which he performed without them*, without coming to know a complete remission of their sins, and living a life of righteousness through faith in the operation of God, and a submission to the work of *his spirit in their minds ;* by which, according to the apostle's exhortation, they can only be enabled to work out their own salvation with fear and trembling. For it is God that worketh in the willing and obedient soul, both to will and to do of his own good pleasure ; but this can only be witnessed by such as experience their own wills to be mortified and slain by the power of the cross inwardly revealed, whereby the true spiritual atonement is made. I was largely opened to communicate on some of these subjects ; and to show to the people wherein the true harmony between the law dispensation, and that of the gospel consisted. It was a season worthy of grateful remembrance ; the meeting closed with thanksgiving and prayer, under a renewed sense of the continued mercy of our gracious God, who is over all, blessed for ever.

Second day. Being unwell with a cold I kept house and read.

Third day. Having the evening before received an invitation to attend the funeral of a deceased neighbour about four miles distant from my dwelling, and understanding it was the desire of the deceased on her death-bed that I would attend; I felt inclined to go, although still unwell. I was glad I gave up thereto, as it proved, through heavenly help, a solemn instructive season, wherein my heart and mouth were opened to declare largely of the way of life and salvation to the people in the clear demonstration of truth. The assembly in general were bowed and humbled, and many hearts contrited; to the Lord alone be the praise, for to him only it is due.

Fourth day. Still unwell: mostly kept house.

Fifth day. Ventured out to our meeting, but was considerably afflicted with my cold and cough. The meeting was held in silence.

The two following days, and the forepart of the next week, I employed, mostly, in preparing for the press a small treatise on slavery; and on the use of the produce of the labour of slaves. I laid it before our meeting for sufferings which met this week; and obtained their concurrence for printing it. As I was in the city, I attended Friends' meetings as they came in course on fourth and fifth days, and returned home on sixth day. Nothing particular transpired on seventh day.

First day, the 13th of 2d month. Was largely opened in communication on divers subjects in a very searching testimony, which brought a covering of great solemnity over the meeting. The honest-hearted were comforted: but it was a season of sharp reproof to the unfaithful and lukewarm.

Fifth day. Attended our monthly meeting, at which nothing opened worthy of particular notice.

Seventh day. I attended the funeral of the wife of John Wine, a Friend of Flushing. We had a very solemn meeting on the occasion, in which I was exercised in a large affecting testimony, tendering and contriting the hearts of the assembly in general. The truth was raised into dominion, breaking down all before its influential searching power; which was cause of

22

deep gratitude and thanksgiving to the Lord our gracious helper, for his unmerited mercy, still dispensed in his longsuffering loving kindness to the children of men.

Feeling my mind inclined to sit with Friends here the next day, which was first day, the people were notified thereof at the close of the foregoing opportunity. It was a full meeting, in which truth favoured and furnished with matter suited to the states of those present; which made it an instructive edifying season. The canopy of love was felt to spread sweetly and very comfortably over the assembly, and I parted with them in the fresh feeling thereof; and with a peaceful mind, and a thankful sense of the Lord's mercy.

Nothing particular occurred in the course of the next week; but the precious savour that was witnessed in the two forementioned opportunities, remained as a canopy over my mind, and was cause of humble gratitude and thankfulness to the blessed Author of all our rich mercies and blessings.

First day, the 27th of 2d month. My mind, in our meeting to-day, after a considerable time of humble quiet waiting, and seeking to be gathered to Shiloh, was led in prospect to view the great and singular advantages which would redound to the children of men by an early acquaintance with the Lord; and by continually looking to him, and relying on him, as the primary and only object of their faith and hope. The prospect enlarged and opened to a communication, and the truth was raised into a comfortable degree of dominion, and spread a solemn covering over the assembly; and many hearts were contrited and made glad from a feeling sense of the Lord's mercy vouchsafed to us at this season. O how good is the Lord, and how greatly to be praised, for his mercy endureth for ever.

The rest of this week I was occupied in my temporal concerns. Sat our fifth day meeting in silence, in which I had to maintain a steady warfare against the intrusion of unprofitable thoughts. O how precious it is to be favoured to gain a complete victory over these, and to have the mind brought to witness a profound stillness, where nothing reigns but Jesus, in his inward spiritual government.

First day, the 6th of 3d month. In our meeting to-day I had again to bear testimony against the prevailing evils of the day some of which I had to expose, and to show how we must enter the church militant, if ever we enter right, and become useful members thereof, and be truly comforted and profited thereby. The communication was introduced by the parable of the supper, which shows that those who have something of the pleasures and treasures of this world to gratify and comfort themselves with, will not come in, although invited : but those who are brought to a full sense of their wretched and forlorn condition, without God and without a Saviour, compared, in the parable, to those who are poor and destitute of every comfort, and scattered in the highways and hedges, will seek a place of refuge ; and having tried every means they had in their power, and every invention that man has sought out in the way of salvation, and after all finding themselves still left in a state of disappointment, are made willing to surrender all up, and sell all ; that so they may be enabled to purchase the field wherein the pearl of great price lies. The word went forth with power, and struck home to many minds, and a very solemn weight appeared to cover the assembly in general.

Second, third, and fourth days. Spent in a quiet attention to my temporal concerns with the attendant blessing of peace of mind ; yet not without some intervals of interruption from the loose and the vain, with which this neighbourhood is too much disturbed. Alas, what has so gained the ascendency in and over the mind of man, as to cause him to delight and take pleasure in wickedness.

Fifth day. Was our preparative meeting, in which the over-seers brought forward information against one of our members, a young man, for deviations from plainness, and being guilty of attending horse races, and suffering his horse to run for a wager ; all which manifest a very thoughtless disposition, and much vanity of mind, very unworthy the least member in our community. The meeting felt tenderly for him, as he had not had a guarded education ; he being left an orphan, when small, by the death of his father. In considering his condition, I was induced to enlist myself voluntarily in the meeting's service, to pay him a visit; and the meeting added another Friend to join me therein. I was likewise engaged in the meeting for worship, to call Friends' attention to the necessity of greater purification both in body, soul, and spirit; as the only medium through which we could gain an inheritance in the kingdom of heaven. I showed by the analogy of reason, that a purified soul could not be content to inhabit a polluted body; and that if the inside was made clean, the outside would be clean also; and that true and genuine Christianity will lead to cleanliness in our persons, in our houses, and in all our concerns. All this will proceed from real love and duty to our Creator, and not from any germ of pride, or vainly to make a show, but from a real desire of effecting holiness in the fear of the Lord.

First day, the 13th. A comfortable meeting to-day, mostly in silence, but closed with solemn supplication, wherein I was led to set forth how our gracious and beneficent Creator, although he sees all our wants, and stands always disposed, before we ask him, to redress all our real grievances, and dispense good to us whenever he finds us in a condition fit to receive: yet as he is a God of justice and truth, he delights to see his people and children grateful and humbly sensible of their dependence on him for every blessing; therefore, he permits them, at times, when he sees meet to influence their minds thereto, to approach his sacred presence in humble and devout prayer, and which also affords to those who are thus devoted, sweet and heavenly consolation and joy.

I passed this week mostly at home overseeing my temporal concerns. Attended our monthly meeting on fifth day, at which we received information, from the women's meeting, of the departure of one of our members, a young woman, who had gone out in her marriage with one not a member, whom they concluded ought to be disowned; with which the men's meeting concurred. This is a weakness among our young members, which is, in general, very pernicious in its consequences, and too often happens through the neglect of care and right concern in parents and guardians, who, for want of living near the truth, and under right religious engagements themselves, are too often led away to seek after riches for their children, and are more desirous that their children should obtain companions who are wealthy and rich in this world's treasure, than such as are truly religious and virtuous. Thus a foundation is often laid, by such indiscreet parents, for many very unhappy connexions, by which the religious improvement and advancement of their tender offspring is often entirely intercepted and prevented, and their prospects of temporal comfort and joy rendered abortive; and they have to drag out a miserable existence until death dissolves their obligations.

First day, the 20th. As I sat in our meeting my mind was brought under exercise in taking a view of the life of Solomon, that wise king of Israel, as delineated by his own pen ; and from which we learn the insignificance of all consolation and joy which have their source in temporal and mortal things, as they must and will end, in vanity and vexation of spirit : and that to fear God and keep his commandments, is not only the whole duty of man, but likewise the only blessed and eternal source of all true joy and never ending felicity. The subject spread on my mind and led to communication, in which I endeavoured, in the ability afforded, by persuasive arguments, to engage the minds of the auditory, both old and young, in the pursuit of that invaluable treasure that waxeth not old, but endureth for ever, which will bring true joy to the immortal soul and adds no sorrow.

Nothing particular occurred in the course of this week, except that a care and fear attended my mind, lest the cares of this world and the increase of temporal things might too much interrupt, and intrude, upon my spiritual concerns ; for riches are ever deceitful, and always promise more than they have in their power to perform.

First day, the 27th. Feeling my mind inclined to sit with Friends at Bethpage to day, I yielded to the motion and attended their meeting; and although I had not a great deal to communicate, yet what I had, appeared to reach home to many minds, and rendered it a comfortable meeting, not only to myself, but to the assembly in general. The subject which opened for communication was the necessity and excellency of integrity ; and that although we might be so wise and knowing as to comprehend all knowledge, yet if we were destitute of integrity and sincerity of heart, we should but share the fate of fools at last, and be not a whit better for all our wisdom and knowledge.

Second, third, and fourth days. Spent in close attention to my temporal concerns, the care for which, and for their right ordering, is constantly necessary; insomuch that I often wonder how it is, that I sometimes hear people say, they seem at a loss how to spend their time; when not only my temporal, but in an especial manner my spiritual concerns, are always urgent and pressing; so that I find not a moment to be idle : so true is that declaration of the Most High verified : " In the sweat of thy face shalt thou eat bread, till thou return unto the ground; for out of it wast thou taken : for dust thou art and unto dust shalt thou return." The wise man also saith : "All things are full of labour" therefore we ought not to repine or murmur at our lot, but receive all, as at the hand of the Lord with thanksgiving.

Fifth, sixth, and seventh days. I attended three funerals, one on each day successively. The first was a very ancient female, upwards of ninety years of age, belonging to Westbury meeting. We had a solemn meeting on the occasion, in which truth favoured, opening suitable doctrine, and bringing it home to the states of those present, who were mostly Friends. The hidden things of Esau, or the first nature, and the secret lurking places of self, were searched out and exposed ; for which my mind, with the honest-hearted present, was made glad in the Lord, and in the apparent working of his power and wisdom. The two last were not members of our society, but were favourably disposed to Friends. They were seasons of favour. A meeting, was held at each, and both largely attended by the neighbouring inhabitants. The doctrines delivered were well adapted to the conditions of the hearers, and were brought home to many minds in the demonstration of truth, breaking and contriting many hearts ; and thanksgiving and praises were returned to the Shepherd of Israel, as a tribute of gratitude for such unmerited mercies.

First day, the 3d of 4th month. Our meeting to-day was

favoured with the overshadowing wing of divine truth, and its power exalted over all, contriting and comforting many minds. But alas, what small advancements are made by many of those who are often dug about and watered by the compassionate Shepherd of Israel, whose mercy is still eminently dispensed to man, the workmanship of his holy hand.

I attended two funerals in the course of this week, one on fifth day, after the sitting of our preparative meeting, and the other on sixth day. Both were young men in the prime of life. The latter unmarried, and was a relation to my wife. His parents had a healthful family of children, and had never met with the like trial before. It was therefore a very affecting scene both to them and their children; they having been before favoured with almost an unbroken scene of worldly prosperity, which made the wound sink deeper. We had a very solemn meeting on the occasion, wherein I was largely opened to preach the gospel in the demonstration of truth; and among other things to show to the people, the necessity and sure felicity of an early preparation for death; and that God was the alone proper object for man to set his heart and affections upon. The auditory were mostly not in membership with Friends. Many of them were much broken and contrited, and a general, and very precious solemnity was spread over the meeting. The hearts of many were made glad, from a sense of the Lord's continued and unmerited goodness and mercy to the children of men; still showing his unwillingness that any should die in their sins, and that all might repent, turn to him and live.

First day, the 10th. I had a hard suffering meeting to-day, in which I witnessed not only deep inward poverty, but had to struggle with unprofitable thoughts, with very little ability to maintain the warfare; yet, under the consideration that it was altogether as good, if not better, than my deserts could justly require, I was preserved from murmuring or complaining at my lot, being willing to receive evil as well as good, at the hand of my gracious and compassionate Lord, when he sees meet to permit or dispense it. "Shall we receive good at the hand of God, and shall we not evil?"

The rest of this week was principally occupied in a close application to my temporal concerns, except attending our monthly and select preparative meetings, which came at this time. My belief was similar to the apostle's, that he who is not carefully industrious to labour for his own and household's comfortable support, may be considered to have denied the faith, and is worse than an infidel; as they are generally careful on those accounts.

First day, the 17th. The meeting to-day was pretty open and comfortable. The rest of the week was mostly taken up in attending our quarterly meeting, held at New-York at this time.

First day, the 24th. Sat our meeting mostly in silence.

Second, third, and fourth days. Were taken up principally in caring for my temporal concerns. Alas, how much precious time is expended for the accommodation of those houses of clay, which must shortly return to the dust from whence they were taken; and which often burden, and too much indispose the mind for heavenly and spiritual meditations, unless carefully watched and strongly guarded against.

Fifth day. I was wholly silent in our meeting to-day; in the course of which I had full evidence of the truth of that saying of the great Master, that of ourselves, without him, we can do nothing.

Sixth and seventh days. Were accompanied with heart searchings, discouragement, and dismay; in which I witnessed the truth of that saying, that vain is the help of man, whose efforts often tend more to sully and weaken, than to brighten and strengthen the minds of those they strive to help. This is principally owing to their dwelling on the surface, and judging from the outward appearance, instead of digging deep in search of the mind of truth, which only can enable to judge with righteous judgment.

First day, the 1st of 5th month. Sat our meeting in silence, and in much poverty of spirit; and when the season for closing the meeting seemed near at hand, I looked over the assembly, which was pretty large, with a degree of sympathy and commiseration, which brought to my remembrance the compassionate

saying of our Lord to his disciples, on, as I apprehended, a similar occasion, viz: "If I send them away fasting to their own
houses, they will faint by the way." This put a stop to my mind
with regard to closing the meeting; and as I knew I had nothing
to give, I looked around to see what was to be done. A friend
then stood up with something comparable to the five loaves and
the two fishes, which were found formerly in the lad's basket.
As they were broken, she handed them to the company, until all
appeared satisfied; for which I was thankful.

Seventh day. The week hath passed away. Oh time, precious time, how swift thou passest on, by us almost unenjoyed
and unimproved! How soon thou wilt land thy travelling pil-
grim in the house appointed for all living; where, oh my soul,
thou knowest there is no repentance nor amendment known!
Prepare then, oh prepare, for thy final change!

First day, the 8th of 5th month. A poor silent meeting until
near the close, when a little light sprang up and dispelled the
darkness, and sweetened all the bitter. By such things we are
instructed, and learn to know our dependent state, and that it is
the Lord's doings, and marvellous in our eyes.

Nothing uncommon transpired in the course of this week,
save as usual, bonds and afflictions for the gospel's sake, spiritually and inwardly experienced, await me; from a view and
sense of the spread of evil, and the great want of faithful testimony-bearers in society; and the languor and weakness which
abound; that I am sometimes almost involuntarily led to cry,
alas for the day.

First day, the 15th. My mind was deeply exercised in our
meeting to-day on divers important subjects, and largely led forth
in communication: but for want of a more full openness and
preparation in the auditory to receive, the labour was arduous
and exercising, yet I trust profitable to some.

The rest of the week was employed in my usual attention to
my necessary temporal concerns, and an unfailing attention to
those of a religious nature. Our monthly meeting was held this
week. The meeting for Ministers and Elders belonging to the
yearly meeting was held on seventh day, at the tenth hour,

which my wife and myself attended. It was, I think, in a good degree a favoured time; as were the public meetings on first day, both forenoon and afternoon. On second day the yearly meeting for discipline opened at the tenth hour, and continued by adjournments until fifth day evening. It was for the most part a comfortable profitable season, evidencing in the several sittings, that the Lord had not forsaken his people, but was still graciously manifesting his presence and power for our comfort and help, in ordering the affairs of the Church. On sixth day Friends turned their faces towards home, where I arrived at evening with my wife and two youngest daughters, who constitute my present family, except servants.

The next day I felt myself in a cheerful readiness to put my hands to whatever they found to do, as right to be done.

First day, the 29th. Felt myself so much indisposed with a cold and considerable pain of body, as to be prevented from attending our meeting to-day ; in reflecting thereon, and how very seldom I had been thus prevented for many years past, my mind was filled with gratitude and thankfulness to our gracious Helper and Preserver, for the portion of bodily health allotted me in the course of his divine providence ; whereby, I have been almost invariably of ability of body for a number of years, to attend all our religious meetings, which I consider and number among our chiefest blessings and benefits.

The latter end of this week I joined our friend William Flanner, who was here on a religious visit from Ohio ; and attended a number of meetings in divers places, where no meetings of our society were held. I had had a prospect of visiting those places some time before. We were out three days and attended five meetings. The first was with Friends at Bethpage, the rest among people inclining to Friends, and those of other professions. They were, I think, all favoured seasons. The Lord's presence and power were manifested for our help, furnishing ability to minister suitably to the different states of the people, in the demonstration of the spirit. Many hearts were humbled and contrited, and the assemblies solemnized, and truth raised into dominion over all ; and our hearts were made glad under an humbling sense of the continuation of the Lord's mercy and compassion, still extended to the children of men. We returned home on first day evening, the 5th of 6th month.

The three following days I was about home, mostly employed in my temporal concerns.

On sixth day attended the funeral of a friend of Westbury meeting. It was a solemn time, in which I found it my place to be an example of silence. Seventh day spent at home. On first day, the 12th of 6th month, I attended two meetings, by appointment, among those not of our society. One in the morning at Cold Spring, and the other at four o'clock in the afternoon at Huntington. They were both seasons of extensive labour, and I hope profitable to some ; and productive of peace to my own mind.

On second day I went to New-York in order to attend the meeting for sufferings, which I accordingly attended the next day, and returned home at evening. On fourth day attended to my temporal concerns with usual industry.

Fifth day attended our monthly meeting, at which several matters occurred producing exercise to my mind, which led to a communication of prospects ; and although some diversity of sentiment was expressed, yet I was favoured so to unfold the subjects, that they were concluded in a general unity.

Sixth and seventh days. Spent in attending to my usual affairs.

First day, the 19th of 6th month. I was led in our meeting to-day, to set forth the excellency of real poverty of spirit ; as it is that only, which can produce that truly humble state, to which the blessing is annexed.

Fifth day. As I was sitting in our meeting enjoying the especial advantages which are attached to silent meetings, when the mind is silently prostrated at the throne of grace, and helped to be sequestered from all intruding thoughts, and wholly centered in and upon Jehovah, the alone object of worship and adoration; a subject opened and spread in a way which led to communication ; in which I had to show, that there were but two proper motives or inducements for our rightly attending religious meetings. The first related to such as were unbelievers, or those who were ignorant of the right way of worshipping God in and under the dispensation of the gospel, which according to our Lord's declaration to the woman of Samaria, is only to be performed in spirit and in truth. The principal benefit to these, is to be informed and instructed; for which more especially, the Lord hath ordained a ministry in his Church, by means of instruments rightly qualified therefor, by the baptismal influence of the Holy Ghost. The second relates to such as are already instructed and informed, whose judgments are convinced, and whose motive as it relates to themselves is, to meet together to wait upon and worship God in spirit and in truth, without any regard or consideration to any external ministry or means whatever : as it is only in a state of entire sequestration from every thing of an outward or external nature, that the soul is permitted to enter into the holy place, not made with hands; and admitted into the immediate presence of Jehovah, and rendered capable of worshipping him, in spirit and in truth, as the gospel requires.

Sixth and seventh days. Spent in my usual vocation as a farmer.

First day, the 26th of 6th month. Attended two meetings by appointment, among those principally not of our society. The first was held in a Friend's house at a place called the Half Hollow Hills. The latter at the fourth hour in the afternoon, at a village called New Babylon, in the township of Huntington. It was held in a school-house, and was a large meeting, mostly of the Presbyterian persuasion. The people behaved very soberly, becoming the occasion. It was a very solemn favoured season ; many hearts were contrited and made thankful for the opportunity ; and my heart was much enlarged in love to the assembly. I trust I felt a mutual return of the same feeling from most present, for which I was made thankful to the Shepherd of Israel ; and for the continuation of his gracious regard in manifesting his presence, and making bare his arm, for the help of his devoted servants ; showing himself indeed to be a God near at hand, and a present helper in the needful time, worthy to be praised and adored by the children of men, throughout all ages, world without end.

The rest of this week I spent mostly about home, being closely engaged in making hay, which for want of suitable help, made it necessary for me to labour myself, beyond what seemed suitable for one of my age; but I felt peace of mind in so doing, although I suffered some pain of body, as the result of my exertion.

First day, the 3d of 7th month. Sat our meeting in silence. At the third hour in the afternoon attended the funeral of a deceased neighbour. Although my mind was brought under some exercise, which led to communication; yet I found very little relief, owing, as I apprehended, to the prevalence of a libertine spirit in many present. For these are generally disposed to mock at, and ridicule every thing serious, or that has the appearance of religion and godliness: rebellious children who hate the light, because their deeds are evil, and who take more delight in revelling and drunkenness than in the fear of the Lord. I often feel sad for such as these, and my mind goes clothed as it were with sackcloth, unseen by the world. O, when will they be awakened to a right sense of their miserable condition! I often fear that some of them have nearly sinned out their day; and to whom the scripture declaration will apply: " He that, being often reproved, hardeneth his neck, shall suddenly be destroyed, and that without remedy."

Second, third and fourth days. Busily employed in my husbandry concerns, with my mind clothed with peace towards all men, and with hope towards God my Saviour: and comforted at times in the remembrance of that apostolic declaration, where it is asserted: " We know that we have passed from death unto life, because we love the brethren."

Fifth day. Attended our meeting in silence, the fire being low on the altar.

Sixth and seventh days. Closely engaged in making and securing hay for the accommodation of my stock the ensuing winter; as I consider it a duty to provide plenty of good provender for them, so as to render their lives as comfortable as may be, whilst under my care.

First day, the 10th. As I sat in our meeting to-day, my mind was led into a consideration and prospect of the excellency and amiableness of justice, and of the vast advantage which would accrue to the children of men by a strict adherence thereto; as it would greatly tend to regulate our conduct, both as it relates to our duty to God our creator, and also to man, our fellow creature : and therefore ought to be the governing principle and main spring of all our conduct, as well in our temporal, as in our spiritual concerns. The subject spread and enlarged and opened to communication; and, I trust, proved an instructive comfortable season to some present; and I felt a reward of peace in my labour.

Second day. Attended the funeral of a deceased neighbour, who was not a member of our society, but being convinced of our principles, and inclined to Friends, the family desired a meeting might be held, which was accordingly agreed to. It was a large collection of people of various denominations, and a considerable number of the looser sort. I had an open favoured time among them, in which the power of truth rose into dominion over all, humbling and contriting many hearts, and a general solemnity was felt to cover the meeting to the praise of Him, who is over all, God blessed for ever.

Third and fourth days. Occupied in my usual concerns, but did not feel that full peace of mind with my fourth day's exercise that is generally my experience, owing, as I apprehended, to a want of a more full attention to a small intimation respecting that day's employment. Remember, oh my soul! that all thy success in temporals, as well as all thy sweet inward heavenly consolations, depend upon thy faithfulness and ready submission to those inward divine intimations; although sometimes small, they ought to be considered by thee, binding and obligatory, as the only source from whence all thy true peace and joy are derived.

Fifth day. This was our preparative meeting, and as it was the one preceding the quarterly meeting, the queries were read and answered; but I apprehended in a way not tending to much profit, either by reason of one or two improper questions being added to the queries of late, which to many Friends appeared inconsistent to be answered; or from the want of a more lively spiritual exercise with the members; or both might have had a share in producing a dull distressing season. No way seemed to open for any relief, so we had patiently to bear it. And indeed I thought it required a large share of patience to sit the meeting through without murmuring; the chariot wheels seemed to go very heavily on, as though almost sunk in the slough of despond; but we did what we could, and so left the matter; and I returned home with a heavy heart, and was preserved, I trust, from mur-muring at my lot.

Sixth day. Spent in gathering in my harvest and some other small exercises. The day closed with a quiet and peaceful mind. What a paradise it is when this is our lot.

Seventh day. Visited two Friends who were under some bodily infirmity. The visits were mutually comfortable. Such opportunities, when rightly conducted, tend to the increase of friendship and mutual love.

CHAPTER VIII.

Visit to Purchase, and engagements at and about home, 1814.

First day, the 17th of 7th month, 1814. Feeling my mind drawn to sit with Friends in their meeting at Westbury, I yielded to the motion. It proved an exercising meeting—but little life to be felt: nevertheless, way opened for a short communication, pointing particularly to the state of the meeting, which I hope was profitable to some. At the third hour in the afternoon, I attended the funeral of a very ancient woman of this neighbourhood, not a member of our society; but the family desiring the company of Friends, a number collected with others. It proved a pretty solemn time. My mind was led to open to the assembly, the especial advantages which would result to us, as rational accountable beings, by a timely preparation for death; and that it was our especial duty, as well as our best interest, to make it, at all times, the primary object of our concern.

Second, third, and fourth days. Spent principally in family cares and my husbandry concerns. What a favour it is for such an active creature as man, possessed of such powers of body and mind, always to have some employment, and something for those powers to act upon: for otherwise they would be useless and dormant, and afford neither profit nor delight.

Fifth day. Attended our monthly meeting. It was an exercising season, especially the meeting for worship, which I think was much hurt by the communication of a Friend in the ministry, who was this day with us. It was attended with so much mere creaturely warmth and animation, as to render it unacceptable, and, as I apprehended, hurtful to the meeting, and the cause it was intended to advance. What a pity it is that any who apprehend themselves called to this very important work, should make such grievous mistakes, and wound the minds of the living sensible members.

Sixth day. Attended our select preparative meeting of Ministers and Elders. It was, I think, a season of profitable exercise, in which some of the hidden things of Esau, or the first nature, were searched out and exposed.

Seventh day. Laboured hard in my harvest field; and, although sixty-six years of age, I found I could wield the scythe nearly as in the days of my youth. It was a day of thankful and delightful contemplation. My heart was filled with thankfulness and gratitude to the blessed Author of my existence, in a consideration of his providential care over me, in preserving me in health, and in the possession of my bodily powers; the exercise of which were still affording me both profit and delight: and I was doubly thankful for the continued exercise of my mental faculties, not only in instructing me how to exert and rightly employ my bodily powers, in the most useful and advantageous manner, but also in contemplating the works of nature and Providence, in the blessings and beauties of the field; a volume containing more delightful and profitable instruction, than all the volumes of mere learning and science in the world.

What a vast portion of the joys and comforts of life do the idle and slothful deprive themselves of, by running into cities and towns, to avoid labouring in the field; not considering that this is one of the principal sources, that the gracious Creator of the universe has appointed to his creature man, from whence he may derive great temporal happiness and delight. It also opens the largest and best field of exercise to the contemplative mind, by which it may be prepared to meet, when this mortal puts on immortality, those immortal joys that will ever be the lot of the faithful and industrious.

First day, the 24th of 7th month. I went to our meeting to-day in much poverty of spirit, and in full expectation of passing it in silence; but I had not sat long before my mind was led into a view of the singular benefit derived to the children of men, by the denial of self, and a daily and faithfully taking up, and bearing the cross; as it is the only way by which we can come to experience real sanctification and justification. The subject spread and opened to communication, in which things were laid home to the states of many present, in a clear manner; and the danger of their situations exposed. It brought a solemn covering over the meeting, for which I was thankful.

Second and third days. I spent in securing my harvest. This week being the time of our quarterly meeting, the meeting for Ministers and Elders opened on fourth day at the tenth hour. It was a season of close search; the deficiencies of Ministers and Elders were laid open; and the hurtful tendency thereof exposed. A number appeared deeply concerned, on account of the prevailing weakness of some in those exalted stations in society. On fifth day the meeting for discipline was held. It was also a very searching time, a season of deep exercise to my mind; in which the hurtful tendency of many apparent deficiencies was laid open and exposed; and Friends exhorted to greater faithfulness and diligence, in the right support of those noble testimonies, given us to bear, for the promotion of righteousness and peace on the earth. On sixth day was a general public meeting, in which my mind was enlarged in gospel communication, wherein truth was exalted and raised into dominion, to the comfort and edification of many minds; and to the sweet peace of my own. After this Friends separated to their several homes in much nearness of affection, and mutual love.

Seventh day. Spent in my temporal concerns.

First day, the 31st of 7th month. A silent meeting to-day, for which I was thankful. Although faithfully labouring in the Lord's vineyard produceth peace and joy to the willing mind, even should it have to bear the burden and heat of the day; yet when permitted, a season of rest is also sweet and grateful.

Having for some days past felt my mind inclined to attend the ensuing quarterly meeting at Purchase, I spent most of this week in that service. On second day I left home, and returned on the following sixth day at evening. I felt but little satisfaction in this short tour of duty, except in one or two visits in Friends' families. Most of the sittings of the quarterly meeting seemed to be clothed with great weakness, and some of them distressingly so.

Seventh day. Exercised in my husbandry business; and the evening closed with a peaceful mind.

First day, the 7th of 8th month. Felt so much bodily indisposition as to prevent my attending meeting; but even this induced thankfulness and gratitude, in recollecting how very seldom this had been my lot for many years. Oh what shall I, a poor worm, render unto the Lord for all his benefits!

Second, third, and fourth days. Spent principally in looking to, and overseeing, my temporal business; and still feeling some slight touches of bodily indisposition, which seemed to announce this language, in unison with every thing that is mortal, *remember to die.*

Fifth day. Attended our preparative meeting: what a privilege! the very name points to care, as saying, "Be ye therefore ready."

Sixth day. Did as Peter and some of his fellow disciples, when not directly employed by their Master, but waiting and watching for his coming.

Seventh day. Laboured in the field; and the day closed with a quiet and peaceful mind, which I esteem the greatest treasure.

First day, the 14th of 8th month. As I sat in our meeting to-day, my mind was impressed with the remembrance of the declaration of the prophet Isaiah, when reproving the house of Israel, under the similitude of a vineyard, for their backsliding and breach of covenant and great wickedness, which he closes with this notable saying: "Therefore hell hath enlarged herself, and opened her mouth without measure: and their glory, and their multitude, and their pomp, and he that rejoiceth, shall descend into it." He showed them thereby the natural tendency of evil, and certain destruction of evil doers, who harden themselves in sin. The subject opened and led to a large exhortatory and cautionary communication; also setting forth the great obligations of parents and guardians to their tender offspring and children under their charge; and the incalculable loss that children sustain where parents and guardians neglect their duty in timely care for their right instruction. It was a solemn time, and I hope profitable to some, by stirring them up to more diligence.

The rest of this week, except attending our monthly meeting on fifth day, was spent in close attention to my temporal concerns. The urgent necessity attending my present business induced me to labour beyond what my judgment approved; which, though somewhat painful to the body, was nevertheless, I trust, free from sin.

First day, the 21st of 8th month. A silent meeting to-day, which closed with a peaceful mind.

Second, third, and fourth days. Passed without any thing transpiring worthy of particular notice.

Fifth day. A silent meeting, as it respects myself.

Sixth and seventh days. Spent in my salt-meadows, about ten miles from home; assisting my men in making and securing hay. On my return visited a poor widow, with the surplus of our provisions, for which she was very thankful.

First day, the 28th. My lips, at our meeting to-day, were closed in solemn silence.

Second, third, and fourth days. Diligently employed in what my hands found to do: for I see no time when it would be right to indulge in idleness.

Fifth day. Sat our meeting in much weakness and poverty of spirit, but felt peace at the close.

Sixth and seventh days. Closely engaged in my temporal business; but did not forget my accountability to my great Lord and Master, for the right use of every portion of precious time, he is pleased to dispense to me.

First day, the 4th of 9th month. My mind, while sitting in our meeting to-day, was led into a contemplation of the great and excellent advantages resulting to those, who have placed their supreme trust in the arm of divine sufficiency; and while musing thereon, and the manifold blessings attendant on such a state, there was brought to my remembrance the exhortation of Solomon: "Trust in the Lord with all thy heart; and lean not unto thine own understanding." The subject spread, and opened to a communication, in which the audience were pressingly invited and encouraged to lay hold and make choice of this only sure rock of refuge, an entire trust and confidence in God, and in the arm of his salvation. For those who trust in the name of the Lord, have never been confounded.

The rest of this week was spent in my usual vocations, except attending our preparative meeting on fifth day. Nothing transpired worthy of particular notice.

First day, the 11th. As I was sitting in our meeting to-day, my mind was led into a train of solemn reflection, from the revival of these expressions of Christ to his disciples : " In the world ye shall have tribulation : but be of good cheer, I have overcome the world." An enlightened view was opened to me of the especial advantages, and deep consolation, derived to the true Christian, by a firm belief therein : as the expressions evidently carry in them an earnest to the true believer, of his being likewise enabled to overcome, as he is faithful in treading in the path of self-denial, agreeably to his heavenly pattern. The subject opened to communication, in which the audience were pressingly invited and encouraged to enter earnestly into this most necessary and interesting warfare ; as nothing short of overcoming the world, the flesh, and the devil, can restore to us an uninterrupted peace, and entitle us to the white stone in which the new name is written ; which none can read, but he who hath it.

The succeeding days of this week were attended to as they passed ; but nothing transpired unusual. Our monthly meeting was on fifth day ; and although we had a pretty trying case before us, yet we got through without interruption, or any breach of Christian harmony.

First day, the 18th of 9th month. A satisfactory meeting to-day, more so than for several weeks past ; the testimony of truth went forth freely, and, I think, clothed with a good degree of power and demonstration of the spirit, which produced a peaceful and thankful mind. The rest of this week I was closely engaged in preparing my fallow ground, and sowing my wheat and rye. I am willing to do my part carefully and industriously ; and then I can with more confidence, place my trust and dependence on a gracious and beneficent Providence, for a blessing on my labour: for if care and industry be wanting, there is nothing for him to bless.

First day, the 25th. A silent meeting to-day, as to any vocal communication ; but my mind was too much intruded upon by unprofitable thoughts, and interrupted by the unchristian commotions and din of war, which are at present mightily prevailing in our land, and by the frequent reports of blood and slaughter witnessed among professed human rational beings: but alas! how inhuman and irrational do they prove and proclaim themselves to be, who can deliberately imbrue their hands in each other's blood for this world's honours and profits ; and dare at the same time to call themselves Christians, although so utterly estranged from the real Christian spirit and life.

The remaining part of this week spent in my usual vocations.

First day, the 2d of 10th month. I was led, in my communication to-day, to show the unreasonableness of some people, in looking to, and depending on, being made Christians, by the ministration of men, and information derived from books and writings; when, alas, the ministration of angels would be entirely insufficient for that purpose. The ministration of the *Son and sent of God*, even the *divine word* that was in the beginning with God, and was God, is only sufficient to effect that great and blessed end : and that, not by any thing which he has *spoken, commanded, or done without us*, but by what he *speaks, commands*, and *does within us ;* we yielding and submitting thereto by faithful obedience. For there is no other way by which any have been, or can be, made real Christians, or true, sincere, sensible followers of Christ, in spirit and life.

Nothing unusual transpired in the course of the remaining part of this week.

First day, the 9th. Whilst sitting in our meeting to-day, there was brought to my remembrance the following portion of Paul's exhortation to his son Timothy, as recorded in his first epistle : " For bodily exercise profiteth little : but godliness is profitable unto all things, having promise of the life that now is, and of that which is to come. This is a faithful saying and worthy of all acceptation. For therefore we both labour and suffer reproach, because we trust in the living God, who is the Saviour of all men, especially of those that believe." The subject spread, and my mind was opened to take an enlightened, and enlarged view thereof; so as to be induced to believe that a necessity was laid upon me to communicate it to the assembly ; and as I yielded thereto, it still enlarged, and led to an open field of doctrine. I was clothed with gospel authority, which produced a most precious solemnity and calm over the meeting. It was evidently the Lord's doing, and it was marvellous in my eyes ; and my spirit was made thankful for the renewed, and unmerited mercy and favour.

Second and third days. Were spent in attending our meeting for sufferings, at which information was received, through one of its corresponding members, that the Legislature of our state, now sitting, were about forming a bill to lay a heavy tax on the members of our society, to be paid in lieu of personal military service ; which, if passed into a law, would be likely to expose many of our members to severe suffering. The subject brought considerable exercise over the meeting, which led into a discussion of our testimony against war ; in which it appeared manifest, that the deficiency of many of our members, in regard to a right support thereof, tended to obstruct, in a very considerable degree, our stepping forward, consistently with the nature of our appointment, to seek redress therein : nevertheless, after a considerable time spent thereon, and many different prospects opened, the meeting so far agreed, as to separate a committee of six Friends, to pay especial attention to the subject : who were directed to proceed therein, as the necessity of the case might require, and way should open for.

Fourth day. Spent in assisting two of my neighbours to settle their business ; and wrote a *will* for each of them. This is a business that every man ought to attend to, and complete, in time of health.

Fifth day. Attended our preparative meeting, and it being the one preceding our quarterly meeting, the queries were to be answered. As one of the overseers was likely to be necessarily absent from the preparative meeting, they met a day or two previous thereto, and prepared essays of answers; and the one who attended, produced them to the meeting at the time of entering upon reading and answering the queries.   As I had long believed, from observation and experience, that this method was inconsistent with the nature of our profession, and right order of our discipline, as well as in its tendency very hurtful and weakening to the meeting, my mind was very much exercised on the occasion; and the more so, in finding several Friends willing to adopt the practice: but, after the matter had been pretty fully spoken to, under a weight of concern, Friends agreed to lay the essays aside, and not notice them; which was a considerable relief to my mind.

Sixth and seventh days.   Passed without any thing particular to notice.

First day, the 16th.   My mind was brought under a renewed exercise in our meeting, from a view and consideration of the very small improvement and progress made by a great portion of our society in religious experience, when compared with the opportunities they were so abundantly favoured with from time to time.   It led to a communication on the subject, which was introduced by a revival of Paul's reprehension of the Hebrews: "For when for the time ye ought to be teachers, ye have need that one teach you again which be the first principles of the oracles of God: and are become such as have need of milk, and not of strong meat."   The subject spread, and brought a solemn weight over the meeting, and Friends were pressingly excited to greater diligence in the right improvement of their precious time; that so when the day of solemn inquisition comes, they may be prepared to give in their account with joy, and receive the desired and peaceful answer of: "well done thou good and faithful servant; thou hast been faithful over a few things, I will make thee ruler over many things: enter thou into the joy of thy Lord."

Our monthly meeting was held on fifth day; and, I think, the business was well and harmoniously conducted.   The rest of the week I was busily employed in my usual vocations; and divers things occurred, which induced gratitude and thankfulness of heart to the blessed Author of all our mercies.

First day, the 23d. A silent meeting to-day. What a precious thing it is, to be taught to know when to speak, and when to be silent.

Our quarterly meeting was held this week at Flushing. It was, I think, through the several sittings, a searching, instructive, favoured season. In the meeting of Ministers and Elders, and meeting for discipline, many of the hidden things of Esau, or the first nature, were searched out and made manifest; and their inconsistency with the gospel dispensation, and hurtful tendency, exposed; particularly that of coveting and grasping after riches; to obtain which, many of the members of our society had launched into extensive business, more particularly in the line of commerce, and, in order to carry it on, had involved themselves in debt beyond their ability to pay; and, to keep up a false credit, had, by a show of friendship, and a deceptive appearance of having great possessions, drawn in others to lend them money, and become their sureties for large sums; until both the borrower and lender were involved in utter ruin, to the great scandal of themselves, the distress of their families, and reproach of our holy profession. Others there were, who, for want of keeping close to the foundation principle of our profession, the inward divine light, and faithful testimony-bearer in the heart and conscience, had given way to busy themselves, and take a part in, the political disputes and controversies among the people, relative to the governments of this world; which at this time ran high, and had produced war and distress in the land; by which, they not only grieved their concerned Friends, but brought much reproach upon themselves and their profession. My mind was deeply exercised on account of these things; and I was constrained to bear a full and faithful testimony against all such inconsistent and unchristian conduct; and to call Friends' attention to the necessity of a more close adherence to the internal principle of divine light and truth, as the only sure Director and Preserver, in times of trial.

The closing meeting, held for worship, was eminently favoured with the Divine presence; and the concurring testimonies borne, gave evidence of his presiding power; and his great name was supplicated, and gratitude and thanksgiving were rendered to him for his continued mercy.

First day, the 30th. In the forepart of our meeting to-day, my mind seemed clothed with great weakness, and much interrupted by the continued succession of unnecessary and unprofitable thoughts: but as I continued to endeavour to draw my attention from them, although to little effect, till towards the close of the meeting, my mind was unexpectedly arrested with a subject very interesting to every immortal soul, that of coming to believe in, and become settled on, the eternal and unchangeable rock of salvation, *Christ the divine light*, as prophesied of, not only as "a light to lighten the Gentiles," but to be God's salvation to the ends of the earth. The subject spread, accompanied with life; which, as communicated under the influence thereof, spread over the meeting, and it became a comfortable refreshing season. It was evidently the Lord's doing, and worthy of thankful acknowledgment, for the unmerited mercy.

Second, third, and fourth days. Busily employed with my workmen, assisting them in securing our corn, &c. It was a bountiful crop, which made the labour pleasant, and the heart thankful.

Fifth day. At our meeting to-day, which was larger than usual, occasioned by the marriage of one of my daughters, I was led to set forth, by public testimony, the excellency of the divine fear, and its blessed and salutary effects on the minds of those, who live daily under an humbling sense thereof; and, by the persuasive language of entreaty, endeavoured to arrest the minds of the tender and beloved youth present, with a sense of the necessity of having it to dwell richly in their hearts, as the only sure means of preservation, from the many evils and temptations which abound in the world. A comfortable calm was brought over the meeting, a fit preparative for the quiet and orderly accomplishment of the intended marriage. It was cause of thankfulness to my mind, having been favoured to have four daughters, out of five, agreeably married, in the comely order of Friends: the other, yet single, a tender precious young woman, observing .with pious submission her parents' counsel. But this is a blessing which few parents enjoy, except those who live under a daily concern, with timely and continued care, to watch over and nurture their tender offspring in the fear of the Lord.

Sixth day. Accompanied our daughter with her husband to his father's house, and returned in the evening.

Seventh day. Spent in my family cares, and ended the week with a peaceful mind.

First day, the 6th of 11th month. My lot was silence to-day. A pleasant lot indeed, when the Master wills it so.

Second, third, and fourth days. Employed diligently in my ordinary affairs. The rest of the week was devoted to religious concerns. We had the company of a ministering Friend from West Jersey on fifth day at our meeting, through whose fervent labour the life was raised into dominion; which made it a comfortable and instructive season. Accompanied him the two following days to Bethpage and Jerusalem, having a meeting at each place; both of which were seasons of favour.

First day, 13th. Passed our meeting again in silence, under the comfortable feelings of a mind resigned either to speak or to be silent.

Second, third, and fourth days. Spent in my usual concerns.

Fifth day. Was our monthly meeting, at which we had the company of the same Friend, who attended our meeting the fifth day preceding. I had near unity with him in his exercise; and had to bear a corresponding testimony, both in the men's and women's meeting. It was a season of favour; and much suitable counsel was administered, tending to excite Friends to greater faithfulness and circumspection in the right ordering of their families, and in bringing up and educating their children, in the nurture and admonition of the Lord, consistent with our holy profession.

Sixth and seventh days. Returned, as respects the mind, like Mordecai to the king's gate; while my hands were busily employed in my family affairs.

First day, the 20th. Having felt my mind for some time increasingly inclined to sit with Friends in their meeting at

Martinicock, I thought it right at this time to attend thereto; but when I came there, my mind felt so vacant and void of concern, that for some time I was ready to conclude, that if my coming was of any use, it would all be included in my personal presence, as an example of silence: but after a time of quiet waiting, a subject presented, and the life rose with it, and opened to a large communication, in which the gospel was preached in the demonstration of the spirit, and with such power attending as produced a very solemn covering over the meeting; and many hearts present were broken and contrited. For this favour my mind was clothed with gratitude and thanksgiving to the bountiful Author of all our mercies and blessings, " who is over all, God blessed for ever."

The rest of this week I spent about home, mostly employed in my temporal concerns. Passed our fifth day meeting in silence; and the week ended with a peaceful mind, which I account an unmerited favour.

First day, the 27th. Feeling my mind drawn to sit with Friends at Westbury, I accordingly attended their meeting, in which I was led to set forth the excellency of the state described by the apostle Paul, which is freed from condemnation, and is effected by a full submission and obedience to the law of the spirit of life in Christ Jesus, which sets free from the law of sin and death. It was an open, and, I trust, a profitable opportunity to some present; and I felt peace in my labour.

Second day. Attended the funeral of a neighbour, whose wife was a member of our society; and, although he had been a very intemperate man, yet, towards his close, he signified a desire to be laid in Friends' burial ground, which was allowed. His widow being desirous I should attend the funeral, I went accordingly with several other Friends. The neighbourhood was chiefly Dutch people, and a considerable number attended. We had a solemn opportunity among them: the testimony borne had a very reaching effect on many, especially among the youth; and I was made thankful for the opportunity.

Third and fourth days. Occupied in laying in my winter store of provisions.

Fifth day. Attended our meeting. It was a quiet encouraging season. Towards the latter part, I was concerned to show to Friends the hurtful tendency of evil thinking, which I introduced by that short saying: Evil be to him, that evil thinks. The subject enlarged, and spread increased weight over the meeting; and many minds were humbled and contrited; and we parted under the solemn covering.

Sixth and seventh days. Occupied in my usual concerns, with attendant peace of mind.

First day, the 4th of 12th month. A quiet silent meeting to-day.

Second, third, and fourth days. Diversely engaged. Part of the time occupied with many other Friends, in collecting some relief for the poor in the city of New-York; the present tumultuous state of public affairs having reduced many of the labouring part of the citizens to a suffering state, for want of the necessaries of life.

Fifth day. In the meeting for worship which preceded our preparative meeting, I felt my mind renewedly engaged to call Friends' attention to a faithful support of our Christian testimonies; particularly those against war and injustice; and that all might with firmness maintain our Christian liberties, without fear, favour, or affection, against every encroachment of the secular powers; as, in the present disturbed state of public affairs, laws had recently been enacted, levying taxes and other requisitions for the support of war; which was now spreading and making its destructive ravages in our once peaceful land. A solemn weight covered the meeting during the communication; and I was favoured to relieve my mind for the present, from the weight of concern and exercise it lay under on those accounts.

Sixth and seventh days. Busily engaged in my family concerns; believing with the apostle, that he who doth not take the necessary care for his own, and families' comfortable support, may be considered to have denied the faith, and in that respect is worse than an infidel.

First day, the 11th. Being invited to attend the funeral of a woman attached to Friends, though not a member; a widow of my acquaintance in our neighbouring town of Hempstead; and feeling an inclination thereto, I attended accordingly. There was a considerable collection, mostly made up of Episcopalians, Presbyterians, and Methodists; among whom my mind was enlarged in gospel love, and led to sound forth the glad tidings of life and salvation, through Jesus Christ the second Adam, the Lord from heaven, a quickening spirit; showing that by a full submission to the inward operation of this spirit, a manifestation of which is given to every man to profit withal, we experience the truth of that remarkable saying of the apostle Paul: For as in Adam, or the first fallen nature, all die; so in Christ, the second Adam, or the renewed and quickened state, all are made alive; and therefore born again, not of corruptible seed, but of the incorruptible seed and word of God, that liveth and abideth for ever. It was a highly favoured season, in which the Lord's power was exalted, and the truth reigned over all, bowing the assembly generally; and many hearts were broken and contrited. It was evidently the Lord's doing, and marvellous in mine eyes; and engaged renewed gratitude and thankfulness of heart for the unmerited mercy.

Second and third days. Spent in attending our meeting for sufferings in New-York, in which an opportunity opened to relieve my mind of a concern I had been for some time exercised under, on account of some recent laws enacted by the general government of this country, and the legislature of the state of New-York; which, in their tendency, were opposite to our testimony against war and injustice; and were likely to produce much suffering to the faithful in our society, who saw they could not yield to the requisition of those laws, without balking their Christian testimonies in these respects. I was led to excite Friends to unity in this concern; as the want of uniformity would very much tend to lay waste those precious testimonies, and increase the sufferings of the society.

Fourth day. Attended our neighbouring monthly meeting of Westbury. My mind was engaged to call Friends' attention to a more close adherence to discipline; the right management of which could not be profitably effected, without keeping to a right and sound form. I felt satisfaction in my labour, in a belief that the honest-hearted were strengthened and encouraged.

Fifth day. Attended our own monthly meeting, at which we had the company of our friend John Winslow, from the district of Maine, in New England. His gospel labours, in the line of the ministry, were acceptable and edifying. At this meeting, I opened to my friends a prospect, which had for some time attended my mind to make a visit to some scattered families of our society, who resided in the outskirts of our quarterly meeting; some of whom, being distant from meeting, but seldom attended. I had also a view of visiting some families who were not members, and of appointing some meetings, among some of the neighbouring inhabitants of other societies. The meeting united with the prospect, and left me at liberty to pursue it, as way might open.

On sixth and seventh days, I accompanied our friend John Winslow to Bethpage and Jerusalem; attending a meeting in each place. The Lord our gracious helper was near, strengthening and qualifying to preach the gospel of life and salvation in the clear demonstration of the spirit, and with power; humbling and contriting many present, and rejoicing the minds of the honest-hearted.

First day, the 18th. I attended our own meeting; and was favoured therein with a lively impressive testimony which produced a very comfortable solemnity over the meeting, and rendered it an instructive edifying season.

On second day, by appointment, I met our friend John Winslow at a meeting in the town of Oysterbay; where we again witnessed the Shepherd of Israel to be near, enabling us to discharge ourselves faithfully to the people; setting the truth above errour, and left it upon them, whether they will hear, or forbear.

On third day evening, had an appointed meeting for the black people in our meeting-house at Jericho. It appeared to be owned in a very especial manner by the Master of our assemblies, who furnished doctrine suited to their states and conditions; and the truth reigned over all, fully evidencing that the Lord our God is no respecter of persons, but is gracious and merciful unto all; and that in every nation, kindred, tongue, and people, those that fear him, and work righteousness, are accepted of him.

Fourth day. Attended an appointed meeting, about four miles easterly from Jericho. It was a highly favoured season; most present were affected by the prevalence of truth, that ran as oil. Surely it was the Lord's doing, and worthy of grateful acknowledgments and thanksgiving, for the unmerited favour.

In the evening we attended another meeting at Cold Spring; and although not so open as the former, yet we were favoured to clear ourselves among them; and left them with the reward of peace in our labour.

Fifth day. Attended a meeting in the morning at the house of a man not a member, at Huntington West Neck; and in the evening one at the west end of the town of Huntington, at Peleg Woods'. The first was a very precious season to the visiters, and, I trust also, to most or all of the visited: the latter a stripping time in the forepart, but ended well.

Sixth day. Visited some families on our way home, which visits, I believe, were mutually comfortable.

Seventh day. Spent partly in repairing the travelling vehicle of our friend aforenamed, who had accompanied me in the above tour.

First day, the 25th. My mind, while sitting in our meeting, was opened on the subject of faith, in the revival of that Scripture passage, viz: "All men have not faith." I was led, in a clear full testimony, to show to the auditory, why all men have not faith; although the means of obtaining it are freely offered to the acceptance of all; yet it is not to be obtained by man's natural wisdom or acquirements, but only by and through the operation and inspiration of the grace and spirit of God, as man yields in obedience and submission thereunto: hence he comes to know God, by the inward experimental touches of his own life and power in his soul; and hence springs up in him, as he patiently submits thereunto, that living operative faith, that works by love to the purifying of the heart; but such as are exercising themselves in their own speculative wisdom, and refuse submission to the manifestations of divine grace, have not faith, because they reject the only means by which it can be obtained. The truth was raised into dominion, to the praise of him who is over all, God blessed for ever.

Second and third days. Busily employed in my husbandry and family affairs; each day closing with a peaceful mind.

Fourth and fifth days. I attended the meetings at Westbury and Cowneck; and previous notice being given of my intention of attending them, they were larger than usual at that time in the week. Through the gracious condescension of Israel's never-failing Helper, my mind was opened to declare to the people of the things concerning the kingdom of God, in two large doctrinal testimonies, one at each place, suited to the states of the auditories. The doctrines delivered distilled as the dew on the minds of many who were present; causing tears of contrition to trickle down their cheeks. Surely such seasons are as a brook by the way to the honest exercised traveller Zion-ward; as they tend to an increase of faith, and inspire with fresh courage to persevere in the heavenly journey.

I also attended an appointed meeting in the intermediate evening at Hempstead Harbour. Although I was led in my communication to treat in a full clear manner divers particular doctrines of the gospel: yet it seemed to have but little entrance in the minds of those present, which made the exercise arduous, and afforded but little satisfaction in the end. This I have found mostly to be the case, in neighbourhoods where the minds of the people are led to adhere to outward, formal and ceremonial performances in religion; and especially where much self-activity and bodily exercise is superadded, which is very much the case with the principal part of this neighbourhood: and those not of this description are, except a few, in a state of lukewarmness and almost entire indifferency, respecting those things which belong to their soul's salvation.

On sixth day, I attended the funeral of a person who died in a Friend's family, wherein he had been a labourer for many years, in the neighbourhood last mentioned. Although but few collected, yet the opportunity was solemn; and the testimony borne had a reaching effect on the minds of divers present especially on several of the youth.   May it be fastened by the Master of assemblies, as a nail in a sure place.

Seventh day.   Occupied in my temporal concerns ; and the week, and the year, ended with a peaceful mind.

First day, the 1st of 1st month, 1815.   My mind, while silently waiting in our meeting, was opened to view in prospect the beauty and excellency of order.   As it spread on my mind, I felt constrained to communicate on the subject ; and to show, that all things, which continued in full subjection to the divine will, were preserved in the same beautiful order they were arranged in from the beginning ; and that all disorder sprang from, and was the effect of, a will separate and distinct from the divine will. For as God is a God of order, and is also the creator of all things, of course there can be no order and right harmony in his creation, but what he is the sole author of : hence the necessity of every created being becoming wholly subject to his heavenly and divine will, as nothing else can possibly restore the creation to its primitive order and harmony : and when this is effected, there will be a perfect subjection of every distinct and separate will, to the will of our heavenly Father.   Then the whole creation will stand in a state of subservience to the divine will ; then will the morning stars again resume their song, and all the sons of God shout for joy.   O ! happy day, may the Lord hasten it in his own time.

Second day.   I attended the funeral of a young man, who was killed by the falling of his horse.   He was in company with a number of loose young men at a tavern, where they had been running horses ; and his horse threw him off in a fearful manner ; nevertheless he escaped unhurt : but shortly after, as he was riding from the tavern, his horse fell with him, and he died with the hurt he received by the fall, in about a week after.   The accident had considerable effect on his young companions ; and impressed their minds with sadness and alarm.   They were generally present at his funeral ; as also were most of the youth in the neighbourhood, for a considerable distance round ; who, with others of riper years, made a large collection.   The Lord, who is always graciously near, and ready to help in every needful time, opened my mouth among them in a large affecting testimony, suiting the occasion. It was a very humbling solemn season, not soon to be forgotten by many present; and my spirit was made thankful for the unmerited favour.

After the funeral, I went, with my wife and daughter Elizabeth, to Islip, to see our grandson, who is in a weakly declining state. We returned home the next evening.

Fourth day. Engaged in my family concerns.

Fifth day. Attended our meeting to-day in silence. We had the company of our friend Phebe I. Merritt, from New-York, who also sat most of the meeting in silence; but appeared towards the close in a short testimony, which spread a good degree of life over the meeting; which was truly gladdening.

Sixth and seventh days. Part of the time occupied in temporal concerns; and part in assisting an ancient Friend, upwards of ninety years of age, in settling his business, and writing his will. He appeared competent to the purpose, both as to memory and understanding.

First day, the 8th. My mind was in unison with the exercise and testimony of our friend Phebe I. Merritt, who was again with us at our meeting to-day; and I found it my duty towards the close of the meeting to set my seal thereto, in a short impressive testimony: and, I trust, the meeting closed under a sensible degree of divine favour, worthy of our thankfulness and gratitude.

Second and third days. While my hands were busily employed in my temporal business, my mind was often led to rise above all temporal enjoyments; and to contemplate on things of an eternal nature. In the course of my meditations I was led to contrast those who are *led and influenced* by the wisdom and will of man, with those who are *led and influenced* by the wisdom and will of God; and it was opened to me that, of necessity, the former must be *ruled and governed* by the wisdom and power of man: hence the necessity of coercion, and hence the necessity of war; as every government of coercion, must of necessity be set up and maintained by the force and fear of the sword, as that is the last alternative, in every government, set up in the wisdom and will of man. But those, who are *led and influenced* by the wisdom and will of God, have no necessity of being governed by any thing else than the divine wisdom and will, through the power of persuasive love ; and no other coercion can ever be necessary in the kingdom of heaven, where nothing reigns but love, peace, and joy undefiled, without intermission. And O! that every rational being was so inspired with a real soul-craving desire, after the enjoyment of this heavenly and peaceful kingdom, as not to rest until he had gained a satisfactory assurance, that his name was enrolled in that city, which hath foundations whose builder and maker the Lord is.

Fourth day. I rode to New-York, in order to attend the funeral of our beloved friend, Matthew Franklin, to take place the next day. He was taken with an apoplectic fit while speaking in the morning meeting in Pearl-street, on the preceding first day. He appeared lively in testimony, but was suddenly stopped by indisposition, and sat quietly down : but soon arose and withdrew, and was followed by some of his friends, and would have fallen as soon as he got out, had he not been upheld by them. In a few minutes he fell into an almost senseless state, as to the body, not being able to speak afterwards ; and quietly expired at about half past seven in the evening of the following day : and, we trust, has safely landed in that celestial port, where the wicked cease from troubling, and the weary soul is at rest.

He appeared amiable in his life and conversation, and was generally beloved by his friends and acquaintance, especially the youth ; for whose improvement and preservation, he often appeared very solicitous. The unusually large attendance at his funeral, and the solemnity that appeared in the countenances of the multitude assembled, (the meeting-house though large not containing perhaps more than two-thirds of those that gathered,) carried full evidence of the correctness of the foregoing representation, as did also the testimonies borne on that solemn occasion.

I attended, besides the funeral on fifth day, two other meetings ; one at Liberty-street in the morning, it being Friends' meeting day at that place, and a meeting for the people of colour in Pearl-street. The latter was very large. My mouth was opened in each assembly to speak of those things which relate to the kingdom of God, especially at the funeral; and in the meeting for the people of colour, my mind was largely opened to preach the gospel in the demonstration of the spirit, and the Lord's power attended, humbling and solemnizing the assemblies. It was evidently the Lord's doing. May all the honour and praise be ascribed to him, for he only is worthy, both now and for ever. Lie low, O my soul! and be humbled in the dust, from a due sense of such unmerited mercy.

On sixth day, I rode to Manhattanville, and attended a meeting there in the evening. It was for the most part, I think, a favoured season. The truth was largely declared, and appeared to have a reaching effect upon most present.

Seventh day. Returned to the city, and attended a meeting in the evening in the Bowery; which I had appointed the day before I left town. It was a very solemn quiet meeting, the power of truth flowed freely, and I hope had a profitable entrance with some. May it prove as a nail, fastened in a sure place.

CHAPTER IX.

Visit to families of Friends in New-York, and engagements at and about
home, 1815.

FIRST day, the 15th of 1st month, 1815. I attended Friends'
meetings in New-York. Was at Pearl-street in the morning,
and the other in the afternoon. My mind was opened to communicate largely in both meetings ; and was led, in the course of the
testimonies, to open divers particular doctrines of the gospel ; and
to distinguish between the law state, and that of the gospel ; and
to show to the people, that as all the shadows of the law stood in,
and consisted of, outward and elementary things, they must end
in the gospel, which is the substance of all shadows ; and of
course supercedes them all. It was a day of favour, in which
the Lord's power was exalted; and his name and truth set above
all errour and untruth.

On second day evening I attended the meeting for sufferings,
which was adjourned to that time on a particular occasion. We
sat again the next day, when we finished the business before
us. In the evening I attended a meeting I had appointed for
the labouring class of the community, and for those in low circumstances. The weather was very inclement ; it being a snow
storm ; which prevented most of the women from attending: but
there was a considerable number of men, who behaved with
great order and solemnity. They received, with much attention,
the truths delivered : which inspired a hope, that the opportunity
would be blest, and a real benefit experienced by many of them.

Fourth day.   I attended Friends' meeting in Pearl-street,
which proved a comfortable, and, I believe, instructive season to
some, especially among the youth. After this, I returned home

with peace of mind, and a thankful sense of the continued mercy of a gracious God to his creature man, amidst all his backslidings and transgressions.

Fifth day. Attended our own monthly meeting; in which I had to lay before Friends the great advantage that would result, not only to us as individuals, but also to society, by individual faithfulness, and a full belief and trust in the divine providence; and a strict and undeviating adherence to the order and discipline of the Church, for which labour I had peace.

Sixth day. I attended the funeral of Charles Valentine, son of David Valentine, at Moscheto Cove. It was very largely attended by Friends and others. I had an open time among them; which was introduced with this scripture exhortation: "Stand fast therefore in the liberty wherewith Christ hath made us free, and be not entangled again with the yoke of bondage." The subject was largely opened, showing that all the works of the flesh did in a lesser or greater degree bring the mind under a yoke of bondage; and that the fear of death was a principal one, out of which many others originated; such as every means of self defence, that consisted in war and warlike preparations. Every ceremonial performance in matters of a religious nature; such as water baptism, and what is called the ordinance of the supper, in the use of outward bread and wine, not being essential bring a yoke and burden on the believer in Christ; as *he* came purposely to set his followers free from all signs and shadows, and bring them into the possession and enjoyment of the substance; whereby we come to know all the shadows to flee away and come to an end; as *Christ manifested*, is the *substance* and end of all shadows. It was a highly favoured season. The truth was raised into dominion and ran freely, humbling and contriting many hearts. May the praise, the honour, and the glory be all ascribed to Him, who opens and none can shut, and who shuts and none can open; and who remains to be " God over all, blessed for ever."

Seventh day. Attended to some necessary repairs about my farm and tenements. For as I am much from home attending to my religious engagements, when I feel a liberty to be at home,

I find it needful to be industriously employed, to keep my temporal concerns in order; so that when I leave home on truth's account, my mind may be at liberty, without thinking much about them.

First day. Attended our own meeting, mostly in silence. The rest of this week was principally taken up in preparing for and attending our quarterly meeting, which was held at Westbury. It was pretty largely attended, both the meeting for discipline, and that for public worship; the latter was somewhat hurt by an unskilful appearance in the ministry, in the forepart, but ended well. In the meeting of Ministers and Elders, as also in that for discipline, a living exercise and concern were prevalent with divers Friends, not only in searching out the causes of the numerous weaknesses and deficiencies that were manifest in society, but also endeavouring for their removal, by much tender and pressing advice and counsel, suited to the states of those who were delinquent. Many minds were brought under an humbling exercise and travail of spirit in those solemn opportunities; and divers young Friends, who were under the forming hand, preparing for usefulness in the Church, came forth at this time, and publicly espoused the cause of truth and righteousness, uniting with their elder brethren in the exercise and travail which were felt to prevail in those favoured meetings. My spirit was led into near sympathy with these, and fervent was the desire and prayer of my mind for their preservation in the path of duty; that so they might grow up and become useful in society, and faithful labourers and pillars in the Lord's house, that should go no more out.

First day, the 29th. We had a comfortable meeting to-day, mostly in quiet silent retirement; except towards the close my mind was quickened and opened to a short communication, in the remembrance of the case of Joseph and his brethren; wherein I was led to recapitulate their envy and hatred towards him, and to show that their wicked intentions in selling him, to prevent his rising to the power and dignity which his dreams appeared to forbode, were the very means in the ordering of divine providence of accomplishing their fulfilment; and of course made their bowing and making their obeisance to him much more humiliating than it would have been had they conducted themselves towards him in the line of true brotherhood, and had he been raised to the dignity and power he was, by some other way. But herein was the true proverb verified : Let envy alone, and it will punish itself. I was led further to open the malignity and baneful effects of those hateful, and very evil propensities. A solemn weight covered the meeting ; and we parted under a thankful sense of the favour.

The rest of this week I spent in my ordinary vocations, and in visiting some friends under bodily affliction.

First day, the 5th of 2d month. I left home in order to proceed again in the concern I had engaged in, to visit some of the inhabitants in some of our neighbouring towns, and some scattered families of Friends and others. I spent the week in this service, and attended nine meetings, all by appointment in places where no meetings are held except one ; and visited eleven families of Friends, and persons not members. Although I left home under much depression of spirit; attended with great discouragement, insomuch that I was brought near to a conclusion that it would be safest to tarry at home, and wait for a more full manifestation ; yet, as I brought the subject to the test in my own mind, and patiently waited for an answer in much abasedness and humiliation, a small degree of light sprang up, in which the voice said, go and trust in the Lord to open the way. My mind was then centered in a state of perfect acquiescence ; and I proceeded accordingly, seeing nothing further when I left home, than to attend the meeting of Friends at Bethpage. This was the first I attended ; but before the close of that meeting, light sprang up, and the way in which I should advance clearly opened ; and as my trust and dependence were fixed in the arm of divine sufficiency, strength and ability were furnished from season to season, faithfully to espouse the cause of truth and righteousness, and to preach the gospel in the clear demonstration of the spirit, and with power ; convincing and contriting many minds, and relieving and comforting my own. My heart was inspired with continual thankfulness and gratitude

27

to the blessed Author of all our mercies. I returned home on seventh day evening, accompanied with true peace of mind.

First day, 12th. Attended our own meeting; and after a pretty long season of solemn silence, my mind was opened to communication, in the revival of the following declaration of the apostle James: "For as the body without the spirit is dead, so faith without works is dead also." The subject was largely and impressively opened, which brought a solemn covering over the meeting, and made it a season of comfort and edification. Surely such seasons administer cause for all the humble and contrite in heart to thank God and take courage; and press forward in the holy and heavenly way.

Second day. I found liberty to occupy this day in my temporal concerns.

Third day. I attended the funeral of a man, not a member, at Jerusalem. There was a very large collection of people, composed of the different classes of civil society; and although it was a time of extreme cold, and the means for rendering the rooms, wherein the people assembled, comfortable, very inadequate for that end, yet they were generally very quiet and orderly, and appeared to pay great attention to the doctrines delivered. My heart and mouth were opened among them, to speak of the things concerning the kingdom of heaven, and to set forth, in a clear and forcible manner, the way and means of man's salvation; and that nothing short of a freedom from sin, and the experience of real righteousness, would be sufficient to effect that great and happy end.

Fourth day. I attended the monthly meeting at Westbury; and had some close searching exercise, both in the meeting for worship and that for discipline, tending to quicken Friends' minds to a more lively concern for the arising of the divine life in their meetings; that so their faith might be productive of good works; and they qualified to serve the Lord in newness of life, and not in the oldness of the letter.

Fifth day. I attended our own monthly meeting. We had but little business to attend to at this time. I found it incumbent, before the meeting closed, to submit a prospect that attended my mind to the consideration of the meeting, to visit the families of Friends of the monthly meeting of New-York; and received Friends' united concurrence therein.

Sixth day. I spent with my family, and in my family concerns; and in the evening attended a meeting I had appointed at Woolver Hollow, a neighbourhood consisting mostly of Dutch people. It was a very solemn quiet meeting, and I had good service among them, to the mutual comfort and edification of most present.

Seventh day. I left home again on my former concern in visiting some more of the scattered families of Friends and others, in the suburbs of our quarterly meeting; having not fully accomplished that service. Our first meeting was the next day at Rockaway, among my relatives and acquaintance, this having been the place of my former residence. Although the meeting at this time was small, partly occasioned by the inclemency of the weather, yet, through the gracious extendings of divine love, it proved a favoured season.

After this, we proceeded eastward on the southern part of the island, and had five more meetings among those not in membership with us, except here and there a scattered family, or part of a family; yet numbers of them appear to be convinced of the truth of the doctrines and principles of Friends; and many of them, I believe, if they continue faithful to their convincement, will in time become members with us. We also had some edifying seasons in the few scattered families of Friends in this quarter, and in a number of families of those inclining to Friends. We returned home on fifth day evening; and I found sweet peace in thus dedicating myself to the promotion of the cause of truth and righteousness in the earth.

Sixth and seventh days. Devoted to the care of my family and household concerns; which I find to be my incumbent duty, when at liberty from my religious engagements and gospel services.

First day, the 26th. Attended our own meeting to-day.

Second day. Attended the funeral of a woman not a mem ber; and the family being inclined to Friends, a meeting was held on the occasion, which proved a profitable edifying opportunity.

Third day. I proceeded to New-York, in order to attend the monthly meeting the next day; in which I opened my prospect of visiting the families belonging thereto, with which the meeting united. But feeling a concern to attend the monthly meeting to be held at Flushing the following day, before entering on the family visit, I accordingly went. The meeting for worship, which preceded that for discipline, was a favoured season, in which truth reigned. I likewise had a large favoured meeting with the inhabitants of the town in the evening; and the next day returned to New-York.

Seventh day, the 4th of 3d month. I began the family visit. Sat with twelve families, in some of which I felt the renewed visitation of the heavenly Father's love, in which the visited and visiters were united in the bond of Christian fellowship; which tended to inspire with strength to persevere and trust in the Lord, who hath graciously promised, that they who trust in him shall not be confounded: but in others, things were much out of order, and darkness spread over us at times as a curtain, when we found it needful to be clothed with faith and patience; and as these were abode in, after a time of suffering with the seed, way was mostly made to set the testimony of truth over darkness and errour. Many were convicted and instructed; and peace afforded to my own mind. Samuel Parsons kindly accompanied me in the greater part of the visit; and cordially united and sympathized with me therein.

First day. I attended the meetings at Liberty-street, both forenoon and afternoon, and sat with four families; and, in the course of the week, seventy more. In these we met with a variety of states and conditions, which renders such services truly arduous and exercising, requiring great inward attention to the divine gift; as nothing else can open to the diverse states of the people, and qualify to speak suitably to their several conditions, to their improvement and help; and give the answer of peace to those under such exercises. I also attended Friends' meetings, held in the middle of the week, at Pearl and Liberty streets. At the former was a marriage. It was a time of unusual favour, in which the descendings of the heavenly Father's love were felt to cover the very large assembly, in an eminent manner. My mouth was opened in a large impressive testimony, in which, in a clear instructive manner, I had to set forth the great difference between a believer and an unbeliever; showing that the former was, by faithfulness and obedience to the inward divine gift of grace, daily improving and advancing in divine wisdom and knowledge, and in the enjoyments and consolations always attendant thereon; while the latter was sinking deeper and deeper into a state of darkness and errour, and the distresses and vexations, which naturally result from unbelief. It was a day of high favour, in which the truth was exalted over all opposition and errour, rejoicing many minds; and bowing my heart in deep thankfulness and gratitude to the Author of every blessing. Surely it was the Lord's doing; therefore let all the praise be ascribed to Him who is over all, blessed for ever.

First day, the 12th. Attended Pearl-street meeting in the forenoon and afternoon. Both meetings were much hurt by a long, tedious and lifeless communication in each, by a Friend, not a resident here, who attended those meetings at this time. It very much shut up my way, and was, I apprehend, a great loss to the meetings; as it very much hurt the solemnity. In the course of this week I sat with twenty-nine families; and attended Pearl-street meeting on fourth day. After this I rode home, in order to attend our own monthly meeting, and returned on seventh day to New-York. On first day, I attended Pearl-street meeting in the forenoon, and Liberty-street in the afternoon, both comfortable seasons. In the course of this week, I sat with seventy-seven families.

First day, the 26th. Attended Pearl-street meeting in the forenoon and afternoon, and an appointed meeting at Liberty-street in the evening. They were large full meetings; and through the condescending goodness of Israel's Shepherd, they were eminently favoured. My mouth was opened in each, to preach the gospel in the demonstration of truth, to the comfort, edification and instruction of many who attended, as appeared by their solemn and satisfactory deportment; and I was truly thankful that I had been enabled to get through this day's exercise, to the peace of my own mind, which I esteem the best treasure.

Second day. Sat with five families in the city, and in the afternoon crossed the ferry to Brooklyn, and visited three families of Friends in that neighbourhood, they being members of Liberty-street meeting. I also had an appointed meeting in the evening, for the inhabitants of Brooklyn. It was well attended, and proved an instructive favoured season, gratefully to be remembered.

Third day. Rode to Manhattanville, and visited the families of Friends in that place, and three families on the way; and returned to the city next morning, and attended Friends' preparative meeting in Pearl-street. It was the time for answering the queries; and it proved an exercising meeting, Friends having too generally got in the habit of making use of words which rendered their answers evasive, and not giving a direct one to the question; by which the deficient members were very much covered; and which tended rather to set them at ease, than to stir them up to more diligence and care. My mind was deeply exercised, things appearing very much out of order with many in this city; and the number of the faithful very small. I endeavoured to discharge myself faithfully among them, and found peace in my labour.

In the afternoon, I had a select opportunity with the Ministers, Elders and Overseers. In this opportunity, I, in a good measure, relieved my mind from a burden I had been under for some time, respecting Friends in those stations. In the evening I had an appointed meeting in the east part of the town, principally among those not in membership with us. It was held in a large, commodious building, erected for the purpose of educating the children of such poor people as did not belong to any society of professed Christians. There was at this time a school held in it, consisting of nearly four hundred such children. The expenses were defrayed by the charitable donations of the citizens at large. It is a benevolent institution, and well conducted. The meeting was large, consisting, as was supposed, of a thousand people; to whom the truths of the gospel were largely opened, com-

forting and instructing many minds, and administering reproof
to the lukewarm, the licentious, and immoral. A general
solemnity spread over the meeting ; and we parted under a deep
and humbling sense of the unmerited favour.

Fifth day. Attended the preparative meeting at Liberty-street,
which was a comfortable meeting. The queries appeared to be
answered with much more consistency than at the other. The
afternoon and evening spent in the family visit ; as also the two
following days.

First day, the 2d of 4th month. I attended Pearl-street meeting in the morning, and that at Liberty-street in the afternoon ;
and public notice being given of my intention of attending the
latter, it was large. I also had an appointed meeting in the
evening at Pearl-street, which was also very large. They were
all seasons of favour, especially those at Pearl-street, wherein
truth reigned, and the people's minds were solemnized, and the
faithful comforted and made glad together, under a grateful sense
of the continued mercy, and longsuffering loving kindness of
Israel's Shepherd to the workmanship of his holy hand.

Second day. Sat with four families in the forenoon ; and, in
the afternoon, had an appointed meeting at Flatbush, near the
west end of Long Island, where no Friends live. The inhabitants were mostly Dutch people, the descendants of the ancient
Hollanders : they had but little acquaintance with us or our
principles. The meeting was held in their court-house. A
respectable number collected, and behaved quietly, becoming the
occasion. Our gracious Helper was near, furnishing doctrine
suited to their states and conditions ; which had a reaching
and salutary effect upon many minds ; and through the prevalence of the power of truth, which rose into dominion, divers
hearts were broken and contrited. We parted from them with
thankful hearts, and returned to the city that evening.

Third day. Attended the meeting of Ministers and Elders,
composed of the select members of the monthly meetings of New-
York and Flushing. It was a solemn, and, I hope, a profitable
time. The next day the monthly meeting of New-York was
held, in which I was favoured to close my visit to Friends there,

in an opportunity with the members generally together, both male and female, select from others. At this meeting I discharged myself fully to the peace of my own mind, and, I trust, to the comfort and encouragement of the faithful; and at the same time administered reproof and correction to the lukewarm, and unsound members, and strength to the weak and feeble-minded. The Lord was supplicated in behalf of his people, that he would still strive with them, both in mercy and judgment, as he may see meet, in his matchless wisdom and loving kindness, and not give his heritage to reproach, lest the people without be led to inquire, where is their God.

Fifth day. I turned my face homeward, having a meeting at Newtown Kilns, at the eleventh hour, and another in the town at evening. They were favoured seasons; although the latter was somewhat interrupted at the close, by a hireling minister, of the Presbyterian persuasion, who took some exceptions to the doctrines delivered respecting water baptism, imputative righteousness, and the hire of ministers. The arguments he advanced in support of these appeared very weak, being unfounded and fallacious; and the scripture passages which he quoted to prove his positions, were in direct opposition thereto. For his proof of water baptism, he made use of the doctrine of the apostle Paul; and especially that part wherein he thanks God that he had baptized but a very small number, positively asserting, that Christ sent him not to baptize; therefore, if so great a minister as Paul had no commission or authority to baptize, that is with water, who had converted so many to the Christian faith, and set up and established many churches, in parts where no other of the primitive ministers had yet travelled, surely he could not think it needful, or otherwise he must have fallen very far short of fulfilling his ministry; but if we conclude, as I apprehend we are all bound to do, that Paul, as he himself asserts, was not a whit behind the chiefest of the primitive apostles, we may then safely conclude that water baptism has no part in the commission of a gospel minister, and consequently is no part of the gospel dispensation, but was only made use of in condescension to the weak state of the Jewish believers, in the same way as circumcision was made use of by Paul. Indeed it is abundantly evident, that the rituals of the law were continued for many years by many of the Jewish Christians. It is clear, however, that it was all in condescension to the weak state that the believers were in, through the force of tradition and custom. Having been long in the use of outward shadows and types, the way did not open to shake them all off at once; but as the light of the glorious gospel should arise, they would gradually recede and give place to the substance, just as when the sun rises above the horizon, all the shadows of the night flee away.

And with regard to imputative righteousness, some Christians affirm that the righteousness of Christ, wrought without us, being imputed to believers, they are thereby justified, without any works of righteousness carried on in us, by and through the operation of the grace of God, we yielding thereunto, and co-operating therewith. But the apostle Paul asserts that " the grace of God, that bringeth salvation, hath appeared to all men, teaching us, that denying ungodliness, and worldly lusts, we should live soberly, righteously, and godly in this present world." Now will any be so inconsistent with truth and righteousness, as to assert, that a man is justified merely by the righteousness that Christ wrought in the outward manifestation, without his coming to know in his own experience, those works of righeousness wrought in him, as above expressed by the apostle; and which he must be a party to and in, or they cannot be wrought. For a mere belief in grace does not do the work of righteousness; but faith in the sufficiency of the grace is the first previous work of the mind of man; but if that belief is not carried into effect, such faith cannot save him; for faith without works is dead, being alone, as a body without the spirit. I think the conclusive arguments of the apostle James are quite sufficient to prove these things to every judicious mind. For although the harlot Rahab had, from what appears, a full belief that Israel's armies would conquer the land of Canaan, and it is likely many thousands more of the Canaanites had the same belief; yet as none of them added good works to their faith but her, none others were saved. Abraham also believed he was required to sacri-

28

fice his son, as the scripture assures us; but had he not gone forward to put it in execution, his faith, instead of being imputed to him for righteousness, would have greatly administered to his condemnation; and instead of becoming the friend of God, he would have been cast out of his favour; so that by his works only was his faith made perfect.

But the great errour, of the generality of professed Christians, lies in not making a right distinction between the works that men do in their own will, and by the leadings of their own carnal wisdom, and those works that the true believer does, in the will and wisdom of God. For although the former, let them consist in what they will, whether in prayers, or preaching, or any other devotional exercises, are altogether evil: so on the contrary, those of the latter, let them consist in what they may, whether in ploughing, in reaping, or in any handicraft labour, or in any other service, temporal or spiritual, as they will in all be accompanied with the peace and presence of their heavenly Father, so all they do, will be righteous, and will be imputed to them as such. And these, and these only, will witness the blessing pronounced by the royal psalmist, where he saith: "Blessed is he whose transgression is forgiven, whose sin is covered. Blessed is the man unto whom the Lord imputeth not iniquity, and in whose spirit there is no guile." And who are those whom the royal prophet here designates; why none but such as have carefully and strictly adhered to the teaching of the grace of God; and who by its teaching and aid have denied themselves of all ungodliness, and worldly lusts; and have come to live soberly, righteously, and godly in this present world.

And in order to prove the consistency of Christian ministers taking pay, and making contracts with the people for their preaching, and letting themselves out to the highest bidders, he brought forward quotations from the same Paul, who is so very severe against hirelings; showing, both by his example and precepts, that it is more blessed to give than to receive; and that parents or leaders ought to care for the children, and not the children for the parents.

The quotations he brought forward were founded principally

on these two passages from the epistle to the Corinthians : " Do ye not know that they which minister about holy things live of the things of the temple, and they which wait at the altar are partakers with the altar ? Even so hath the Lord ordained, that they which preach the gospel should live of the gospel."

In order to understand correctly how far proof will arise from these passages of scripture, it will be necessary to consider the ground upon which the priesthood was established under the law ; and likewise the reason and ground, upon which their maintenance was instituted : for it was all a work of perfect wisdom. And first, the dispensation of the law was outward and local ; so likewise was the priesthood : none being eligible to that office but the family of Levi : and in consequence of their being appointed to that office, they were deprived of having their portion or allotment in the land ; but the Lord was to be their portion : except that they were to have room for residence, and some suburbs about their dwellings, for their convenience. Their office was to kill and prepare the sacrifices which the people brought of their holy things, as offerings to the Lord ; so that they were under the necessity of doing a great deal of manual labour for the people. Therefore, in order that they might have a livelihood among their brethren, the Lord had let one-twelfth, that is Levi's lot, to farm among his brethren ; and they were bound to return to their brethren, the Levites, one-tenth of their increase ; to reward them not only for the abundant manual labour they were bound to do for them, but also in consideration of their having the improvement and profits arising from Levi's portion of the promised land.

Now to make a right bearing between the shadow and substance, and render it eligible under the gospel for its ministers to take pay, they must be such as are immediately called, as was the house of Levi ; and be deprived of any allotment in the land, except room for residence, and some small suburbs : they must likewise be under the unavoidable obligation of doing a great deal of manual labour in outward things, or otherwise they are not entitled to any outward pay : and all this only as their duty to him, who hath called and appointed them, without making any contract with the people at all for their service ; for this was not admissible under that dispensation : and all that did were reproached by the Lord's prophets as hirelings. An instance to the point is the case of Micah, who had a house of idol gods ; and he hired a Levite to be his priest, and gave him for his service ten shekels of silver by the year, and a suit of apparel, and his victuals. Indeed we have in this Levite a true specimen of a hireling ; for when the Danites proposed to his consideration, which would be best for him, whether to be a priest to the house of one man, or to a tribe and family in Israel, he soon solved the question ; and it made his heart glad, and he took Micha's ephod, teraphim, and graven image, and added theft to covetousness ; and went with the Danites, and became their idol priest.

Secondly, we are next to consider the perfect analogy between the service of the priesthood under the law, and their wages, agreeable to Paul's expressions : " Do ye not know that they which minister about holy things, live of the things of the temple, and they which wait at the altar, are partakers with the altar ?" Now the things of the temple and of the altar were all the Lord's things ; and as the priests and ministers were also the Lord's, he rewarded them out of his own holy things, and justice required that it should be so. Therefore the priests under the law had no right to call on the people for any pay, because there was no contract between them: so likewise under the gospel, the Lord's true ministers must be such as are immediately called of God, as was Aaron : but as there is no outward holy land under the gospel, so neither is there any outward holy offerings or sacrifices, nor any outward holy temple or altar of man's building ; so likewise no outward victims to be slain or consecrated, hence no outward reward : but the Lord's ministers under the gospel are all called and commissioned by his spirit, and clothed with his power and authority to preach the gospel, not with wisdom of words, lest the cross of Christ should be made of none effect. For the preaching of the cross is to them that perish foolishness, but unto such as are saved it is the power of God. Hence those who preach the gospel live of the gospel ; that is, as the gospel is the power of God, which is communicated to the people by gospel ministry, by which they are fed and comforted spiritually, as the Israelites were outwardly, by their outward sacrifices, of which the priests who ministered took their share with the people : so likewise the ministers of the gospel, who minister to the people spiritually in holy things ; they also take their share, and are made to rejoice together spiritually and mutually. And herein consists the true analogy between the shadow and substance; the first being the type, which consisted in outward things, and the latter the antitype, consisting in spiritual things. For if the reward of the Lord's ministers under the gospel for their gospel labours is to consist in outward temporal things, and likewise the reward of the Lord's ministers under the law was of the same kind, then it would no longer hold as is generally agreed by Christians, that the first is type, and the latter its antitype : but it will be only type for type, and shadow for shadow ; of course we must look for another dispensation in order to do away the shadow, and make way for the substance. " But thanks be to God, which giveth us the victory, through our Lord Jesus Christ." He is the end of the law to all those who believe, and are witnesses of his spiritual appearance in their hearts, to take away sin and finish transgression, and fulfil all righteousness, in those who willingly deny themselves, and take up their cross daily, and follow him in the way of regeneration. Even so let it be, saith my spirit, with the spirits of the faithful. Amen for ever.

Sixth day. I had an appointed meeting in the town of Jamaica, at the third hour in the afternoon. It was for the most part a favoured meeting, although long in gathering. The truths delivered had an affecting reach on many minds, and I was made thankful for the precious solemnity which prevailed over the meeting, and we parted under a comfortable sense thereof. After this I returned home, and found my family well; and my mind was clothed with peace, which favour inspires grateful acknowledgments to the bountiful Author of every blessing.

Seventh day. Rested with my family.

First day. Attended our meeting to good satisfaction. The

three following days spent with my family, and in my family concerns.

Fifth day. Attended our preparative meeting, previous to the sitting of which, I attended a funeral of one of our neighbours. The corpse was laid in our burial-ground, and the people, after the interment, came into the meeting. It was a large collection, to whom the truths of the gospel were largely opened, and the humbling power of truth spread over the assembly, contriting many hearts.

Sixth and seventh days. Spent in my family concerns.

First day, the 16th. Attended our own meeting, sat it through in silence. It was exercising in the forepart, in which I felt reduced into a state of baptism, with and for the dead : but as I abode in the patience, toward the close light sprang up and I was relieved from the burden.

Second day. I spent in my temporal concerns. What a strict and continual guard and watch it requires, when engaged in any worldly business, to keep the mind free and loose from every thing of a terrestrial nature; so that, at the first beck or motion of the divine intelligence, we may be ready to obey, and submit willingly to its holy requiring, without consulting with flesh and blood.

Third day. I attended the funeral of a deceased Friend. A meeting was held on the occasion at the place of her residence. The neighbourhood were mostly of the Presbyterian order, many of whom attended. I had an open time among them, to declare of the things pertaining to the kingdom of heaven ; and many gospel truths were plainly set forth and exalted over all untruth and errour. It was indeed a season thankfully to be remembered, and my heart was bowed in grateful acknowledgments to the great and blessed Author of all our mercies.

Fourth day. At the funeral yesterday, I was requested by several of my friends to attend the funeral of an individual who had been a professor among the Methodists, but whom I had for some time believed was pretty fully convinced of the principles of our profession ; but the trial of parting with his fellow professors, and making a full surrender, had kept him back.

until being brought on a bed of languishing, he yielded and acknowledged to the truth, and desired that in future his family would attend Friend's meetings : and towards his close, in order to give full testimony to his belief, requested in a solemn manner that after his decease his body might be taken into Friends' meeting-house at Bethpage, which was not far from his dwelling, and a meeting held there at his funeral, and desired that I might be requested to attend. On consideration of the subject, Friends were easy to comply with his request, and a meeting was held accordingly. It proved a very solemn affecting time ; many hearts were tendered, and much brokenness and contrition were manifest in the meeting, through the prevalence of the divine power which accompanied the word preached. Surely it was the Lord's doing, and truly marvellous in the eyes of his people. And oh ! saith my spirit, what shall we render unto the Lord for all his benefits, for his mercies are new every morning.

Fifth day. Attended our monthly meeting, and on sixth day our preparative meeting of Ministers and Elders. In both of these, my mind was engaged to stir up Friends to more watchfulness and circumspection, for the right ordering of the concerns of the society, and maintenance of our Christian discipline.

Seventh day. Spent in my family concerns, and ended the week with a quiet mind.

First day, the 23d. Attended our meeting in silence. It was rather an exercising dull time ; but we ought not to murmur, for if we had had our deserts, it might have been more so.

The rest of this week principally taken up in attending our quarterly meeting in New-York. It was in general rather an exercising time ; for not only the answers to the queries from the several monthly meetings, manifested many deficiencies as to the right support of our Christian testimonies and discipline, but the diversity of sentiment among the active members respecting the full support of our testimony against war, also produced much exercise to the faithful ; especially with regard to the active compliance in the payment of a tax, levied by the general government of the United States, for carrying on war, and other purposes of the government, which many Friends believed could not be

actively complied with, consistently with our testimony on that
head. For refusing the payment of this tax, a number of
Friends had suffered in their property by distraint, to a considera
ble amount more than the tax demanded, some even three or
four fold ; whilst some others actively complied and paid the tax,
and justified themselves in so doing, which caused considerable
altercation in the meeting : nevertheless, I believe, Friends were
generally preserved in a good degree of harmony with each
other.

My mind was deeply baptized into the weak state of society,
and I laboured in the ability received to stimulate and encourage
Friends to faithfulness and perseverance, that so all our precious
testimonies for the Prince of Peace might be held up and exalted
as a standard to the nations.

First day, the 30th. A silent meeting. The rest of this week
spent in my family cares, except attending our fifth day meeting,
which I sat in silence.

First day, the 7th of 5th month. I sat our meeting again in
silence. The repeated seasons of rest that I have witnessed,
since returning from my arduous labour in New-York, have
brought to my remembrance the saying of the dear Master to
his disciples, when they returned from the service they had been
sent about, in visiting and preaching repentance to the Israelites,
and healing their sick, &c. : " Come ye yourselves apart into a
desert place, and rest awhile." I accounted it a favour, for which
I was thankful to the bountiful Author of all our blessings.

No particular call to any religious service during this week,
except in attention to our preparative meeting. Silent in the
meeting for worship.

First day, the 14th. Indisposition of body prevented my
attending meeting. I therefore spent the day quietly at home ;
and in reading a portion of Moshiem's Ecclesiastical History of
the Fifth Century, and which is indeed enough to astonish any
sensible, considerate man, to think how the professors of that
day could be hardy enough to call themselves Christians, while
using every artifice that their human wisdom could invent to
raise themselves to power and opulence, and endeavouring to

crush down their opposers by almost every cruelty that power, envy and malice could inflict, to the entire scandal of the Christian name; and changing the pure, meek, merciful, and undefiled religion of Jesus, into an impure, unmerciful, cruel, bloody, and persecuting religion. For each of those varied sects of professed Christians, in their turn, as they got the power of the civil magistrate on their side, would endeavour, by the sword, and severe edicts, followed by banishment, to reduce and destroy all those who dissented from them, although their opinions were not a whit more friendly to real genuine Christianity, than the tenets of their opposers; for all were, in great measure, if not entirely, adulterated and apostatized from the true spirit of Christianity, which breathes peace on earth, and good will to man.

The rest of the week I spent in my family cares, except fifth day, which was the time of our monthly meeting; in which the women's meeting brought forward, for our consideration and concurrence, requests to be joined in membership for eight individuals. Six of these were children, at the request of their father; another, a minor of about ten years of age, who appeared very desirous of membership: she sent forward her request, joined by her parents. The other was an adult of a promising aspect, the mother of several children. She had been brought up and educated in the Episcopal profession; but being favoured with an opportunity of attending Friends' meetings, she was convinced of the truth as held by us; and cheerfully submitted to the cross, accounting the reproaches of Christ a greater treasure, than all the comfort and delights that could be found among her former associates in an outside pompous profession. Their requests were all admitted by the meeting; and it was, I think, a comfortable instructive season.

First day, the 21st. While sitting in our meeting my mind was led into a consideration of the testimony of the apostle John, where he assures us, agreeably to truth and right reason, that God is love, and that they who dwell in love, dwell in God, and God in them. My mind was opened to set forth to the people the excellency of this state and the certainty of its attainment, by all such as sincerely desire salvation; and in order therefor, are

29

willing, through and by the leading and teaching of divine grace, which the apostle Paul assures us, agreeably to our own sensible experience, has appeared to all men, to forego all our selfish and creaturely inclinations, and to deny self; and by bearing our cross daily, come to a full crucifixion of the old man, with all his corrupt and ungodly deeds. We thereby come to know a putting on the new man, even Christ, or a salvation state, agreeably to another declaration of the same apostle, where he asserts: "Therefore, if any man be in Christ, he is a new creature; old things are passed away, behold all things are become new, and all things are of God." I was likewise led to show the good fruits that would be the natural result of such a state, as certain as good fruit is produced by a good tree; for we should no longer love as man loves in his fallen state, from a selfish motive, self being slain; but we should love as God loves, with a disinterested love, and then we should love, not our friends and neighbours only, but our greatest enemies also; and we should become qualified sincerely to pray to God for them. We should then be brought to discover, that all such among Christians as pray for the downfall, or overcoming of their enemies by force of war, or by any other means than pure disinterested love, pray not in a Christian spirit, nor by the leading and influence of the spirit of God; but in their own spirit, and by the leading and influence of the spirit of antichrist. Therefore, such prayers are not heard, but are an abomination in the sight of a pure and holy God, who cannot behold iniquity with approbation. My mind was largely and impressively opened on the subject; and with solemn weight I left it upon the auditory, which was larger than usual: may it have its desired effect, is the sincere desire of my spirit.

Second day. I attended the funerals of two elderly men of Bethpage meeting. They were neighbours; and were both interred in the meeting's burial-ground at the same time. One of them was a member; and the other was educated among Friends, but had lost his right. A meeting was held on the occasion, and there was a large collection of people. It proved a solemn, and, I trust, an instructive time to some present: may it fasten as a nail in a sure place.

The rest of this week, except the usual weekly attendance of our meeting, was spent in family cares, and in preparation for the attendance of our approaching yearly meeting. Indisposition in a branch of my family, prevented my attending the meeting for Ministers and Elders; but got to the city in time to attend the first day meetings. In the morning I was at Pearl-street, and in the afternoon at Liberty-street; and although the latter was pretty large, and in a good degree solemn, yet it was an exercising season to the living sensible members.

In those large meetings, where Friends are collected from various parts, the weak and the strong together, and especially in those for worship, it is essentially necessary that Friends get inward, and wait in their proper gifts, keeping in view their standing and place in society, especially those in the ministry. For otherwise there is danger, even from a desire to do good, of being caught with the enemies' transformations, particularly with those that are young, and inexperienced; for we seldom sit in meetings but some prospect presents, which has a likeness, in its first impression, to the right thing; and as these feel naturally fearful of speaking in large meetings, and in the presence of their elderly friends, and apprehending they are likely to have something to offer, they are suddenly struck with the fear of man, and thereby prevented from centering down to their gifts, so as to discover whether it is a right motion or not; and the accuser of the brethren, who is always ready with his transformations to deceive, charges with unfaithfulness and disobedience, by which they are driven to act without any clear prospect, and find little to say, except making an apology for their thus standing; by which they often disturb the meeting, and prevent others, who are rightly called to the work, and thereby wound the minds of the living baptized members.

On second day the meeting for discipline opened, and continued by adjournments until sixth day. Although divers weaknesses were manifest, in transacting the business, for want of a deep indwelling with the pure spring of life, and each patiently abiding in his own proper gift, without envying others, yet, I think, in the main it was a favoured meeting

Divers brethren were largely opened to speak to subjects of concern, which came before us, in the life, and in the clear demonstration of the spirit, as scribes well instructed, bringing out of the heavenly treasury things new and old.

First day, the 4th of 6th month. Being invited to the funeral of a young woman within the compass of Westbury meeting, I attended that meeting, which was very large, much more so than usual, occasioned in part by the funeral. Although the forepart of the meeting was dull and exercising, yet, as my mind centered under a patient exercise and travail, way gradually opened to communication, in which I was enabled, through adorable condescension, largely and livingly to declare to the people of the things concerning the kingdom of heaven, and their own present and everlasting peace. It was a season of great favour, thankfully to be remembered.

The rest of this week I spent at home, in peace of mind.

First day, the 11th. My mind was brought under exercise, as I sat in our meeting, in remembrance of Paul's declaration, where he says, "For all seek their own, not the things which are Jesus Christ's." As I continued under the exercise, way opened to communication, which brought a comfortable solemnity over the meeting.

Second and third days. I spent in attending our meeting for sufferings in New-York; an appointment which I have been under for nearly forty years.

Fourth day. Most of this day spent in some necessary repairs about my house. Much is saved by timely and prudent care.

Fifth day. Was our monthly meeting, at which we had the acceptable company of our friend John Comly, a fellow-labourer in the gospel, with whom I felt near sympathy and unity in travail. I accompanied him the next day to a meeting he had appointed at Martinicock; in which he was favoured with a pretty large testimony, in the plainness and simplicity of the gospel. I took my leave of him and his companion Stephen Comfort that afternoon, and returned home.

Seventh day. Spent in my common avocations, and the week closed with a peaceful mind.

CHAPTER X.

Engagements at and about home, 1815.—Visit to the monthly meetings within the circuit of Nine Partners quarterly meeting, 1815.

FIRST day, the 18th of 6th month, 1815. My mind towards the close of our meeting, was opened into a view of the excellency and advantage of having our minds actuated invariably, by a principle of strict and impartial justice, and of having just ideas and apprehensions of the divine character. For nothing short of this, is able to establish our faith in God on its right basis, and to give us an unshaken hope and trust in his divine sufficiency, and bring us to experience that love of our benevolent Creator, and of our fellow creatures which casteth out all fear. As I communicated, the prospect enlarged and brought a solemn weight over the meeting, and we parted under a sense of the favour.

The rest of the week was spent in close attention to my temporal concerns, except attending our fifth day meeting.

First day, the 25th. Sat our meeting to-day in solemn silence, being much depressed in mind on account of the improper conduct of some of my friends, fellow members in society, by which I apprehended the noble cause we had espoused was in danger of being hurt, and the unity of the Church broken, which to me was a cause of real sorrow of heart.

Except attending our fifth day meeting, which I sat in silence, the rest of this week was occupied in my common avocations, and ended with a peaceful mind, which is a hidden treasure of more value than the golden wedge of Ophir.

First day, the 2d of 7th month. As I sat in our meeting, my mind was early impressed with that important scripture passage

of the psalmist : " Let God arise, let his enemies be scattered."
It led to communication, in which I was largely opened to set
forth the very necessary truths it comprehended, especially as it
regards man's salvation. For it shows clearly that man may
prevent his thus arising, and thereby hinder his own salvation :
and it also shows, that unless we know him to arise and become
supreme and chief ruler in our hearts, agreeably to his own good
will and pleasure, we cannot be saved nor come to know his enemies to be scattered. Therefore it becomes us as poor helpless
creatures, patiently to wait, and quietly to hope for his arising,
with penitent hearts and willing minds, ready to receive him in
the way of his coming ; although it may be "as a refiner with fire,
or as a fuller with soap." It is also necessary for us to know this
arising to be within us and not without us ; and to be with
power, binding the man of sin and son of perdition, which is
self, or the strong man armed ; whose goods, while he rules, are
at peace : but when we permit a stronger than he, who only is
God, to come in or arise with power, " he will bind the strong man
armed, and cast him out ; and then he will spoil his goods," that
is, cleanse the heart from all the old rubbish of sin and uncleanness, and purify his temple and make it a fit receptacle for his
holiness to dwell in. It was a season of favour. Many gospel
truths were clearly opened to the auditory who gave solid attention ; may they fix as a nail in a sure place.

I was under considerable bodily indisposition most of this week.
On fifth day, so much so, as almost to give up the prospect of
getting to meeting ; but I put on my usual resolution and went,
and was glad in so doing, as there I met with that peace of God
that passeth all understanding, which is only known by being
felt. I had to declare to my friends how good it is to trust in the
Lord with all the heart, and lean not to our own understandings,
lest they fail us.

On sixth day I attended the funeral of a kinsman, a neighbour, who had spent much of his life in a careless irreligious
manner, very seldom attending any religious meetings, and was
very ignorant as it respected the things of God and his own salvation ; but for a year or more before his death, he was greatly

afflicted with bodily indisposition, from which he suffered long and very deeply. It brought him to a solemn consideration respecting his latter end, and I had a hope it worked for his good, as he manifested a state of resignation; so that he bore his affliction with much patience and quietude of mind. My heart and my mouth were opened on the occasion, to warn the people, and to call their attention to the necessity of an early preparation for death; showing them that it bordered even on presumption, for such poor impotent helpless creatures as we are, whose time is dealt to us by moments, even to dare to close our eyes to sleep, without first being well assured that our peace was made with our great and gracious Creator. Many minds were considerably humbled, and I hope the labour will not be lost, but be as bread cast upon the waters, that some may gather after many days.

First day, the 9th. We had a comfortable favoured meeting to-day. My mind was set at liberty to preach the gospel in the clear demonstration of the spirit; and to show unto the people that the reason why they were not healed of their many infirmities, was not because there was not " balm in Gilead," and "a Physician there;" but because they were not willing to seek him in the right way, and receive him in the way of his coming, which is inwardly, as a refiner with fire, or a fuller with soap; to purify from all the old leaven of self, and to cleanse the heart from all self-righteousness, and self-sufficiency; that a thorough crucifixion of the old man, with all his unrighteous deeds may be witnessed; and the creature set at liberty to serve the Lord in newness of life. The meeting closed with solemn supplication and thanksgiving to the Lord for his continued mercy.

Second, third, and fourth days. Spent in my family affairs, mostly attended with sweet peace of mind; although accompanied with much bodily pain, which is more or less my common lot. But what a great portion of severe bodily pain may be endured without a murmuring thought, while accompanied with true peace of mind, and a conscience void of offence toward God and man: a rich consoling treasure.

Fifth day. This being the time of our preparative meeting, at which our queries were answered, I had to admonish Friends to feel deeply after their own states. For as it is by individuals that meetings are composed, so every individual ought to know how far his particular state corresponds with what is queried after ; that so by a united labour, and an inward investigation of our own particular states, we may be enabled to form true and righteous answers to the superiour meetings. For if they are false, it will be accounted lying and that not unto men, but unto God ; and thereby our queries be rendered very hurtful to us, instead of being helpful.

Sixth and seventh days I occupied myself in my usual business, not feeeling any particular religious draft ; except the necessity of keeping up the daily watch, that no intruding thoughts lead into temptation, or prevent my daily converse with the God of my salvation ; whose presiding fear, I have long experienced to be the only sure antidote against all evil.

First day, the 16th. My mind was led forth in our meeting to-day in a large clear testimony, clothed with gospel authority, which was introduced with the following apostolic exhortation : " Let love be without dissimulation. Abhor that which is evil ; cleave to that which is good. Be kindly affectioned one to another with brotherly love ; in honour preferring one another." I was led to show that this undissembling love was not to be known by man in his fallen nature ; but only by the regenerated soul, the new man in Christ, who had come to know, in degree, a partaking of the divine nature, as no other nature is congenial with this love ; a love, which the beloved apostle tells us, casteth out all fear. It was a season of favour, thankfully to be remembered.

The remaining part of this week was principally employed in helping to gather in our harvest, except attending our monthly meeting on fifth day, and preparative meeting of Ministers and Elders on sixth day : both of which were rather dull, poor meetings. Alas ! how the cares and cumbers of this world, like thorns and briars, choke the good seed and prevent its bringing forth fruit. Be watchful, O my soul ! that so thou mayest know thy seed time and harvest not to fail.

First day, the 23d. My present allotment is a state of depression and poverty of spirit; but considering myself deserving thereof, I do not complain. In this condition I accompanied my family to meeting as the best thing I could do, not feeling the least qualification to be in any degree useful to myself or to others; except in a voluntary surrender of myself to be any thing or nothing, as He, who has a right to dispose of his own workmanship at his own pleasure, should see meet. But I had not sat long in this submissive state, before a prospect presented to my mind, that opened to a field of labour, in which I had to espouse the Master's cause, and demonstrate to the people present the just and indubitable right he had to them and all their labours, without the promise of any reward: and that our true and real felicity, in time and in a future state, solely depended on this complete and willing surrender of ourselves and all we have, to his holy and gracious will; as nothing short thereof can produce our real sanctification and adoption.

Second and third days. Nothing occurred worthy of particular notice.

Fourth day. Was our quarterly meeting of Ministers and Elders, held at Westbury. I attended under great depression and poverty of spirit, which sealed my lips, as to any communication, the greater part of the meeting. I sat resigned to my lot, and heard my friends, or some of them, express their exercise, which was principally directed to Ministers and Elders, especially in regard to an honest, careful exercise of their gifts as such; and also alluding to the dulness and want of life that too generally attended those meetings. I felt very little effect wrought in the meeting from their labour, and could take no part in it; but as I sat patiently waiting, and endeavoured quietly to endure the cloud that was spread as a veil over the meeting; it clearly opened on my mind, that it was not brought over us in consequence of a deficiency in ministers, as it respects their ministerial gifts, nor from a want of care in elders in watching over them; but from a much more deep and melancholy cause, viz: the love and cares of this world and the deceitfulness of riches; which, springing up and gaining the ascendency in the mind, choke the good seed like the briars and thorns, and render it fruitless;

and produce such great dearth and barrenness in our meetings. As the matter spread with a degree of animation on my mind, I found it my place, near the close of the meeting, to open the prospect and sound an alarm to Friends, which appeared to have a quickening effect on many minds, and enabled us at parting, to renew our trust in the Almighty arm of divine sufficiency, and still to believe that the Lord had not altogether forsaken his people, but was mindful of the seeking remnant of his heritage, and continued his gracious calls to his backsliding children.

Fifth day. Was the meeting for discipline. It was likewise rather an exercising season, but I hope attended with some profit.

Sixth day. Was the parting meeting held for public worship. It was a large crowded meeting, but was somewhat hurt in the forepart, by the appearance of one young in the ministry standing too long, and manifesting too much animation: yet, I believed, he was under the preparing hand, fitting for service in the Church, if he only keeps low and humble, and does not aspire above his gift, into the animation of the creature. For there is great danger, if such are not deeply watchful, of the transformer getting in and raising the mind into too much creaturely zeal, and warmth of the animal spirit, whereby they may be deceived, and attribute that to the divine power, which only arises from a heated imagination, and the natural warmth of their own spirits; and so mar the work of the divine spirit on their minds, run before their gift and lose it, or have it taken away from them. They thereby fall into the condition of some formerly, as mentioned by the prophet, who, in their creaturely zeal, kindle a fire of their own, and walk in the light thereof; but these, in the end, have to lie down in sorrow.

Towards the close of the meeting, as Friends kept quiet and solid, way opened for further communication, which brought a comfortable solemnity over the meeting; and we parted from each other with gladdened hearts, under a grateful sense of the Lord's mercy to his unworthy creatures.

Seventh day. I turned my hand again to my usual industry in my family affairs, with a peaceful mind.

First day, the 30th. Devoted this day, as usual, to the attendance of our own meeting, in which I had not sat long, silently musing, before my mind was opened into a view of the divine attributes, especially that of God's unchangeableness, and with which I had to contrast the changeable and unstable state of man. I was led, in the view thereof, to show to the people, that all our infelicity arose out of our unsettled state, and for want of being established, or fixed on some steadfast and invariable principle; and as there is no other but God, consequently all our true felicity and salvation depends on our being entirely settled and fixed in and upon him, by which we are brought to witness an unchangeable state, having the feet of the mind established on the immoveable rock, *Christ, the light of the world*, and the real spiritual life of all true believers. For nothing short of this experience ought to satisfy, or give rest to any seeking, pant ing soul after God its redeemer.

The rest of this week I attended to my family avocations with, generally, peace of mind, attending our fifth day meeting, as it came in course; nothing unusual occurring, but having daily and continual cause of thankfulness to the bountiful Author of every blessing, both temporal and spiritual.

First day, the 6th of 8th month. My lot was to suffer the greater part of our meeting to-day, until near the close, when I found it my place to unite in a short testimony with a female fellow labourer, in calling the attention of the people to an inward exercise and faithful improvement of the gift or talent committed to them, while time and opportunity are afforded, that so when called, they might be prepared to render up their accounts with joy.

Spent the remainder of this week as usual, at and about home, feeling no call abroad to any religious service; but felt it my incumbent duty simply to wait, and to watch at the King's gate.

First day, the 13th. Towards the close of our meeting, my mind was led to view the great and singular advantages which would result to mankind, by a full surrender of their wills to the divine will, not only in religious concerns, but also in things of a temporal nature, and indeed in every thing they do. The subject became very impressive, insomuch that I found it my place to spread it before the auditory; and to set forth the inconsistency of people, in first acknowledging the entire supremacy of the divine Being, and their own dependant state, as tenants at will of the sovereign Lord of the universe; and at the same time presumptuously exercising an independent will and judgment in their temporal, and, mostly so, even in their religious concerns. Therefore, without breach of charity, we may safely conclude, that the generality, even of professed Christians, serve and worship the creature, more than they do the Creator. To this we may refer the source of all the misery and wretchedness of man; and that to rise out of his fallen state, he must come to know a complete sinking down into a state of nothingness of self, and a full surrender of his will to the divine will, and not to move in any thing without being conscientiously satisfied it is in correspondence therewith; then should we move on safely, and peace of mind would be our daily attendant.

In the course of this week I was indisposed, being afflicted with much bodily pain; but was enabled to attend our monthly meeting on fifth day, at which we received extracts from our yearly and quarterly meetings, with the printed epistle from London. They furnished suitable advice on several subjects, particularly relative to a right attendance of our religious meetings. I was impressed also with a similar concern, to call the careful attention of Friends thereto, as that upon which our religious advancement greatly depends.

First day, the 20th. Feeling a draft on my mind to sit with Friends of Bethpage, I yielded thereto. I sat the meeting mostly in silence, it being rather a dull, low time, and but little life discoverable in the meeting; yet near the close, I felt a small motion leading to communication, and as I gave way thereto, a small stream of life arose, and ran through the meeting, and we parted under a sense of its comforting influence, with thankful hearts.

First day, the 27th. My mind was solemnly exercised during the greater part of our meeting, and deeply impressed with the spirit of prayer and supplication. Oh, how awful is the prospect

of approaching the Majesty of heaven in solemn prayer! How
it reduces the creature, and shows him his entire unworthiness
and helpless state. Well might the prophet thus exclaim:
"When I heard, my belly trembled; my lips quivered at the
voice; rottenness entered into my bones, and I trembled in
myself, that I might rest in the day of trouble." As I sat under
the humbling prospect, I was strengthened, towards the close of
the meeting, with a bowed down mind and bended knees, to
address my humble petition, on behalf of myself and my friends,
to the throne of grace, expressive of the desire of my soul,
that we might be kept, both old and young, at all times, under
an humbling sense of the divine fear, as that on which all our
safety and preservation depends.

Second and third days. I spent with a family of my friends
some distance from home, my wife accompanying me. I had
been for some time under considerable exercise and concern on
account of some uneasiness and disunity which subsisted among
them, greatly to their hurt. I entered fully into the subject, and
was favoured, through patient perseverance, to bring matters to a
peaceful close, for which I was thankful, as the harmony of the
family had been for several years very much interrupted.

Fourth day. We returned home.

Fifth day. Attended our meeting held this day, in which I
was silent.

Sixth day. I spent principally in assisting a friend, who was
somewhat straitened in getting along with his husbandry concerns; he having been indisposed.

Seventh day. Attended the funeral of a very ancient woman
Friend, an elder in society. She lived to the age of ninety-
seven years, an example of prudence and plainness; of an innocent life and conversation, and generally beloved by her acquaintance. A large collection of Friends and others attended it. I
was led to set forth the great advantages the true believer has
over the unbeliever; and to show to the people the great necessity of care that we did not place any confidence in a mere traditional or historical belief, without coming to a real experimental
knowledge of God and Christ. It was a solemn time; many

hearts were tendered with the savour of truth, that spread over the meeting.

First day, the 3d of 9th month. Feeling a small draft of love and concern to sit with Friends of Westbury meeting to-day, I yielded thereto. It proved rather a low dull season, very little life felt to be stirring in the meeting; but a little before the close, I felt my mind quickened with the remembrance of the occurrence which took place with Jesus and his disciples a short time previous to his being taken prisoner, and carried before Pilate; but, in a particular manner, my mind was impressed with the proceedings of Judas the traitor. It opened on my mind that he was a true figure of self in man, which is the son of perdition, and man of sin. I was led, in the opening, to warn Friends to beware of him, each one in themselves, for otherwise he would deceive, and betray them, as Judas did his Master; and who will as certainly destroy the precious life in us, as he brought Christ to his crucifixion; his delight is to scatter and expose to trial and temptation. It spread with weight over the meeting, and many minds were solemnly affected. Surely the Lord's mercy is still great towards his backsliding people, as he continues striving to gather and preserve them from all evil.

The rest of the week I spent as usual, nothing particular occurring.

First day, the 10th. This day I was pretty closely engaged. Attended our own meeting in the morning, and an appointed meeting at Jerusalem in the afternoon. Both were meetings of favour, and comforting seasons to the upright in heart.

Second day. Visited a sick brother. Found him very ill, his case being such as to render his recovery very doubtful. It caused much distress in the family. Oh! how wise it is for such dependant creatures as we are, and whose stay here is so uncertain, to be always in a state of readiness to meet every event. What consolation it affords in such trying seasons, when we can come to say, Lord, thy servant is ready.

I returned home on third day evening. Fourth and fifth days employed as usual. On sixth day paid him another visit, and found him much better, and the family cheerful. Oh, how unstable a creature is man! full and empty, joyful and sorrowful, as things go well or ill. All this is for want of having the mind centered in and on God, its alone proper object and sure balance.

I tarried until first day, and had an appointed meeting in the neighbourhood; and although not so large as I have sometimes had in that place, yet it was in the main an open favoured season, exciting thankfulness to the blessed Author of all our mercies. I returned home that evening, leaving my brother in a favourable way of recovery, with a hope that the visitation will be profitable to him and his family, if they rightly improve it.

The rest of the week I spent at and about home. Attended our monthly meeting on fifth day, and the funeral of a female relative on sixth day, who was taken off very suddenly with an apoplectic fit. Such instances speak a language to survivors very urgent and expressive : " Be ye therefore ready also."

First day, the 24th. After a considerable time of silent waiting in our meeting, my mind was quickened in the remembrance of the following declaration of the apostle Paul: " For by grace are ye saved, through faith; and that not of yourselves: it is the gift of God: Not of works, lest any man should boast." The subject opened to communication, wherein I had to unfold to the people the utter incapacity of man, in his fallen or natural state, doing any thing that would, in the least degree, further his salvation, or be acceptable to God, as a part of his necessary duty or service to him. For it would be very unwise and dangerous to presume or attempt any such thing : unwise, because it is impossible for him to effect it, and dangerous, lest he should do something that might warm or stir up his own passions, or those of others, in such manner as to apprehend that a degree of the divine power attended. For this would tend to lead to a very fatal errour, a continuance in the presumption ; which can produce no other, than darkness and death to the soul. In this state he could not possibly avoid boasting, and thereby counteract the apostle's doctrine ; and indeed it would be justifiable to boast, if we could do the least thing of ourselves, without the immediate aid of divine grace. For strict justice cannot deny the ascription of merit to any cause that produces a real good work; but as no mere man can possibly ever be such a cause, so he can never merit any good from his own works, and therefore he never can have a right to boast. All this the truly humble are abundantly sensible of, and therefore dare not attempt any thing in a religious way, in their own time and will, but wait patiently for the immediate inspiring of divine grace, to whose power only, as the procuring cause of our salvation, all merit is due.

The rest of the week I spent in my usual avocations, not omitting my religious duties as they opened on my mind.

First day, the 1st of 10th month. My mind, while sitting in our meeting to-day, was led into the consideration of the real necessity there was for each individual to know God, before he could worship him acceptably, in spirit and in truth. For if we are ignorant of him, our worship would be no better than the worship of the Athenians to an unknown God. The subject enlarged and opened to the communication of divers gospel truths, and gave cause gratefully to acknowledge the mercy and goodness of our heavenly Father to his backsliding children.

The six following days I was occupied at and about home, with a grieved mind most of the time, on account of the conduct of some of my neighbours, particularly one of my tenants, and one other, who spent the week principally attending horse races; a most pernicious practice, leading to more evil than almost any other wicked custom that the loose and the vain are so foolishly addicted to; for it is not only spending our precious time in a vain and wanton manner, but likewise manifests great ingratitude to the Author of all our blessings, if not a total disbelief in him: for how can it be supposed that a rational mind, that has a real belief in God, could have hardiness enough to drive a horse in a race, to gratify a number of idle and vain spectators; and if for a bribe or a wager, it adds greatly to the sin, as it is then accompanied with covetousness and dishonesty. When we consider that the horse is one of the great temporal blessings conferred on man, by a gracious and beneficent providence, to abuse him without cause, by driving him in a race, is both cruel and wicked; for his life, and the life of his rider are both at stake, as it sometimes happens that both are killed. And not one single real good ever has arisen, or ever can be looked for, from it: for the truth of which, I dare appeal to any rational man who was ever in the practice, that it has never produced one hour of real peace to the mind.

First day, the 8th. As I sat in our meeting, the declaration of Paul, introductory to his epistle to the Hebrews, presented to my mind, and opened to a very interesting communication, showing that "God, who at sundry times and in divers manners, spake in time past unto the fathers [in Israel] by the prophets, hath in these last days spoken unto us by his Son, whom he hath appointed heir of all things." This renders it necessary for every true follower of him, to hear him in all things, as now, under the gospel dispensation, we have no other sufficient teacher but the Lord Jesus Christ, by his spirit in our hearts; therefore, they who do not hear and obey him, cannot be saved, but, agreeably to the testimony of Moses, "the wrath of God abideth on them."

Second and third days. Were taken up in attending our meeting for sufferings. The rest of the week I was occupied in my temporal concerns, except attending our preparative meeting on fifth day.

First day, the 15th. Although in going to meeting to-day my mind was under the impression of poverty and spiritual want, yet I had not sat long, ere light sprang up, and opened to the communication of divers weighty gospel truths. In the unfolding of these, I was led to open to the people, that every birth was clothed in its own proper nature, and which must be congenial to the spring or source from whence the birth derived its existence. Hence, agreeably to the apostle Paul's declaration, "The first man is of the earth, earthy; the second man is the Lord from heaven; and as we have borne the image of the earthy, we shall also bear the image of the heavenly." Therefore, as the earthy or animal part in man, must draw all its succour and support from the earth, and cannot be comforted nor subsist without earthly food; so neither can the spiritual part, or the

31

immortal soul of man, be comforted or subsist in its true life, without spiritual food.

This, and much more, I was led to open in the light of truth, at this solemn time; for the Lord's power spread over the meeting in a very weighty and sensible manner, and we parted under the precious covering. Oh that our hearts might be continually warmed with gratitude for such unmerited mercy!

Fifth day. Since first day, I have been busily employed in putting my family affairs in order, so as to leave home in company with a committee appointed by the yearly meeting, to visit the quarterly meeting of Nine Partners, with the monthly meetings constituting it, this being the time to set out. I also attended the funeral of a deceased neighbour, on fourth day, where I had a favourable opportunity of expostulating with a large assembly, on the fallen, weak, and helpless state of man, and the necessity of his witnessing, through the aid of divine grace or spirit of his Creator, a redemption therefrom, as the only means whereby he can be saved, and be again renewed into his divine image and become a partaker of his real nature, as no other nature can be happy in the enjoyment of him.

I accordingly left home on sixth day, the 20th of 10th month. My wife and daughter Elizabeth set out with me, with a view of bearing me company in part of the visit. We rode through New-York to Westchester, and lodged with our kind friends Thomas and Elizabeth Underhill, in our way to West Hartford, in Connecticut, that being the first monthly meeting we were to attend, in the arrangement made by the committee. On seventh day we continued our journey to Middlesex, and lodged with our friends Samuel and Phebe Bishop. On first day attended Friends' meeting there; and some notice being given to the neighbouring inhabitants, of our intention of attending it, the meeting was large, and through the condescending goodness of the Shepherd of Israel, it proved a comfortable edifying season. The doctrines of the gospel were freely and largely communicated, and the truth raised into dominion above all, to the glory of him who is over all, God blessed for ever. On second day we proceeded on our journey, going by way of Bridgeport, in order to visit a female Friend of our acquaintance who lived in that town, far separated from her friends and relatives; and whose husband being a seafaring man, was from home on a voyage. She was comforted, and glad of the visit, although short. After dining with her, and staying as long as our time would admit, we proceeded that afternoon to Woodbury, and lodged with Elijah Sherman, a person of the Methodist persuasion, and an old acquaintance, where we were hospitably entertained. The next day we rode to West Hartford, and put up with our kind Friend Ruth Gilbert, widow of Charles Gilbert. Fourth day, being the day their usual meeting was held, we attended it; and although small, was nevertheless a precious favoured season. The states of those present were spoken to in the fresh flowings of gospel love, tendering and contriting the hearts of most present. Surely it was the Lord's doing, and worthy of deep thankfulness to him, as the alone author of every blessing.

Fifth day. Was their monthly meeting, held at this time out of its usual course to accommodate the yearly meeting's committee. It proved a satisfactory season. The few Friends constituting it, appeared to conduct the business which came before them, in a good degree of propriety and harmony.

On sixth day we took leave of our friends there, and rode to Oblong; a long journey of about fifty-five miles, and the way rough and hilly. We lodged with our friend Azariah Howland, and the next day attended Oblong monthly meeting, which proved, through heavenly help, particularly the part for worship, a comfortable edifying meeting. Near the close, feeling a draft on my mind to be there the next day at their first day meeting, I informed Friends thereof before we parted; and notice being given to the neighbouring people of my intention, the meeting was large; and through the unmerited condescension of our gracious Helper, ability was given to preach the gospel in the clear demonstration of the spirit, and with power. The spirits of most present were humbled and contrited, and the truth raised into dominion, to the praise of Him, who calleth us to glory and virtue.

After this favoured meeting, we parted with our friends, under a lively sense of the Lord's goodness, and rode that evening to Nine Partners and took quarters with our kind relations Isaac and Anne Thorne.

The two following days we attended the monthly meetings of Nine Partners and Oswego, which were, in the main, solemn edifying seasons.

On fourth day we rode to Cornwall, leaving my wife and daughter with our relations at Nine Partners. The three following days, attended the monthly meetings of Cornwall, Marlborough, and Rosendale Plains. With grateful hearts, we had abundant cause to acknowledge the goodness, and never-failing loving kindness of our heavenly Father, in condescending to be with us from day to day, making bare his arm for our help and furnishing with ability for the work we were engaged in, both in meetings for worship, and those for the right ordering of the affairs of the Church. The several opportunities were crowned with His gracious presence, solemnizing and tendering the hearts of the people, and comforting and gladdening the sincere in heart, who prefer the prosperity of Zion to their chiefest joy.

First day. We attended Marlborough meeting; and some notice having been given to those of other societies, of our intention of being there, the meeting was large, and the house much crowded. Through divine favour extended to us, it proved an awakening precious season; the testimony to the power of truth went forth and reigned victoriously over all. We tarried here until the next day, and then returned to Nine Partners, in order to attend the quarterly meeting, which opened the next day with a meeting for Ministers and Elders. Here I again met my wife and daughter. The quarterly meeting closed on fourth day afternoon, and was in the main an instructive favoured season, although considerably interrupted by the imprudence of a Friend, in his unwarrantable opposition to a concern, which was opened to draw Friends off from the too free and unnecessary use of articles, which were the produce of the labour of the poor enslaved black people; and which was wrung from them, while in a state of cruel bondage, by their hard-hearted task masters. For the sufferings of those oppressed people, my mind was deeply exercised.

Fifth day. Rode to Stanford, and attended the quarterly meeting of Ministers and Elders, which through condescending goodness proved a comfortable edifying opportunity, as was that for discipline. The following day the quarterly meeting closed, with a meeting for worship on seventh day. It was a season thankfully to be remembered by every sensible mind present; for he that opens and none can shut, and shuts and none can open, was graciously near, and condescended to open many deep doctrines of the gospel, in a full and clear manner, in the demonstration of the spirit, attended with power; humbling and solemnizing the minds of most present, and exalting the truth, which was raised into dominion, and ran sweetly over all.

We returned that evening to Nine Partners, intending to sit with Friends there the next day; and some public notice being given that we were there, the meeting was large. Although it proved rather an exercising season, and the labour hard, yet, I trust, it was a season of profit and instruction to many.

After this meeting, feeling myself released from any further service, the committee having fulfilled their appointment, and my wife feeling anxious to return home, we took leave of our friends on second day afternoon and rode to our friend Enoch Dorland's at Beekman. The next day we rode to Croton, and lodged with our friend James Jordan. On fourth day we proceeded on our journey to Manhattanville, and lodged with our friend Joseph Byrd; and the following day, attended the little meeting of our friends at that place. After this we rode down to New-York, and took up our quarters at the house of our friend and kinsman Whitehead Hicks. We tarried in town until seventh day morning, and then took leave of our friends and rode home, where we arrived just before evening.

We were from home about four weeks, in which time I travelled four hundred and eighty-four miles, and attended two quarterly meetings which held five days; seven monthly meetings, and five particular meetings. We had especial cause of gratitude and thankfulness of heart, to the great and beneficent Author of every blessing, in that our journey was prosperous, and ourselves preserved in a comfortable degree of bodily health during the time, although a season of very general indisposition with those among whom we travelled.

First day, the 19th of 11th month. I sat with our friends again in our own meeting, and found it my place to set them an example of silence, feeling my situation like Mordecai's when sitting at the king's gate : a state as grateful to an humble mind as riding the king's horse, and more safe, as there is less danger of falling.

Fifth day. Another silent meeting.

Seventh day. Attended the funeral of a deceased neighbour. My mind was largely opened, to set forth to a large auditory assembled on this solemn occasion, the great and blessed effects of a firm belief and faith in the living God; as it has proved an antidote to all evil in every age of the world, and to every individual who has had this true and living faith. For it is that by which the just live, and this the apostle saith, is our victory, even our faith ; and without it, it is impossible to please God. The Lord's power accompanied the communication, and many hearts were broken and contrited by its heavenly influence ; may it not pass away as the morning dew, but fasten as a nail in a sure place, driven by the Master of our assemblies, is the fervent desire and prayer of my mind.

First day, the 26th. I passed our meeting to-day mostly in silence, except just before the close, I found it my place to remind the meeting of the complaint of the apostle Paul in his epistle to his beloved Timothy, concerning some in that day, who were ever learning, and never able to come to the knowledge of the truth. The occasion of this was, as it opened on my mind, their neglect of practical duty, and unfaithfulness in what they styled little things ; and thereby rendered themselves unfit and unworthy of being made rulers over more ; and yet were continually seeking after knowledge in greater things, through the medium of the outward ear, and creaturely comprehension ; loving to hear the truth declared and doctrines communicated, but unwilling and neglectful of putting them in practice ; and therefore made no advancement in true learning. I had to warn my friends to be careful not to render themselves liable to the same reprehension, and found sweet peace in this small portion of duty.

The rest of the week I spent about home, being somewhat indisposed. Sat our fifth day meeting in silence, quietly waiting as at the king's gate, for renewed instruction.

First day, the 3d of 12th month. My mind has been much shut up since I returned home. Sat our meeting again to-day in silence; but felt a daily exercise and concern relative to a religious visit in New England, which has for months past, been ripening on my mind; but have a prospect of some services about home, ere I engage therein. Lay low, oh my soul! that thou mayest be rightly and wisely directed therein; for thou well knowest the greatness, and vast importance of the work thou art called to; and that of thyself, thou art utterly destitute of any right ability to perform it to thy own good, or to the glory and honour of thy chiefest good, who is the Lord alone, thy gracious and all-sufficient helper.

Second and third days. Attended to some necessary concerns about home, preparatory to the approaching winter. On fourth day afternoon rode to Flushing, in order to attend the monthly meeting the following day, with a further prospect of having two other meetings on sixth and seventh days, one at Newtown, and the other at the Kilns, in my way to New-York, where I felt drawings on my mind to be on first day. Accordingly after attending the monthly meeting, having the company of my kind kinsman Isaac Hicks from Westbury, with the assistance of some Friends of Flushing, we procured the appointment of a meeting the next evening at Newtown at the sixth hour, principally for those not in membership with us. As there were no Friends residing in the village, the meeting was held in a large upper room at an inn, which was nearly filled with sober and orderly behaved people. Through heavenly help, it proved a comfortable edifying season; the doctrines of the gospel were freely and largely opened, apparently to the general satisfaction of those present, and many hearts were humbled and contrited.

The next day we attended an appointed meeting in Friends'

meeting-house at the Kilns. Although not large, yet it proved a precious tendering opportunity to most present, worthy to be remembered with thankfulness and gratitude to the blessed Author of all our multiplied favours and blessings. After this we dined with our kind friend Jane Betts, and then proceeded to the city.

First day. We attended Pearl-street meeting in the morning, and that at Liberty-street in the afternoon. In the former, the testimony of truth went forth with power, and its dignity and excellency were exalted over all opposition, to the praise of Him who is calling and leading all his devoted and obedient children out of darkness into his marvellous light, wherein they are brought to witness a full remission of their sins, and an inheritance among all those that are sanctified. The latter meeting I sat mostly in silence; but towards the close, I was led forth in a short searching testimony, which brought a solemnity over the meeting, under which covering the meeting closed.

Second day. I attended a committee of the meeting for sufferings, and in the afternoon a funeral of one not a member, but whose parents were inclined to Friends, and frequently attended Friends' meetings. They hearing of my being in town, requested my attendance at the funeral; and being disposed thereto, I attended accordingly, and had an open time to declare the truth to those present, suited to the occasion, and many minds were humbled.

Third day. I attended the meeting for sufferings, and on fourth day the meeting held in the middle of the week at Pearl-street, at which there was a marriage; which occasioned the meeting to be quite large, and in which my mind was exercised in an unusual manner. For the subject which first presented, after my mind had become silenced, was the remembrance of the manner in which the temporal courts among men are called to order; and it became so impressive, as to apprehend it right to make use of it as a simile, much in the way the prophet was led to make use of some of the Rechabites, to convict Israel of their disobedience and want of attention to their law and law-giver. I accordingly was led to cry audibly three times, " O yes, O yes, O yes; silence all persons, under the pain and penalty of the displeasure of the court." This unusual address had a powerful tendency to arrest the attention of all present, and from which I took occasion, as truth opened the way, to reason with the assembly, that if such a confused mass of people as are generally collected together on such occasions, and from very different motives, and many from mere curiosity to hear and see the transactions of the court, should all in an instant so honour and respect the court, as immediately to be still and silent at the simple call of the crier: how much more reasonable is it, for a collection of people, promiscuously gathered to the place appointed in a religious way, to wait upon, and worship the Judge of heaven and earth, to be still, and strive to silence every selfish and creaturely thought and cogitation of the mind. For such thoughts and cogitations would as certainly prevent our hearing the inward divine voice of the King of heaven, and as effectually hinder our worshipping him in spirit and in truth, as the talking of the multitude at a court of moral law, would interrupt the business thereof. As I proceeded with this simile, the subject enlarged and spread, accompanied with gospel power and the evident demonstration of the spirit, whereby truth was raised into victory, and ran as oil over all. The meeting closed with solemn supplication and thanksgiving to the Lord our gracious Helper, to whom all the honour and glory belong, both now and for ever.

We left the city that afternoon, under a grateful sense of the Lord's goodness, and rode to Flushing, where we had a large public meeting that evening, mostly of those not in membership with us. It was a solemn season, instructive and edifying. I returned home the next day, and found my family in a reasonable state of health; surely may I not, with propriety and humility of heart, exclaim with one formerly: "What shall I render unto the Lord for all his benefits towards me?" Are not his mercies new every morning? his faithfulness faileth not.

Sixth and seventh days. I was industriously occupied in my family affairs, and the week ended with peace of mind.

First day, the 17th. I was led in our meeting to-day, to call Friends' attention to the cross; assuring them, that if we lived without the cross, we must expect to die without the crown. For

32

as the cross consisted only in doing right, and doing right only in a conformity to the will of our heavenly Father, and doing all our works agreeable to his good pleasure and not our own, therefore, doing right is always a cross to our fallen nature, as nothing can do right in the sight of God, but a birth or child of God. For although a man in his fallen state may do a moral act, that in itself is a right work, yet, doing it for his own pleasure and will, and not because it is agreeable to the will and pleasure of his Creator, it cannot be accepted as a good act, because the motive and principle were evil, being selfish and not of God.

Second day. Busily employed about home and in home affairs.

Third day. Visited a sick friend at his request. Assisted him in settling his business and wrote his *will.* Surely this is a work which requires sound judgment and discretion, therefore ought always to be done in time of health, with proper deliberation, and not in haste.

Fourth day. Attended Westbury monthly meeting, to my own, and I trust, my friends comfort and satisfaction. I believe it was a season of instruction and profit to many who were present ; may it fasten as a nail in a sure place.

Fifth day. Attended our own monthly meeting. The meeting for worship, through close labour, proved a quickening tendering season to many present. In the meeting for discipline, I found it my duty to spread before my Friends, a concern which had for many months been, at times, very impressive on my mind, to pay a visit in gospel love, to Friends and others in some parts of the yearly meeting of Rhode Island. After due deliberation thereon, they united with it and gave me their certificate, leaving me at liberty to pursue the prospect, as truth might open the way. This brought me under serious reflections, in a view and consideration of the great responsibility which naturally attaches to those who thus go out on this solemn embassy, with the concurrence of their Friends. For not only their own reputation as ministers of the gospel, must rise or fall, according to their good or ill conduct, but likewise that of their Friends, and the society they profess to be ministers of; and also, the truth which they seem to espouse, instead of being advanced, may be retarded thereby. Lay prostrate, O my soul, at the throne of grace, and seek that wisdom which is only profitable to direct, that thou mayest be thereby strengthened to endure hardness, as a good soldier and servant of the Prince of Peace.

Sixth and seventh days. Busily employed in so arranging matters at home, as to leave it with a peaceful mind.

First day, the 24th. A profitable edifying meeting with my Friends at home. I was led to sound forth a gospel message among them, in an arousing searching testimony, by which many minds were humbled and contrited.

Second and third days. Employed in making preparation for my proposed journey.

Fourth day. Attended Friends' meeting at Westbury, at which there were two marriages accomplished; which occasioned the meeting to be very large. Many of other societies came out of curiosity to see the manner of our marriages, amongst whom, I was largely opened in communication, to set forth many gospel truths necessary to be believed and witnessed in our own experience, in order to our salvation. It was a season of favour, and a very solemn time; may it be blessed and sanctified to the lasting benefit of all who were present, is the fervent desire and travail of my spirit.

Fifth day. Attended our meeting in silence. The two following days busily engaged in arranging my temporal concerns, and putting them in order, that I may leave home with a peaceful mind.

First day, the 31st. A solemn meeting to-day, in which my mind was led forth in humble supplication for support and preservation in my proposed journey; and that the Lord our gracious helper, in his guardian care, would be pleased to be near my dear family and friends at home, and be their comfort and strength in every needful time; and that all those who sit in darkness and the shadow of death, might be redeemed therefrom, and translated into the kingdom of God, that so his truth might prosper and spread from sea to sea, and from the rivers to the ends of the earth; that his great and excellent name might be praised and magnified by all the nations of the earth, from the rising of the sun, to the going down thereof, world without end. Amen.

Second and third days. Still busily engaged preparatory to leaving home, with a prospect of setting out on fourth day morning, if way should open.

CHAPTER XI.

General visit to Friends in New England, 1816.

FOURTH day, the 3d of 1st month, 1816. After taking a solemn and affecting opportunity with my dear wife and children, I took leave of them under a sense of the Lord's goodness and gracious regard, and proceeded on my intended journey. Called on my kind kinsman Isaac Hicks, of Westbury, who had previously concluded to go with me as a companion. We proceeded that afternoon to New-York, where we tarried over the next day. On sixth day morning we left the city, and arrived at Bridgeport, in Connecticut, on seventh day evening, where we had a small though comfortable meeting, the next day, at the house of Thomas Woodward, whose wife was a member of our society. After this we proceeded to New Haven, and lodged. On second day we rode to Hartford, and lodged.

On third and fourth days, rode to Leicester, and lodged with our friend Pliny Earle. On fifth day had an appointed meeting there, at the eleventh hour. A number of the neighbouring people, not of our society, attended with Friends, among whom was their priest. It was, I think, a season of favour, in which my heart and mouth were opened, under, I trust, the influence of gospel love, to declare the way of life and salvation to the people; proving from the scriptures, and clear rational demonstration, that nothing short of the inspiring spirit of truth, could enable any rational creature to make the least progress in a real Christian life, or qualify to worship the Father of spirits, in spirit and in truth; and that a confession to all, or any creeds or forms of religion, however specious in their appearance, without the immediate aid of this inspiring spirit, would, in the end, leave the soul in utter disappointment. I was also led to show the unreasonableness and inconsistency of the doctrine of unconditional election and reprobation, and that it was impossible to be drawn from a right and enlightened view of the divine character.

There occurred one circumstance in the meeting, which, as it was in itself improper, and gave some interruption to my mind, I am willing to mention as a caution. When the meeting had got pretty quietly settled, and my mind opened with a prospect to stand up, just before I was about to rise, there came in a stranger, in appearance; and a Friend who sat near me spoke to him to come forward, and called him *parson,* meaning a priest, which I was very sorry to be informed of: for I think that Friends ought to be exceedingly careful, never to inform travelling ministers the state or condition of those who attend their meetings, as it not only has a tendency to close up the way very much, of real gospel ministers, but when close and plain things are delivered, they often are judged of having outward information of the condition of those to whom it applies; which, if it be the case, it would most likely be the means of rendering their labour useless; but if from inquiry such find that the speaker was utterly ignorant of them, from any outward discovery, it is then much more likely to fix on their minds and become useful.

After dining with our friends, we proceeded on our journey about thirteen miles that evening, with a view of endeavouring to get an opportunity with Friends at Bolton, the next day; but the morning opened with a pretty severe snow storm, which rendered it impracticable. However, we proceeded in the morning through the snow, and with much difficulty reached that place, where we tarried until first day. We had then a very comfortable edifying meeting with Friends; and continued there, at the house of our kind friend John Fry, until second day morning, and then proceeded to Lynn.

On third day, the 16th, we proceeded to Seabrook, in order to attend the quarterly meeting, which opened the next day with a meeting of Ministers and Elders. On fifth day was the quarterly meeting for discipline, preceded by a meeting for worship. It was a season of favour, especially the meeting for worship, wherein my mind was largely opened to preach the gospel in the demonstration of the spirit, to the comfort and edification of the upright in heart; many being reduced into a state of humble contrition and thankfulness for the unmerited mercy.

On sixth day we proceeded to Epping, where, by previous notice, we had a meeting in the evening, in which the Lord's power and presence presided in a very eminent manner; and his truth rose into victory over all, and ran as oil, quieting and solemnizing every thing that stood in opposition to its pure holy influence. I scarcely ever was at a meeting, wherein all were so swallowed up in a profound solemnity, that when the meeting closed, it was sometime before any removed from their seats. Surely it was the Lord's doing.

From thence we went the next day to Lee, and had a small comfortable meeting at the eleventh hour, and then proceeded to Dover. On first day attended Friends' meeting there at the eleventh hour, at the close of which, feeling a draft of love towards the inhabitants of the town at large, with the unity of Friends, there was a meeting appointed in the evening, and general invitation given; at which there was a very large collection of the various sects, amongst whom my mind was largely opened, and my tongue loosed, I trust, by Him who opens, and none can shut, and shuts and none can open, to declare of the things concerning the kingdom of God, and to point out to the people, in a very clear manner, the way of life and salvation, unfolding many important doctrines of the gospel, in the clear demonstration of the spirit, bowing and humbling many minds present, and rejoicing the hearts of the faithful; under a sense whereof my mind was bowed in deep abasedness for the favour.

Next morning we proceeded to Berwick, and had an instructive edifying meeting there in the evening, wherein many hearts, with mine own, were made thankful. The next day we proceeded to Portland, a town on Casco Bay. The following day, being the fourth of the week, we rode to Falmouth, and attended their select meeting, constituted of the Ministers and Elders belonging to Falmouth meeting. It was small, and the business conducted in a very weak, and, in my view, a very improper manner; for, previous to the meeting, it appeared that the clerk had, at his leisure, entered the business of the meeting, as though at meeting, and made answers to all the queries; so that when the meeting collected, they had nothing to do, but to hear him read over what he had before written, and which, without any alteration, was approved; some representatives to the quarterly meeting appointed, and the meeting closed. On taking a view of the subject, I was led to believe that meetings, held in such a way, brought no honour to the cause, nor strength nor profit, to those who attend them.

At the close of the meeting, we rode to our friend John Winslow's, and lodged; and the next day attended Falmouth monthly meeting. The two following days we attended the select meeting at Windham, and their monthly meeting. First day attended Windham meeting; and on second day, an appointed meeting at Gorham. On third day we rested, and wrote. On fourth day their quarterly meeting opened at Windham, which closed on fifth day. Sixth day, had an appointed meeting at Falmouth. On seventh day rode to Durham; and on first day attended their meeting, which was large, notice having been given to the neighbouring inhabitants of our coming. Second day, rode back to Portland, and had an appointed meeting with Friends and others that evening. On third day attended an appointed meeting at Cape Elizabeth, and then returned to Portland, and had a large public meeting in the evening. On fourth day we were at Scarborough.

I then felt my mind released from any further service in this quarter; but before I proceed, am led in humble gratitude and thankfulness of heart, to acknowledge the goodness and mercy of Israel's Shepherd, who, in his never-failing love, was graciously near from place to place, and clothed the assemblies with his presence and power, opening my mind in every meeting for worship, to preach the gospel, humbling and contriting many minds, and comforting and edifying the willing and upright in heart. Surely it is the Lord that worketh in us and for us; magnified and adored be his right worthy name, both now and for ever, to whom all the praise belongs: nothing due to man.

After the meeting at Scarborough, I went with my kind friend William Cobb to his house at Gorham, he having taken me in his chaise from Portland to Scarborough; for our way of travelling was with a sled: but the snow on the seacoast was so wasted as to render it difficult getting along with it. It was therefore concluded that my companion should go back into the country to Gorham, where the snow was more abundant; and William accompanied me as aforesaid. We met again in the evening at his house, and the next day returned to Berwick, and the day following to Dover.

On seventh day I proceeded to Rochester, accompanied by Thomas Stackpole. My companion being unwell, it was thought best for him to rest until our return. We attended the upper meeting in that town in the evening; and the next day, at the eleventh hour, were at the lower meeting. After this we returned to Dover, to attend a meeting in the evening, which had been concluded to be appointed previous to my going out; and general notice having been given, it was very large. They were all seasons of favour, in which the Lord's presence was felt to preside, and truth raised into dominion; particularly the last, wherein my heart and mouth were largely opened, and the gospel preached in the demonstration of the spirit, attended with power, solemnizing this large assembly. Truth reigned, and the meeting closed with humble supplication and prayer to the Lord.

Second day, the 12th of 2d month. We returned to Seabrook, to the house of our kind friend Joseph Phillbrick, and had an appointed meeting there that evening. The next day proceeded to Almsbury and Newbury, and had a meeting at each place, the latter in the evening. They were open favoured seasons, particularly the meeting at Almsbury, in which truth prevailed, and ran as oil over all. A ministering friend observed, after the meeting, that he believed the witness was raised in every mind present. It was indeed a precious strengthening opportunity to my own mind: may the honour and praise be all ascribed to Israel's Shepherd, to whom it is altogether due. How deeply humbling

33

are such continued mercies, dispensed to us poor unworthy creatures. Lay low, O my soul! for thou well knowest that it is the Lord's power only, clothed in righteous judgment and never-failing mercy, that has raised thee from the dunghill, where thou hadst plunged thyself by thy own follies; yea, it is he who has plucked thy feet out of the mire and clay of sin, and set them on a rock, and strengthened thee in faith to believe, that as thou dwellest in deep humiliation before him, resting on his mercy, until self is fully mortified, and the old man with his deeds is utterly crucified, he will establish thy going, and put a new song into thy mouth, even eternal praises to thy God. Even so be it. Amen.

We left Newbury on fourth day morning, and returned to Salem, and attended their meeting, the next day, as it came in course, at which there was a marriage accomplished between two worthy Friends, elders in society. It was a comfortable edifying season, in which I was led to set forth the deep and solemn obligations which mutually attach to the parties entering into the marriage covenant—obligations that can never be rightly and harmoniously fulfilled, so as to render the parties truly happy together, unless they are of one mind and one heart, in all matters of importance, but more especially in regard to their principles of religion and faith; for if these are diverse, it will most likely imbitter their enjoyments, and produce discord in their family, and tend to wound and distract the minds of their children, should they be favoured with any. It therefore bespeaks great presumption and folly in young people to risk the attempt, especially on such slender reasons as are commonly brought forward as a plea, that one of the parties may change their opinion, and come to unite with the other. This, however, is very fallacious, as such change is uncertain; and no man of reason will trust thereto in the most trivial matters, for each generally suppose themselves in the right, and look for the other to condescend and conform; and therefore the breach often becomes greater.

On sixth day evening, we had an appointed meeting for the inhabitants of the town in general. It was very large, consisting of the various religious sects, and some of almost every description of people, who commonly reside in such populous towns. I was largely opened among them in the line of the ministry, in which I was led to set forth the excellency of man's primitive state, before the fall, in which he was placed by the wisdom and goodness of his all-wise and gracious Creator, and furnished with sufficient light and understanding to know that he was altogether the work of his almighty power, and that he derived his life and existence, with every other blessing he had, or could have, from his bountiful hand; under a just sense whereof, while he stood in this happy state, every desire of his soul flowed with a continual ascent to him, as his only comforter and preserver. In this state he realized the condition the apostle reminds us of in this exhortation: "Rejoice evermore; pray without ceasing; and in every thing give thanks:" this being the only true delineation of a faithful servant of God. But from this happy state man fell, by a wrong use and abuse of those powers and capacities conferred on him as a free agent, and without which he neither could have known nor served his God: therefore, man's fall was altogether an act of his own choice, contrary to known duty; and had it not been so, he could not possibly have felt guilt and condemnation for what he had done.

I was also led to open to the people that the great end of Christ's coming was to introduce the gospel, which is the last and most blessed dispensation of God to the children of men, as by it only can man be restored to this primitive state, and without which restoration he cannot effectually serve God in spirit. This gospel our Lord told his disciples his Father would send them in his name, and which is the Holy Ghost or power of God sent down from heaven, which well agrees with the doctrine of the apostle Paul, where he tells us, that the gospel of Christ "is the power of God unto salvation, to every one that believeth." This therefore supposes, that those who do not obey the spirit of truth, or Holy Ghost, which convinces them of sin, do not believe the gospel, and therefore are not benefitted by it: of course they remain under the power and dominion of sin.

After this favoured meeting, I felt myself much indisposed

with a very severe cold and fever, and had to keep house until the next third day, when we proceeded to Lynn. The following day we attended their meeting held in the middle of the week; and notice being given of our intention of being there, it was large. The power of truth went forth freely, tendering many minds, and comforting the faithful and upright in heart.

The next day we proceeded on our way to Long Plain, where we arrived the day following, about noon. Had a meeting there that evening. The day after had a meeting at the eleventh hour, at Accushnet. They were both favoured meetings.

We then proceeded to New Bedford; and the next day, the first of the week, and 25th of 2d month, we attended their forenoon and afternoon meetings. In these my mind was largely opened in gospel communication, tending to expose the man of sin and son of perdition, manifesting that he was nothing but self in man, and showing that, in his mysterious workings, in leading man to endeavour to imitate God, in doing good and performing acts under the show of religion and religious worship, but all done in his own will and time, the whole mystery of iniquity is comprehended. For in man's thus turning away from God and the inspirings of his holy spirit, consists his fall, as he takes upon himself an independent state, and assumes the right of self-government, and becomes his own director; therefore, his salvation wholly consists in surrendering up this self-ability, letting it die on the cross, and returning into a state of full submission to the leading and sole guidance of the inspiring spirit of God. My mind was largely opened on these and other truths of the gospel in those meetings, whereby truth was raised into dominion over all, to the comfort and peace of my own mind, and to the apparent satisfaction, instruction, and edification of the rightly exercised and seeking minds present.

The three following days we attended meetings at Newtown, Centre, and the monthly meeting of Dartmouth, or Aponegansett. In each of these I was largely opened in gospel communication, particularly in the last. The truth was powerfully raised into dominion over all, spreading a precious solemnity over the meeting, and much contrition of spirit was manifested. It was the

Lord's doing, and to him belongs all the praise of his own work, nothing due to the creature but blushing and confusion of face.

Fifth and sixth days. We had meetings at Acoaksett, alias West Port, and Little Compton. In both the gospel was preached in truth's authority; the latter especially was a powerful melting season to most present, inspiring the mind with deep thankfulness and gratitude to the bountiful Author of every blessing.

On seventh day we proceeded to Newport, on Rhode Island, and attended Friends' forenoon and afternoon meetings on first day. On second day, had an appointed meeting at Portsmouth. After this, with peace of mind, we left the island that afternoon, and went to Tiverton, and lodged with our kind friend Joseph Barker. We had an appointed-meeting there the next day, and the day following were at Swansey. Truth was eminently exalted in these meetings, especially the latter, which was a powerful baptizing season, in which the Lord's presence was witnessed, and much brokenness and contrition of spirit was spread over the meeting. This was witnessed, not only by Friends, but by many others not in profession with us, encouraging and gladdening every sincere mind for the unmerited favour. After this solemn meeting, we took leave of our Friends, and rode that afternoon to Providence.

The next day we attended Friends' meeting there, as it came in course, in which my mind was led to exemplify and set forth, the excellency and blessed effects of true and strict justice in all our dealings and commerce between man and man, as rational social beings; which was introduced into my mind by the remembrance of this saying of the wisest of men, viz. Solomon: " Righteousness exalteth a nation, but sin is a reproach to any people." My mind was opened to show the great and essential difference there is, between the righteousness of man, as comprehended in, and tolerated by the laws, customs, edicts and traditions of men, and the righteousness of God, which is altogether comprehended in pure, equal, impartial and unchangeable justice: showing that every act of man, which is not in conformity to this pure and impartial justice, is sin; and that whatever we do that has a tendency, either directly or indirectly, to counteract this pure, simple, impartial justice, cannot be considered as any part of that righteousness which exalts a nation, as it cannot bring glory to God ; for no righteousness, but God's righteousness, wrought in man by this pure principle of justice, can possibly glorify him, as this must be the foundation of every virtue in man.

It was a season of close searching labour, by which the hidden things of Esau, or the first nature, in which the serpentine wisdom works, deceiving multitudes; was brought to light and exposed : especially that cunning sophistical reasoning in the wisdom of this world, which many people are making use of to justify themselves, and thereby stifle and put to silence the convictions of conscience, while acting in direct opposition to this pure principle of justice ; by continuing a traffic in, and making themselves rich, by a commerce in the produce of the labour of the poor, afflicted and deeply oppressed Africans and their descendants, held in a state of slavery by the mere force of war, and which is wrested from them without their consent. Truth was exalted over all, and unrighteousness exposed, and its evil effects on societies and individuals manifested.

After this arduous meeting, not feeling myself clear of the town, I appointed another meeting in the evening. Public notice being given, it was large, not only of the white inhabitants, but a large number of the people of colour also attended. It was a season of favour, and much doctrine was communicated, suited to the states of those present ; tending to the edification and instruction of the seeking minds of the varied sects, many of whom were collected in this solemn assembly. I closed with a peaceful mind, and the next day we proceeded to Scituate, and had a very edifying tendering meeting there.

The day following, being the first of the week, we were at Friends' meeting at Foster. It was a small meeting of Friends, but a very considerable number of the neighbouring people came in of different persuasions. I was led to open and explain among them many essential doctrines of Christianity, which, crossing the carnal views of these outside professors, and striking at their creaturely activity in their religious services, I felt as I proceeded a strong spirit of opposition in some of this description, but truth favoured so that no outward opposition was manifested, and the meeting closed under a covering of solemn quiet.

On second day evening we attended an appointed meeting in Friends' meeting-house at Plainfield. There are but few Friends belonging to this meeting, the whole consisting of but three families; but a considerable number of their neighbours came in and sat with us. We likewise appointed another meeting the next day at a Friend's house in the northern part of this town, at the second hour in the afternoon, which was well attended by the neighbouring people. These two last meetings closed my visit to Friends and others, in the compass of Rhode Island yearly meeting. They were opportunities of favour, in which much gospel instruction was communicated, to the general edification, comfort and satisfaction of the people, and which was acknowledged by many of them. In parting with them I felt the incomes of sweet peace, as a crown to all my deep exercises and ardent gospel labours, in this visit to Friends and others in the compass of that yearly meeting : a sense of which humbles my mind in deep thankfulness and gratitude, to the bountiful Author of all our mercies and blessings, who is over all, God blessed for ever.

We proceeded from thence on fourth day, directly to the city of Hartford; and on fifth day evening had a large meeting there, held in a meeting-house belonging to the Baptists. I was led forth among them in a large doctrinal testimony, showing that Christ's coming in the flesh, was designed to supersede the dispensation of Moses, which stood in mere legal righteousness, consisting of carnal ordinances, and relating only to the outward or animal body, made up of circumcision, outward sacrifices, elementary washings and cleansings, and the blood of slain beasts, &c. : all which were only outward, and therefore could not affect the soul, nor make the comers thereunto perfect, as pertaining to the conscience.

I was likewise led to open the nature of the true Christian Sabbath, which is the antitype of the typical one, and does not consist in a rest to the body merely for a day, but in a perpetual rest to the soul by its coming into Christ, and submitting to the government of his spirit, and entirely ceasing from its own willings and runnings, by which reconciliation is witnessed, and peace made with our heavenly Father. These things and much more, I had to open to the people, in the fresh feelings of the love and life of truth, which was exalted over all. The next day we rode to Woodbury, with a prospect of obtaining a religious opportunity with the people; but way not opening for it, we proceeded the day after to New Milford, and the next day being the first of the week, we had a comfortable edifying meeting with Friends, and a large collection of their neighbours with them.

After this, we rode that afternoon to Oblong, and the next day attended the monthly meeting there. In the meeting for worship, the Lord's power was eminently exalted, and truth was raised into dominion; the season was deeply instructive and edifying. The day after we had an appointed meeting in the town of Patterson, where no Friend resides. It was held in a school-house, and proved, through divine favour, an instructive baptizing season. From thence we proceeded to the Valley, and the following day had a precious strengthening opportunity with Friends and others, in Friends' meeting-house there.

We then rode to North Salem, and the next day being their meeting day in the middle of the week, we attended it: and notice being given that we were there, it was considerably enlarged by a number of the neighbouring inhabitants coming in. The forepart of the meeting was exercising: my mind, in silent waiting, was dipped into a deep sense of poverty and darkness, and as I sat patiently under the impression, I was led gradually into a view of the cause, which appeared to be too much creaturely activity and a froward will. As light began to arise and expel the darkness, there was brought to remembrance these expressions of Solomon: "Keep thy foot when thou goest to the house of God, and be more ready to hear, than to give the sacrifice of fools: for they consider not that they do evil:" and also, "But the talk of the lips tendeth only to penury." These were opened in a way that led to communication, in which I had to show the very hurtful tendency of creaturely activity in matters of religion and religious worship, and the absolute necessity of a complete redemption from self, and all self motives, in the great work of our salvation. As I proceeded, the life rose, and truth prevailed and spread over the meeting in an eminent manner. After this favoured meeting, I found there was sufficient cause for my exercise; and I was glad that I was altogether ignorant of it from any outward information.

The next day we had an appointed meeting at Amawalk. It was favoured with the Lord's presence and power; and many hearts were contrited and made thankful, under a sense of his continued mercy.

We proceeded from thence to Peekskill, where, by previous appointment, we had a meeting the following day, which was crowned with the Lord's blessing. Surely the Lord is good and gracious, and his mercy endureth for ever; for did he deal with us according to our deserts, surely we might ere now all have been consumed: for as I passed along from place to place, I discovered great unfaithfulness, and want of right submission to the divine will, with many Friends as well as others ; under a feeling sense whereof, I was often led in a line of close searching doctrine, by which the hidden things of Esau, or the works of the first birth or fallen nature were brought to light and exposed, in a way that showed it was the Lord's doing : and my heart, with the hearts of the faithful few were made glad in his power, and his everlasting loving kindness to the children of men.

The next day being the first of the week, we attended Croton meeting. The number of Friends there is small, but the meeting was large for that place, for many of other societies came in. The doctrines of the gospel were freely and largely preached among them, to the instruction and edification, I believe, of most present, and to the peace and comfort of my own mind.

Our next meeting was at Shapaqua, which was large, and a favoured season. The two following days we had meetings at Croton Valley and North Castle, in both of which I was helped to clear myself among the people in a line of plain doctrine. The next day and the fifth of the week, we had an appointed meeting at Purchase, which was a large satisfactory meeting. The two

34

following days we attended meetings at Mamaroneck and Westchester; in both of which, the Lord's power was manifested for
our help, and the gospel preached in the demonstration thereof,
and its divine influence tendered and contrited many hearts;
especially in the latter, which being the last meeting I had in
this journey, it proved a crowning season, in which truth was
aised into victory over all, and the Lord's name praised and
magnified for his goodness and marvellous loving kindness to the
children of men. After this solemn meeting I felt myself at
liberty to return home, where I arrived safe that evening, and
found most of my family in usual health.

I was from home nearly three months in this journey, travelled upwards of one thousand miles, and attended fifty-nine particular, three monthly, and two quarterly meetings.

First day, the 31st of 3d month, 1816. Having returned from
my aforesaid journey last evening, sat with Friends in our own
meeting to-day. I felt things to be very low in a religious sense,
and my mind clothed with much poverty, which appeared to me
in the openings of truth, to be occasioned by Friends suffering
their minds to be too much overwhelmed with the surfeiting cares
of this life, which I was led to open to them in a plain though
tender manner. It had a reaching effect on the meeting, and
contrited many hearts; may it fasten as a nail in a sure place, is
the fervent desire of my mind.

Fifth day. Since first day I have been somewhat circumstanced as Mordecai formerly at the king's gate, waiting and watching in much poverty of spirit; against intervening temptations,
while making some necessary arrangements respecting my temporal affairs; being desirous that they may all be so conducted,
under the ordering and limitation of truth, as to accord with the
will of my heavenly Father, and thereby bring glory to his excellent name. Sat our meeting to-day in silence.

Sixth and seventh days. Nothing transpired requiring particular notice.

First day. I was led in our meeting to-day, under a sense of
the great want among mankind in general of a right concern to
become acquainted with their Creator, to set forth the great loss

and suffering which must necessarily result to them from this state of ignorance, and want of the true knowledge of God, and of his will concerning them.

Seventh day, the 13th of 4th month. This week has passed since first day, without feeling sufficient to warrant making a short note; but being at present musing on the past time, and feeling no condemnation, although I had passed the present week mostly in caring for my temporal concerns; yet not so much, I trust, from the love I have for the world or the things of it, but more especially from a sense of duty, that I may honestly provide for the outward welfare of myself and family, and have, through the blessing of a kind and benevolent Providence on my frugal industry, a sufficiency when called from my home and from every temporal enjoyment there, for the gospel's sake, to keep the gospel free from charge, and that I abuse not my power in the gospel. For this care, I often fear is too much wanting by some who go out on that solemn embassy; which, if not guarded against, may not only tend to frustrate the end of their labours, but prove a stone of stumbling to many seeking minds. For how inconsistent it must appear in those who profess to have taken up their cross to self and the world, to follow their self-denying Saviour in the plain path of duty, to be anxious about what they shall eat or drink, or what they shall wear; or manifest a desire after praise or applause from their Friends or others, or have their hands and hearts open to receive the gratuities of the rich. For all these may be considered when sought after, as bribes to the receivers, and it places such under the appellation of hirelings; for although there may not have been any previous contract, yet, receiving benefits in that way, I conceive, will bring the receiver under obligations to the giver, and place the individual in a situation not fit for a free minister of the gospel.

First day. Sat our meeting to-day mostly in silence, and in suffering with the seed, that lies oppressed as a cart under sheaves, in the minds of most of the professors of Christianity; but towards the close a gleam of light broke forth, in the remembrance of that saying of Christ, where he tells us, that the kingdom of God is within, and that it doth not come through outward observation. The subject opened in a lively manner on my mind, which led to communication, and brought a solemn weight over the meeting, and we parted under the favour.

The three following days I kept much within, being under very considerable bodily affliction, although, at intervals, so as to pay some necessary attention to my family affairs, not being willing to let any portion of precious time pass away unimproved, as I cannot suppose that any part of our time is dispensed to us for nought.

Fifth day. This was the time of our monthly meeting, at which the queries were answered, and accounts prepared to go up to the yearly meeting. How deep and solemn our deliberations ought to be on such occasions, not only that our answers may be consistent with truth, without any false colouring or evasion, but that all may be done under the influence of that divine power, which humbles and abases the creature, and which only can qualify for the Lord's work and service, whether in ministry or discipline. At this time I returned the minute I had from the meeting, to perform my late visit to Friends in New England, with a short account of my journey.

Sixth day. Attended our meeting for Ministers and Elders, at which nothing unusual occurred.

Seventh day. Quietly spent in my temporal concerns.

First day, the 21st. My mind, in our meeting to-day, was brought under a deep feeling exercise, in sympathy with backsliders, and such as, having been often reproved, continue still to revolt. The power of truth went forth to these in a searching arousing manner : may it prove effectual to produce in such more stability and faithfulness to the convictions of divine grace, which, as they become fully obedient thereunto, will work their salvation; otherwise these may share the fate described by one formerly : "He that, being often reproved, hardeneth his neck, shall suddenly be destroyed, and that without remedy."

The rest of this week I spent principally in attending our quarterly meeting, held at this time in New-York. It was for the most part a favoured season, but would have been more so, had not some in the ministry quite exceeded the mark by unnecessary communication. For very great care ought to rest on the minds of ministers, lest they become burthensome, and take away the life from the meeting, and bring over it a gloom of death and darkness, that may be sensibly felt.

First day, the 28th. A silent meeting to-day.

Second day. In the afternoon of this day I accompanied a friend to a meeting he had appointed at Jerusalem. There was a considerable collection; but the meeting proved trying, not only in the silent part, but when our friend was communicating, there seemed to be a great weight of death over the meeting, and the people appeared generally very dull and lifeless. I was very much borne down under a feeling sense of it, so that I had not the least prospect that I should have any thing to communicate, as I felt nothing in myself to offer, nor did there appear any disposition or fitness in the people to receive; but just before the close, some time after the Friend had sat down, there was a small presentation opened on my mind, attended with a degree of life, which, as I yielded thereto, it spread a comfortable calm over the meeting generally, insomuch that I thought that the fragments which were left, after each had had their portion, were more than the whole stock in the beginning, like the fragments of the loaves and fishes, when the multitude were fed formerly.

I accompanied the aforesaid Friend on fourth day to Bethpage, but sat the meeting in silence. He appeared in a pretty long testimony, but it was rather a dull heavy season, and but little life to be felt, so true is that saying, that, "Except the Lord build the house, they labour in vain that build it; except the Lord keep the city, the watchman waketh but in vain." He returned with me and attended our meeting the next day, and had a pretty favoured time in the meeting, and was led to open divers passages of scripture in a pretty clear manner, which rendered the season instructive and satisfactory.

Sixth and seventh days. Passed without any thing transpiring worthy of remark.

First day, the 5th of 5th month.   Being invited to attend the funeral of one of my wife's cousins, on Cowneck, I accompanied her thereto.   There was a large collection of people ; but by their untimely and irregular gathering, the opportunity was much interrupted ; yet, through the condescending goodness of Israel's Shepherd, the power of truth went forth freely to the people, tendering and contriting many hearts, particularly among the youth : may it fix on their minds as a nail, driven by the Master of assemblies, in a sure place.

The rest of this week I spent about home, being somewhat unwell ; yet not so much so, but that I attended our preparative meeting on fifth day.

First day, the 12th.   Feeling considerably indisposed, I did not get out to meeting to-day ; yet had to reflect how very seldom I had been prevented by indisposition for many years past, being generally preserved in health, a favour worthy of grateful acknowledgments.

Fifth day.   Attended our monthly meeting.   It was a low dull season, through the greater part of the first meeting ; but just before the close, a small gleam of light appeared, which, with a short communication from a female, brought the meeting to a pretty comfortable conclusion.

Sixth and seventh days.   Spent in my family avocations, clothed with poverty of spirit, yet not altogether cast down, being encouraged at times with the remembrance of the divine promise succeeding the flood, that, " While the earth remaineth, seed-time and harvest, and cold and heat, and summer and winter, and day and night, shall not cease." As in my past winter journey, I witnessed summer and harvest, so now I may rest patiently in the divine promise, with the assurance, that as winter in due course has succeeded summer, so likewise summer by and by, in its turn, will succeed winter, and the time of the singing of birds will come, and the drooping spirit will again rejoice in the Lord, and joy in the God of its salvation.

Nothing requiring a note the following week, except, that on seventh day, the 25th of the month, I proceeded to New-York, in order to attend our approaching yearly meeting, which opened for Ministers and Elders at the tenth hour this morning; but the morning being rainy, we did not arrive in season to attend the first sitting. The meeting continued by adjournments until the following sixth day, and was in the main, I think, a favoured meeting, the Lord graciously manifesting himself to be near, suppressing forward spirits, that would now and then start up to the hurt of the meeting, and uniting the living baptized members in a joint travail for the promotion of right order, and the increase of the Messiah's kingdom in the earth. We returned home on seventh day.

First day, the 2d of 6th month. Attended our meeting in the morning in silence; but in the afternoon meeting, appointed by a friend from Pennsylvania, I had a pretty full opportunity, after the Friend who appointed the meeting had relieved his mind, to call the people's attention to the only sure guide, the light of God's spirit in their own hearts and minds, which reveals to every man and woman all things that they had ever done, as Jesus did to the woman of Samaria, reproving for the evil, and justifying for the good: and were men and women all as faithful to themselves, as this divine reprover is to them, they would all witness the blessing of peace; and if they held out in faithfulness and obedience to the end, the answer of " well done, thou good and faithful servant", would be the happy portion of them all.

Fifth day. Attended our meeting in silence.

First day, the 9th. Had the company of two female Friends from Philadelphia, who were travelling in the ministry, at our meeting. It proved a hard trying season : one of them was exercised in public testimony, and although she appeared to labour fervently, yet but little life was felt to arise during the meeting. This makes the work hard for the poor exercised ministers, who feel the necessity publicly to advocate the cause of truth and righteousness, and yet obtain but little relief, by reason of the deadness and indifference of those to whom they are constrained to minister. I found it my place to sit silent, and suffer with the seed.

Second day. Went to New-York, in order to attend our meeting for sufferings, which was held the next day at the ninth hour in the morning. I accordingly attended, and returned home that afternoon.

The rest of the week I spent about home. Attended our preparative meeting on fifth day. The meeting for worship was held in silence, and was a hard trying meeting.

CHAPTER XII.

Engagements at and about home, and within Westbury quarterly meeting, 1816 and 1817.

FIRST day, the 16th of 6th month, 1816. My wife being under an appointment to meet some women Friends at Bethpage meeting, I accompanied her thither. It proved an exercising meeting, especially in the forepart; but as I submitted cheerfully and patiently to endure the present baptism, which, indeed, as the experienced Paul well observes, is being baptized for the dead, towards the latter part of the meeting, that all-quickening and vivifying power that raises the dead to life, was felt gradually to arise, by which my mind was quickened and led to minister to the states of many present. Life spread over the meeting tendering many hearts, and we parted under a grateful sense of the Lord's mercies; so that indeed the query of the royal Psalmist is worthy to be had in continual remembrance: "What shall I render unto the Lord for all his benefits towards me?"

Spent the rest of this week about home. Attended our monthly meeting on fifth day, but nothing unusual transpired.

First day, the 23d. Had the company of our friend Mary Post from Westbury, she being engaged in a visit to the families of Friends in our monthly meeting, a very useful service when rightly entered into. My mind in this meeting, was brought under exercise, in the remembrance of the following exhortation of the wise king Solomon, viz: "Keep thy heart with all diligence, for out of it are the issues of life." From a consideration of which, I was led to believe there was a very great want of care among people generally, in duly guarding their rising

35

cogitations and thoughts, as it is the avenue by which all temptations enter, and get place in the mind; and, if suited to our natural propensities, too often overcome and lead to undue conduct. The subject spread on my mind, and led to an impressive, and, I trust, to some, an instructive communication; for which my mind was made gratefully thankful to the Author of every blessing.

Fifth day. Had the company of our aforesaid Friend at our meeting to-day, whose simple and plain communication, tended to quicken. A comfortable degree of life accompanied my mind during the meeting, which I accounted a favour, having for some time past witnessed much poverty of spirit in our meetings. The rest of the week I attended to my temporal concerns, as much as my state of health permitted; but being much indisposed with bodily pain, it was but little I could do, except to take some oversight of my business. This I consider one, among many other such like mementos, to remind me of the approach of my bodily dissolution. Be attentive, O my soul! that so thou mayest be in a state of readiness when the midnight cry is heard: "Behold the bridegroom cometh."

First day, the 30th. My mind was led into close exercise and travail, in the prospect of the very great apparent want of truth and justice among the generality of the professors of Christianity, even of the foremost classes of the different sects. The subject spread and opened to communication, in which the attention of the auditory was impressively called to the subject, as one of the greatest moment, both in respect to our temporal, and, in a very especial manner, our spiritual good; as every other virtue must fail, and prove abortive, where truth and justice are wanting.

The rest of this week passed away without any thing worthy of remark, except great poverty of spirit being almost continually my attendant.

First day, the 7th of 7th month. My mind was opened and enlarged in communication in our meeting to-day, on the subject of the universal love of God to the children of men. For he not only extends his gracious call to all, but causes them to hear it; yet, agreeably to that scripture testimony, " all have not obeyed the gospel." There are also many other plain testimonies in the scriptures of the same import; clearly showing, that man's destruction and misery are altogether the result of his own misconduct, and disobedience to divine requisition, without any necessity laid upon him by his gracious Creator to err, or to swerve from the path of rectitude; so that the Lord will be clear of the blood of all his rational creation, as saith the prophet: "O Israel, thou hast destroyed thyself, but in me is thy help;" and there are many other passages which express the same. My mind was led to open these subjects in a clear manner to the people, and to show that the want of a right faith in God and Christ, as inwardly revealed, was one of the greatest obstacles to their living a just and righteous life in the sight of their Creator, as the just can only live by faith. The meeting was large, and many hearts were convicted, comforted and contrited; to the Lord only belongs all the praise, nothing due to man but blushing and confusion of face.

In the course of this week I was much unwell, forewarning me that my glass is almost run, and my day of labour drawing to a close. My indisposition prevented my attending our preparative meeting on fifth day. These things all unitedly conspire to sound forth this language, *remember to die.* Oh that I might witness with the worthy Paul, more and more a daily death, to every thing that tends to hinder my steady walking in the path of duty, that so my day's work may be finished in the day time.

First day, the 14th. Having so far recovered from my indisposition as to get to our meeting to-day, my mind was opened in a living powerful testimony to the excellency of the gospel dispenpensation, in which Christ by his light and spirit was come to teach his people himself; a Teacher not to be removed into a corner, a Shepherd ever present to lead and feed all his sheep that hear his voice and follow him; and do not follow the stranger, nor listen to the voice of any outward hireling teachers, although they charm ever so wisely. It was a season of favour, and many hearts were warmed and contrited by the prevalence of truth, and the Lord's name was praised, who is over all worthy for ever.

Fifth day. Attended our monthly meeting, at which the queries were read and answers prepared to go to the quarterly meeting. To judge from these, it would appear that we were generally an upright people; but I fear our answers are becoming too much like many of us, more in show and outside appearance, than in spirit and substance. For by this formal way of answering them, unless great care is taken, our queries may do us much more harm than good; and this fear often attends my mind, and induces me to call the attention of my friends from the letter of discipline, to the spirit and substance; without which all letter and outward order, however beautiful in the outward appearance, is but as sounding brass or a tinkling cymbal, and will in the end only deceive and disappoint us, and unveil our nakedness.

Sixth day. Was our preparative meeting of Ministers and Elders, in which our answers made a similar appearance; insomuch, that there was but little to find fault with. I hope it may stand the test in the day of trial; this we ought carefully to consider, otherwise, in the end, we may fall short when it may be too late to retrieve the loss.

The rest of the week I attended to my temporal business as far as my bodily infirmity would permit, although at times my exercise produced very acute pains. I find it needful however, to keep up a continual watch, that I do nothing to promote or encourage idleness, that bane to every Christian virtue; and especially at such a time as this, when most of our capable well-looking young men are running into cities and populous towns to engage in merchandise, or some other calling by which they may live by their wits, being unwilling to labour with their hands: although it is the most sure way marked out by divine wisdom for our truest comfort and peace here, and a right preparation for eternal joy hereafter. And, although many fatal consequences have befallen many of those who have thus run out in trade and mercantile business, apparently to the ruin of both body and soul, and the great injury and distress of their families: yet, because some few have made themselves rich in temporal things by those pursuits, it has so blinded the minds of many that they will not take warning, but go on in their wilful way to their own utter ruin.

First day, the 21st. This day at our meeting, my mouth was opened in a full testimony introduced by this scripture passage: "Wherewithal shall a young man cleanse his way? by taking heed thereto according to thy word." I was led in my communication to show to the people, that in this word was comprehended the great gospel privilege, the word nigh in the heart and in the mouth; and that it was not a *literal or outward word*, nor any created thing, but the *uncreated word, Christ*, by whom all things were created, or at first spoke into existence and order. For nothing else could enable us to cleanse our way, or live a righteous holy life; and that it was only by a living faith in this inward, operative, powerful word, that any could please God or be acceptable to him, and was the only means by which we could be saved: and that it was offered to the acceptance of all, and therefore all were encouraged to lay hold of the offered mercy, and not slight the day of their visitation.

Second and third days. I was busied in overseeing my temporal business, attended, at times, by much bodily pain; and which, I trust and hope, I endured without improperly complaining or murmuring. The three following days, I attended our quarterly meeting, held this time at Westbury. I think, in the main, it was a favoured season. The meeting was large and solemn: the divine presence and power were evidently felt to preside, humbling many minds and producing contrition of spirit, and the gospel labours were instructive and edifying.

First day, the 28th. A quiet day. Sat our meeting in silence.

Fifth day. A silent meeting. The rest of the week, as to bodily exercise, mostly occupied in my temporal affairs.

First day, the 4th of 8th month. My mind settled in quiet with the exercise of this day. Besides the usual care and industry necessary in my temporal concerns, that all things might be rightly arranged, I attended, in the course of this week, our preparative meeting on fifth day, and the funeral of a deceased neighbour on sixth day. At the funeral was a large promiscuous assembly, amongst whom my mouth was opened in a large searching testimony, suiting the occasion; whereby many hearts were tendered, and much brokenness appeared in the meeting. The truth delivered being brought home to the consciences of many, by the prevalence of the divine power, which was eminently in dominion over all.

First day, the 11th. I trust the exercise and travail of our meeting to-day tended to profit.

Second day. I attended the funeral of our friend Edmund Pearsall, of Flushing. His corpse was carried into the meeting-house there; and a large solid meeting was held on the occasion.

Third day. I attended our meeting for sufferings in New-York, which, I think, was an instructive season.

Fifth day. Attended our monthly meeting, in which I opened to Friends a prospect, which had for several months attended my mind, to pay a religious visit to the bordering inhabitants of our quarterly meeting; and had their unity therein.

Sixth and seventh days. I spent in my usual avocations.

First day, the 18th. My mind, as I sat in our meeting, was opened into a view of the great benefits, and supreme felicity, which man derives, and only can derive, from the true knowledge and right fear of his Creator; and which knowledge and fear no man can witness or have experience of, but by the revelation of the spirit of God, or by the aid of that light, which Jesus Christ told the Jews was the condemnation of the world, or of all those who did not believe in and obey it; and which is an *inward* and not an *outward light;* and all its manifestations are in the mind or heart of man. I was led to show to the people, that this doctrine was altogether the most rational, and such as no man of right reason could doubt or dispute. I hope the season was instructive to some, and might tend to remove doubts from some doubting minds, as, from the sensations which I had, I was led to believe there were some such present.

Second, third, and fourth days. I attended to my temporal concerns, clothed with much poverty of spirit; yet, not altogether cast down nor discouraged, respecting my spiritual welfare.

Fifth day. A silent quiet meeting.

Sixth and seventh days. Paid some attention to my temporal business, although, at times, in much bodily pain, which, more or less, attends me daily, and has for several months past.

First day, the 25th. According to the prospect opened at our last monthly meeting, I attended two appointed meetings in the neighbouring town of Hempstead; one in the morning, at the eleventh hour, at the house of Samuel Carman, a person inclining to Friends, and the other at the fourth hour in the afternoon, at John Raynor's, about four miles distant from the former, he also being kind and well disposed towards Friends.

These were both pretty full meetings, there being as many people as the rooms could well accommodate. Through the gracious condescension of the Shepherd of Israel, the word went forth freely among them, in a full impressive testimony at each place, tendering and contriting many hearts, and to the increase of love to the truth, and to the promoters of it. I took my leave of them in the fresh feelings of mutual Christian affection, and returned home that evening with a quiet peaceful mind, the assured reward of faithfulness.

The rest of the week I spent in my usual avocations, not omitting the attendance of our meeting on fifth day, which I sat in silence.

First day, the 1st of 9th month. I attended an appointed meeting among my relatives and acquaintance at Rockaway, the place of my former residence, when young, while living in my father's house. The meeting was not large, but proved a precious tendering season. Many hearts were much broken and contrited by the prevalence of divine love and power that accompanied the testimony borne, and spread generally over the meeting, to the praise of His grace who is calling us to glory and virtue.

A concern for the guarded education of the youth among Friends has for many years past exercised our yearly meeting; and many advices and recommendations have been issued therefrom to the quarterly and other subordinate meetings, in order to stir up Friends to vigilance and care therein, that proper schools might be established among them, under the care of pious tutors, that so Friends' children, while getting their necessary school learning, might be religiously instructed, and preserved from evil examples, and the company of such children as are viciously inclined; by which their tender minds might be wounded, and led from the simplicity of truth. In order further to stir up Friends to this concern, our last yearly meeting directed the quarterly meetings to appoint committees to visit the monthly and preparative meetings, to encourage Friends therein. As I was one among other Friends appointed by our quarterly meeting for that purpose, we attended the monthly meetings of New-York and Flushing, in the course of this week. And I am thankful in believing that the service was owned by the Head of the Church, who was graciously near, and furnished with matter suited to the occasion; insomuch, that I have cause to believe that the opportunities at each place were instructive and edifying, affording encouragement to the willing-minded.

First day, the 8th of 9th month. I found it my place to be at home to-day, and of course attended our own meeting. Although most of the forepart of the meeting, I apprehended I should be permitted to sit it in silence; yet about the middle thereof, my mind was quickened in the remembrance of the testimony of Solomon, where he tells us, that "Wisdom is the principal thing." As the subject spread on my mind, I was led to consider how it is that all men speak highly of it, and yet, at the same time, are not at all rightly acquainted with its beginning; and are therefore mostly living all their days without the right knowledge of, and acquaintance with it. For it is not to be derived through any other medium than the true fear of the Lord, which we are told is the beginning of wisdom; and as it is only begun in man by this true fear, so likewise it is the middle and the end; as every advancement in true wisdom is only by the fear of the Lord: surely, then, it is the most precious of any thing to the children of men.

I spent the rest of the week about home. Attended our preparative meeting on fifth day. The meeting for worship was held in silence. Our yearly meeting's minute of advice on the subject of schools was at this time received; but as it was expected that the quarterly meeting's committee, on that subject, would shortly attend the preparative meeting, the consideration thereof was deferred to the time of their attendance.

First day, the 15th. By appointment I attended two meetings; one at Cold Spring at ten o'clock in the morning, and the other in Friends' meeting-house at Oysterbay, at the third hour in the afternoon. Both were pretty well attended by the neighbouring inhabitants, among whom I was helped to preach the gospel in the demonstration of the spirit, accompanied with such a degree of the Lord's power and presence, as to produce a precious solemnity over the assemblies, especially the latter, wherein many truths of the gospel were largely opened, humbling and contriting the hearts of a number present. Surely it was the Lord's doing, to whom all the praise and glory are, and ought to be ascribed, both now and for ever.

In the course of this week, I attended our own and Westbury monthly meeting, in company with the quarterly meeting's committee, on the subject of schools. These were both favoured opportunities. The concern was opened in a very impressive manner, and spread weightily over the meetings, the men and women sitting together while this subject was before them. And I have a hope that Friends will be strengthened and encouraged to persevere in the concern, and keep it on its right basis, that is, a concern for the religious and moral instruction of our youth, while at school, by placing them under the care of pious tutors, who may co-operate with the endeavours of religiously concerned parents, who are more desirous that their children may be brought up and educated in the fear of the Lord, and in his nurture and admonition, than that they should make great advancements in scholastic science, or obtain the riches and popularity of the world; all of which are of momentary duration, and unworthy of much of the care of a rational immortal being, especially when compared with the blessings attendant on a truly moral and religious life, and walking in the fear of the Lord.

First day, the 22d. In prosecution of the concern I had engaged in to visit the neighbouring inhabitants, notice was sent to Friends of Martinicock, that I proposed to attend their meeting at this time; and desiring that public notice might be given to their neighbours who were not members, it was accordingly done. By this means the meeting was very large, more so than I had ever seen it before; among whom I was helped to labour in the cause of the gospel, opening many important scripture passages, tending to elucidate and confirm many points of our doctrine and principles, to my own, and apparently to the general satisfaction of the assembly. At three o'clock in the afternoon I attended another meeting at Moscheto Cove, held in the house of the widow Hannah Valentine. This was also a large favoured meeting, in which many truths of the gospel were clearly and satisfactorily opened. I returned home that evening with peace of mind, from an inward sense that I had faithfully discharged myself among the people, concerning the things which relate to their salvation.

The rest of the week I was at and about home, attending to my usual occupations. Sat our fifth day meeting in silence.

First day, the 29th. I attended Friends' meeting at Cowneck; and previous notice having been sent of my intention to be there, the meeting was large, and favoured in a good degree with the overshadowing of the divine presence, enabling to preach the gospel in the demonstration of the spirit, and with power; breaking and contriting many hearts. At the third hour in the afternoon, by previous appointment, had a meeting at Hempstead Harbour, at the house of Daniel Robbins. This was rather a hard exercising meeting, yet, I trust, in the main a profitable season.

The following part of the week I spent mostly in the oversight of my farming business. Sat our fifth day meeting again in silence, at which we had the company of our Friends Isaac Martin and Henry Shotwell, from Jersey.

First day, the 6th of 10th month. Attended our meeting in silence. It was in the main, I think, a weighty, solemn season. At three o'clock in the afternoon, I had an appointed meeting in the neighbourhood for the people of colour. It was held in one of their houses, and was a season of favour. I hope it may prove profitable to them. For this portion of dedication to duty in the cause of righteousness, I felt peace in my own mind.

Second day. A Friend from the western part of this state, being on a religious visit among us, had an appointed meeting at our place at the eleventh hour. It proved a comfortable edifying season. After this I rode to New-York in order to attend our meeting for sufferings, held the next day at the ninth hour. In the course of the business that came before us, the meeting was led into an exercise, on behalf of that portion of the descendants of the Africans who are still held in bondage in our state. A proposition was made for addressing our state legislature on their account, in order, if possible, to obtain a law for their emancipation; apprehending, that as the greater part of these long-oppressed people had now obtained their freedom, those who were still held, felt their condition much more aggravating, and their bondage more intolerable; insomuch, that it appeared to us altogether just and consistent with the duty of the legislature, to restore to them the just right of freedom. After due consideration, the proposition was acceded to, and a committee named to draft an essay of an address accordingly.

Fifth day. This being our preparative meeting, in which our queries were read, and answers prepared to go to the quarterly meeting, I felt my mind exercised on account of the many deficiencies apparent, particularly in the non-attendance of our religious meetings, as a failure in that often leads to greater deficiencies in other respects.

First day, the 13th. My mind was pretty largely opened in testimony to the sufficiency of the divine light. The season was solemn, and I hope instructive and profitable to many present.

At three o'clock in the afternoon, I attended an appointed meeting in Woolver Hollow, a neighbourhood composed mostly of the descendants of the Dutch. The season was instructive, and tending to edification; and I parted with them under an humbling sense of the favour.

Fifth day. Our monthly meeting being held at this time, answers were received from our preparative meetings, to the five queries usually answered, in which divers deficiencies were stated ; but this being frequently the case, it produced little or no concern to the greater portion of the members ; and I have been afraid at times, that the queries would become a snare to us, and prove rather hurtful than helpful.

First day, the 20th. Had a conflicting season in the forepart of our meeting to-day with a worldly spirit, and the benumbing consequences of a desire after riches. And while labouring under a feeling of these states, with their stupifying effects, which were even intolerable to bear, it often ran through my mind, that " the cares of the world, the deceitfulness of riches," and the lust of other things, like briars and thorns, choke the good seed and prevent its growth. And as I continued patiently under the labour, towards the close of the meeting light sprang up and dispelled the darkness; in which strength and ability were dispensed to communicate in a lively and clear manner, showing the pernicious effects of those things, wherever they obtained the ascendency in the minds of men and women ; elucidating the subject by the parable of our Lord, concerning the rich man and Lazarus the beggar. It was, I believe, a season of real instruction to some present, which I hope may not be soon forgotten.

At three o'clock in the afternoon, I attended a meeting I had previously appointed in a neighbouring village. It proved a satisfactory season to my own mind, and generally so, I believe, to all who attended. These favours are not to be lightly esteemed, but held in grateful remembrance.

In the course of this week was our quarterly meeting, held at this time at Flushing. Although some of the sittings were exercising and arduous, yet in the main, I think, it was a favoured edifying season ; and we parted at the close of the public meeting on sixth day, under a thankful sense that the Shepherd of Israel had not forsaken his people, but was still graciously near, a present helper to all his faithful and devoted children. In the course of this meeting, on the evening of fifth day, I had an appointed meeting in the town of Jamaica, among those not in profession with us, which proved a very satisfactory season. The people's minds appeared to be gathered into true stillness, a situation most suitable to be taught and instructed.

First day, the 27th. Sat our meeting mostly in silence, but towards the close my mind was opened and led to communicate a short, but lively testimony, which was introduced by the greatest part of the first psalm of David: in the opening of which, the meeting appeared generally to be gathered into a sweet, comfortable solemnity, and we parted under a solemn sense of the unmerited favour.

In the course of this week, I attended, in company with most of the committee of the quarterly meeting on the concern relative to schools, the two preparative meetings in New-York, and that at Flushing; also an appointed meeting at Brooklyn on third day evening, and one at Newtown on fifth day evening. The last was a very instructive favoured meeting.

First day, the 3d of 11th month. Sat our meeting to-day altogether in silence. Spent the rest of the week principally in attention to my temporal concerns, which I believe to be a Christian's reasonable duty; except that I attended in company with some of the quarterly meeting's committee on fifth day, the preparative meeting at Cowneck. I sat the meeting for worship in silent suffering; but was led in the preparative meeting, pretty largely to open the nature and design of the concern of the yearly meeting, with regard to the pious and guarded education of the youth of our society, particularly while young and at school, in getting their necessary school learning; that they might as much as possible, be kept out of harm's way, by being placed at schools under the care of pious religiously concerned persons, members in society; who would be likely to co-operate with the religious concern of their parents, in endeavouring, as much as might be, to bring them up agreeably to apostolic exhortation: "In the nurture and admonition of the Lord." For there is nothing that can more nearly and necessarily engage the minds of rightly exercised parents, next to their own souls, than the religious welfare of their children: for parents who can live in the neglect of this great and incumbent duty, must be dead to every right exercise and concern for the preservation and everlasting welfare of their tender offspring.

First day, the 10th. Sat our meeting in silence: then rode

several miles to visit a person who was sick, and returned the next day.

I had to reflect on the great and serious loss sustained by a large portion of mankind, from the want of due attention and a right perseverance in the way of known duty while young in years ; that when they are advanced in age, and bodily infirmities interfere and increase upon them, they are tossed up and down in their minds, and can find no sure place of refuge for their souls; like a ship in the midst of the ocean without a helm, and which can find no safe anchoring ground.

On fourth day attended the funeral of a young woman on Cowneck, who was taken away very suddenly, with about three hour's illness. I had an open time among the people that were assembled on this solemn occasion, and was led to call their attention to the propriety and necessity of an early preparation for death; and to show that it manifested great presumption in such a poor impotent creature as man, who was so sensible of the uncertainty of time, to dare to lay his head down at night to take his natural rest, without knowing his peace made with his God.

Fifth and sixth days. Attended, in company with some of the committee of the quarterly meeting on the subject of schools, the preparative meetings of Martinicock and Bethpage; both of which were open favoured seasons, while the subject of our appointment was under consideration.

On seventh day I attended the funeral of a very aged man of my acquaintance, being upwards of ninety years old, who lived in the town of Hempstead. There was a pretty large collection of the neighbouring inhabitants present, among whom I was led and strengthened to open divers necessary and important doctrines of the gospel, in the clear demonstration of the spirit ; and, I trust and hope, to the edification and religious instruction of many present. Surely it was the Lord's doing, and to him belongs all the praise and honour of his own works, and nothing due to man.

First day, the 17th. Sat our meeting in silence. It was a quiet solid season. The rest of the week I was occupied in my husbandry business, except attending our monthly meeting on fifth day.

First day, the 24th. My mind in our meeting to-day, was led into an humbling exercise, under a sensible view of the great ascendency of evil over the good among mankind in general, not excepting the best regulated society among men. I was also led, under the saddening prospect, to communicate to the meeting the feeling impressions of my mind thereon, together with the causes of this great degeneracy from the simplicity of the gospel of Christ; and that it was the effect of a spirit of ease and carnal security, and being led and governed in our conduct and works by custom and tradition, without taking the pains to examine whether they were founded in truth and righteousness or not; and when at times they are awakened by the convicting evidence of truth on the mind, instead of willingly submitting thereto, they call to their aid all the powers of their reasoning faculties to drown the reprover's voice, that so they may rest secure in their ceiled houses. Alas for these in the trying hour of final decision! how dreadfully saddening will be their prospects in a dying hour!

First day, the 1st of 12th month. I sat with Friends at Westbury. The meeting was for the most part a dull exercising season; but towards the close I had a short testimony given me to communicate, in which the state of the meeting was so opened as to have a very reaching effect on most present; which spread life over the meeting, and much tenderness and contrition were apparent. Surely have we not cause for these favours, often to say with one formerly: "What shall I render unto the Lord for all his benefits towards me."

Second day. I attended the funeral of a near kinsman at Far Rockaway, at which I had a very open time amongst the people collected on that solemn occasion.

I returned home on third day, and the weather being cold and inclement I was indisposed for several days after, which prevented my attending our meeting on fifth day; a circumstance which very seldom happens, as I am generally preserved in the enjoyment of such a state of health, as to attend meetings when at

home without much omission : and which I consider as one
among many especial blessings and favours, dispensed by a kind
and beneficent Providence to me, a poor unworthy creature.

First day, the 8th.   I left home this morning and rode to New-
York, and attended Friends' meeting at Pearl-street in the afternoon, in which I had to suffer, being dipped into a state of death.
I felt as though baptized for the dead, but as I patiently endured
I was helped towards the close to spread my exercise before the
meeting, and a degree of life was felt to arise, and some were
quickened, but with too many there appeared to be a great want
of a right inward engagement and travail of spirit, and these
were sent empty away.

I tarried in town until fourth day, it being the time of our
meeting for sufferings.   In the course of this meeting, we prepared a memorial to lay before the legislature of our state, on
behalf of the black people still held in bondage among us.   A
committee was separated to attend therewith, and we have a hope
that it may prove effectual for their relief.

Fifth day.   Attended our preparative meeting, and had to
spread before my Friends the exercise of my mind, on account
of the neglect of too many among us in respect to the due observance of discipline; which is a source of great weakness to society,
and especially so to those who are delinquent.

Sixth and seventh days.   Spent in my usual vocations, accompanied with quietness and peace of mind.

First day, the 15th.   Almost as soon as I had taken my seat
in our meeting to day, there was brought to my remembrance
the following exhortation of the apostle, accompanied with a
degree of life : " To do good, and to communicate, forget not."
As I quietly attended to the impression, it led to communication
and opened to a field of doctrine, tending to show the indispensable
obligation every real Christian lies under, let his allotment in the
Church or in the world at large be what it may, to comply
therewith, it being a divine requisition.   It is therefore reasonable to suppose that by a life of steady and uniform industry, and
from which man derives great earthly felicity, and through the
divine blessing, most individuals would be enabled to fulfil the

obligation ; by which means all the misery and distress that arise
from poverty and want would be done away from the Church of
Christ, and agreeably to the prophecy of Isaiah, no wasting or
destruction be found within her borders; and Christians would
witness in their own experience, that it is more blessed to give
han to receive; as we should thereby approach nearer to our
divine original, from whom we receive every blessing both spirit
ual and temporal.

The following part of the week I spent in my usual occupations, except attending our monthly meeting on fifth day.

First day, the 22d. This day I attended the funeral of my
brother Stephen Hicks at Rockaway. There was a pretty large
collection of people on the occasion, among whom I was led to
labour fervently in the gospel, and largely to declare of the things
concerning the kingdom of God. The season was solemn, and
by the prevalence of the divine power that attended, many hearts
were contrited and a precious solemnity was spread over the
assembly, worthy of our deepest gratitude and thankfulness of
heart. I returned home that evening with sweet peace of mind.

Having for some time felt a draft on my mind to appoint a
few meetings in some adjacent neighbourhoods, to the south and
east of us, I left home on the seventh day of this week, accompanied by my neighbour Jacob Willits, jr. We rode that afternoon
to our friend James Rushmore's, at the Half-way Hollow Hills ;
where, by previous notice, we had a comfortable satisfactory
meeting in the evening, mostly made up of those not in membership with us. The next day, the first of the week, we had two
meetings ; one in the town of Islip in the morning, at the residence of my son-in-law Joshua Willits, the other at the third
our in the afternoon, in the school-house at the village of Baby-
on. These were very solemn affecting meetings, wherein many
truths of the gospel were largely and livingly opened, in the
demonstration of the spirit, attended with a power that humbled
and contrited many hearts, and brought a general solemnity over
the meetings.

The next day we rode to our friend Thomas Whitson's, on
the south side of our township. Had an appointed meeting there

37

that evening, which was also favoured with attendant gospel power ; whereby my mind was opened and led to sound forth an arousing testimony, in order to stir up many present, who, for want of faithfulness and obedience to manifested duty, were much behind in their day's work : and which, as it opened on my mind, I expressed to them to be not only a cause of great loss and disadvantage in a religious sense to themselves, but also to their families and their tender offspring. Things were laid close home to these, and they excited to more faithfulness and religious engagement.

At this place I was informed of the death of our Friend and neighbour Elizabeth Jones, wife of Samuel Jones, whose funeral was to be the next day. This information induced us to return home early in the morning in order to attend the same. As she had many connexions, there was a very large collection of people on the occasion, many of whom were of divers persuasions. My heart and mouth were opened to preach the gospel among them, and to explain to the people the principles of the Christian religion, in a full and clear manner, in the authority of truth. It was a highly favoured season, in which truth reigned triumphant; and the Lord's name and power were praised and exalted over all.

Fifth day, the 2d of 1st month, 1817. I attended our meeting as usual. It was quiet and comfortable. Near the close I had a short testimony to communicate, to the excellency and exalted privileges of the Christian state, which brought a precious covering over the meeeting.

First day, the 5th. Very soon after I took my seat in meeting to-day, my mind was brought into a feeling sense and view of the superiour excellency of the true Christian religion ; and this can only be known and possessed by a full and entire subjugation of our wills to the divine will, and living in the practical part of that reasonable injunction of our blessed Lord, to seek first the kingdom of God and his righteousness ; then every other blessing that is needful and comfortable for us will be added, in the openings of the divine counsel. But alas, how few there are who pay any right attention to this excellent requisition, but on the contrary go on in their own wills, and in the prosecution of their own schemes of profit and pleasure, most generally at least 'until they marry, and settle themselves in the care and concerns of a family. In all this time, scarcely one in ten thousand of the human family even think of seeking first the kingdom of God and his righteousness, or even asking counsel of him in the weighty concern of marriage ; upon a right procedure in which, their present and future happiness greatly depend, and for want of this previous care, they are often very unequally yoked together ; and when these have a family of children about them, without any right ability and qualification to instruct them, confusion and disorder ensue ; and the poor children are left to grow up without right cultivation, as brambles in the wilderness, a lamentable case indeed : a view of which has often clothed my mind with mourning. I was led largely to open these subjects to the meeting under the influence of gospel love, and found peace in my labour, the sure reward of faithfulness to manifested duty ; and whether the people will hear or forbear, it is not the business of the instrument to be careful about, as the word that goeth forth will not return void, but will accomplish the thing whereto it is sent ; either to instruct and comfort, or to reprove and condemn.

The rest of the week I was mostly employed in my temporal concerns, except attending our preparative meeting on fifth day. The meeting for worship was, I think, a favoured season.

First day the 12th. A silent meeting to-day.

Fourth day. Feeling my mind drawn to attend the monthly meeting of Westbury, which was held to-day, I proceeded accordingly. In the meeting for worship, I was led to show to Friends under the similitude of Israel's travel, that it was not enough to be delivered from our former sins, nor from the red sea of trials and obstructing temptations, so as to rejoice on the banks of deliverance, and be fed with heavenly manna, even angels' food ; nor to journey on towards the promised Canaan, as far as Korah and his company ; and to see like them, the wonder-working power of Jehovah in the wilderness, unless they also came to witness a complete death to their own wills, so as to be entirely submis sive to the will of our heavenly Father ; for otherwise they would be left to encompass as it were, a mountain in the wilderness, until the old man, that is, self-will, is entirely worn out and dies there, on this side Jordan : for nothing short of that will open Jordan's streams, and enable us to go through on dry land. I had largely to open to Friends the mystery of our redemption, in the demonstration of the spirit, showing the necessity of continual perseverance and making progress in our heavenly journey, otherwise we shall be liable to fall into a state of ease and carnal security ; and thereby make shipwreck of faith and a good conscience, and our latter end be worse than the beginning ; like those of Israel, who fell in the wilderness and never obtained the promised land.

Fifth day. Attended our monthly meeting. As it was the time of answering our queries, I was engaged to stir up Friends to more diligence, by faithfully scrutinizing their own individual states through the medium of the queries, by which means they would be truly useful to us ; for otherwise the reading and answering them would become a dead lifeless form.

First day, the 19th. A silent meeting to-day, in which my spirit was grieved, as is too often the case in our meetings, from a sense of the great want of real spiritual life, and the apparent deadness and formality which too generally prevail ; whereby it often happens that a number appear drowsy and nodding, and some falling asleep, to the great trouble and exercise of the living concerned members, who are often led to mourn in secret on these accounts.

In the course of this week I attended our quarterly meeting held at this time at Westbury. It was a season of close solemn searching, and through the animating influence of the divine light and life, the hidden things of Esau or the first nature, were brought to light and judged. Although some, who had long covered themselves as with thick clay, and were solacing themselves in their ceiled houses, kicked like Jeshurun of old, when they were made to feel the piercing edge of that sword which divides between soul and spirit, joints and marrow, and is a discerner of the thoughts and intents of the heart ; yet the truth had its way over all their opposition, and in the closing meeting reigned triumphant over all. Blessed be the Lord for his unspeakable gifts dispensed to his faithful children.

First day, the 26th. My mind in our meeting to-day, was led to reflect on the excellency and powerful effect of true faith. As the subject opened, I found it my place to spread the prospect before the meeting ; in the communication whereof, life sprang up and the truth was raised into dominion over all, and my heart was made thankful for the unmerited favour.

The rest of the week I was busily employed in my domestic affairs, and in taking the oversight and care of my stock ; the weather being very cold and frosty, and the earth covered with snow. Attended our meeting on fifth day, at which there was a funeral of a deceased Friend, an ancient maiden. I sat the greater part of the meeting in silence, in which time there were two short testimonies delivered, but without much apparent effect, as the seed of immortal life was too much pressed down, as a cart with sheaves ; and nothing is sufficient to raise a meeting from such a state of death and stupor, but the life-giving presence and powerful word of Him, who raised Lazarus from the grave. As I patiently endured the necessary baptism for the dead, towards the close of the meeting a little gleam of light appeared, in which was brought to my remembrance that passage of the wise man, that "Righteousness exalteth a nation." And as my inward eye was kept to the opening, it spread, and light sprang up, in which I felt the truth of that saying, that " the Lord's people are willing in the day of his power ;" and as I yielded to communication, the life was raised into dominion, and ran as oil over all. Surely it was the Lord's doing and marvellous in mine eyes.

CHAPTER XIII.

Engagements at and near home, 1817.—Visit to some parts of the yearly meetings of Philadelphia and Baltimore, 1817.

FIRST day, the 2d of 2d month, 1817. I was largely led forth in our meeting to-day, on the different dispensations communicated to man by his gracious Creator, in order for his recovery out of the fall, and pointing out to the people the difference between the law state and that of the gospel : showing that the former was a mere figure or prelude to the latter, and that the first, with all its elementary rituals, ceased where the latter begun ; the first only affecting the body, the latter principally the soul ; the first only the shadow of good things, the latter the substance of all good to man ; by which he is altogether redeemed from sin and death, as he submits willingly and fully to the power of the gospel, and is thereby prepared for an inheritance in eternal life.

In the course of this week, besides giving the necessary attention to my temporal affairs, I made several friendly visits to the families of some particular friends, in company with my wife and daughter Elizabeth. Although I met with some occurrences, one in particular, which produced considerable exercise on my mind, yet I had satisfaction in the visits; believing that when they are properly made, they often prove mutually comfortable and encouraging. Sat our meeting on fifth day in silence.

First day, the 9th. Had a silent meeting to-day. This week afforded occasion of deep inward exercise, and seasons of heart-searching, in a view of the manifest declension of many among us from that honest simplicity and faithfulness which so eminently characterized our worthy predecessors, as also the increase of vanity and immorality among the people without; and which I fear may have been increased by the want of faithfulness among us, in the right and full support of our Christian testimonies.

First day, the 16th. Soon after I took my seat in our meeting to-day, my mind was quickened and led into a sympathetic feeling with the state of Elijah, when he fled from the wrath and persecution of Ahab and Jezebel, and when under great discouragement and dismay he bemoaned his condition; saying, that they had pulled down the Lord's altars, slain his servants, and he only was left and they sought his life; but the Lord told him for his encouragement, that there were seven thousand yet left in Israel, who had not bowed their knee to the image of Baal. But these no doubt were so scattered and dispersed among the people, that Elijah could scarcely find one to whom he might open his mind, and therefore felt himself as one alone. This no doubt is the lot of some of the Lord's most faithful servants in the present day, and was it not for the same divine help and succour that Elijah experienced, some of these at times would be altogether cast down and discouraged.

The subject spread and enlarged, and opened to a field of doctrine; wherein I was led to show to the people that the mystery of iniquity had wrought in and under every dispensation of God to the Church through its varied transformations, and always resembling as much as may be, an angel of light; by which it lies in wait to deceive, and has generally deceived, and still deceives, the greater part of the people of all the nations under heaven; setting up its post by God's post, and leading its votaries to perform their worship and works just like the Lord's servants, with only this difference, that it is done in a way and time of their own heart's devising. But the Lord's children are all taught of the Lord, and they are made to know it; for in righteousness they are established, and great is the peace of these children; and there is no peace to the wicked, to such as walk in their own wills, and in the way of their own heart's devising.

On fifth day of this week, was our monthly meeting, at which we had the company of a Friend in the ministry from one of our upper quarterly meetings. He preached the truth to us in a pretty correct manner; but I thought I never saw, with greater clearness than at this time, that ministers might preach the literal truth, and yet not preach the real gospel: and herein is witnessed the truth of that saying of the apostle, that "the *letter*," however true, "*killeth;*" "but the *spirit*," and the spirit only, "*giveth life.*" And it is a great thing when ministers keep in remembrance that necessary caution of the divine Master, not to premeditate what they shall say; but carefully to wait in the nothingness and emptiness of self, that what they speak may be only what the Holy Spirit speaketh in them; then will they not only speak the truth, but the truth, accompanied with power, and thereby profit the hearers.

First day, 23d. A silent meeting to-day. Nothing transpired in the course of this week, which required particular notice. Sat our meeting on fifth day in silence.

First day, the 2d of 3d month. Having felt my mind for several weeks past drawn to visit Bethpage meeting, I rode thither to-day in company with my wife. It was rather a low dull time, but as I continued in the patience, a small prospect opened on the excellency of justice, and the right bringing up of children. It led to a communication instructive and edifying, for which I was made thankful.

First day, the 9th. This day as I sat in our meeting, my mind was led to view the exalted and precious state those enjoyed, who were brought by their faithfulness to witness in themselves the fulfilment of the first and great commandment, that of loving God above all; as they would thereby likewise know the fulfilment of the second, that of loving their neighbour as themselves. As the subject spread on my mind I believed it right to express it to the assembly, which brought a precious solemnity over the meeting, and, I trust, it was an instructive season to some present.

This week principally spent in the care of my temporal concerns and in lending assistance to the needy, and in the course of which my mind was often attended with comforting ejaculations after this manner. "The Lord is my strength and my song, the lifter up of mine head and my salvation; therefore I will not fear what man can do unto me. He leadeth me about and instructeth me, and preserveth me from the snare of the fowler, and from the strife of tongues."

First day, the 16th. Our meeting to-day was large and solemn, and mostly silent. A little before the close, an exhortation of the apostle Peter was brought before the view of my mind: "Be sober, be vigilant; because your adversary the devil, as a roaring lion, walketh about seeking whom he may devour." As the subject opened I found it my duty to spread it before the meeting, with some observations thereon, tending to excite the people to diligence, inasmuch as there could be no doubt of the truth of the apostle's testimony; hence it was necessary for each one to keep the watch, resisting him steadfast in the faith. The communication though short, was so attended with the quickening power of the gospel, as to reach, affect, and tender many minds, and brought a solemn awe over the meeting. Such seasons are worthy of grateful acknowledgments to the blessed Author of all our rich mercies.

Spent this week mostly at and about home, enjoying sweet peace of mind, and the solace of heart-felt thankfulness to the Shepherd of Israel for the unmerited favour. Attended the funeral of a deceased neighbour on fourth day and our monthly meeting on fifth day. The funeral was largely attended by the neighbouring inhabitants, among whom I was led forth vocally to espouse the cause of the gospel, in a large impressive testimony. Many hearts were humbled, and the assembly in general solemnized; may it be to these as bread cast upon the waters, gathered after many days.

First day, the 23d. Our meeting to-day was a season thankfully to be remembered. The subject that arrested my mind and led to communication, was a comparative view of man with the rest of the animal creation; showing that man, although endued with a rational understanding, and blessed with a measure and manifestation of the spirit of God, to guide him infallibly in the way of his duty, had nevertheless swerved much further from the state of rectitude in which he was created, than any other creature; and was much more changeable and unstable than

38

they. This is a sure mark of his fall: and although continually liable and willing to change, to gratify his own will and the humour of others, in following the changeable customs and manners of a vain world; yet averse to that necessary and laudable change, whereby he might regain paradise and renew communion with his Maker. This and much more I was led to open to the auditory, in the demonstration of the spirit, showing the way of man's return; whereby many minds present were humbled and contrited, and solid satisfaction and comfort afforded to my own.

On fourth day, I attended a marriage at Bethpage. It was, I think, a solid instructive season. On fifth day attended our own meeting which was held in silence. The rest of the week I was busily attentive to my usual avocations.

First day, the 30th. I attended Westbury meeting, wherein my mind was opened into a view of man's primitive state, the manner and means of his fall, and the way whereby he only can be restored, all which I had largely to spread before the meeting. In addition to this, I had also to caution Friends, particularly the youth, against letting their minds out in their own will and wisdom, into a search and pursuit after forbidden knowledge, particularly that of the *origin of evil*, which in the present day is a subject of much conversation and inquiry. For man in the beginning was forbidden the knowledge of good and evil, and that command is as binding and obligatory in the present day as it was in the primitive state; therefore all those who presume in their own wills and creaturely wisdom, independent of the teaching of the spirit of God, to know good and evil, do thereby desert God, and so become dead to the divine life; and this is man's fall, and leads to Deism and Atheism.

I was much engaged in the course of this week in endeavouring to arrange and settle some difficulties in the neighbourhood, and in regulating some of my own temporal affairs. Sat our meeting on fifth day in silence.

First day, the 6th of 4th month. Sat our meeting to-day in silence. In the afternoon at the fourth hour, we had a meeting appointed by a Friend from abroad, who was accompanied by another Friend in the ministry, both of whom appeared in public testimony.

Most of this week I was occupied about home. Attended our preparative meeting on fifth day, which being the time of answering our queries to go forward to the yearly meeting, I was led to make several remarks to Friends to stir them up to more faithfulness, in order that we might profit by the queries, and be prepared to answer them with more clearness and propriety, according to truth and justice.

First day, the 13th. Sat our meeting to-day in silence. This week our monthly meeting was held, at which the state of society as represented by the answers to the queries from our preparative meetings was attended to, and a summary thereof forwarded to the quarterly meeting to be held the following week. This order of reading and answering the queries quarterly, if rightly attended to, and Friends were generally kept lively in spirit, and were zealously engaged for the promotion of truth, would, I believe, be productive of much good to the society : but alas! there are so many who seem lulled asleep in the lap of the world, and their minds clothed with so much indifferency, that it is to them but a dead lifeless form. Surely these reap little or no advantage from their right of membership among us.

Sixth day. Was our preparative meeting of Ministers and Elders, in which nothing transpired worthy of notice.

First day, the 20th. Our meeting to-day, as well as at some former times, has been rather heavy and dull. In the course of this week I attended our quarterly meeting, held at this time at New-York. It was in general rather a low time, although not without some manifestations of divine favour : therefore we had no cause for murmuring but rather of rejoicing, in that we were not cast off and forgotten.

First day, the 27th. Sat our meeting again in silence. My present allotment is to be mostly at home, generally engaged in temporal concerns for myself and others. But, I trust, instead of increasing my love to the world and the things of it, I am fast weaning from it, and my love continually increasing and strengthening to higher and better objects ; as my attention to the world and its cares arises from necessity and duty, and not from love, except that I love to do my duty in all respects to God my Creator, and man my fellow creature, believing that there is no real Christianity without it.

Our fifth day meeting was quiet and solemn, wherein I had to remind Friends that it was not enough to say with Peter, when queried of by his Master whether he loved him, " yea Lord," for this is no more than every professor is ready to say, although they may be quite void of any true sense thereof ; but we must come to know him and love him in such manner, as when brought to a full trial of our faith and love, we can say as Peter did in his third answer : " Lord thou knowest all things, thou knowest that I love thee." For this is the situation of mind which prepares to be at his disposal, and to endure hardness for his sake in the Christian warfare.

First day, the 4th of 5th month. My mind was led into an interesting view and reflection on the following gracious invitation of our Lord : " Come unto me, all ye that labour and are heavy laden, and I will give you rest. Take my yoke upon you, and learn of me : for I am meek and lowly in heart, and ye shall find rest unto your souls." As the subject spread on my mind attended with a degree of life, I was constrained to communicate the prospect, showing that Christ's yoke was nothing less nor more than the revealed will of his, and our, heavenly Father ; which, as it is faithfully submitted to, yokes down and keeps in subjection every desire and propensity of the human mind which stands in opposition thereto. So that the creature hereby knows God's kingdom to be come, and his will to be done, in earth as it is done in heaven ; and the reward of rest and peace promised in the closing part of the invitation is experienced.

The following part of this week spent principally in my usual vocations, except attending our preparative meeting on fifth day ; and at the third hour in the afternoon, the funeral of our Friend Joshua Powell of Westbury, who was taken from us after a short illness, by a sudden inflammation and mortification in one of his arms. How true is that saying of the prophet : "All flesh is grass, and all the goodliness thereof is as the flower of the field ;

the grass withereth, the flower fadeth ;" just such is man, alive to-day, to morrow is dead. This subject very sensibly impressed my mind at the funeral, and led to an awkening communication, which had a very reaching effect on the assembly. I hope the word that went forth will not return void, but prove a blessing to some who were present.

First day, the 11th. Our meeting to-day was a trying season, but little felt of the real virtue and life of religion. It seemed as though we were in a worse condition than the multitude formerly; for there was a lad found among them with five barley loaves and a few fishes, which served for the blessing to operate upon and enlarge, so as to suffice the multitude and leave fragments remaining; but we were almost, or altogether destitute of any thing for the blessing of heaven to act upon. Therefore we ought not to murmur, although we were sent empty away.

Except attending our monthly meeting on fifth day, and assisting some of my neighbours to settle their business in which a dispute had arisen, I was principally occupied in my temporal concerns through the week.

First day, the 18th. A silent meeting to-day. The rest of this week busily employed preparatory to leaving home to attend our aproaching yearly meeting. Left home early on seventh day morning, and got into the city seasonably to attend the opening of the yearly meeting of Ministers and Elders at the tenth hour. On second day at the same hour, the meeting for discipline opened, and continued by adjournments until the seventh day following. In the forenoon of that day at about eleven o'clock it closed, under a comfortable evidence that the divine presence presided; and which, with thankfulness and gratitude we have humbly to acknowledge, has, in gracious condescension, been vouchsafed to us in the several sittings of our large solemn assembly, in as great, if not greater degree, than has been witnessed in any previous season : tending to unite all the rightly concerned members in a living travail, for the promotion of the cause of truth and righteousness, and the spreading and exaltation of those precious testimonies given us as a people to bear for the Prince of Peace.

First day, the 1st of 6th month. Attended our own meeting to-day in humbling silence. Spent the week at and about home, except attending the funeral of our ancient Friend Isaac Underhill of Flushing, on sixth day; on which occasion a meeting was held in Friends' meeting-house at that place. It was a very solemn, and, I trust, a profitable season to some present. My mouth was opened among them to testify of the things concerning the kingdom of God, in a large affecting testimony, whereby many hearts were contrited and made humbly thankful for the present favour, and I was glad in believing that the Lord is still mindful of his people, and is graciously disposed to strengthen and support them in the needful time; as their eye is kept single to him, looking to him only for help and salvation.

First day, the 8th. Had a comfortable meeting to-day. The testimony to the power of truth went forth freely to the people, comforting and contriting many minds present. This is the Lord's doing and is worthy of grateful acknowledgments from his people, for such continued yet unmerited mercy.

On third day I attended a meeting at Bethpage, appointed by our friends Elizabeth Coggeshall and Ann Shipley of New-York, who were now among us on a religious visit. It was, I think, a season of great favour; not only the two women appeared in seasonable and appropriate testimonies, tending to gather the minds of the people into a very comfortable solemnity, but also, my heart and mouth were opened in a large affecting testimony, which found a ready entrance into the minds of most present, breaking down all opposition and contriting many hearts by the prevalence of truth, which ran as oil over all. After this, our friend Elizabeth closed the service in solemn supplication. It was a day of favour, worthy of grateful remembrance.

On fifth day I attended our preparative meeting, in which I had some service for the promotion of truth's cause. The four other days of this week, I spent in my usual necessary avocations.

First day, the 15th. Nothing in particular to remark respecting the exercise of this day.

On the fourth day of this week, our monthly meeting was held, in which I was led into some close searching exercise, in order to stir up Friends to more diligence and circumspection, that so their light might shine forth to the help of others, and their conduct appear consonant with their profession. In this meeting I found it expedient and consistent with my duty, to open to Friends a prospect and concern which had for a considerable time rested on my mind, to pay a visit in gospel love, to Friends and othe s in some parts of the yearly meetings of Philadelphia and Balti more. The subject obtained the solid attention of the meeting, and some Friends were appointed to confer with me on the subject, and, as way opened, prepare an essay of a certificate for that purpose, and produce it to our next meeting.

First day, the 22d. Whilst sitting in our meeting to-day, my mind was led into a view of the great and singular advantages that would accrue to the children of men, from their having right and just ideas of religion, the want of which was the principal cause of all the distress and misery that fell to their lot, both here and hereafter. The subject spread, and, as I communicated, opened to a large field of doctrine, which had a very reaching effect upon the assembly, and a very precious solemnity was spread over the meeting; for which my heart was made truly glad, with that gladness that hath no sorrow with it.

The rest of the week I was busily employed in the care of my temporal concerns, which nevertheless has no tendency, if kept within right bounds, to prevent internal religious exercises, and spiritual meditations and soliloquies. Sat our fifth day meeting in silence.

First day, the 29th. I sat our meeting to-day in a sense of great weakness, in which I realized the truth of David's testimony: "Verily every man at his best estate is altogether vanity."

Except attending in silent meditation our fifth day meeting, and the funeral of the only daughter of my brother Samuel, on seventh day, I was engaged as usual during the week, in my family cares; which indeed is an arduous task, if rightly performed, and every department duly cared for in its right season, consistent with our moral and religious duty. The funeral mentioned above was a solemn one, in which I was largely led forth to testify of the things concerning the kingdom of God; opening the way of life and salvation to the people, in the demonstration of the spirit. The assembly were generally solemnized by the efficacy of the power which attended, and truth raised into victory over all. Such favours are truly worthy of deep heart-felt gratitude and thanksgiving to the God and Father of all our sur mercies, who is over all, worthy for ever.

First day, the 6th of 7th month. Soon after I took my seat in our meeting to-day, my mind was opened into a view of the great need man stands in of a Saviour, and that nothing can give him so full and lively a sense thereof, as a true sight and sense of his own real condition; by which he is not only brought to see the real want of a Saviour, but is also shown thereby, what kind of a Saviour he needs. For it must not only be one, who is continually present, but who is possessed of a prescience sufficient to see, at all times, all man's enemies, and every temptation that may or can await him; and have power sufficient to defend him from all, and at all times. Therefore, such a Saviour as man wants, cannot be one without him, but must be one that is always present, just in the very place man's enemies assault him, which is *within*, in the very temple of the heart: as no other Saviour but such an one, who takes his residence in the very centre of the soul of man, can possibly produce salvation to him: hence, for man to look for a Saviour or salvation any where else, than in the very centre of his own soul, is a fatal mistake, and must consequently land him in disappointment and errour.

I was led forth to communicate largely to the people on the subject; and on the blessed effects that do, and will result to all those who find such a Saviour, and who, in humility and sincerity of heart, follow him faithfully in the way of his leadings It was a solemn season, and a day thankfully to be remembered

I was taken up principally the rest of this week, except attending our preparative meeting on fifth day, in my hay harvest. It is a laborious season; and is made much more so by reason of there being so few faithful labourers, among those who offer themselves as such. Most of them are more anxiously careful how they may obtain the highest wages, than to be engaged honestly to strive justly to earn them. This makes the care and oversight of such business rather irksome and unpleasant, which otherwise would be agreeable and often delightful.

First day, the 13th. I sat our meeting in silence. This week I was mostly taken up in caring for and assisting in, my hay harvest. For by the fertility of the season, our fields have brought forth plenteously. On fifth day our monthly meeting was held, in which Friends united with the concern I had laid before them at the preceding monthly meeting, to pay a visit in gospel love to Friends and others, in some parts of the yearly meetings of Philadelphia and Baltimore. A certificate was prepared for the purpose, leaving me at liberty to proceed therein, as way should open.

First day, the 20th. A solemn, and, I trust, a profitable meeting to-day, in which the gospel was preached freely in the demonstration of truth, and a precious covering was felt to spread over the assembly; and sweet peace clothed my mind at the conclusion. Surely the Lord is a bountiful and rich rewarder of all his faithful servants, who serve him, not for reward, but for the sake of that love wherewith he loveth them, and which he so abundantly sheddeth abroad in their hearts, that they are thereby drawn to love him above all; and in and under the influence of this precious love, they are led and constrained to serve and worship him freely for his own sake, because he is worthy, and not for any reward to themselves, because they are altogether unworthy; and because that precious love wherewith he hath loved them, and with which he hath filled their hearts, hath banished and dispelled therefrom every germ of self-love, and all kind of selfishness. Nevertheless, of his own rich bounty and free will, without any real merit on our part, he abundantly and plenteously bestoweth his blessings upon all his faithful servants and children, whereby their love to him is continually increased, until he becomes their all in all, their alpha and omega, and they are brought into the possession of that perfect love that casteth out all fear; and in which they are enabled continually to worship and adore Him who liveth for ever, and who only is everlastingly worthy of all blessing and praise.

39

In the course of this week was our quarterly meeting, which was held at this time at Westbury. It was a season of exercise to all who were concerned for the promotion of right order in the Church; and much counsel, reproof, and admonition, were communicated, under right influence, to stir up the negligent and refractory members to more faithfulness and attention to their several duties, and a more full submission to the manifestations of divine grace in their own minds, that they may be thereby strengthened to arise, and shake themselves from the dust of th earth, and separate themselves from those hindering and annoying things, which divert and turn them aside from their Christian duty, and those things in which their best interest consists. The meeting for worship was likewise a favoured season. Many very important truths of the gospel were clearly opened in the demonstration of the spirit; and the meeting closed under a thankful sense of the unmerited mercy; and the living among us separated to their several homes with grateful hearts.

I laid before this meeting my prospect of a religious visit as aforementioned, and received the unity and concurrence of the men's and women's meetings; and an endorsement thereof was made on my certificate. Being now left at liberty, and separated to the work whereunto I believed myself called by the Holy Spirit, and knowing my own insufficiency, and that of myself I can do nothing, all that remains for me is to cast my care wholly on him, in full faith, who hath called me; and, as I abide in the patience and in a full submission to his heavenly will, he that putteth his servants forth, will in his own right time go before them and make way for them, without which there is no way; and will make darkness light before them, and not forsake, but safely carry them through and over all the opposition and discouragements, that either men or devils may or can cast in the way, to the exceeding praise of his grace, and to the glory and exaltation of his great and excellent name, who is over all, God blessed for ever.

First day, the 27th. My mind while sitting in our meeting to-day, was led into a view of the great necessity there was of more faithfulnes and attention to the inward principle of divine truth, or inward teacher in the mind, as professed by us as a people. For want of this, many were led into divers errours and deficiencies, which in their tendency not only led to great weakness, but to the encouragement of evil doers in their evil practices; a sight and sense of which had for some time been a cause of much exercise to my mind. The subject became very impressive, insomuch that I found it necessary to spread it before the meeting in a large arousing testimony; laying before the auditory the great danger many were in for want of a living concern to work out, through the assistance of divine grace, their salvation while the day of visitation was lengthened out. For nothing short of a full submission to the operation of divine truth on their minds could fit and prepare them for the awful approaching season, when the pale-faced messenger shall arraign us before the judgment seat of Him, whom we can neither awe nor bribe, to give an account of the deeds done in the body, whether good or evil. A solemn weight spread over the meeting and many minds appeared to be deeply humbled. May the exhortation be fixed in their remembrance, as a nail in a sure place that may not be moved, is the fervent desire of my mind.

The rest of this week I was busily employed in endeavouring so to arrange my temporal matters, that when I leave home on the prospect before me, I may feel my mind at full liberty therefrom, and that no occasion may be given, through the medium of any of my temporal engagements, for the enemies of truth to gainsay or find fault, to the disadvantage or reproach of the great and dignified cause I was about to embark in. For I have been led to believe some who have gone out on this solemn embassy, for want of this care have given too much occasion for censure, and have thereby wounded the cause they have proposed to promote, and brought much exercise on the minds of the faithful.

On fifth day at our meeting, my mind was deeply bowed in commemoration of the Lord's continued mercies, and that indeed it might be said of us as it was of Israel formerly, that it was of the Lord's mercies we were not consumed; and I was made thankful in believing, that there was a small remnant who were preserved faithful to his name and cause, and who were the salt of the society, and for whose sake he would not utterly cast us off nor forsake us. Surely it is of his unmerited mercy that we are not swallowed up in the mass of the people, and numbered among the unstable multitude who have no sure and solid foundation to rest their hopes upon, but are trusting in a ceremonial religion, of man's invention; all which in the day of trial will fail them, and afford no succour to the soul.

First day, the 3d of 8th month. My mind was brought under exercise in our meeting to-day, in a view of the great want of diligent attention to the light within, or that measure of the spirit given to every one of God's rational creatures to profit withal; even those who were so far convinced as to acknowledge its excellence, yet were almost daily neglecting its reproofs, and turning aside from its teachings; by which their understandings became darkened, and they were left in a dwarfish unstable condition, without any solid ground of hope. The subject spread, and my mind was led into a large arousing testimony, setting forth the danger of such a state, and the fatal consequences that would naturally and certainly follow such delinquency if continued in. Truth prevailed, and many minds were sensibly bowed and affected by its power, and a very general solemnity spread over the meeting, to the praise of Him who is calling all his faithful and obedient children out of darkness into his marvellous light. The rest of the week spent as usual without occasion for any remark.

First day, the 10th. A peaceful quiet meeting to-day in silent waiting. The rest of the week, except attending our meeting for sufferings and preparative meeting on fifth day, was taken up in my outward business; with a steady view to my religious engagement, that with all readiness I might be prepared to embark therein when the full time arrived.

First day, the 17th. A silent meeting. This week was taken up preparatory to my journey. Attended our monthly meeting on fifth day, and feeling my mind drawn towards an opportunity with the people of colour before I left home, I mentioned it to the meeting; and with the unity of Friends, a meeting was appointed for them on the following first day at the fourth hour in the afternoon. I also gave Friends of Bethpage meeting information, that I felt my mind drawn to sit with them in their meeting the next first day, and left them at liberty to inform their neighbours thereof.

First day, the 24th. Agreeably to my prospect I attended Bethpage meeting in the forenoon. It was large, and I think, greatly favoured with the overshadowing wing of divine kindness. Truth rose into dominion, and bowed the assembly by the prevalence of its power, for which my spirit was made deeply thankful.

The meeting for the coloured people was held at the fourth hour, and I was enabled to clear my mind among them, although it was a season of hard labour. After this I felt my mind clear to set forward on my intended journey.

Fourth day, the 27th of 8th month. I left home in the afternoon in order to accomplish my contemplated visit to Friends and others, in some parts of the yearly meetings of Philadelphia and Baltimore. My son-in-law Valentine Hicks, accompanied me in the journey. Feeling my mind drawn to attend the meeting of Friends at Flushing the next day, we rode there and lodged. Notice being given in the neighbourhood of my intention to be there, the meeting was large, and the Lord graciously manifested himself to be near, and enabled me to discharge myself faithfully among them under the feeling influence of gospel love. Many hearts were contrited and truth appeared in dominion over all, for which favour I was made reverently thankful, not only on my own account and the account of those present, but especially so on account of my dear family and friends at home, who gave me up with great reluctance on account of my present bodily indisposition, being under the pressure of a heavy cold and very hard cough, which, in their apprehensions, rendered me unable to travel in so arduous a service until I might be recovered therefrom. But the time appearing to be come for my setting out, and the way appearing open, I considered it safest to cast my care wholly upon Him in faith, who, I believed, had called me to the work; and that as I continued to go forward, as he was graciously pleased to open the way and make it clear before me, all would be well, whether it terminated in life or in death.

The next day, being the sixth of the week, we had an appointed meeting in Friends' meeting-house, at the Kilns, in Newtown. The meeting there, had been discontinued for a number of years, and now there was but one member of our society left in the neighbourhood. There was, however, a considerable number of people of other persuasions collected; and the Lord graciously condescended to enable me to preach the gospel among them, and to open divers doctrines of the Christian religion, suited to their several conditions, in the demonstration of truth, for their consideration and instruction. The people were very solemn and quiet; and, I hope, the labour will not prove in vain, but be to some of them, as bread cast upon the waters, gathered after many days. We rode, after this meeting, to New-York, and rested on seventh day.

First day, the 31st. We attended Pearl-street meeting in the morning, and that at Liberty-street, in the afternoon. They were both full meetings; and, although I was still under considerable bodily indisposition, yet, through condescending goodness, I was strengthened to discharge myself faithfully in both opportunities, and felt peace in my labours of love among them; being led in each meeting to declare largely of the things concerning the kingdom of God, and to point out to the people, in a clear manner, the way to peace and salvation.

On second day afternoon, we proceeded on our journey to Newark, a town in New Jersey, where we attended a meeting at the fourth hour, previous notice having been given in the town, of our coming. I had had several meetings there before; but this was larger than usual for the place. There is no member of our society residing in the town; the inhabitants being principally of the Presbyterian order. All was quiet, and a general solemnity spread over the meeting; and truth and its testimony were raised into dominion. Surely, it is the Lord's doing, and my spirit was made gratefully thankful for the unmerited favour.

The next day we attended a meeting appointed for us in Elizabethtown. Here, likewise, there is no member of our society.

The meeting was small, yet through condescending goodness it proved, I trust, a comfortable instructive season to some present; and I parted with them in peace of mind, the sure reward of faithfulness.

From this place, we rode home with our kind friend Henry Shotwell, of Rahway, who met us here. The next day we attended Friend's meeting at Plainfield. Notice having been given that we intended to be there, the meeting was large, in which the Lord's power was manifested, and his arm made bare for our help; and through which, way was made and utterance given, to preach the glad tidings of life and salvation to the people, in the demonstration of the spirit. Many hearts were broken and contrited by the prevalence of its power. May the glory and the praise be all ascribed to our gracious Helper, for such continued mercy; for he only is worthy thereof, as nothing is due to the creature, but blushing and confusion of face.

After this favoured meeting, we rode back, towards evening, to Rahway. The next day, being the fifth of the week, we attended Friends' meeting there. The meeting was much enlarged by many of the neighbouring inhabitants coming in, who were not members. Many gospel truths were opened to their consideration, and its power ran as oil over the assembly, silencing all opposition, and a perfect calm was witnessed to spread over all. I have not often beheld such a perfect quiet; such seasons are truly encouraging, and worthy of thanksgiving and praise to the blessed Author of such unmerited favours.

On sixth day morning, we took leave of our kind friends at Rahway, and rode to Mendham, alias, Randolph. The next day we had an appointed meeting there, at the tenth hour, which proved a solemn, instructive season. I left them with peace of mind, and proceeded that afternoon to Hardwick. The following day being the first of the week, we attended Friends' meeting there. It was large for the place, as notice had been given that we expected to be there. And, through heavenly help, the gospel was preached in the demonstration of the spirit; and, by the influence of its power, a general solemnity was spread over the assembly, and many hearts were broken and contrited.

On second day we proceeded to Stroudsburgh, in Pennsylvania, where we arrived about three o'clock in the afternoon. Here we had a meeting, by appointment, the next day, at the third hour. It was well attended by the Friends of that place, and many of the neighbouring inhabitants; and was a very solid, instructive season. Surely, such unmerited favours greatly enhance our obligations to our all-gracious Benefactor, and tend to inspire the minds of his humble dependant children with gratitude and thanksgiving.

From this place we proceeded to Richland, and attended Friends' meeting on fifth day. It was much enlarged by many who were not members coming in. From thence we went to Plumbstead, where, by previous appointment, we had a meeting the next day. Both these meetings were seasons of favour. Surely, it is cause of deep humiliation, when we consider the many sorrowful deviations which are obvious among us from the simplicity and purity of our holy profession, and the great want of faithfulness in the support of those noble testimonies given us to bear, for the Prince of peace : yet, nevertheless, in the midst of all our backslidings, the condescending goodness of our heavenly Father is such, as to break the bread and distil the water of life, often, on our gathered assemblies; satisfying the hungry and thirsty soul, and causing his heavenly rain to descend on the thoughtless and worldly-minded professors, whose hearts are like the dry and barren ground, in order that they may be softened and rendered fit for the seed of his heavenly kingdom to take root in and grow, to the praise of his grace, and the glory of his great and excellent name.

From Plumbstead we proceeded to Buckingham, and rested on seventh day, as I was still unwell with a cough, although much better than when I left home. On first day we attended Friends' meeting here, which was large, and favoured with the over-shadowings of the heavenly Father's regard, which caused the faithful to rejoice. On second day we rested with our ancient and worthy friend, Oliver Paxton, who was under deep bodily affliction, and appeared drawing fast towards his close. He was lively in spirit, and cheerfully and patiently resigned to his heavenly

Master's will. It was comfortable and instructive to be in his company.

On third day we were at Solebury meeting, of which our aforesaid friend was a member ; and, although in much weakness and affliction of body, he accompanied us thereto, and a blessed meeting we had. After this, I parted with him in near unity of spirit, which was a final parting to us, as to the body: for he lived but a short time after. He was an elder and judge in Israel ; and his memory will be precious to all the living, who were acquainted with him, and knew his worth.

The three following days we attended meetings at Wright's Town, Makefield, and Newtown. These were all large, favoured meetings, in which the power of truth was exalted over all opposition.

On seventh day we rested, and wrote to our families.

On first day, the 21st of 9th month, we attended Horsham meeting, which was very large. Strength was afforded me to communicate to the people, and open many gospel truths, to the relief of my own mind, and, I trust, to the general satisfaction, comfort and instruction of the assembly, which was composed of various denominations of professed Christians, besides Friends.

Second and third days. We attended meetings at Upper Dublin and North Wales. In both of these meetings the heavenly Father's power and presence were felt to preside, in an eminent degree, breaking down and reducing by its blessed influence all opposing and contrary spirits, and covering the assemblies with a precious solemnity, especially the latter, in which truth reigned triumphantly over all.

On fourth day we had an appointed meeting in a village called Norristown. It was held in their court-house, there being only a few scattered members of our society living in the place. The meeting was pretty large, principally of people of other professions; among whom was the chief judge, and several lawyers and priests. All were quiet, and through the condescending goodness of the Shepherd of Israel, it was, I trust and believe, to most present, a very instructive and precious season.

Fifth and sixth days. We were at Friends' meetings as they came in course, at Plymouth and Providence. Notice having been given of our coming, they were much enlarged by the attendance of the neighbours who were not members. These were precious opportunities, in which help was afforded to preach the gospel of life and salvation to the people, accompanied with a power which broke down and subjected all to its blessed influence ; for which unmerited favour, the hearts of the faithful were made to rejoice, and in deep humiliation, to return thanksgiving and praise to the benevolent and gracious Author of all our blessings.

On seventh day we rested at Charlestown. On first day attended the meeting at that place, which was large, many more attending than the house could contain. The three following days we attended meetings at the Valley, Pikeland, and Nantmill. These were all precious meetings, in which the Lord's presence and power were manifested for our help.

On fifth day we proceeded to Columbia, a town situated on the east side of the river Susquehannah. We had an appointed meeting there the next day, in which truth prevailed ; nevertheless, a hireling priest who attended the meeting, afterwards made some objection to the doctrine delivered, as it counteracted his traditional belief concerning the atonement, the carnal ordinances of water baptism, and the outward bread and wine, and preaching for hire, and the scriptures being the only rule of faith and practice ; the fallacy and inutility of all which had been laid open and exposed. This roused his opposition ; and indeed, it is not to be wondered at, as it goes to overthrow all their craft, by which they have their wealth.

We proceeded from thence to Little York, and rested on seventh day. On first day, attended Friends' meeting there. It was a pretty large, favoured meeting, but not feeling my mind fully clear, I proposed another meeting in the evening ; and, notice being given accordingly, it was very large, more than the house could contain. It was a blessed meeting, in which the Lord's presence and power were manifested, and truth raised into dominion over all.

The four following days, we had meetings at Newbury, Warrington, Huntington and Monallin. In these opportunities my mind was much engaged to turn the attention of the people from man, and from all dependance on any thing without them, to the inward principle of divine light and truth, the great gospel minister; which, as it is heeded and obeyed, leadeth into all truth, and out of all errour; and without whose teaching, the true and saving knowledge of God and Christ, which only brings eternal life to the soul, can never be obtained, although we may be favoured to sit under the most powerful gospel ministry, through the instrumentality of man, however divinely qualified to that end, from youth to old age. For all that the best outward instrumental help, either from reading the scriptures, or hearing the gospel preached in the clear demonstration of the spirit, can do for any man, is only to point to, and lead the minds of the children of men home to this divine inward principle, manifested in their own hearts and minds.

These were all favoured, instructive seasons, worthy of grateful remembrance.

From Monallin we rode to Baltimore, in order to attend the yearly meeting at that place, where we arrived on sixth day evening, the 10th of 10th month. The yearly meeting of Ministers and Elders opened the next day at the tenth hour, and the yearly meeting for discipline at the tenth hour, on the following second day; and continued by adjournments until the next sixth day at evening, when the meeting closed under an evident sense of divine favour, and which had been graciously extended through the several sittings of the meeting. I had much general and particular service in the course of the meetings, both in those for worship, and those for discipline; tending to gather Friends' minds, to an inward, faithful exercise for the support and promotion of those noble testimonies, that we, as a people, are called to bear for the Prince of Peace; and for the exaltation of truth and righteousness in the earth. The Lord our gracious helper, by his presence and power, manifested himself to be near, setting home the doctrines delivered to his witness in the hearts of most present; whereby Friends appeared generally to be united in spirit, and comforted together under a renewed sense of the Lord's goodness; and we parted from each other with thankful hearts.

The meeting being ended, we left the city the next morning, in order to take a few meetings which lay westerly, or south-westerly from this place. We were out from the city about two weeks, and attended the following meetings, viz: Pipe Creek, Bush Creek, Fairfax, Goose Creek, South Fork, Alexandria, Washington, Sandy Spring, Indian Spring, and Elk-Ridge. All favoured meetings, in which the Lord's power and presence were manifested for our help, enabling to preach the gospel in the authority of truth, to the comfort and instruction of the honest seekers, and rejoicing the hearts of the faithful, and administering reproof and caution to the disobedient and ungodly, and to such as are living at ease without God in the world. I felt sweet peace in my labours of love among them.

After the latter meeting, we returned again to Baltimore on sixth day afternoon, the 31st of 10th month. Here we continued until the 11th of 11th month, not only attending Friends' usual meetings as they came in course in the city, but likewise their monthly meetings, and quarterly meeting, which were held during the time. In all of these I was led into much exercise and religious labour, both in the ministry and in the discipline and order of the Church. We had, likewise, during our stay in the city, three very large, satisfactory evening meetings with the citizens at large. Two were for the white people, and one for the people of colour. I was led forth among them, and strengthened largely to declare of the things concerning the kingdom of God, and to open to their consideration divers important doctrines of the gospel, in the authority and demonstration of truth, apparently to their general satisfaction, and to the comfort and edification of my friends, and the solid peace of my own mind. I then took leave of them, under the precious uniting influence of the heavenly Father's love, and the covering of deep thankfulness and gratitude for the unmerited favour.

On third day, the 11th of the month, we left the city and proceeded to a place called the Bush, where there is a small meeting of Friends. The three following days we attended meetings at that place, at Deer Creek, and East Nottingham, all favoured seasons. After the latter meeting on seventh day, we proceeded to Wilmington, and attended Friends' meetings there the next day, both forenoon and afternoon, in which truth favoured with ability to preach the gospel in the demonstration of the spirit, suited, I trust, to the states of many, or most, of the people which composed those large assemblies, and I left them with peace of mind.

On second day I rode to London Grove, accompanied by my kind friend William Poole of Brandywine, my companion being disposed to tarry a day longer at Wilmington. On third day the quarterly meeting opened there with a meeting of Ministers and Elders; in which I was led to open to Friends of that meeting, the great obligations and accountability which attached to those who consented to take seats in such meetings. For it placed us in the front of society, and consequently we were looked to as the leaders of the people; and therefore if we should fall short in faithfully holding up those precious testimonies we are called to bear for the Prince of Peace, and in leading forward the flock by advancing the reformation as truth opens the way, we shall become stumbling blocks in the way of the honest travellers, and thereby shut up their way to improvement, by which they may be discouraged and fall back and be lost; in consequence whereof it is to be feared, their blood might be required at the hands of such unfaithful and dilatory shepherds. It was an instructive searching opportunity, in which truth prevailed in an humbling degree.

The next day was the meeting for discipline. It was also a very favoured searching season, in which many of the hidden things of Esau or the first nature were brought to light and exposed, and the careless worldly-minded professors reproved, and the honest-hearted comforted and encouraged.

After this, feeling a draft of love to those not in membership with us, I proposed an opportunity for them the next day; and Friends uniting therewith, a meeting was accordingly appointed. It was a large gathering and mercifully owned by the Head of the Church, by the gracious manifestation of his divine presence;

under the blessed influence of which, the gospel was preached in the demonstration of the spirit, and I parted with them under a thankful sense of the Lord's mercy, accompanied with a peaceful mind, and rode that afternoon to Concord.

On sixth day we rode to Darby and lodged with our kind friend Edward Garrigues, who accompanied us the next morning to Philadelphia. Here we continued about a week, attending Friends' meetings in the city as they came in course. As information of our coming had spread in the town the meetings were greatly thronged, and at some places many more than the houses could contain; people of varied professions, and some of almost every description, high and low, appeared eager to attend. It seemed a renewed visitation to the people in general, Friends and others; and not only at meetings but in Friends' families where we visited, large numbers, especially of the younger classes, would soon collect; so that those opportunities were made seasons of instruction and edification. For the Lord, I believe, beheld them with a gracious eye, and opened my heart and mouth in converse and communication, to the comfort and satisfaction of their inquiring minds, and enabled me in each meeting to communicate in the line of the gospel in large impressive testimonies, affording instruction, comfort and edification to the assemblies in general; and I felt a great power of love to flow freely towards them, which caused my heart to rejoice; and I was made glad in believing that it was the Lord's doing. and it was marvellous in mine eyes.

After I had got through Friends' meetings, I felt my mind drawn to have a public opportunity for those not of our society; and Friends uniting therewith, it was concluded to be held on the evening of sixth day. Friends apprehending that the numbers who would be desirous of attending would be very great, it was appointed at Mulberry-street, their largest house. As the notice was given at the monthly meeting at that house, Friends likewise appointed a large committee of men and women to have the oversight of its gathering, and to keep Friends out until their neighbours should first have seats: but the number that collected of other people was so great, that it was supposed as many went away after the house was filled, and the yard around the house as far as they could hear, as there was in the house. Every avenue in the house was filled with people, standing as close as they could crowd together. Such a collection of people I never saw together before on any such occasion. It was with great difficulty that I got into the meeting, and when I had taken my seat, in viewing the crowded state of the multitude, I was ready to fear that the pressure of the people upon one another would destroy the solemnity of the meeting; but as I centered down to the gift, life and strength sprang up, and faith was increased; and the Lord made bare his arm for our help, and soon opened my mouth among them, which brought a precious calm over the assembly. Indeed I could scarcely have thought it possible had I not seen it, that such a large promiscuous multitude, made up almost of every description of people, should in a few moments be brought into such a perfect state of quiet and remain so for hours, until the meeting closed; especially as in the midst of the meeting while I was communicating, some ill advised persons, in order to disturb the meeting, made a great cry of fire, rattling their engines along the street near the house, but it had no tendency to break the solemnity of the meeting. My heart and all that was alive within me, was bowed in humble thankfulness to the Lord our gracious helper, for such a marvellous and unmerited favour. As my whole man was filled with a flow of heavenly love to the multitude, it was likewise very comfortable to feel a mutual return from them, for all that could come near me manifested it, both by conduct and converse; such a time I never witnessed before: surely it was the Lord's doing, and to him belongs all the praise and glory of his own work, nothing due to the creature but blushing and confusion of face. So let it be. Amen, saith my spirit.

After having got thus favourably through my service in the city, the next morning I took an affectionate farewell of my friends there, in much unity of spirit, and passed over the Delaware to Newtown, in Jersey; where by previous appointment I had a meeting at the eleventh hour. A considerable number of Friends accompanied me thither from the city. Here we had another precious instructive meeting. The next day being the first of the week, we attended Friends' meeting at Woodbury; and notice being spread of our intention of being there it was unusually large; and through the condescending goodness of Him who opens and none can shut, my heart and mouth were opened in a large effective testimony, in which was opened to the people divers of the most essential doctrines of Christianity, I trust, to the general instruction and edification of those present, and to the comfort and peace of my own mind.

The seven following days we attended meetings at Mulica Hill, Upper Greenwich, Penn's Neck, Piles Grove, Salem, Alloway's Creek, and Lower Greenwich. These were all large favoured meetings, particularly the one at Salem; at which place the county court was then sitting, which was adjourned by the judge in order to give the people generally an opportunity to attend the meeting, which they did; the judge and lawyers with the rest of the court also attended. The gospel was preached to them and the doctrines of Christianity largely opened, apparently to the satisfaction of all; and truth was raised into dominion over all that was contrary to its blessed influence.

From the latter place we proceeded on second day, the 8th of 12th month, to Morris River, alias Port Elizabeth, where we had a very instructive edifying meeting the next day. The day following we rode to Little Eggharbour; and the next day being the fifth of the week, we attended Friends' monthly meeting there. The meeting for worship was favoured, and truth prevailed by way of testimony; and many gospel truths were opened to the consideration of the people, whereby many hearts were humbled and contrited.

The meeting for discipline was very weakly conducted. The order of truth being at a low ebb with Friends of this place, and but little hope of improvement, unless the younger classes in society come forward in more faithfulness than their elder brethren have done. For most of the few that are left appeared to be settling on their lees, without any thought or prospect of advancing the noble testimonies we are called to bear.

Our next meeting was at Barnegat: the day being rainy it

was small, yet a precious favoured season. The next day being the seventh of the week we rode to Squan, and the two following days attended the meeting at that place and at Squancum; but the weather being still rainy, these were also small meetings: but the power of truth being present for our help, rendered the opportunities instructive and edifying. After the latter meeting we proceeded to Shrewsbury, and on third day, the 16th of 12th month, we had an appointed meeting there which was large and satisfactory. Many gospel truths were fully and clearly opened to the apparent satisfaction, and, I trust, to the instruction and edification of the assembly in general. It was a very solemn meeting, in which truth was raised into dominion, humbling and contriting many hearts; and which brought my religious labours in this journey to a peaceful close.

After this, the three following days I passed directly home, and found my dear wife, children, and grand-children in usual health, to our mutual rejoicing. For this favour, together with the continued evidence of the divine favour which had accompanied me in this journey, strengthening and enabling me from day to day, faithfully to perform the work and service the Lord had appointed me, my mind was impressed with deep thankfulness and gratitude for the unmerited mercy.

Praise the Lord, O my soul! and forget not any of his benefits, for he hath dealt bountifully with thee, and set thee above all thine enemies, to the exaltation of his own glorious name and power; and who is God over all, blessed for ever.

CHAPTER XIV.

Engagements at and near home, and within the limits of Westbury quarterly meeting—Visit to some parts of the yearly meeting of New-York, 1818.

FIRST day, the 21st of 12th month, 1817. I again met with my friends at home, in our own meeting, and was glad to see them; having been absent nearly four months, in which time I travelled about eleven hundred miles, and attended eighty-five meetings for worship, and eleven for discipline. And now, at home, I find no time to be idle; for in this first meeting, my mind was brought under exercise, and I had to tell my friends, that if we would be Christians, we must be united to Christ, and learn by his example to do good for evil; as it is no certain mark of a real Christian, to be in the practice of mutual returns of good offices to one another. For sinners give and lend to sinners, to receive as much again. I found afterwards that there was just occasion for my exercise, as some of my neighbours, members of society, had been disputing and differing about trivial matters of property. Alas for such! what peace can they have on earth, and much less can they hope for any in heaven, when done with time. For such dispositions cannot possibly be happy in the presence of a just, holy, and merciful Being, who is love ineffable.

I sat our meeting on fifth day in silence, and nothing unusual occurred the rest of the week.

First day, the 28th. I was led, while sitting in our meeting to-day, into a view of the great want generally manifested by the people, of living in the fear of the Lord, and of seeking to be initiated into his kingdom of peace and love; as nothing short of it can administer to any the joys of salvation, or produce a real redemption from the power of evil. The subject spread on my mind, and opened to a pretty full communication, in the line of close caution and warning to the indolent and unconcerned, respecting the necessary preparation for our final change. A solemn weight spread over the assembly, and I have a hope the labour will not be all lost, but sink deep and remain on some minds.

In the course of this week my case seemed to resemble Mordecai's of old; after riding the king's horse, he had to retire to the king's gate, and there wait for fresh direction. I also felt my mind brought into a waiting quiet state, in poverty of spirit. Attended our fifth day meeting mostly in silence, except just before the close I had to remark to Friends the great advantage that accrued to us by being embodied together in religious society, under the influence of truth, as our duties and religious obligations became more binding upon us, especially the diligent attendance of meetings for worship, which gave us frequent opportunity of inquiring into our own states, and how far we stood accepted in the divine sight, and were at peace with Him and with all men; for this is a very requisite care which ought not to be neglected, but always be first in our minds.

First day, the 4th of 1st month, 1818. Having felt my mind for several days drawn to sit with my friends at Martinicock, I accordingly went on this day, accompanied by my wife and daughter Elizabeth. Although the meeting was not altogether so large as at some other times on this day of the week, the weather being cold, yet the opportunity, through the manifestation of divine regard, by which I was enabled to preach the gospel in the demonstration of truth, was rendered an instructive edifying season, and we were comforted together under a renewed sense of the Lord's goodness.

Second day. I attended the funeral of a neighbour. It was a promiscuous gathering of different societies of professed Christians. I was largely led forth among them to declare of the things concerning the kingdom of God, and to open to the people in a clear and impressive manner, the way and means by which we may come to have an inheritance therein, and that nothing short of our coming into a passive state without a will of our own, as a little child, agreeably to the doctrine of our Lord, will ever qualify us for that blessed inheritance, where nothing that worketh an abomination or maketh a lie can ever enter. It was a season of favour, in which truth had the victory, and I felt peace in my labour of love among them.

On third day I went to New-York, accompanied by my son-in-law Valentine Hicks, in order to attend the monthly meeting of Friends there, which came the next day. I attended it accordingly. It was a pretty full meeting, in which I was led in a close, searching line in my testimony, which agitated some of the worshippers in the outer court, and made them fretful. Alas for such professors! what will they do in the end, when the winds blow and the rains descend? Surely their sandy foundation will fail them; then will they be made to call to the rocks and mountains of their own exalted self-righteousness, to cover them from the prevailing indignation which they have brought upon themselves, by their own neglect of a right improvement of the talent with which they had been entrusted, and which they had buried in an earthly mind; but their cries will be in vain, as the hypocrite's hope will perish.

Fifth day. I attended Friends' meeting held in the middle of the week at Flushing, at which there was a marriage, which caused it to be much enlarged, by many of the neighbouring inhabitants coming in who do not usually attend. It was a favoured season, in which I was led to communicate divers important doctrines of the Christian religion, and to open the true ground of the marriage covenant, whereby male and female may be rightly joined together, so as to become true helpers and blessings to each other. After this, I returned home that evening with the blessing of peace, the sure reward of faithfulness, and retired willingly to the waiting gate of inward trust, and poverty of spirit.

First day, the 11th. My mind was led into a view of the necessity of doing all our works to please God, and not to please ourselves, or one another; and the only way to please our neighbours to edification, was to do all to please the Lord, who hath promised that if our ways please him he will make our enemies to be at peace with us. The subject spread and led to communication, in which the people were invited to acquaint themselves with God, and be at peace with him by doing his will, and not our own, whereby good would come unto us; hence we should please one another to our mutual edification and comfort.

On fifth day our monthly meeting was held. It was a season of exercise, occasioned by a case of difficulty being improperly introduced into the meeting.

I saw clearly the meeting could not get along with it in its present form, as it had taken ground which was not tenable. It was therefore agreed to dismiss the subject for the present, and let it be taken up anew, unless on a further investigation by the overseers, it should be settled.

How necessary it is for those who take an active part in the discipline of the Church, to wait for a right qualification, and not to put a hand to the work until they are rightly called and furnished, with that wisdom which is profitable to direct; for otherwise, instead of advancing the cause of righteousness, they may retard its progress, and do harm to themselves, like Uzza of old, when he put forth an unsanctified hand to steady the ark.

I opened in this meeting to my friends, a prospect I had of paying a religious visit to some of the neighbouring inhabitants not in membership with us, within the borders of our quarterly meeting; with which the meeting united, and left me at liberty to pursue the prospect as way might open for it.

The rest of this week was spent in the care of my necessary temporal concerns, and the week ended with peace of mind and a thankful heart, for the continued blessings of a gracious Providence.

First day, the 18th. Our meeting to-day was favoured, and the power of truth exalted, and the gospel preached in its own authority, and a precious solemnity spread over the meeting, which ended in thanksgiving for the mercy, and solemn supplication for the continuance of divine regard.

In the course of this week our quarterly meeting was held at Westbury. It was a favoured season, particularly the last day or closing meeting for public worship, in which the Lord's presence and power were manifested in an eminent degree, and truth was exalted and a precious solemnity spread over the assembly, convicting, contriting, and comforting many hearts; to the praise of Him who is calling us out of darkness into his marvellous light.

First day, the 25th. A silent meeting on my part to-day. How comfortable it is to sit silently under the shadow of our own vine and our own fig-tree, where none can make afraid.

Second day. I attended the funeral of my eldest and last surviving brother. I am now the last and only survivor of six brethren, and am myself arrived nearly to the age of three score and ten ; therefore cannot expect many more days, as I continually feel time making its ravages on the animal system, and which, as a faithful herald, exclaims repeatedly to the inward ear, "prepare to die." There was a large promiscuous collection of people of different societies attended the funeral. I was largely led forth among them to declare the way of life and salvation, and to open many very important doctrines of the Christian religion. The assembly were generally very quiet and attentive, and, I believe, to many, it was a season of solid instruction and edification. I left them with peace of mind and a thankful heart.

I attended our fifth day meeting as usual, and mostly in silence. On sixth day I attended the funeral of a person not in membership. It was principally made up of the poorer kind of people, who made little or no profession of religion, except a few Friends and some of the Methodist society. I was deeply baptized into a feeling of their weak state, in which I was led to communicate according to their capacity to receive ; which brought a comfortable solemnity over the assembly to their general satisfaction, and I felt peace in my labour of love among them.

First day, the 1st of 2d month. As I sat musing in silence in our meeting, my mind was led into a view of the great mischief and harm which result to mankind, by their giving way to harbour and indulge vain and evil thoughts. The subject spread and led to communication, in which I had to show to the assembly that our redemption and salvation principally depended on a right government of our thoughts, and that if men and women were as fearful of evil thinking as they are of evil doing, and as desirous of avoiding one as the other, they would soon find themselves empowered as fully to avoid evil thinking as to avoid evil doing; and this would be a suppression of sin in its first rise: and there is no other way for any man or woman to become righteous and holy in the sight of God, who as certainly at all times sees our evil thoughts, and more so than man can see our evil actions: yet nevertheless poor blind forgetful man will please and entertain himself with abundance of evil thoughts in the open view of his Maker, while at the same time he would dread to expose them by overt acts, in the view of men. This shows how much more predominant the fear of man is with the most of mankind, than the fear of God their Creator. I hope the opportunity was profitable and instructive to some present.

Second day, the 9th. I rode to New-York in order to attend the meeting for sufferings which came the next day, and which I attended accordingly. After this I spent several days in the city and neighbourhood, in prosecuting the concern I opened before our last monthly meeting. My kinsman Isaac Hicks accompanied me.

I attended Pearl-street meeting as it came in course on fourth day, and had an appointed meeting at the same place in the evening, for the inhabitants of the town at large. It was a very full meeting, many more collected than the house could contain. The next day I attended Friends' meeting at Manhattanville, and in the evening had a public meeting in the city, at Friends' meeting-house in Liberty-street. These were all full favoured meetings, in which truth reigned and subjected, at least for the present, all contrary spirits, which was cause of humble thankfulness to my mind.

We left the city on sixth day and had an appointed meeting at Brooklyn in the evening. On seventh day we had two meetings in Newtown, the first at Friends' meeting-house at the Kilns, and the latter at the town in the evening. These three last meetings were principally made up of people of other societies, who behaved very commendably and appeared well affected with the meetings; and truth's testimonies were largely and satisfactorily opened in each meeting, comforting and contriting many hearts, and to the solid peace of my own mind.

On first day, the 15th, I attended Friends' meeting at Flushing, and some notice having been spread of my coming, it was large ; and was added to by a number from Newtown, of other societies who had attended the two meetings held there the day before. This was also an open instructive meeting, in which divers doctrines of the gospel were communicated in the life, to the edification of the people. The next day I returned home and found my family well, which, with the peace of mind that accompanied, produced thankfulness of heart to the blessed Author of all our mercies and blessings.

Fifth day. I attended our monthly meeting. It was rather a dull exercising season, in which I was led into some painful labour.

On sixth day, I proceeded again on the visit to some of the neighbouring inhabitants. Had an appointed meeting in the evening at Hempstead Harbour, and the next evening at the lower part of Cowneck. Both were full meetings. In the former I was largely opened by way of testimony, and many important doctrines of the gospel were communicated for the instruction and edification of the people, and I left them with peace of mind. In the latter I was mostly silent. On first day I attended Friends' meeting at Cowneck, which was well attended ; many of the neighbouring inhabitants coming in that were not members, who behaved soberly. It was a favoured satisfactory season, in which truth reigned.

In the evening I had a pretty large instructive meeting in the village of Herricks. It was a solemn time, in which many truths of the gospel were clearly opened, apparently to the satisfaction and edification of the assembly in general, and I returned home next morning with peace of mind.

On fourth day I attended Bethpage meeting, at which there was a marriage, which occasioned the meeting to be very large. I think it was much the largest I had ever seen in that place. There was a large number of young people, and although many of them appeared raw and undisciplined, yet they generally behaved orderly during the meeting, and I had a pretty open time among them. I was led to set forth the nature and dignity of the marriage covenant when rightly entered into, and the sad reverse, when rashly and unadvisedly undertaken ; and especially so when unequally yoked together, and of different persuasions as to religion : for being disunited in the main point, it most certainly must tend to disturb their quiet and imbitter their enjoyments. And the offspring of such connexions are greatly to be pitied; attached by nature to both parents, how confused must be their ideas with regard to which they shall follow ; and as it often happens, the boys going with their father, and the daughters with their mother ; hence, children which ought to be bound together in the strongest ties of natural affection and consanguinity, are in early life divided in principle and in conduct, by which they become alienated from each other. To avoid which the youth were earnestly and affectionately invited and admonished to put in practice the exhortation of Jesus Christ to his immediate followers, and the people which resorted to hear him, viz : To seek first the kingdom of God and his righteousness, in a full belief that as we comply therewith, all other things needful and consolatory will be added.

I attended our own meeting the next day in silence, and feeling a stop in my mind as to proceeding further at present in the visit before me, I turned my attention to my family concerns, not being willing to spend any of my precious time in idleness.

First day. Sat our meeting in silence. It is a precious thing and very consoling, to all Zion's exercised travellers in the path of duty, to be instructed how and when to speak, and when to keep silence.

Fifth day. A silent meeting. Spent the rest of the week in attention to my family concerns.

First day, the 8th of 3d month. A favoured open time in our meeting to-day, in which the gospel was preached in its own authority, and in which the excellency and reality of the divine principle of grace and truth was opened and explained ; showing it to be the same breath of life which was breathed into man on the day of his creation, and which constituted the divine image in man, and is the Lamb or innocent life of God, and which

42

innocent life was slain in our first parents by their first transgression. Hence it is called the Lamb slain from the foundation of the world, agreeably to the scriptures; but no otherwise slain than by man's rejecting it, and turning away from it, into the serpentine wisdom; by which man became dead to this divine life, and that dead to him. Hence the denunciation was fulfilled on man, in the day thou eatest thereof, that is, in the day thou turnest away from this divine life, and presumest to know good and evil for thyself, thou shalt, or wilt, surely die; which was accordingly fulfilled on our first parents in the day of their transgression, and consequently on all their offspring who have followed their example. Agreeably to the apostle Paul's doctrine, it then follows, that as in Adam all die, that is, as in our transgressing like Adam, we take upon us Adam's nature in the fall, which nature is a state of death; so on the contrary, as we turn inward to the divine light and law, and repent of our transgressions, and become sincerely obedient thereunto, by denying ourselves and taking up our cross daily, we then come into the obedience of Christ; not doing our own will, but the will of our heavenly Father. We then put on Christ and become partakers of his divine nature, and thereby come to witness in our own experience, not only that in Adam, that is, in Adam's nature in the fall, which we have taken upon us by our own transgression, and not by Adam's, we die or witness a state of death to the divine nature: so likewise in our coming into the obedience of Christ, we take upon us his divine nature; and are thereby made alive and come to witness the Lamb which was slain in us, while we remained in Adam's nature, to rise from the dead and become Christ in us the hope of glory, or the Lamb of God which taketh away the sin of the world. Therefore all the varied names given in scripture to this divine light and life, such as Emmanuel, Jesus, sent of God, great Prophet, Christ our Lord, Grace, Unction, Anointed, &c. mean one and the same thing; and are nothing less nor more, than the spirit and power of God in the soul of man, as his Creator, Preserver, Condemner, Redeemer, Saviour, Sanctifier and Justifier.

Spent the rest of the week at and about home. Attended our preparative meeting on fifth day. The meeting for worship I sat mostly in silence.

First day, the 15th. In the course of our meeting I felt constrained to communicate some plain truths in doctrine and in caution, to the unguarded and refractory; but which seemed too much to rebound, for want of a disposition in such to receive the word preached, as they are apt to kick against the truth when it is plainly told them ; this causes hard labour to the messengers, who, although they feel the woe and are constrained to labour, yet find little satisfaction therein, except in the consciousness of having faithfully done their duty to their careless and deficient brethren and fellow creatures.

In the afternoon I proceeded in the concern before expressed, in visiting some of the neighbouring inhabitants. Had an appointed meeting at Jerusalem in the evening, and on second day, a meeting about four miles westerly from thence. On third day I had one further on, in a southwesterly direction, among a people in moderate circumstances as to this world, but whose minds seemed generally open to receive the doctrines of truth. I also had a meeting in the evening of this day in the town of Hempstead. These were all large favoured meetings, especially the last, which was unusually so, and in which the truths of the gospel were largely communicated, apparently to the satisfaction and edification of the assembly, and to the peace of my own mind. We returned home the next day, attending Westbury monthly meeting in our way.

Fifth day. Attended our monthly meeting. In the meeting for worship I was led to open to Friends the many precious advantages and privileges resulting from a firm faith and sincere trust in the Almighty Jehovah. For thereby we come to witness all those great and precious promises fulfilled which the scriptures mention, and know in our own experience that they who trust in the Lord are never confounded.

The rest of the week I was busily employed in a variety of temporal concerns, as I find no time to be idle, either in body or mind, for nothing affords so much true peace as a con-

sciousness of the right improvement and employment of precious
time.

First day, the 22d. By previous appointment I attended a
meeting at the house of our friend James Rushmore, at the Half-
way Hollow Hills, at the eleventh hour, and in the evening at a
place called Babylon, on the south side of the Island. These meetings, by the extreme inclemency of the weather, were small, especially the first, where it was like the two or three as to number, yet
I found a good degree of satisfaction in faithfully attending to the
appointment, although I had to ride a dozen miles or more
through the storm, which was so extreme as to prevent nearly
all the neighbours from attending the meeting, and in our passing from one meeting to the other, the wind blew with such
violence, that our carriage seemed several times near blowing
over ; but we got along safe, and had a comfortable meeting at
the latter place in the evening. After this I rode to my son-in-
law Joshua Willits', at Islip, and lodged. I spent most of the
next day at his house, and on third day at the eleventh hour had
a pretty large favoured meeting at the house of our friend Thomas
Whitson, at Oysterbay South. After this I returned home.

In our fifth day meeting I was made an example of silence.

First day, the 29th. In our meeting to-day I was led into an
enlightened view of the excellency of faith, and its blessed effects
on the minds of those who come to witness its lively operation.

The subject opened to communication in a large affecting testimony, recapitulating its wonder-working power in the holy
ancients, and showing that its efficacy was the same now as in
former days, to those who become rightly initiated into it through
faithful obedience to divine requiring, as nothing else will establish
us in that living faith which works by love, and gives victory over
the world.

Fifth day. Attended Friends' meeting at Martinicock, in
which I was an example of silence. At the second hour in the
afternoon, I attended the funeral of Charles Thorne, a person
inclining to Friends, in the neighbourhood of Moscheto Cove.
There was a large collection of the neighbours, among whom I
was led to communicate and open divers essential doctrines of

the gospel, and to set forth the design and end of the types and shadows of the law dispensation given to Israel, and to Israel only ; and to show that they were finished and abolished by the introduction of the gospel state, or the diffusion of the spirit of truth, or Holy Ghost, in the minds of the believers, by which only we can come to have a living faith made perfect by good works, because faith without works is dead.

First day, the 5th of 4th month. A silent meeting to-day. This week busily employed in my temporal concerns, even so as to occasion wearisomeness at times. What a comfortable state would even this world afford, if men and women were all honest enough to do their right portion of labour, for want of which thousands in every country are inventing pitiful and unrighteous schemes to obtain a livelihood from the labours of others. These, let them be high or low, learned or unlearned, rich or poor, make up that class of mankind, who grievously oppress and grind the faces of the poor.

First day, the 12th. I had a precious open time in our meeting to-day, in which I was led largely to open many truths of the gospel, in a clear instructive manner, which brought a precious solemnity over the meeting, and which closed under the sensible covering of divine favour.

Fifth day. Attended our monthly meeting. It was the time for preparing answers to the queries to go up to the yearly meeting, and was, I believe, a season of profitable exercise.

First day, the 19th. I had good service in our meeting to-day, and through the overshadowing wing of divine kindness, it proved a precious opportunity. In the course of this week I attended our quarterly meeting, held at this time in New-York. It was a favoured season in the several sittings of it, affording encouragement to the honest-hearted, to persevere on in their heavenly way without turning aside to the right hand or the left, through fear, favour or affection. The labour in the line of com munication fell mostly to my lot.

First day, the 26th. I was made an example of silence through our meeting to-day. Nothing of particular notice occurred in the course of this week.

First day, the 3d of 5th month. I attended the funeral of our ancient worthy friend Jacob Underhill, of Cedar Swamp. There was a very large collection of Friends and neighbours assembled on the occasion, he being very generally beloved and esteemed by his acquaintance and Friends. A very solemn meeting was held at the meeting-house at Martinicock, on the occasion, in which I was largely led forth in ministry and doctrine, so that many hearts were contrited, to the general satisfaction and edification of the assembly, and to the peace of my own mind.

In the afternoon I had an appointed meeting at the house of Amos Cheshire, about four miles easterly from our village. Through divine favour it was made an instructive, profitable season, in which truth was exalted over all opposition.

Fifth day. I attended the funeral of my kinswoman the widow Sarah Albertson. A solemn meeting was held on the occasion, at Friends' meeting-house at Westbury, in which I had good service. I was led to open in a clear manner, the superiour excellence of the divine principle of light and truth, borne testimony to by the society ever since we have been a people, and showing that, where that is wanting, or is not given heed to, every thing else will and must fail of effecting the great work of our salvation, as no other means are adequate to that end. It was a season of favour, in which I was largely opened to declare of the things concerning the kingdom of heaven, and to open to the people many truths of the gospel, in the demonstration of the spirit, accompanied with power; which solemnized and tendered many minds. Surely it was the Lord's doing, and to him belongs all the praise : nothing due to man.

First day, the 10th. A hard trying meeting, mostly silent.

Fifth day. Had the acceptable company of our friend Mary Naftel, from England. She laboured in the ability afforded for our help and encouragement, which honest travail does not fail of meeting its own reward, true peace of mind, the richest treasure.

First day, the 17th. Silent in our meeting to-day.

Fifth day. Attended our monthly meeting, at which we had the company of our esteemed friend Phebe Field from Scipio.

Her company, together with her lively, simple, plain testimony, corresponding with our profession, were truly acceptable and refreshing.

Seventh day, the 23d. I left home early in the morning in order to attend our yearly meeting, accompanied by my wife and daughter Elizabeth. We arrived in New-York in time to attend the first sitting of the meeting of Ministers and Elders, which opened at the tenth hour. The meeting for discipline opened the following second day at ten o'clock, and closed on fifth day evening. It was shorter as to time than usual; but I think, in the main, it was a favoured meeting, and closed well, under an humbling sense of divine condescension and regard, and Friends separated to their several homes, under a feeling sense of brotherly love.

First day, the 31st. Attended our meeting in silence, and in much poverty of spirit, and although we had the company of a Friend who was travelling in the ministry, and who appeared pretty large in testimony; yet it seemed void of life to me, which I was willing to conclude was my own fault. We had another meeting appointed at the fourth hour in the afternoon, by two women Friends from West Jersey. This was also a meeting of exercise to me, without laying any thing to the charge of my friends.

Fifth day. A silent meeting. The rest of the week laboriously exercised in my temporal concerns. Oh how killing too much bodily labour is to our best spiritual life, and although it may be no more than is our duty to do, in order comfortably to accommodate our families, and the timely payment of our just debts, and the punctual performance of all our contracts, yet even then divine wisdom has so wisely ordered the events of things, as to impress caution on our minds, by not suffering us to reap much spiritual content or inward enjoyment from bodily exercise, or worldly care, lest as man is naturally prone to seek earthly things, he might become so swallowed up in his temporal enjoyments, as to neglect the one thing needful, that of laying up treasure in heaven.

First day, the 7th of 6th month. We had a large meeting to-day, and having been made an example of silence for a number of meeting days past, I also looked for the same at this time, till nearly half the time of our meeting was expired. I sat clothed in darkness, a darkness which could be felt; but after wrestling for about an hour a gleam of light sprang up, and a prospect revived, which had presented at the opening of the meeting, and enlarged with increasing weight until it led to communication. In the course thereof, the original state of man was considered, and presented to the view of the audience; and the state of rectitude in which he was placed by his gracious Creator; also the way shown, by and through which he fell, in a way clearly to discharge and exculpate the all-equitable and perfect Jehovah from any blame, as having any part or hand in man's fall and ruin, and placing it wholly on his own turpitude, by making a wrong use of his liberty, and by making his election to evil instead of good, when both lay open before him, at his own choice. Therefore, if he would pursue evil instead of good, he had none to blame but himself: the Lord would be clear, and his faithful servants would be clear; his blood will be upon his own head.

Fifth day. Attended our preparative meeting. My exercise and testimony led to show the excellency and necessity of silence to man, in all his attempts to approach the divine Being in solemn spiritual worship; not only the body but also the mind must be silenced, according to that saying of the prophet, " Be still and know that I am God ;" with which the testimony of Christ well agrees, where he assures his disciples, " That he is the vine, and they are the branches; and except the branch abide in the vine it withereth," and that "without him they can do nothing." As it is the sap from the vine that can only quicken and vivify the branch; so nothing short of the will, life and power of the Creator, spiritually dispensed to the creature, can enable him to perform worship in spirit and in truth. For nothing but man's assuming an independent will, in opposition to the divine will, and becoming active therein, occasioned his fall and separation from his Maker; so likewise nothing but a renunciation of that will, and a cessation from all self-activity as an independent creature, can unite and restore him again, or enable him to worship in spirit and in truth.

First day, the 14th. Having not fully performed my contemplated visit to our neighbouring towns and villages, and way opening for a further procedure, I attended two appointed meetings to-day, one in the morning at Cold Spring, and the other at the fourth hour in the afternoon at Huntington. Both these were pretty full meetings, in which my exercise was laborious, but I had a hope they were profitable meetings to some present. I returned home in the evening.

Fifth day. Attended our monthly meeting, at which we had the company of a Friend from Pennsylvania. His plain lively testimony, together with his company and solid deportment, did my heart good, as it brought to my remembrance some of our primitive worthies.

Sixth day. I attended the funeral of our friend Jacob Smith of Westbury. His death was very sudden and unexpected, which made it the more trying to his family. A meeting was held on the occasion, which was largely attended by his friends and the neighbouring inhabitants. The opportunity was solemn and instructive, and the gospel was preached in the demonstration of the spirit, and many hearts were humbled and contrited. Thanks be to God for his unspeakable gift.

First day, the 21st. I proceeded again in order to accomplish my aforesaid visit to the neighbouring towns and villages. By previous notice, a meeting was appointed at Cow Harbour, about twelve miles to the eastward, at the fourth hour in the afternoon, at the house of a person by the name of Henry Scudder, which was large and favoured. The five following days, I attended meetings appointed at the following places, viz: at Elias Smith's, in the west part of Smithtown, on second day, at the fourth hour in the afternoon; at the Branch on third day, at the eleventh hour; at Stony Brook, on fourth day at eleven o'clock; at Setauket on the same day, at the fourth hour in the afternoon; on fifth day had one at a place called the Haupauge, at the fourth hour in the afternoon; on sixth day at the eleventh hour, one near Commack, at the house of our friend Jacob Harnad, and at the fourth hour, had our last meeting in this town, at the house of Jonah Wood, at Dixhills. This is a grandson of Jonah Wood

43

deceased, who resided in the same place, where I often had meetings while he was living. He was a man convinced of the principles of Friends, but never came forward to join the society, which I apprehended was a loss to himself and family. These meetings were all owned by the Master of our assemblies, although great weakness and ignorance were manifest in many who attended, nevertheless the Lord was graciously pleased to conde scend to their low estates, and opened my mouth in doctrine suited to their states and conditions. I returned home on seventh day, with a thankful heart and a peaceful mind, the result of faithfulness in the Lord's work.

First day, the 28th. Attended our own meeting, which I sat the greater part in silence; but towards the close had a short testimony to deliver, which was introduced by the remembrance of the account given by the evangelist of the pool of Bethesda, and our Lord's healing the impotent man who had long waited there to be healed, but was not; therefore our Lord had compassion on him, and healed him. This shows how good it is to have a steady persevering faith and hope in the means God appoints for our salvation.

Fifth day. A silent meeting. The rest of the week I was busily employed in the oversight of my hay harvest, and in assisting in getting it into the barn; the fields having brought forth bountifully, which greatly enhances our obligations to the benevolent Giver.

First day, the 5th of 7th month. My mind in our meeting to-day, was humbled under an awakened sense of my own imperfections, and the impotency of our common nature. In this humiliated state, my mind became clothed with the spirit of prayer and supplication, which gave utterance vocally to present a petition to our heavenly Father for the continuance of his mercy; and that he would increase our faith and confident dependance on him, as our only source of help and salvation.

Fifth day. Attended our preparative meeting. The meeting for worship was a lively meeting, although silent or nearly so. The diffusion of real friendship and brotherly love was warmly felt.

First day, the 12th. I sat our meeting in silence, endeavouring to be edified by a communication from a young minister from Cowneck, which was sensible and in a good degree lively. How much more comfortable it is to sit under a testimony that comprehends good sense, and by which the understanding of the people is spoken to, than such as are delivered in a high sound of many words, and yet so unconnected, as to render it difficult to comprehend the subject matter the speaker really aims at; or such as are delivered in a kind of prophetic strain, without power, which some speakers are too apt to fall into; so that we are sometimes ready to doubt their call to that highly important and dignified office. These often cause deep exercise and concern to the living baptized members.

Fifth day. Attended our monthly meeting, at which the queries were read and the usual number answered, in order to represent our state to the quarterly meeting. Things appeared well with us, if the answers given in, were a true representation of our state.

First day, the 19th. I was again made an example of silence. In the course of this week our quarterly meeting was held. It was, I think, in the main a favoured season, in which divine goodness manifested a renewed extension of unmerited mercy to us poor, helpless and unworthy creatures. We had at this quarterly meeting the company of our esteemed friend Gerard T. Hopkins from Baltimore. He appeared lively in his gift, to our mutual edification.

It fell to my lot in the meeting for discipline, to revive the concern for the melioration of the condition of the Africans and their descendants; not only as it respected those who are still held in a state of abject bondage and oppression, but also on behalf of those who have been set free, but who, nevertheless continue, in a very general manner, in a degraded and helpless state, for want of being placed upon the ground of equality with the rest of the inhabitants, as strict justice would dictate, if rightly adhered to by the people and government. And I am fully in the belief, that divine justice will not be satisfied, nor the black stain of shedding innocent blood and cruelly oppressing this people, ever be taken from the inhabitants of this land, until strict justice is done them, and they placed by the laws of our country, in the same state of equality in every respect as the rest of its inhabitants, and in the enjoyment of the full right of civilized man. This is their just and righteous due, and these privileges, if duly and rightly administered to them, would bring them to be as good and useful citizens as those of any other nation.

I was also led to call upon my Friends to persevere in this noble and righteous concern, that nothing might be left undone on our part, in restoring strict justice and right to this deeply oppressed part of our fellow creatures ; not only on their account and for their relief, but on our own account also. For, I believe, we are in a very peculiar manner called upon, agreeably to our profession, of being led and guided by an unerring principle of perfect righteousness, to exalt the standard of truth and righteousness in the earth : and believing, as I do, that it is not in the power and wisdom of man to effect this, by all the coercive laws which can be enacted, nor by all the force of the arm of flesh. For nothing can destroy and put an end to sin and wickedness, but a principle in man of perfect righteousness and justice ; and this adhered to by man in so full and complete a manner, as to have no fellowship or communion, either immediately or remotely, directly or indirectly, with any acts of injustice or oppression. Hence, I believe, that if we as a people were faithful and obedient to this first principle of our profession, we should be led thereby to abstain from all kinds of commerce or dealings in the produce of our country or elsewhere, which we had cause to believe originated out of, or through the medium of, the labour of slaves, wrung from them and sold by their tyrannical masters. And I am well assured that nothing short of such an exalted testimony to truth and righteousness will ever put a full end to oppression and injustice; and, I believe, He who called our worthy predecessors to exalt the testimony of truth in the earth, and who is still calling us to advocate this noble cause, is looking for this testimony of strict justice and righteousness at our hands.

O, saith my soul! that we as a people, called as we are to be a light to the world, might so persevere in faithfulness and obedience to the teachings and inspirings of light and truth in our hearts, by which we should be enabled to unite together for the exaltation of this noble testimony, and the increase of the Messiah's kingdom of truth, righteousness, and peace in the earth; and which in its progression will break down and dissolve all the kingdoms of this world, until they become the kingdoms of our Lord and of his Christ, and he comes to reign whose right it is.

The subject spread with unusual weight over the meeting, and many brethren appeared deeply affected therewith, and divers came forward by expression to encourage its progress, and to stimulate each other therein ; so that my heart was truly gladdened under a sense of the prevalence of truth, which was felt to preside in the meeting, clearly manifesting that the concern was owned by the Head of the Church.

First day, the 26th. A silent meeting to-day. Passed this week in much poverty of spirit, accompanied with a peaceful mind. Sat our fifth day meeting in solemn silence.

First day, the 2d of 8th month. Feeling my mind disposed to sit with Friends in their meeting at Bethpage, I went thither to-day accompanied by my wife. Although my mind felt rather depressed from a sense of the low state of things among them, yet I was led to communicate some plain things ; showing that true religion did not consist in going to meetings and making a profession of it, but in works of real righteousness, and in a strict and daily conformity and submission to the cross, and a steady obedience to the law of the spirit of life in Christ Jesus, which only can set free from the law of sin and death.

Fifth day. A silent meeting on my part. The rest of the week I was taken up in temporal matters, having workmen of various kinds to overlook and assist, even at times to a degree of wearisomeness; insomuch that was it not from the calls of necessity and duty, I should endeavour to quit them all and be free from their cumber and interruption; as they do often interfere with better concerns, and those of a higher and more excellent nature.

First day, the 9th. A silent meeting

Fifth day. Was our preparative meeting. Silence was my lot in the meeting for worship.

First day, the 16th. Our meeting was larger than usual by the attendance of strangers, who did not usually attend. Very soon after taking my seat, my mind was impressed with a view of the baneful tendency of pride, and its hurtful effects on the children of men universally. The prospect led to communication, and opened into a pretty full testimony, tendering and humbling many minds. May it fasten as a nail in a sure place, that so it may continue in remembrance for many days and bring forth fruit, is my fervent prayer.

Fifth day. Attended our monthly meeting. In the meeting for worship I renewed the example to silence.

First day, the 23d. In the course of our meeting, my mind was led into a view of the necessity of the cross, consistent with that saying of the lip of truth : " If any man will come after me, let him deny himself and take up his cross and follow me." The subject spread and led to the necessity of communication, in which the way and work, and its effect upon the man of sin or self, was opened ; showing that when the cross is submitted to and borne, the transgressing nature in us is reduced and subjected by the operation of its power, through which true liberty is known, and the captive soul set free, and made to rejoice on the banks of deliverance.

Fifth day. Attended our meeting in silence. In the afternoon attended the funeral of a man inclined to Friends, at which there was a large collection of people of various professions. My mouth was opened to testify among them of the things concerning the kingdom of heaven, and to open the way of life and salvation to the people, and the only means by which it ever was or can be effected, viz : by the grace of God or light of truth, revealed in the hearts and consciences of men and women, as a swift witness against all manner of sin and iniquity. Life sprang up and the gospel was preached in the demonstration of the spirit, wherewith many were affected and edified.

First day, the 30th. The consideration of the great advantages which would result to the children of men, were they possessed of right ideas, and a right understanding of the divine character opened to an exercise and concern, from an impressive belief that there was a great shortness in that respect, even among professing Christians in a general way; and a great want of a right improvement of the talent or talents dispensed by our gracious Creator to his creature man, or that manifestation of the spirit given to every man to profit withal. For this, if rightly improved, would bring us to know and witness the true and saving knowledge of God, and give us right ideas of the divine character; and by which, if rightly adhered to, our salvation would be effected. I was led to communicate on the subject, which brought a very comfortable solemnity over the meeting.

Fifth day, the 3d of 9th month. A silent meeting to-day.

First day, the 6th. Having for some days past felt drawings on my mind to attend Friends' meeting at Westbury, and way opening for it to-day, I went thither accompanied by my wife. It was rather a trying exercising season in the forepart, but towards the close my spirit was set at liberty, and an opening presented, attended with life; in which I was led to open and show to those present, the necessity of an entire renunciation of self, in order to come to a saving knowledge of God, and a qualification to worship him in spirit and in truth; and of an entire cessation from all our own willings and runnings, both in body and spirit and in thought. Although this is an attainment which man cannot arrive at by the dint of his own sufficiency, yet, nevertheless he may, by a right faith in God and in the sufficiency of his power. Therefore we ought not to let in discouragement from a sense of our own impotent state, but continue to strive to enter in at the straight gate of self-abasement and renunciation, and persevere therein, leaving the rest to the Lord; and then, no doubt, we may be brought to the experience of one formerly who exclaimed: "Thou wilt ordain peace for us, for thou also hast wrought all our works in us."

Fifth day. Attended our meeting as usual when at home. I was much cumbered in the forepart of the meeting with unprofitable thoughts, such as relate to our temporal concerns. For these produce poverty of spirit in religious meetings, and ought to be strove against in order to obtain a release from them: and, although it is what we cannot do in our own time and strength, yet as we continue to strive and do not give over the struggle, but persevere in faith and patience to obtain the blessing, as Jacob did when he wrestled with the angel, we shall witness an overcoming in the Lord's time and strength, and know our light to rise out of obscurity, and our darkness to be as noonday. Then are we qualified to worship the Father in spirit and in truth, in the beauty of holiness, and nothing can hinder or let. Then can we do the Lord's work with a willing heart agreeably to his will, without the fear or favour of mortals. We can then minister, if called thereto, in the demonstration of the spirit, accompanied with power, which causes it to be instructive and edifying to the hearers.

First day, the 13th. My mind, as I sat in our meeting to-day, was led under exercise from the remembrance of the following passage of Isaiah: "Look unto me and be ye saved, all ye ends of the earth; for I am God, and there is none else." I was largely opened on the subject, and as I communicated, truth was raised into dominion; whereby the minds of many were humbled and contrited, the meeting generally solemnized and edified, and sweet peace afforded me in the labour.

Fifth day. This was the time of our monthly meeting. We had the company of our friend William Rickman from England, now on a religious visit in this country. Having felt my mind drawn for some considerable time past, to make a visit in the love of the gospel, to Friends in the compass of our yearly meeting, with a view also to appoint some meetings among those of other persuasions, it appeared right to spread the concern before my Friends at this time; who, after due consideration, united with me therein, and directed the clerk to furnish me with a minute of concurrence with my prospect, leaving me at liberty to pursue it as truth might open the way.

Fifth day, the 24th. A quiet silent meeting. On seventh day I attended the funeral of a young Friend, a kinsman, who, for more than a year previous to his dissolution, had been in a declining state of health. There was a large collection of Friends and neighbours on the occasion. The corpse was taken into the meeting-house, and a meeting held before it was interred, which is mostly the case among Friends in this part of the society. It proved a very exercising season in the forepart, and although divers ministers were present, yet all seemed shut from any communication, until the meeting seemed drawing to a conclusion, when my mind was set at liberty from its bonds, and a degree of light arose and dispelled the darkness, in which I was led to open the cause and ground of the prevailing darkness which had been so generally spread over us; and to show that it was owing to the people's living too much to self, and serving self, when they ought more faithfully to serve the Lord and live unto him. I was led, in a brief way, in a close, searching testimony, which I hope will have its use, at least with some present.

First day, the 27th. In our meeting to-day, my mind was largely opened into the substance of things referred to by the shadows and symbols of the law, or outward dispensation. As the prospect spread and enlarged, I found it necessary to spread it before the assembly, and to show the difference between the law state and that of the gospel, and that as the shadows and symbols of the outward law dispensation, stood and consisted in real essential and substantial things, suited to our outward nature and life; so likewise the substance of those shadows, as they were intended to point to spiritual things, must also consist in real, essential and substantial things, suited to our inward and spiritual nature and life, and therefore of course all the shadows of the law are at an end, where the gospel state is known and experienced. It was a season of favour, and renewedly strengthening to my mind, and I believe, instructive and edifying to many present. Thanks be given to Israel's Shepherd, for his continued mercy.

Fifth day. Attended our preparative meeting, at which the queries were read, and answers given to the usual five, to go to the quarterly meeting; and I thought, from the tenour of the answers, if correct, we were a favoured people.

First day, the 11th. Our meeting was large, in which the gospel axe was laid close to the root of the corrupt tree; showing that
44

every tree which did not bring forth good fruit must be hewn down, let it have ever so specious an outward appearance.

Fifth day. Attended our monthly meeting, at which answers to the queries were produced from the preparative meetings. Although I feared the answers from our preparative meeting made us appear more correct than we really were, yet those from the other branch of the monthly meeting were still more perfect, and although I felt some doubting, yet a degree of gladness attended in a hope that we were improving.

After this meeting, nothing in particular transpired, until I proceeded on my intended journey, which was on the 21st of 10th month, 1818, and fourth day of the week. Samuel Willis, a member of our meeting, and an elder, joined me as a companion. We proceeded to Flushing, in order to attend our quarterly meeting, which opened with a meeting of Ministers and Elders at the tenth hour. The next day was the meeting for discipline, and the day following a public meeting for worship. Through the condescending goodness of the Shepherd of Israel, the several seasons were truly comfortable, instructive and edifying, in which the power of truth was exalted over all opposition, to the praise of Him who is calling us to glory and virtue.

From Flushing we proceeded to Newtown, on sixth day afternoon, and attended a public meeting in the evening, of those belonging to other societies.

The next day we had an appointed meeting in Friends' meeting-house at the Kilns, and another in the evening at Brooklyn, generally composed of those not in membership with us, and many not in strict fellowship with any religious society. And we had thankfully to acknowledge, that He who opens and none can shut, was graciously near for our help, and opened doctrine suited to the states of those who attended in the several opportunities, to the peace and comfort of my own mind, and, I trust, to the instruction and edification of the people.

From thence we proceeded to New-York, and attended the meetings in the city, on first day. They were large : many not in profession with us came in, as previous information had been given of our intention to be there. The gospel was freely preached among them in both opportunities, particularly that at Pearl-street, wherein truth was raised into dominion over all.

On second day we attended a meeting by appointment at West-Chester, which was also a precious edifying opportunity. After this we proceeded to Purchase, in order to attend the quarterly meeting at that place, which opened the next day at the eleventh hour, and continued three days. The meeting for discipline was well conducted, in which I was led to call upon Friends, to rally to our standard, the *light within*, which is a principle of perfect rectitude and justice, and if rightly attended to, will lead us to withdraw from all kind of conduct and commerce, which is in the least degree tinged with injustice and oppression. And in a particular manner from a commerce in, and the use of, articles which are the product of the labour of slaves; the injustice of which was clearly opened and brought home to Friends' minds, showing them that nothing short of a principle of immutable justice, which may so pervade the minds of mankind, as not to have any intercourse with the oppressor, in the produce of the labour of the oppressed, will ever be sufficient fully to suppress that monstrous evil, and put a final end thereto. It was a very solemn season. The meeting for worship was likewise favoured, in which the divine presence was witnessed for our help and comfort.

The four following days we attended meetings at North Castle, Salem, Oblong and the Branch. These were all large for the places, and favoured with the overshadowing of heavenly regard, in which ability was received to preach the gospel, in the demonstration of the spirit, and wisdom afforded to divide the word to the different states of those present. Each meeting was composed of a variety of professions and conditions; and such was the gracious condescension of the Shepherd of Israel, as not to send any away empty, if they were willing to receive the portion iustly allotted them; and if they refuse, because it is not agreeable to their own inclinations, the Lord will be clear, and his faithful servants will be clear; and if they are not saved, their blood will be upon their own heads. These several seasons were comfortable and encouraging to the honest-hearted, and strengthening to

my exercised mind ; a sense of which filled my heart with gratitude and thanksgiving to the blessed Author of all our mercies.

After these meetings we proceeded to Nine Partners. On third
day, the 3d of 11th month, their quarterly meeting came on.
The meeting of Ministers and Elders opened at the tenth hour,
and the meeting for discipline the next day. These were both
profitable instructive meetings to many present, in which way
opened fully to relieve my own mind ; and I felt sweet peace in
my labours of love among them.

The three following days we attended the quarterly meeting at
Stanford. I had but little active service in the meeting of Ministers and Elders, yet I found it my place to remind Friends of the
danger and bad effects of covering or hiding, and of the advantage
of laying ourselves open to the just witness, and of entering into
an individual investigation, when answering the queries, lest we
overlook some things even in ourselves, and so make our answers
more clear than truth and equity will warrant. And when the
answers to the queries came to be read, I thought there was occasion for the caution, as their answers were generally full and
clear.

In the meeting for discipline, I was led to call Friends' attention to the fundamental principle of our profession ; and to show
the drift and design of those precious testimonies, as good fruit
naturally emanated from a good tree ; especially those two, the
most noble and dignified, viz : against war and slavery. And
whether while we were actively paying taxes to civil government
for the purpose of promoting war or warlike purposes in any
degree, we were not balking our testimony in that respect ; and
pulling down with one hand, what we are pretending to build
with the other. And in like manner with regard to slavery. For
although we had freed our own hands from holding, by active
force, any of this oppressed people, the Africans and their descendants, in unconditional slavery ; yet, whether so long as we voluntarily and of choice, are engaged in a commerce in, and the free
use of the fruits of their labour, wrested from them by the iron
hand of oppression, through the medium of their cruel and unjust
masters, we are not accessary thereto, and are partakers in the

unrighteous traffic of dealing in our fellow creatures, and in a great measure lay waste our testimony against slavery and oppression. These subjects were largely opened, and the inconsistency of such conduct placed before the minds of Friends; accompanied with strong desires, that they might have their proper effect, in convincing them of the unrighteousness of such conduct.

The meeting for worship, or closing meeting, was mostly made up of such as were not members. It was a favoured, solemn meeting, and, I trust, instructive and comfortable to many present; as it was to the satisfaction and peace of my own mind.

First day, the 8th of 11th month. We returned and attended the meeting at Nine Partners. As notice was given of our intention of attending it, it was very large; the house was filled with a mixed company of various professions, besides Friends. I was largely led forth among them, to declare of the things concerning the kingdom of God. Truth was raised into dominion, and a precious solemnity spread over the assembly. May all the praise be ascribed to the Shepherd of Israel, for the unmerited favour.

In the course of this week, after resting on second and third days, in which time I visited some of my relatives, we attended meetings at Chestnut Ridge, Apoquague, Beekman, and Oswego. These meetings were generally well attended, and were, I trust, profitable and instructive to many who attended them.

First day, the 15th. I attended West Branch meeting in the morning, and that at Pleasant Valley in the evening. They were both very crowded gatherings. At the latter meeting, there were many more than the house could contain, composed, principally of such as were not in membership with Friends, being of the varied religious professions common among us; and many who were not in strict fellowship with any. At such seasons, where, of course, there must be a great variety of states and conditions, I have found it necessary to dwell deep, and wait patiently for the arising of the pure spring of gospel ministry, which alone can enable and qualify to divide the word aright, so that each may have his due portion, and be spoken to in his own language;

a language which sets home the truth to every mind, as was the case on the day of Pentecost.

On second day evening, we had a very large meeting in Poughkeepsie. It was held in their court-house, which was a very commodious room for the purpose, being well seated, and was thought sufficient to hold nearly a thousand people. It was much crowded, and proved a very solemn, quiet opportunity, in which truth had the dominion.

The five succeeding days, we attended a large meeting by appointment at Crumelbow, the monthly meetings of Oswego, Nine Partners, Creek, and Stanford. In all these meetings I had good service; the several opportunities being favoured with the overshadowings of heavenly regard.

First day, the 22d. We had a very crowded meeting at Little Nine Partners. The next day we were at an appointed meeting, in Friends' meeting-house, in the town of Northeast, which was likewise a very full meeting. In both of these the gospel was freely preached, and its doctrines largely opened, and set home to the minds of the people; and the fallacy and emptiness of all formal and ceremonial religion exposed, and the people pressingly invited to gather inward, to the immutable principle of *light* and *truth* in their own souls, as the *sure rock of ages*, and the *only means* whereby we can be enabled to work out our salvation. The Lord's power was felt eminently to preside in those solemn assemblies, to the praise of his great and excellent name, who is over all worthy for ever; and I parted with them in true peace of mind, the sure result of faithfulness.

On third day we rode to Canaan, a town in Connecticut, and the next day had an appointed meeting there, with the few Friends at that place, and some of their neighbours. It was a comfortable, instructive season. The following day we had another meeting by appointment, in an adjacent neighbourhood which was held in a school-house. This was also a favoured meeting. Divers present were much broken and contrited, and truth reigned over all.

On sixth day we proceeded to Hartford, and on seventh day evening had an appointed meeting in the city. It was held in a meeting-house, belonging to the Presbyterians; as there were only two or three members of our society in the place. The meeting was small, occasioned, as I supposed, by the inclemency of the weather, and want of proper notice; nevertheless the divine presence was felt to preside, and truth was declared among them in the demonstration of the spirit; and I parted with them, unde a thankful sense of the Lord's mercy.

The next day, being the first of the week, we attended Friends' meeting at West Hartford. This was likewise very small, Friends being but few in number in that place, and those mostly appeared in a lukewarm state; and I apprehended they had taken but little care to inform their neighbours of our intention to be there, although we had seasonably requested them so to do. Such conduct manifests great insensibility, and want of regard for their friends who have left all their outward enjoyments, for the promotion of the gospel, and the religious improvement of the people; and are going up and down in travail and labour, as with their lives in their hands, as truth leads the way; and yet, Friends whom they visit in some places, either think it too much trouble, or are so unconcerned as to take little or no care to give their neighbours notice; a sense of which caused me to take leave of my Friends at this place with a heavy heart.

From thence, on second day, we proceeded to Woodbury, and put up at the house of a person of the Methodist society, where we had a large meeting the next evening with the neighbouring inhabitants, composed of Methodists, Episcopalians, Presbyterians and some others, not in strict fellowship with any religious society. It was a very solemn, favoured meeting, in which the Lord's presence and power were felt eminently to preside; and many hearts were broken and contrited, and manifested much satisfaction with the opportunity, especially the man at whose house we were, who in much brokenness of spirit, and with gratitude and thankfulness of heart, acknowledged the favour.

The next morning, after a tendering opportunity in the family, we took leave of them in mutual affection, and rode to Middlesex, upwards of forty miles. Here we lodged with our kind friend Samuel Whiting, who, with his affectionate wife and children, received us with marks of true friendship, which is a brook by the way to the weary traveller; and which was our case at this time. What added further to our comfort, was the readiness of mind and concern they manifested, in giving their neighbours information of our intention to attend their meeting the next day, which we accordingly did. The Lord graciously condescended to open my mouth among them, in a living, powerful testimony to the truths of the gospel. It was a season of great favour. May the word preached not return void, but accomplish that to which it was sent, is the fervent desire of my spirit.

After this solemn meeting we proceeded on our journey, and rode that afternoon to our friend Charles Field's, at a place called the Saw Pitts. Here we had a meeting the next day at the eleventh hour. There is but one family of Friends in this village, the Friend and his family above named, and one other member. The inhabitants consist of the various professions common among us, and some others not in communion with any religious society. A considerable number assembled, with whom we had a very solemn instructive opportunity, to the comfort and peace of my own mind.

The evening of the next day, we had a precious favoured meeting at Manhattanville on New-York Island, with Friends of that place. It was attended by a considerable number of the neighbouring inhabitants, who conducted themselves very soberly, suiting the occasion. Many hearts were broken and contrited, and we parted with them under an humbling sense of the Lord's goodness, and with grateful hearts for the unmerited favour.

First day, the 6th of 12th month. We rode to the city. As Friends of the monthly meeting there had recently opened a new meeting in the eastern part of the town, we attended it both forenoon and afternoon. And as notice was given at the close of the forenoon meeting of our intention to attend in the afternoon, it was a full meeting, more than the house could well contain. These were both memorable meetings, in which the Lord's presence and power were manifested in an eminent degree, breaking and contriting many hearts, and truth reigned over all. It was the Lord's doing, and marvellous in our eyes, that he should thus condescend, in matchless mercy, to notice us poor unworthy creatures.

At evening, we had a very large meeting by appointment, in Friends' meeting-house in Pearl-street. Although I was much worn down by arduous labour in the three foregoing meetings, yet I was strengthened to communicate in this, in a full plain testimony, opening to the people the danger and disadvantage of resting in the forms and empty shadows of the law state; and continuing in the traditions and ceremonies introduced into the professed Christian Churches, in the time of the apostacy from primitive simplicity; and the hurtful tendency of observing days and times, like the carnally-minded in the Galatian Church; for which they were sharply reprehended by the apostle Paul, in his epistle to that Church. The people were very quiet and attentive, and a precious solemnity was spread over the meeting, which closed in a solemn manner. Thanks be given to Israel's unslumbering Shepherd for the unmerited favour.

We tarried in town until third day, in order to attend the meeting for sufferings which came in course at that time. We also had an appointed meeting in Liberty-street, on second day evening. It was pretty well attended, in which I was led to open to the people the way of redemption by Christ, the only Mediator between God and man; and the way of his working in man, in the accomplishment of his salvation. I also opened to them the emptiness of all shadows and outward ordinances, under the Christian dispensation; such as water baptism, and the ordinance called the supper or communion; also the hurtful tendency of observing days and times, such as a seventh day sabbath, days of thanksgiving, and fast days of man's appointing They were shown that all these were of Jewish or Heathenish original, being a part of the law dispensation, and of course ended with it, and therefore the continuance of them under the gospel dispensation was irrational, non-essential, and contrary to truth; tending to keep the minds of Christian professors under the veil of carnal ordinances, and greatly retarded the progress of reformation, and the advancement of real Christianity. I was led to use great plainness of speech, and the people sat very quiet and attentive, and the word preached appeared to have free course. It was a highly favoured season, and the honest-hearted were made to rejoice, under an humbling sense of the Lord's mercy, and I parted with them in true peace of mind. The next day, after attending the meeting for sufferings, we rode home and found our families well, which I considered as an additional favour from my heavenly Father, whose mercy is over all his works.

I was from home at this time about forty-nine days, and attended forty-nine meetings, and travelled about four hundred and fifty miles.

CHAPTER XV.

General visit to Friends of the yearly meeting of New-York, 1819.

I CONTINUED at and about home, until the commencement of the year 1819, attending our meetings as they came in course. I also attended two funerals, at which I had good service; and the meeting at Westbury, on a first day, in which I was led to open to Friends the three principal requisites to the being, and well-being, of a Christian. The first being a real belief in *God* and *Christ, as one undivided essence,* known and believed in, *inwardly* and *spiritually.* The second, a complete passive obedience and submission to the divine will and power inwardly and spiritually manifested; which, when known, brings to the Christian state, through a crucifixion of the old man, with all his ungodly deeds. The third, in order for the preservation and well-being of a Christian, it is necessary that they often meet and assemble together, for the promotion of love and good works, and as good stewards of the manifold grace of God. For this purpose the Lord's people and children have been led by his spirit to appoint times and seasons in which to present themselves before him. Of these times, all being apprized, and living within a reasonable distance of the place so appointed, it becomes their bounden duty to attend, in order to wait upon, and thereby become qualified to worship God, in spirit and in truth; and no temporal concern of the greatest magnitude ought to be considered as a sufficient excuse for omitting this great and necessary duty. For the experience of many ages has shown, that those who suffer their temporal business to divert them from a steady attendance on their religious meetings, never make any real proficiency in religion, or the true spiritual life. The communication was impressive, and reached the witness in many minds, and truth was exalted, and the honest-hearted comforted, and I was made glad in believing that my labour had not been in vain. Such seasons are truly worthy of grateful remembrance.

As, on my return home, I did not feel myself released from a further prosecution of my concern, and visit to Friends of our yearly meeting, with the concurrence of my friends, I retained the minute I had received for that purpose, and on the 2d of 1st month, 1819, I again left home, and proceeded in the engagement. My son-in-law Valentine Hicks joined me as companion in the journey. We proceeded to New-York; and, the next day being the first of the week, we attended Friends' meeting at Pearl-street in the morning. After this, in the afternoon, we proceeded on our journey as far as our friend Thomas Walker's, at West Farms, near West Chester, where we had a meeting, at the sixth hour in the evening. On second day, we had an appointed meeting at Mamaroneck. These meetings were in a good degree favoured, in which the presence and love of our heavenly Father were felt to preside.

On third day we had another opportunity, by appointment, at White Plains, in the court-house. It was rather a season of hard labour, as the truths communicated did not appear to have free course, in any general way; but, I trust, some were instructed and edified. On fourth and fifth days, we attended Friends' meetings at Purchase, and Shapaqua. As notice was given of our intention to attend them, they were large; and through divine condescension, they proved seasons of favour, in which the truths of the gospel were largely declared in the demonstration of the spirit, to the edification of the assemblies, and peace of my own mind.

The two following days we attended meetings at Croton Valley, and Amawalk. They were well attended by Friends, and some others. I was led to open among them many essential doctrines of the Christian religion; and to show to the people, in the openings of truth, the way and means by which, and by which only, our redemption and salvation can be effected. The testimonies had a very reaching effect upon the auditories; many present were much broken and contrited, and truth was raised into victory, and a precious solemnity was spread over the meetings, to the comfort and edification of the honest-hearted, which was cause of thankfulness and gratitude to the beneficent Author of all our mercies.

First day the 10th. We attended Friends' meeting at Croton in the morning, and at Peekskill in the evening. Both were full meetings, in which the power of the gospel was felt to preside, furnishing with wisdom and strength to divide the word, to the several states present, in a way which seemed to give each his due portion, and none sent empty away, but those who refused to take their own part. Many hearts were broken and contrited, and the honest-hearted comforted; and the Lord's name and power praised and exalted over all, who is worthy for ever.

On second day we rode to Nine Partners; and on third day evening had an appointed meeting at Dover. It was held in a pretty large school-house, there being no other place so convenient in the neighbourhood; but it was too small to contain the people who assembled, some being obliged to stand without, for want of room. It was a very solemn, instructive meeting.

On fourth day we attended Pleasant Valley meeting; and notice being given of our expectation to attend it, the meeting was large. A considerable number of other societies were present who behaved soberly, consistent with the occasion. It was a season of great favour, under a sense of which the honest-hearted were made to rejoice.

After this, we proceeded to Poughkeepsie, and attended an appointed meeting in the evening, at the sixth hour. It was held in their court-house, a large convenient room, but not sufficient to contain the people who assembled; many were obliged to withdraw for want of room. It proved, through the condescending goodness of our heavenly Father, a blessed meeting to myself, and, we had cause to believe, to the assembly in general. Thanks be to God for his unspeakable gift: yet we have reason to believe there were some present watching for evil, as carpers and opposers, if we may judge from the conduct of the hireling priests, since I was there a few weeks before, as I was informed at this time, that they had joined together to calumniate me, and endeavour to lay waste the testimony I then had to bear. We tarried here most of the next day, visiting some of our friends.

On sixth day we proceeded to Hudson, where we arrived at evening. The following evening, we had an appointed meeting in the town of Claverack, about four miles distant from Hudson. The inhabitants were mostly Dutch; a considerable number attended, and behaved pretty soberly; and way opened to communicate divers truths of the gospel, in a clear and impressive manner among them, to which they paid good attention, and appeared to be generally well satisfied. The next day, being first day, we attended Friends' meeting in Hudson, and an appointed meeting in the evening. The latter was very large, more than the house could contain. These were favoured meetings, in which I was largely led forth in testimony to the truths of the Christian religion, setting forth, in a clear manner, the ground and source from whence all true religion and true worship have their spring and origin. A general solemnity prevailed, and truth was raised into dominion over all.

On second day, we proceeded to Kinderhook, and had a meeting in the evening in a school-house, and on third day afternoon, we had an appointed meeting in Spencertown. These were both crowded meetings, mostly made up of the different societies common among us; many of them were the descendants of the old Dutch inhabitants, not much acquainted with our customs and order; yet they generally behaved soberly, and gave good attention to the testimonies borne. Many gospel truths were opened to their consideration, and the Lord's presence and power were felt to crown these solemn assemblies; and I parted from them in true peace and thankfulness of heart.

On fourth and fifth days, we attended Friends' meetings at Kline Kiln, and New Britain. In both of these meetings, I had good service for truth and its blessed cause, and the hurtful tendency of a dependance on forms, and outward ordinances and ceremonies in religion and worship, was laid open and exposed.

On sixth day, we proceeded to Troy, where we rested on seventh day, and wrote to our families. On first day, we attended Friends' meetings at Troy, both forenoon and afternoon, and, information being given that we were there, they were large. At the forenoon meeting, more assembled than the house could contain; and that gracious Being, who never leaves nor forsakes his dependant children, whose trust is fixed on him, was near for our help; and opened my heart and mouth in both meetings, to declare largely of the things concerning the kingdom of God, and to open many gospel truths to the people, and to show the fallacy and hurtful tendency of all ceremonial religion, which consists in the observance of days and times, and outward ordinances. The people were generally attentive; and I found solid peace in my labours of love among them.

On second day, we proceeded to Pittstown, and the next day had a meeting appointed there, at the eleventh hour, which was a large, favoured meeting. After this we proceeded to White Creek, and attended Friend's meeting as it came in course the next day; and, information being given that we were there, it was largely attended. The Lord's presence was felt to preside, and truth was raised into victory. Oh my soul! what wilt thou, or canst thou render unto the Lord, for all his benefits; "for his mercies are new every morning, and great is his faithfulness."

On fifth day we attended an appointed meeting in the town of Shaftsbury, on our way to Danby. In this place, none of our society reside, except one female member, the wife of a well-disposed man, at whose house we put up, and were very hospitably entertained. The meeting, although small, was attended by the governor of the state, and divers of the judges and magistrates. It was a season of favour; many essential doctrines of the Christian religion were opened to them, in the demonstration of truth, and I parted with them in thankfulness of heart, and with a peaceful mind; and the next day rode to Danby.

On seventh day, we attended an appointed meeting near a village called the Borough, in the east part of the town; and on first day, attended Friends' meeting on the Hill. Both were fully attended by Friends, and the neighbouring inhabitants; and were both solemn instructive seasons, in which the power of truth was felt to preside, enabling to preach the gospel in the demonstration of the spirit, to the comfort and encouragement of the living, faithful few, and to the instruction and edification of the honest inquirers, whose faces were turned Zion-ward; likewise spreading caution and reproof to the indolent and careless.

On second day we proceeded towards Ferrisburg, where we arrived on third day afternoon, and the next day attended the monthly meeting at that place. The four following days, we attended meetings in the following order: On fifth day we had an appointed meeting at Monkton. It was large, and proved a very solemn, favoured meeting, in which the power of truth prevailed, silencing all opposition, and ran as oil, to the comfort, encouragement and instruction of the honest-hearted. Bless the Lord, O my soul, and forget not any of his benefits! On sixth day we attended Friends' monthly meeting at Starksborough. On seventh day had an appointed meeting in a school-house, in the southeast part of the town, where Friends hold a small meeting; and on first day was at Friends' meeting at Lincoln. These were all favoured meetings, in which I had good service for truth and its cause.

On second day, we returned into the south part of Monkton, and had an evening meeting in a kinsman's house, by the name of Stephen Haight. He was convinced of the principles of Friends, but failed in the practical part. This proved a pretty exercising season, by reason of the unsettled state of some who attended; especially in the silent part of the meeting: for being brought up and educated in the belief that, unless they are engaged in some bodily exercise, such as outward and vocal singing, praying, preaching, and the like, there is no meeting; being so instructed by their teachers, it is very difficult to get them into stillness, or into any right condition to hear. This makes hard work for the true gospel minister, whose labour and travail is to get into, and bring others into, a state of true solemn silence; that he may therefore become baptized into the state of the people, and be qualified to administer to their real conditions; for otherwise preaching is vain. But as I continued patient in travail, my mouth was opened in a large searching testimony, showing the fallacy and emptiness of all outward ceremonial worship; and that it must inevitably land all those who trust therein, in a state of sad disappointment, in the end. I was led also to open, in a clear manner to the people, the most essential doctrines of the Christian religion, to the information and satisfaction of the honest inquiring minds.

The next day we returned to Ferrisburgh, in order to attend the quarterly meeting which opened on fourth day, with the meeting of Ministers and Elders, which I attended, and had good service among them. I was led to open in the life the order of true gospel ministry, and the necessity all are under, who are called to that solemn and important office, of keeping their vessels clean, not only from sin and every pollution of flesh and spirit, but also in their ministry from all the dregs or remains of former offerings. For if, through the strength of memory, any act upon former offerings, such communications tend to produce death, rather than life. We find, under the law, that the vessels in the Lord's house were not only at first made pure and holy, but when they were made use of in the Lord's offerings, and had been filled with the Lord's holy things, when that season of offering was over, they were then cleansed from all the remains and dregs of such offering, and put up in their places clean and empty. This also agrees with the doctrine of Christ to his apostles: "Every branch in me," he says, "that beareth fruit, my heavenly Father purgeth it, that it may bring forth more fruit." It was, I trust, an instructive season, there being a number present who were young in the ministry.

After this meeting we rode to Vergennes, and attended an appointed meeting at six in the evening. It was pretty well attended by the inhabitants of the town, who generally behaved soberly. I was led to open divers important doctrines of the gospel for their consideration, and to caution them against having any fellowship with, or affording any support to the dark, and what I esteem, pernicious system of Free Masonry. They were generally attentive, and withdrew quietly.

The two following days, we attended the quarterly meeting for discipline; and the parting meeting for worship. These, I trust, were profitable opportunities. The latter was a highly favoured meeting, in which truth reigned over all; and I took leave of my friends in the sensible feeling of true gospel fellowship.

We rode, that afternoon and evening, to Shoram, and lodged with our kind friends Zebulon and Elizabeth Frost. The next day at evening, had an appointed meeting there, which many of the neighbouring inhabitants attended. It was a solemn time, in which many doctrines of the Christian religion were opened for their instruction and consideration; and I parted with them with a peaceful mind.

The next day we rode to Granville; and the following day had an appointed meeting there, at one o'clock in the afternoon. This was a greatly favoured opportunity, the power of truth breaking down and dispelling every opposite spirit, humbling and contriting many hearts, and comforting and strengthening the honest-hearted. Surely it was the Lord's doing; a sense of which inspires gratitude and thankfulness of heart, for the unmerited favour.

On third day we rode to Easton. On fourth and fifth days we attended their quarterly meeting for discipline, and public meeting for worship. Their meeting of Ministers and Elders was held on third day previous to our arrival. On sixth day we had an appointed meeting at Cambridge. These meetings were all comfortable instructive seasons, in which the doctrines of truth were largely opened, for the information and edification of the people.

We rested on seventh day, feeling myself pretty much worn out with such continual and almost incessant labour in travelling and in meetings. On first day I again attended Easton meeting which was also a large favoured meeting, in which the power of truth was exalted.

On second day we proceeded on our way to Queensbury, and attended a meeting in our way, which I had previously appointed at a large village called Whipple City. It was largely attended by the neighbouring inhabitants. There were no members of our society in the place. It was, I think, a favoured opportunity, in which I was enabled to declare the truth among them, in a large, effective testimony. Many present were humbled and contrited, and I parted with them in true peace of mind.

After this we proceeded to Queensbury, where we arrived in the evening. The three following days we attended the quarterly meeting held there at this time for Saratoga and Queensbury. I also attended two evening meetings in two neighbouring villages, which I had appointed for the benefit of those of other societies, who pretty generally attended. I think the quarterly meeting in general was an instructive favoured time. The two other meetings were exercising seasons; the minds of the people appeared to be very much veiled, and in a state of much ignorance; being generally too much swallowed up in worldly pursuits, and self-gratifications. This makes hard work for the devoted traveller, who is engaged for the advancement of the cause of truth and righteousness in the earth. But as I waited, and patiently endured the baptisms necessary to be brought into a feeling of their real conditions, way opened to communicate doctrine suitable for their instruction and help; and, although there did not appear much effect wrought for the present, yet I had reason to hope, that the labour would not be all lost; nor the word return void, but would, in the end, accomplish the thing whereunto it was sent, and be as bread cast upon the waters to return after many days. My hope in this respect was strengthened from the satisfaction and true peace I felt in the ardent labour I passed through, in these seasons of exercise.

The quarterly meeting being over, we proceeded to Saratoga, and on sixth day had an appointed meeting there at two o'clock in the afternoon. This was a large favoured meeting, in which truth was raised into victory over all, and under its precious influence the gospel was preached in the clear demonstration of the spirit. Thanks be to God for his unspeakable gift.

From thence we proceeded to Milton, and on first day, the 28th of 2d month, we attended Friends' meeting there. It was largely attended by Friends and others, and through the condescending goodness of Israel's unslumbering Shepherd it proved an instructive edifying season.

The five following days, we attended meetings at Greenfield,

Galloway, Providence, Mayfield, and Northampton. Although things in most places, as it regards the life of religion, appeared rather low, and considerable rawness was apparent in many in that respect, yet such is the unmerited kindness of the heavenly Father, that he graciously condescended to break the bread, and caused it to be distributed to the people, in these several opportu-·nities, so that none were sent empty away, except those who either neglected or refused to take the portion allotted them ; and my spirit was comforted, under an evident sense that I had faithfully discharged my duty among them.

From Northampton we proceeded to Newtown, and on first day the 7th of 3d month, we attended Friends' meeting at that place ; and, information being given that we were there, it was large. A very considerable number more assembled, than the house could contain, who were obliged to stand without. For these I felt much sympathy and concern, as the weather was very cold, and those without, not willing to lose the opportunity, continued until the meeting ended, which held nearly three hours. But I had cause to hope they did not go away unrewarded, as the season proved a very favoured one, in which the divine presence was felt to preside, enabling to preach the gospel of the grace of God to the people, in the demonstration of truth, and to the comfort and peace of my own mind.

On the evenings of the two following days, I attended meetings by appointment, at Waterford and Troy. Both were largely attended by those not in membership with us. On fourth day, attended Friends' monthly meeting at Troy. On fifth day evening, had a very large meeting in Albany, which was held in the state-house, a large, commodious room for the purpose. In these several meetings truth was felt to arise into dominion, and ability afforded to discharge myself faithfully in communication to the people who assembled, I trust, to their general satisfaction and edification ; may it instructively fasten on their minds, as a nail·in a sure place, driven by the Master of assemblies, that so the word preached may tend to real profit, and not return void, but accomplish the end to which it was sent.

From thence we proceeded to Bern, within the compass of

Duanesburgh quarterly meeting, where we arrived on sixth day evening, and lodged with our kind friend Samuel Cary, who, with his affectionate wife and children, treated us with great hospitality. The next evening we had an appointed meeting at a village about four miles distant, where no member of our society resides. We intended to return and attend Friends' meeting at Bern, on first day ; but a snow storm coming on seventh day, and increasing towards evening and all next day with such violence, that, although we got to the evening meeting, which was small, by reason of the storm, we were not able to return until the following second day, and then it was with great difficulty that we got along, the snow was so deep, and the roads drifted full. We however made the attempt to return on first day morning, and got on our way about half a mile, but could proceed no farther. We then called at a house on the way, a good looking mansion belonging to a professor among the Presbyterians. Here we tarried over first day, not being able to proceed. We held a little meeting there with this family, and three of their friends, who were with them on a visit, in which my mind was opened to communicate to them the grounds of our profession, and the doctrines of the Christian religion, as held by us. This had a very considerable effect on the man's wife, so that she openly acknowledged to the truths, delivered, and assured all present that she should vindicate them, as certain undeniable truths, which she felt to be so, in her own experience.

On the following fifth day, we attended Friends' meeting at Bern. The weather being again stormy and inclement, it was small. The roads were blocked up, so as to prevent many from attending. The next day we proceeded to Duanesburgh, and had a meeting there on seventh day, which was a large favoured season. On first day we attended meetings at Charlestown in the morning, and at Carlisle in the evening. On second day we proceeded to Middleburgh, and the next day had a meeting there. The day following, had meetings at Oakhill in the morning, and at Rensselaerville in the afternoon. After this we returned with our friend Samuel Cary to his house, who had kindly accompanied us in this little tour. I felt true peace of mind, from a consciousness that I had faithfully discharged myself in the service allotted me, in those several meetings, void of any influence from the fear or favour of man.

On fifth day, we attended Friends' monthly meeting at Bern. The meeting for worship was attended by a very considerable number of the neighbouring inhabitants, not in membership with us, who behaved themselves soberly, and were very attentive to what was communicated. Many were broken and contrited by the prevalence of truth, which was raised into dominion in this favoured meeting. Not only the meeting for worship, but likewise that for discipline was a comfortable instructive season.

The two following days, we had meetings at New Baltimore, and a village where several families of Friends reside, by the name of Dickenson, from whom they call the meeting "Dickenson's meeting;" and at Coeman's, alias, Stanton Hill. I had good service in those several meetings, in which Friends appeared to be brought near together, in the feeling influence of the truth, and in the oneness of the spirit. In a sense of this, we had gratefully to acknowledge that the Lord is still mindful of his people, fulfilling all his promises to those who seek him with sincerity of heart; and they that seek him early will find him to be near at hand, a present helper in every needful time.

After the latter meeting, we proceeded to Athens; and, the next day being the first of the week, and the 28th of 3d month, we attended Friends' meeting there in the morning, and had another meeting by appointment in the afternoon. These were exercising meetings, particularly so in the forepart of the latter. A great power of darkness seemed so to prevail, as entirely for a considerable time, to close up the way to any public service; but as I patiently submitted to the baptism and willingly became baptized, with and for the dead, for it is only through death, that the resurrection from death can be witnessed, a little glimmering of light appeared, in which I felt the necessity of standing up; and as I proceeded, keeping my eye single to the light that led the way, the light more and more arose, and the darkness vanished; and He that opens and none can shut, and shuts and none but himself can open, made way for the promotion of his own righteous cause, and the exaltation of truth's testimonies. It was the Lord's doing, and marvellous in mine eyes.

We left here on second day morning, and proceeded to Alexander Young's at the east part of Esopus, about forty miles. This was a day of very hard travel, both for man and horse, the roads being bad, as the winter was just breaking up; but we arrived safe in the evening, and were kindly received by our friends, which made up in part for the toil of the day.

At this place we had an appointed meeting the next day. The five following days we had meetings at Rosendale Plains, Paltz, Plattekill, Newburgh Valley and Marlborough. Attending these meetings, with the exercise of travelling on the heavy, rough roads, produced a large portion of exercise, both to body and mind. But the Lord's strengthening and consoling presence, vouchsafed from season to season for our help, carried us through and over all, to the praise of his grace, and to the comfort and peace of our own minds.

On second day, the 5th of 4th month, we proceeded to Cornwall, and attended a meeting by previous appointment, at the eleventh hour. The next day, had an appointed meeting at Smith's Clove, and the day following were at a place called the Upper Clove, alias Blooming Grove. In these several meetings I was led largely to open to the people the law state, or dispensation of figure, as comprehensively set forth in the Old Testament, and to show the difference between that and the gospel, and that the first ends where the latter begins, and are as distinct from each other, as the body is from the soul. The first comprehends the salvation of bodies from outward servitude, the latter the salvation of the soul from sin, and the death consequent on it. I also set forth the use and necessity of the rituals, or shadows of that dispensation, during its continuance; and that they were all abolished under the gospel, and have no part nor lot under that dispensation. I had much service in these meetings, and great cause of gratitude and thankfulness to the bountiful Author of all our multiplied favours.

The next day, we attended Friends' meeting at Kakiat, alias Hempstead. We had a tedious time in getting there, the road, part of the way, being deep with mud and wet, and much cut up. But the Lord richly rewarded us for all our toil, in giving us a precious meeting with our friends, and a considerable number of the neighbouring inhabitants. It was truly a season of grateful remembrance, both by us and our friends ; we were made to rejoice together for the unmerited favour.

After this we proceeded to Tappan, to the house of our friend John Lawrence. Here is not any meeting of Friends; but feeling the way open, we appointed a meeting there at two o'clock next day. Although it was not large, yet, I trust, it was a comfortable instructive season to some present.

This meeting closed our visit, and the next morning we proceeded to New-York, where we heard of the decease of my kinsman Benjamin Hicks, with information that he was to be interred the next day.

This induced us to proceed home that afternoon, where we arrived between eight and nine at night, much wearied, having travelled in the course of the day upwards of fifty miles, and some of the way but indifferent travelling. Finding, however, our dear families well, accompanied with sweet peace of mind, it made rich amends for all our toil, and my heart was inspired with gratitude and thankfulness to the great and gracious Author of all our blessings.

I was from home in this journey fourteen weeks, attended seventy-three meetings, three quarterly meetings, four monthly meetings, and travelled one thousand and eighty-four miles.

The next day I attended the funeral of the aforesaid Friend, which was on first day the 11th of 4th month, 1819. It was largely attended by Friends and others, he being a man much esteemed by his friends and neighbours, and a useful member of society, both in a religious and moral relation, and his memory will be blessed. It was a very solemn time, in which my heart and mouth were largely opened to declare to the people of the things concerning the kingdom of God ; and to point out to them in a full and clear manner, the only way and means by which an entrance therein is attainable by the children of men. It was a season of favour, and many hearts were made to rejoice under an humbling sense of the gracious extending of heavenly regard to the workmanship of His holy hand.

After this my lot seemed similar to Mordecai's of old, when sitting at the king's gate; I had but little public service when at and about home. This brought to my remembrance, the saying of our Lord to his disciples, on their return from the service he had sent them out to perform in the land of Israel. When they had given him an account how well they had succeeded, he invited them to retire awhile and rest. I was mostly silent in our meetings at home, and was not from home, except to attend a funeral in a neighbouring town, and our quarterly meeting at New-York, until our yearly meeting.

This opened on seventh day, the 22d of 5th month, with a meeting of Ministers and Elders. The yearly meeting for discipline opened on the following second day, and closed near evening, on the fifth day following. It was, I think, in general, a favoured meeting, although the weaknesses and deficiencies still among us, as manifested by the accounts from our quarterly meetings, were cause of exercise and travail to the honest-hearted who are engaged for the promotion of the cause of righteousness and peace in the earth; yet the condescending goodness of the Shepherd of Israel, in manifesting his life-giving presence for our encouragement and support, inspired the hearts of the living with thanksgiving and gratitude for his unmerited mercies. We returned home the next day.

I now found it my duty to pay some attention to my temporal concerns, and to see that all accounts between myself and others were truly adjusted and settled, as is my general rule from year to year. A rule which every honest man will be led to pursue to prevent trouble and preserve harmony; as a contrary course often leads to vexation and litigation, by which both parties are often hurt and wounded.

First day the 30th of 5th month. I attended our meeting as usual, when at home. Had a short communication, tending to excite Friends to faithfulness, and an inward labour, that the true end of our meeting together might be answered. I was busily employed in the course of this week, in my temporal concerns. Attended our fifth day meeting; and closed the week in quiet.

First day, the 6th of 6th month. I was led, in our meeting, to show Friends the fallacy of trusting in the outside appearance of things, without coming to possess the real substance, as the day is hastening when every foundation will be tried, and all will receive according as their works have been. I was considerably enlarged, and the power of truth was exalted over all.

I found it my place at this time, to keep close at home, both in an inward and outward sense, to arrange my temporal concerns, and set things in order; not knowing how soon I may be called to leave them all, and surrender them, with myself, to the guardian care and disposal of a gracious Providence, who doth not suffer a sparrow to fall to the ground, without his heavenly notice. I attended our preparative meeting on fifth day, and the meeting of the Charity Society, for educating the children of the poor black people, on seventh day; in both of which I felt satisfaction and peace of mind.

First day, the 13th of 6th month. Towards the close of our meeting to day, I had to open to Friends the necessity of our individually coming to know what life we are living; whether it be a life after the flesh, which worketh death to the immortal soul; or a life of the spirit, by which we become spiritually-minded. For if we live after the flesh, it will prove in the world to come an eternal death to the soul; but if it be a life in the spirit, and in the things of heaven, it will prove an everlasting life to the soul, in the world to come; and will crown it with joy unspeakable, and full of glory, at God's right hand for evermore.

From this time to our monthly meeting in 7th month, I was pretty steadily at home. Attended our meetings as they came in course; and was very busily and necessarily engaged in my temporal concerns, having a prospect before me of attending the ensuing yearly meeting of Ohio, and also some other meetings in that, and in the compass of Baltimore and Philadelphia yearly meetings. This concern I spread before my Friends, at our monthly meeting the 15th of 7th month; and obtained their unity and concurrence.

First day, the 18th of 7th month. Attended our meeting. We had the company of our ancient honest friend Thomas Titus. He communicated for our consideration, some plain truths, in order to stir up and encourage Friends to industry and faithfulness in those things which belong to their everlasting peace and welfare. I felt unity with him in his exercise, and found it my place and duty to make some addition, to bring the matter close home to the minds of Friends. It was a favoured solemn meeting, and most minds seemed well affected with the heavenly power which was felt to preside.

In the course of this week our quarterly meeting was held at Westbury. It was well attended by Friends; and the public meeting was very large. It was in the main a favoured meeting. I likewise opened to this meeting, my prospect of attending the yearly meeting of Ohio; and produced the minute of unity and concurrence from our monthly meeting. It was fully united with by the quarterly meeting, and an endorsement thereof made on my certificate.

First day the 25th. A silent meeting to-day. When such meetings are attended with full acquiescence, and entire peace of mind, how precious they are. Thus are the Lord's dedicated children led and instructed; taught how to suffer want, and how to abound; being content in every dispensation of his divine will and pleasure: and in this condition, all things work together for good to these. Hence we are led to "Rejoice evermore. Pray without ceasing. In every thing give thanks."

The rest of this week I was diligently employed in preparing for my intended journey; and in arranging my temporal concerns, that no occasion might be given to the adversaries of truth, to reproach the truth, or its cause, by any neglect or omission on my part; and endeavouring that all things might be left sweet and quiet at home, that so I might leave it with peace of mind, freed from every burden and care on that account; and be fully at liberty to devote myself wholly to the service of my great and good Master, until the allotted portion is accomplished, which he hath called me forth to fulfil. For to him belong obedience and worship, who is over all, God blessed for ever. Amen.

First day the 1st of 8th month. At our meeting to-day, my mind was led into a view of the excellence and necessity of a right faith in God and Christ; it being that by which the just live. For nothing else can qualify to live a life of true righteousness and justice, but a true and living faith in God and Christ; and without this faith, it is impossible to please God. The subject spread and led to communication in a large testimony, by which many minds were reached and comforted, and a precious solemnity spread over the meeting; and we parted from each other with grateful hearts for the unmerited favour.

On fifth day I was led to call the attention of my friends to first principles, and to recur to the uprightness, simplicity, and faithfulness of our worthy predecessors, and to recount the great and sorrowful deviations therefrom by those who are making the same profession in the present day, in departing from a full reliance and dependance on the power and spirit that actuated and governed them. Hence weakness and darkness pervade their minds, by which great reproach is brought upon the society, and occasion given for many to speak evil of the truth, and the principle we hold out to the world, as the only sure guide to blessedness; to the wounding of the faithful few, who are yet preserved in a good degree of gospel simplicity, and who live under a daily exercise for the promotion and advancement of the Messiah's kingdom here on earth, and that it may arise and become the peace and glory of all nations.

CHAPTER XVI.

Journey to Ohio in 1819.—Visit to the neighbouring inhabitants in 1819.—Visit to Farmington and Duanesburgh quarterly meetings in 1820.—Visit to some parts of Pennsylvania, and to Baltimore, in 1822. Visit to some of the lower quarterly meetings in 1823.

HAVING, as before noted, had it on my mind to attend the next yearly meeting of Friends in the state of Ohio, and some other meetings in going there and returning home; and having obtained a minute of unity and concurrence from our monthly and quarterly meeting, I left home in order to accomplish the service, the 17th of 8th month, 1819, and proceeded to New-York. The next day, being first day, I attended Friends' meeting in Pearl-street in the morning, which proved a favoured season, in which I witnessed a renewal of strength, and a satisfactory evidence that my proceedure was under right direction; for which my mind was reduced into a state of humble gratitude for the unmerited mercy; having left my home in weakness and poverty of spirit, and nothing to lean on in crossing this Jordan, but my slender staff of faith. I attended the meeting at Liberty-street in the afternoon, which, although small, was in a good degree comfortable, and encouraging to my much exercised mind. As our meeting for sufferings was the succeeding third day, I staid in town and attended that meeting.

After this I proceeded on my journey, accompanied by my kind friend and neighbour Willet Robbins, who had joined me as a companion in this journey. We attended the quarterly meeting at Rahway on our way, which opened the next day with the meeting of Ministers and Elders. The meeting for discipline was held the day after; and a meeting for public worship, as a parting meeting, the succeeding day. In these several opportunities, way opened to discharge myself faithfully in the exercise of gospel communication to my friends and others who attended, fully to the relief of my own mind, and, I trust, to the instruction and encouragement of many who attended ; the Lord having been graciously pleased to manifest his presence and power for our help, to the glory and praise of his own excellent name, who is over all, God blessed for ever.

After these solemn opportunities were closed, we took leave of our friends, and proceeded on our journey ; and arrived at Easton on seventh day evening.   This is a town on the west side of the river Delaware, in the state of Pennsylvania. Having felt my mind led to pass through this town, attended with a concern to have a religious opportunity with the inhabitants, we tarried with them the next day, and had a meeting appointed, which was held in their school-house, at the fourth hour in the afternoon.   It proved, through heavenly help, a favoured, and, I trust, an instructive season to many ; several of their ministers and most of the principal people attended, and appeared all to go away satisfied ; and many apparently with thankful hearts for the present favour ; and I parted with them in true peace of mind.

The next morning we proceeded on our journey, and rode to Maiden Creek, and lodged with our kind friend Isaac Penrose. The day following being third day, we had an appointed meeting at Reading, about eight miles farther on our way.   It was held in their court-house.   Many of the inhabitants of the town attended, and behaved soberly ; and the gospel was preached among them in the plain demonstration of truth, and, I trust, was as a sword or hammer to some present, who were not prepared to meet sound doctrine ; but was comfortable and instructive to others, such as were tender in spirit, and were honestly seeking the way to peace.   It was a solemn, and, I trust, profitable opportunity.

After the meeting I made a short visit to a sick woman, who appeared to be drawing fast toward her close.   She was comforted in the visit, and when I parted with her, appeared in a quiet resigned state of mind.   Her bodily affliction, which had attended her for a considerable time, had, I believe, wrought a good work in her. After this opportunity we proceeded immediately on our journey, which we continued the four following days, through a number of towns and villages, where no Friends live.

We arrived on seventh day evening at Dunning's Creek where there is a monthly meeting of Friends. They lie very much detached from the body of society; the nearest meeting to them is about sixty miles distant. We attended their meeting on first day, which proved, through heavenly help, a comfortable, strengthening opportunity. We lodged with our kind friend Thomas Penrose.

The next morning we proceeded on our journey, having the Alleghany, and several other mountains and high and rough ridges of land to pass over, in our way to the settlements of Friends in the Redstone country. The roads were excessively bad, and in some places almost impassable; but with two days hard travelling we got safe to Connelsville, on the west side of the mountains, on third day evening. We put up with a man by the name of John Gibson, who had once a right of membership in our society, but by some means had lost it; yet he appeared to retain his love to Friends, and was very kind and benevolent, and appeared very glad of the opportunity of entertaining Friends. His family likewise appeared very kind and friendly, and signified it as a matter of considerable regret, that they were so far distant from Friends, as not to have the privilege of attending their meetings. There was one family of Friends in the town; and one of their children, an infant of about eight months old, had died a little before our arrival; and the funeral being the next day, we attended it. It was a very solemn opportunity, in which many hearts were contrited by the tendering power of truth, which was felt to cover the assembly in a very general manner. Such seasons are as a brook by the way, to the poor exercised travellers, who often go mourning on their way, from a sense of the prevalence of sin and iniquity in the land.

After this solemn opportunity we proceeded on our journey, and the next day attended Friends' monthly meeting at Westland, in Redstone quarterly meeting. I had some service, both in the meeting for worship, and that for discipline; but things appeared rather low as to the right order of the gospel, in both meetings. It being a day of ease and outward tranquillity; and this hath a tendency to produce lukewarmness, if not watchfully and diligently guarded against.

From this place we proceeded directly to Mount Pleasant, in Ohio, where the yearly meeting is held; where we arrived on seventh day, the 28th of 8th month. On first day, the 29th, attended Friends' meeting at Short Creek in the morning, and had an appointed meeting at Mount Pleasant in the afternoon. They were both largely attended, and proved very instructive satisfactory meetings, in which I had good service; and found sweet peace as the result of my labours of love amongst them.

The five following days, meetings were appointed for us at Concord, St. Clairville, Plainfield, Flushing, and Harrisville. These were all full meetings; generally more collected than the houses could contain; but Friends were industrious, and provided seats out of doors, about the house, by which the people were generally accommodated.

On seventh day the yearly meeting of Ministers and Elders opened; and continued by adjournments until fifth day. I think they were generally favoured opportunities. The Head of the Church graciously condescending to manifest his presence for the help of his devoted, dedicated children; and this is the crown and diadem of all our religious assemblies. On first day public meetings for worship were held, both forenoon and afternoon, in both Friends' meeting-houses in the neighbourhood; that in the town of Mount Pleasant, held in their new meeting-house, which is one of the largest I ever saw belonging to Friends, was very large. I attended that meeting both forenoon and afternoon, in which I had much service by way of testimony; which appeared to be much to the comfort and general edification of the assemblies, and resulted in the solid peace of my own mind.

On second day, the yearly meeting for discipline opened, and continued by adjournments until seventh day toward evening.

It was a season of much travail and exercise to the rightly concerned active members ; having before them, in addition to their usual business, the revisal of their discipline. I was led under close exercise on the account, and a very considerable portion of active service fell to my lot, with other Friends. It was thought, I believe, by Friends generally, to have been the most favoured yearly meeting they had had since its institution, and was worthy of grateful remembrance.

I tarried here over first day, and attended their meeting at the old meeting-house. It was a season of deep travail in the forepart of the meeting, in which my spirit was led into deep baptism with, and for, the dead ; and I was brought into sympathy and fellowship with the suffering seed, which appeared to me to be pressed down in the hearts of the formal professors, as a cart under sheaves. This, I believed, was too much the situation of a considerable number in that assembly; but as I continued patiently to endure the exercise, and kept up the inward travail, light sprang up and dispelled the darkness, accompanied with a motion of life to stand up ; and my mouth was opened in a large searching and effective testimony, whereby the dead were raised, the lukewarm stirred up, the honest seekers encouraged, and the rightly exercised minds comforted and edified. It was the Lord's doing, and marvellous in mine eyes.

The six succeeding days, meetings were appointed at the following places, which we attended. On second day, at a little village called York, where a few Friends were privileged with an indulged meeting ; a meeting not being established. On third day at Smithfield ; on fourth day at Cross Creek ; on fifth day at Franklin, where was also only a small indulged meeting. On sixth day, at Augusta, at the tenth hour in the morning, and at Sandy Spring, at the third hour in the afternoon ; on seventh day at New Garden. These were all seasons of favour, wherein I was strengthened to labour in the work of the gospel, and to declare largely to these several assemblies, of the things concerning the kingdom of God ; endeavouring, by persuasive arguments, founded in the clear demonstration of the spirit, accompanied with a lively evidence of divine

48

power to gather the minds of the people to the *light of Christ,* or *Christ the light, in their own hearts ; as the only sure guide to blessedness,* and *foundation rock on which to build all our hopes of redemption and salvation.* A precious solemnity was felt to prevail in those several meetings, most of which were crowded gatherings, many more often collecting than their meeting-houses could contain ; and truth was exalted over all, to the praise of Him who is over all, God blessed for ever.

After the latter meeting we proceeded to Salem, intending to be at Friends' meeting there the next day, which was first day, the 19th of 9th month. We attended the meeting in the forenoon, but not feeling myself clear, I was led to appoint an afternoon meeting; which was accordingly held at the third hour, and was largely attended by Friends and others; among whom way opened fully to discharge and clear myself, and I found peace in my labour of love among them.

On second and third days, I attended meetings by appointment at Springfield and Goshen, two neighbouring villages. These were likewise very solemn instructive seasons, wherein I was largely led forth in ministerial labour, apparently to the comfort and edification of most present. From Goshen we returned back to Salem, intending to be at their monthly meeting to be held the next day, which we accordingly attended. I had good service among my Friends, both in the meeting for worship and that for discipline.

After this we took a final leave of them, in the fresh feelings of mutual love and Christian fellowship, and proceeded on our journey that afternoon to Fairfield, where we had a meeting the next day. On sixth day, was at Columbiana. On seventh day, at Middleton. And on first day, the 26th, had two meetings; one in the morning at Elk Run, and the other at the third hour in the afternoon at Carmel. These meetings were all well attended ; wherein I was led forth largely in testimony, apparently to the general satisfaction and edification of the people, and to the comfort and peace of my own mind.

On second day we proceeded to New Lisbon, and attended a meeting in their court-house at the eleventh hour. It was a large collection, mostly made up of other societies, there being but few Friends residing in that place. I was led to open several doctrinal points of our profession, and to show the great difference between profession and possession; and that no profession of religion was worth esteeming as any thing, unless it was the effect of the real possession of the thing professed; as no profession of a thing, could of itself give any a possession thereof; but a real possession, will manifest itself by its fruits. It was a day of great favour, in which truth reigned over all.

On third day, we proceeded to Beaver Falls. Had a meeting there the next day to good satisfaction. After this we travelled on our way to Pittsburg, where we arrived the next day about noon, and had an appointed meeting there in the evening in their court-house. It was a large spacious building, but more collected than the house could contain. I had much service among them, and the Lord's power was felt to preside, quieting and solemnizing the assembly; and many hearts were humbled and contrited, and truth raised into dominion over all.

On sixth day afternoon, we left Pittsburg on our way to Brownsville, where we arrived in the afternoon of the next day. On first day we attended Friends' meeting there; and notice being spread among the people at large that we were there, it was a very crowded assembly, more than the house could well contain. Through the condescending goodness of the Shepherd of Israel, I was helped to discharge myself faithfully among them, in an effective testimony to the truths of the gospel; proving from clear scripture testimony, accompanied with the demonstration of the spirit, in harmony with right reason, that nothing short of a full belief in, and obedience to, the revelation of the spirit of truth, (a manifestation of which is given to every man and woman to profit withal,) as the only rule of faith and practice, can make a real Christian, and produce redemption and salvation to an immortal soul. It was a very solemn instructive season, worthy of grateful remembrance.

On second day we had an appointed meeting at Sandy Hill, at the tenth hour; and another in the evening at Uniontown, held in their court-house. These were both seasons of favour, producing solid peace to my own mind, and, I trust, instructive and edifying to the people in general who attended. These meetings closed my labours among Friends and others, in the compass of the yearly meeting of Ohio.

On third day we set out on our journey over the mountains, towards Winchester in Virginia; in order to attend the meetings of Friends in that neighbourhood, on our way to Baltimore. The distance was about one hundred and sixteen miles. It took three days to accomplish the journey, with hard travelling; a considerable part of the way being very rocky, as well as mountainous. We arrived among Friends at Pughtown, on fifth day evening; and had a meeting appointed there the next day, at two o'clock in the afternoon, which we attended accordingly. On seventh day had a meeting at the Ridge. On first day at Centre, near Winchester; and the two following days had meetings at Hopewell and Berkley. I was largely led forth in these meetings, to show to the people the inconsistency and unrighteousness of holding our fellow creatures in bondage, and the evil tendency of bringing up our children and families on the fruits of their labour, wrested from them by violence, without paying them an adequate reward for the same. I likewise opened to them the folly and deception of all their profession of worshipping that Being, who is perfect in justice, purity and holiness, while their hands are full of violence and oppression, and they living in luxury and idleness on their unrighteous gain. The Lord's power was exalted in these meetings, and truth reigned.

After the latter meeting we proceeded on our way towards Baltimore, where we arrived on seventh day evening; attending meetings at Fredericktown and New Market, on our way thither. On first day, the 17th of 10th month, I attended Friends' meetings in that city; the Western District in the morning, and the Eastern District in the afternoon. I was silent in the former, but in the latter, I was largely led forth in gospel communication. As notice had been spread among the citizens of other professions, the meeting was large, and the divine power was felt to preside, which brought a precious solemnity over the meeting, and truth was raised into dominion.

Here we met with our friend Elizabeth Coggeshall from New-York, with her companion Judith Coffin, from Nantucket; also our ancient friend William Rickman, from England. We were mutually glad in seeing each other. Elizabeth felt a concern to see the members of our society, select from those of other societies in each meeting, accordingly a Friend, at her request, in the morning meeting when the service of the first meeting was over, proposed the same to the assembly ; when those who were not members quietly withdrew, and our dear friend had good service among them. This also opened an opportunity for me to throw in my mite, and set a seal to the service. A similar opportunity was likewise had with Friends at the close of the afternoon meeting in the Eastern District, which was also a favoured time.

And as I had felt my mind somewhat similarly engaged in coming into the city, it opened the way to spread my exercise before Friends ; which was that of the more select service of seeing the active members and heads of families of both sexes together. I had an opportunity with those of this description in the Western District, and afterwards with those of the Eastern; and was glad in believing that divine love was near, favouring with His enlivening, reconciling presence ; which raised a hope, that through the divine blessing, the opportunities would not prove altogether unfruitful, for some disunity and jealousies had prevailed among the members of society in this city.

The next day being Friends' meeting day, I felt most easy to stay and attend it. I also found my mind led to some further service among the citizens at large : for although I had had a public opportunity on first day evening, which seemed for the present to ease my mind, yet a renewed exercise on that account induced a belief it would be right to give the citizens generally another invitation ; which Friends readily agreed to, and spread the notice accordingly. It was a very large meeting, and through gracious condescension a highly favoured season; the Lord's power was felt to preside, and a precious solemnity spread over the assembly, and I took my leave of them in much peace of mind.

This closed my service among them. The two following days we rode to Wilmington, where we arrived on sixth day evening. On seventh day evening we had a large meeting by appointment, with Friends and the inhabitants of the town. This was a solemn instructive season, worthy of grateful remembrance. We also attended the morning meeting of Friends the next day, and then proceeded to Chester, parting with my Friends in much sweet peace and unity. Here we had a large solemn meeting in the evening, among the few Friends of the place and the inhabitants of the town. I trust, through heavenly goodness, it proved an instructive edifying season to many.

The two following days, I attended the monthly meetings of Providence and Darby. On fourth day morning we proceeded to Philadelphia. We staid in the city until the following third day, and attended all the meetings of Friends there; some by appointment, and the others as they came in course. We were at two of their monthly meetings, and their quarterly meeting. The meetings were generally crowded, and at several many of the people were obliged to stand outside of the doors, for want of room. Through unmerited mercy the Lord's power was felt to preside, producing a precious solemnity over those large promiscuous gatherings, and by which truth was raised into dominion. Surely it was the Lord's doing, and marvellous in mine eyes. It was, I trust, a time of renewed visitation to many, especially to the beloved youth.

We left the city on third day morning, and proceeded to Germantown, where by previous appointment we had a large meeting at the eleventh hour. The two following days we attended Friends' quarterly meeting at Horsham; and on sixth day, had a large public meeting at Byberry. These were all favoured instructive seasons, in which the Lord's presence was manifested for our help, and were worthy of grateful remembrance.

On seventh day we attended a meeting at Bristol; and at evening crossed the river Delaware to Burlington, and attended Friends' forenoon and afternoon meetings on first day. These were large favoured meetings, in which truth reigned.

On second day, the 8th of 11th month we proceeded to Trenton and had a large meeting there in the evening, with the few Friends of that place, and the inhabitants of the town, in which divers essential doctrines of the gospel were opened to the consideration of the assembly. It was a solemn meeting, and I parted with them in true peace of mind, which is the certain and consolatory result of disinterested obedience, and faithfulness to manifested duty.

We proceeded on third day, on our way to New-York, where we arrived the next day in season to attend Friends' meeting in Pearl-street; it being their usual meeting day. The meeting was generally gathered when I got in, having had some distance to travel to reach there, which occasioned my being a few minutes after the time. My mind, soon after taking my seat, was brought under a renewed exercise, on account of the members of our society mixing in with the associations of other people, in their governments and politics, their Bible and Missionary societies, and pretended charity associations ; which had a very hurtful tendency, by leavening the minds of Friends, and leading them to assimilate with the spirit of the world ; and turning them away from the simplicity, of our profession, thereby neglecting to support our Christian testimonies, as it regards plainness of speech, deportment, and apparel. Such conduct is particularly wounding to some of the beloved youth, for they seeing their elder brethren, and especially some who' were sometimes active in our meetings for discipline, join with such associations, it leads them into a free familiarity and friendship with such as are light and vain in their conversation and deportment, by which their tender minds are greatly wounded ; and they led off from the cross, and a strict regard to that sobriety of conduct, which truth requires of all its professors. I was led to communicate largely on those subjects, in a close searching testimony ; and the Lord's power was felt to prevail, and the meeting generally brought under a solemn covering. It proved a season of favour, and the right-minded were made to rejoice.

Feeling my mind impressed with a concern to appoint a meeting for the citizens at large, the appointment was accordingly made at seven o'clock the ensuing evening. It was a very large collection, more than the house could contain; and was a highly favoured season. A very precious solemnity was spread over the assembly in general; and when I sat down, after standing nearly two hours, I turned my eyes over the congregation, and all was quiet and still, and every countenance seemed expressive of the solemnity felt, which united us together and clothed us as with a mantle of love. Surely it was the Lord's doing, and marvellous in our eyes.

The next day I attended Friends' meeting near the Bowery, as it came in course; and some notice being given of my intending to be there, we had the company of a number of their neighbours of other societies. This was also a very instructive favoured season.

The ensuing evening I had another appointed meeting for the citizens at large, in Friends' meeting-house at Liberty-street. This was rather a trying meeting; as many who attended were such as had settled down in a form, and were difficult to reach, which makes hard labour for the truly exercised ministers. However I had a hope the season would prove profitable to some, and I left them with peace of mind.

This meeting closed my labours in this journey, and the next morning we rode home, the 12th of the 11th month, 1819. I found my family and friends in usual health, and glad to see me, which rendered it a cause of mutual joy, and filled my heart with gratitude and thanksgiving to the God and Father of all our sure mercies, who had led about, instructed and preserved me, through all, to the praise of his great and excellent name.

I was from home in this journey about three months, and travelled nearly twelve hundred miles, and attended eighty-seven meetings:

First day, 14th. I sat with my Friends in our own meeting, in which I was largely led forth in ministry, setting forth, as it opened on my mind, the cause why so little progress was made in reformation, and the true spiritual or real Christian life ; and showing that it was principally, as it then appeared in the openings of truth, occasioned by the visited children of our heavenly Father, not keeping close to that which first visited them, and opened their understanding ; but letting their minds out to worldly things, and that by opening the way to a free and familiar converse with the people of the world, many were led and induced thereby to join with them in their manners, maxims, interests and worldly policies, by which means they were so yoked together in a free and open friendship, as thereby to become weakened and brought into bondage to them; so as to be ashamed and afraid to stand upright, and bear a faithful testimony against this worldly spirit and its fruits; by which the testimonies of truth were in a great measure let fall, for fear of offending these their worldly-minded associates, by which the promotion of the cause of truth was greatly obstructed, and its faithful testimony-bearers grieved, and made to go mourning on their way.

Fifth day. Attended our monthly meeting, in which I also had some close searching labour to stir up Friends to more diligence and faithfulness in the support of our Christian testimonies ; and cautioning them against a worldly spirit, which would lead to extortion and grinding the faces of the poor ; for this is very reproachful for any Christian professor, and more so for us, who are making a more exalted profession than any others who go under the Christian name.

First day, the 21st. My mind to-day was led into a near feeling sympathy with such as had been visited with the day-spring from on high, but who had not so fully given up to the pointing of truth, in what are generally termed little things, as they ought : the natural tendency of which is to lead the mind into a doubting state. For when the creature, in his own will, takes the liberty of judging for himself, of what is little, or what is great, he departs from the true standard, and has no certain

49

evidence to walk by; for if he has a right to judge for himself in one case, why not in every other. Here doubting will arise in his mind, of what is, or is not, agreeable to the divine will; as nothing can give the mind certain evidence, but faithfully complying with the evident sensations which the light of truth opens upon it, let them be what the creature may judge to be small or great; for we have no more reason or right to refuse complying with a small requisition, than we have a great one, if the requisition proceeds from the same source. The subject was so opened as to affect many minds with tenderness and contrition; and had an humbling, solemnizing effect on the meeting in general, and was, I believe, gladdening to many minds.

Fifth day. Attended our meeting in silence, which was very acceptable to me.

First day, the 28th. Mostly silent in meeting to-day.

On my return home from my late journey, I felt my mind drawn in sympathy, attended with a concern to pay a religious visit to the neighbouring inhabitants in the compass of our quarterly meeting. This concern I opened to my friends the first monthly meeting after my return, and received their full unity therein; but taking a severe cold soon after I came home, I continued indisposed for some weeks, which with some necessary concerns, prevented my entering on the visit, until after our succeeding monthly meeting. The fourth day following, the 22d of 12th month, I proceeded therein, accompanied by my wife and my kinsman, Isaac Hicks, of Westbury. We were from home five days, and attended six meetings, mostly among those of other societies. It was a time of deep exercise to me, being led in the line of searching labour, pointing to a reform in manners and conduct; and showing the fallacy of all ceremonial religion in the observation of days, and complying with outward ordinances; which do not in the least tend to make the comers thereunto a whit the better, as it respects the conscience, but lead the observers thereof into a form, without the power.

We returned home the following second day. I tarried at home until the beginning of the next week, when feeling my mind drawn to attend the monthly meeting of Friends in New

York, I again left home, accompanied by the aforesaid friend. We were at the monthly meeting on fourth day, in which I had some close exercise, the meeting having much business before it, and one case in particular was very trying, in which Friends were divided, and two or three unqualified individuals seemed determined, for a considerable time, to compel the meeting to comply with their unsanctified wills; but as Friends who were rightly exercised, patiently kept up the travail, and withstood them, truth was raised into dominion, and by its power silenced all their cavilling, and united the meeting in a right conclusion. The meeting for worship and that for discipline continued upwards of six hours.

We left the city soon after the close of this long meeting, and passed over the river to Brooklyn, where by previous appointment we had a meeting that evening, composed of the different professions of the inhabitants of that place, very few Friends residing there. The meeting was pretty large, and in the main satisfactory. The next day we proceeded to Flushing, and attended their monthly meeting. I was silent in the meeting for worship, but had some good service in that for discipline. We also had an appointed meeting in the evening for the inhabitants of the town, which was large and solemn. The next day we returned to Newtown, and had a meeting at Friends' meeting-house at the Kilns in that place, at the eleventh hour; and another in the evening at the sixth hour, in the village. They were both favoured meetings. We returned to Flushing after the latter meeting, and lodged with our kind friend Walter Farrington, and the next day rode home and found my family well.

First day, the 9th of 1st month, 1820. I sat with my friends at home in our own meeting to-day, which I considered as no small privilege.

On second day morning I was early informed, that my kinsman and kind fellow traveller Isaac Hicks, was taken with a severe illness, about ten o'clock the preceding evening, and lay at the point of death. I hastened to see him, and found him nearly breathing his last, being past noticing any thing by his external senses.   It was a sudden and unexpected trial to me, to be thus almost instantaneously separated from such a kind and valued friend, who had for a number of years devoted himself in divers ways, to promote the cause of truth and righteousness in the earth; and in particular, by encouraging and accompanying Friends in the ministry, when travelling in truth's service, especially myself, having been with me in several long journeys, as well as divers short ones.   I parted with him at the close of one of the latter, on the seventh day afternoon before his death, at his own house, and apparently in usual health: although he had been for a considerable time previous there, much afflicted, at times, with severe pain in his breast and short- ness of breath, which created great suffering during their con- tinuance.   He had a return thereof the evening before I last parted with him, which occasioned him to observe to me, that he thought he should ere long be taken off in one of those attacks; but I then thought quite otherwise, as in other respects he appeared to be in very good health, and had a very healthy countenance.

Such sudden attacks prove with indubitable evidence, that mortality is so closely interwoven in the very constitution of these animal bodies, that the present moment is the only time we can call our own; and which continually announce the impressive language : " Be ye therefore ready."

Such sudden and unexpected separations from our endeared friends make the loss seem greater, not only to their families and near connexions, but to their friends in general, and particularly so to those who knew their real worth.   But it ever affords a soothing consolation, and induces to acquiesce in the divine will, when we have evident cause to hope that our loss, which is but for a short time, is their eternal gain.

I attended the funeral of my beloved friend, which was large and solemn; and I was led forth in an impressive testimony to the truths of the gospel; inviting the people to inquire, and see, and taste for themselves, that the Lord is good.

I continued at home until the following seventh day, when I again proceeded on my visit to the neighbouring towns and villages. I was from home about thirteen days and attended fifteen meetings, returning home on sixth day, the 11th of 2d month, 1820. My service in many of those opportunities was very arduous; the lukewarmness and insensibility of the people, as to any right religious concern, make hard work for the honest labourers, in this day of ease and carnal security. But true peace of mind, the sure result of faithfulness, crowns the attempts at doing good, as it makes hard things easy and bitter things sweet.

I tarried at home until the latter end of the next week, in the course of which I had a very severe attack of bodily indisposition, occasioned by the gravel, with which I have been afflicted at times, for near twenty years. These warnings are designed to spur us on to our duty, as they continually announce to the enlightened mind this very useful memento: "Remember to die."

In the latter end of the week, there came to my house my much esteemed friend and kinsman Edward Hicks, from Newtown, in Bucks county, Pennsylvania, on a religious visit to our parts, with his companion James Walton, an elder. I accompanied them the next day to a meeting they had appointed at Westbury. It was very large, in which Edward had very good service, being largely led forth to open to the people many important doctrines of the Christian religion. I accompanied him to all the meetings he had among us except one; and in some of them had a portion of the service laid upon me, particularly in the meeting at Bethpage.

I accompanied my friend to four meetings after this, in which he was generally favoured to open things suitable to the states of the people; his gift being searching and lively. After his service was over in the meeting at Cowneck, on first day, I was led forth in a short testimony; and the meeting closed under an evident sense that truth reigned. Our next meeting was the day following at Rockaway, on second day, the 28th of 2d month. It was in the main a favoured opportunity. My part was to sit in silence. After this meeting I parted with my beloved friend and his companion, in the fellowship of the gospel; they proceeded towards New-York, and I returned home that evening, and found my family well.

First day, the 5th of 3d month. I attended our own meeting, which through heavenly help proved a very precious instructive season. It was larger than usual, many coming in who did not often attend, to whom the gospel was preached in the demonstration of the spirit, through which truth was raised into dominion, causing the hearts of many to be warmed within them by the influence of its power, and manifesting itself by much brokenness and contrition of spirit.

Second day, the 13th. Attended the funeral of our friend Charles Frost, at which there was a large collection of friends and neighbours. A meeting was held on the occasion, which was a favoured one, and, I trust, a profitable opportunity to some present, and worthy of grateful remembrance.

In the fall of 1820, being, with several other friends, on an appointment from the yearly meeting, requiring our care and attention in the northern quarters, and having for some time previously felt my mind drawn to visit some of the meetings of Friends, within the compass of Farmington and Duanesburgh quarterly meetings, I obtained the unity and concurrence of my Friends at home to attend thereto, after accomplishing the service of the yearly meeting. I accordingly set out in the 9th month, and was favoured to go through the visit with peace to my own mind; for He, who is the alone sure helper of all his dependant children, graciously manifested himself to be near, for my help and encouragement in the travail and exercise that I was engaged in, for the promotion of his noble cause of truth and righteousness in the earth; and in a way, that was often marvellous in mine eyes, tending to inspire my soul with deep and humble gratitude and thanksgiving, for the unmerited favour.

In the summer of 1822, I opened to my Friends a prospect, which for a considerable time had been impressive on my mind, to make a visit in the love of the gospel, to Friends and others in some parts of the yearly meeting of Philadelphia; and, if way should open for it, to visit some of the families of Friends in that city, and also to attend the yearly meeting at Baltimore. They united with me in the concern, and left me at liberty to proceed therein. I set out in the 7th month, with David Seaman as my companion. We had a large favoured meeting at Flushing, which was strengthening and comforting to my mind, in first setting out in this arduous engagement, and excited gratitude for the unmerited mercy. After leaving Flushing on our way to New-York, my prospect of a meeting at Hester-treet, which I had a view of several weeks before I left home, revived with renewed weight; and although from the consternation and interrupted state of the citizens, owing to the prevalence of fever in the city, I had given up the prospect on leaving home, yet I now saw that I could not depart from the city with a quiet mind, unless I had a meeting agreeably to my former view. Accordingly, when I got into town I opened my concern to some of my friends there, who readily united therewith, and notice was given; and one of the Friends who attended about the door at the gathering of the meeting, said there were more people collected than had ever been at any former time in that place; several hundreds, he said, went away, who could not get into the house for want of room. I had a full opportunity to clear my mind among the people, most of whom were very solid and attentive. Thus we have great cause of gratitude to the gracious Care-taker of his faithfully devoted children, who opens a way for them, when some are ready to conclude there is no way. But he opens a way for those, which none but himself can shut, to the praise of his own great and adorable name, who is over all, blessed for ever.

We then proceeded to Newark, and had a meeting in the court-house. There was a pretty large collection of the inhabitants, among whom I had strength and utterance given to open many important doctrines of the Christian religion, in a clear and impressive manner, which appeared sensibly to affect and impress the minds of the sober and well inclined; but many appeared very ignorant and inexperienced as to the real truths of the gospel. But having fully cleared my mind among them, I left them with the answer of peace, and proceeded to Plainfield. We attended the meeting there, which was large for the place; and it was favoured in an eminent manner, to our mutual comfort. We then rode to Kingwood, and had a full and comfortable meeting there; after which we went to Solebury, in Pennsylvania, and had a meeting at the sixth hour in the evening. It was a large meeting, in which I was led to discharge myself faithfully in a close searching testimony. It was a very solemn quiet opportunity, and I parted with them in peace of mind.

We afterwards attended meetings at Buckingham, Plumbstead, Wrightstown, Makefield, and Newtown: and we have abundant cause to bless the name of Israel's unslumbering Shepherd, who hath graciously condescended to manifest his presence and power for our help and support, opening my way in a marvellous manner in all the meetings I have attended since I left home, uniting my friends in a joint travail for the promotion of his blessed cause; truth prevailing in every meeting, and running as precious ointment over the assemblies, bearing down all opposition, and spreading, by its power, a sweet and precious solemnity over all. Surely it is the Lord's doing, and marvellous in our eyes: and what is the greatest cause of gratitude and thanksgiving to the benevolent Author of all our richest blessings, is, that he causes all these favours to bow my spirit in deep humiliation and fear before him, as unworthy of the least of his mercies. To the sufficiency of his grace, may all the praise and glory be ascribed, nothing due to man.

We then attended meetings at Horsham, Upper Dublin, North Wales, Plymouth, Providence, Pikeland, Westchester, London Grove, and Deer Creek; and my spirit is humbled in a deep feeling sense of the Lord's goodness vouchsafed for our help, opening a way in the minds of my friends generally to receive the testimonies given me to bear, for the promotion of his righteous cause, with marks of apparent joy and satisfaction, and to our mutual comfort. We reached Baltimore on the 25th of 10th month; and the meeting of Ministers and Elders was opened on the next day at the tenth hour. The yearly meeting continued till sixth day evening, and was acknowledged to be the largest and the most favoured meeting they had known for several years past. The unity of Friends with my exercises in the public meetings, and in those for discipline, was truly grateful, and tended to humble and inspire my mind with gratitude and thanksgiving to my heavenly Father.

I did not feel myself at liberty to leave the city at the close of the yearly meeting, believing that some more public service among the people was required of me. I had accordingly a public meeting in the Eastern District, on seventh day evening. It was very large; and among the various subjects that opened for communication to those assembled, I was led to expose the iniquity and deformity of the cruel practice of holding our fellow creatures in bondage, and the injustice and inconsistency of Friends doing any act where the right of slavery was acknowledged and supported; and, I think, I was enabled to do it in a more full and impressive manner than ever before. We had a very interesting and solemn meeting; truth appeared to gain the victory, and reigned over all. On first day I attended Friends' meetings for the Western District, both in the forenoon and afternoon. They were very large; and I had a full opportunity in the morning of clearing myself among them. We had a precious, powerful meeting; and among the divers states addressed, the slave-holders were peculiarly the objects of my exercise and concern. The afternoon meeting I sat in silence, except the expression of a few words just at the close, in taking leave of them, and bidding all farewell.

In the evening I had a precious interesting opportunity with the coloured people, in Friends' meeting-house in the Western District. It was said by Friends to be much the largest known in that place. It was a very quiet, solemn meeting; and the minds of all, both white and coloured, seemed animated with gladness and joy for the favour dispensed, and gave manifestations of their thankfulness and gratitude for the opportunity.

We then proceeded towards Philadelphia, attending several meetings on our way, which were greatly favoured, and crowned with the divine presence and power, in such a manner as to be marvellous in our eyes.

We arrived in Philadelphia in the early part of 12th month; and I immediately entered on the arduous concern which I had had in prospect, and which I was favoured soon comfortably to accomplish. We visited the families composing Green-street monthly meeting, being in number about one hundred and forty; and we also attended that monthly meeting, and the monthly meeting for the Northern District. This closed my visit there, and set me at liberty to turn my face homeward. We left Philadelphia on the 25th of 12th month, and attended several meetings in Pennsylvania and New Jersey, on our way home, which were large and solemn opportunities. We were favoured to reach our homes with feelings of thanksgiving to our gracious Preserver, and with the enjoyment of that precious peace, which is experienced by those whose minds are stayed on God; as the prophet declared in his appeal to Jehovah: "Thou wilt keep him in perfect peace, whose mind is stayed on thee, because he trusteth in thee." And he subjoins, for our encouragement: "Trust in the Lord for ever; for in the Lord Jehovah is everlasting strength." May we all dwell here; then nothing can hurt or harm us; for the Lord our Preserver will turn all the designs and cunning devices of those that rise up against us upon their own heads, and cause them to fall into their own pit.

In the latter part of 1823, I felt myself engaged to make a religious visit to Friends and others in several of the lower quarterly meetings; and having obtained the unity of my friends, I set out in the 10th month, with Samuel Willis as my companion. After having meetings at Westchester and Mamaroneck, we attended the select quarterly meeting at Purchase, which was small, many of the members being absent. They appeared to be clothed with much weakness: I was led into a feeling sympathy with them, and way was opened to communicate to their states, in a way that was comforting and encouraging to the honest-hearted. The next day was the quarterly meeting of discipline. It was large; and, I think, in the main it was a favoured instructive season, although considerably hurt by a long tedious communication from a Friend, not sufficiently clothed with life to make it useful. But the society is in such a mixed and unstable state, and many who presume to be teachers in it are so far from keeping on the original foundation, *the light and spirit of truth*, and are so built up in mere tradition, that I fear a great portion of the ministry amongst us is doing more harm than good, and is leading back to the weak and beggarly elements to which some seem desirous to be again in bondage.

After leaving Purchase, we had a pretty large and favoured meeting at North Castle; and next day we went to Oblong, and attended their meeting on first day. It was large, and I had an open time among them, through the prevalence of that power which opens and none can shut, and when he shuts none can open. Truth reigned, and the people generally, I believe, were instructed, comforted, and edified. I parted with them in true peace of mind, which leads my heart into deep humility, and inspires it with gratitude and thanksgiving to the great and blessed Author of all our mercies. We had a meeting at the Branch, and then proceeded to Nine Partners, and attended the select quarterly meeting. It was much like some other meetings of this kind, hard and not very fruitful. The members of those meetings are too generally falling more short of coming up faithfully, according to their stations, than most of the other departments of our society. We attended the quarterly meeting for discipline, also that at Stanford, and soon after turned our faces homeward; where we arrived, accompanied with the fresh feelings of that love that many waters cannot quench; even that powerful love that is stronger than death, and binds together in an indissoluble bond, all the new-born children of the heavenly Father. May we all seek for it, and dwell in it. It will cast out all fear, and clothe with that innocent boldness, which will enable us to withstand all the dark powers of antichrist and his agents, and all their deceivableness of unrighteousness; and will raise above the fear of death, with all his mis-shapen and ugly forms, and clothe with the joys of God's salvation here and for ever, as we continue steadfast in the faith that overcomes the world.

CHAPTER XVII.

Visit to Baltimore to attend the yearly meeting in 1824.—Visit to the inhabitants
of the eastern part of Long Island in 1825.—Visit to Scipio quarterly meeting
in 1825.—Visit to Southern and Concord quarterly meetings in Pennsylvania
in 1826.—Visit to the families of Friends in Jericho and Westbury monthly
meetings in 1827.—Visit to Friends in some parts of New Jersey, Pennsylvania and Ohio in 1828.

In the summer of 1824, I had the concurrence of my friends
to attend the quarterly meeting of Cornwall and Stanford, which
I accomplished to my own peace and comfort. And in the fall
of the same year, they also united with a concern which had
impressed my mind, to attend the ensuing yearly meeting in
Baltimore. This engagement, through the mercy of Him who
has hitherto helped me, I was favoured to accomplish to the
peace and satisfaction of my own mind. The yearly meeting
for discipline opened on second day, and continued by adjournments until the following fifth day, in the afternoon of which it
closed, under a comfortable evidence of divine favour attending.
I think it was, in its several sittings, one of the most satisfactory
yearly meetings I ever attended, and the business was conducted
in much harmony and brotherly love.

In Philadelphia, on my return, I had a severe attack of bodily
indisposition ; so that, for some time, there seemed but little
prospect of my recovery. I lodged at the house of my very
kind friend Samuel R. Fisher, who, with his worthy children,
extended to me the most affectionate care and attention ; and I
had also the kind sympathy of a large portion of Friends in
that city.

In the summer of 1825, I obtained the concurrence of my
friends to make a visit, in gospel love, to the inhabitants of the

eastern part of Long Island, and I proceeded therein, with Samuel Willis as my companion. The people appeared open to receive us, and the meetings at the several places we visited, were pretty fully attended. Many minds were humbled and contrited, and truth's testimonies exalted, and the people generally comforted, and, I trust, edified.

In the fall of 1825, being on an appointment of the yearly meeting to attend the opening of Scipio quarterly meeting, I obtained the unity of my friends to attend some meetings among Friends and others, on my way going and returning. The quarterly meeting in its several sittings, was conducted in much apparent harmony and condescension; the truth was so effectually raised into dominion over all, that if there were any discordant spirits present, they were all kept down and subdued by the prevalence of its power; and Friends were united in the bond of brotherly affection, and the faithful were made to rejoice for the unmerited favour. The meeting closed on the 30th of 9th month, with a very large solemn public meeting; the public service therein fell to the lot of Thankful Merritt and myself, and Thankful closed the meeting in sweet solemn supplication. In returning home, I attended several meetings which were large, and, through the condescending goodness of the Shepherd of Israel, were favoured satisfactory seasons, in which truth was raised into dominion, and a precious solemnity prevailed.

In the latter part of 1826, my friends united with a concern, which had been for a considerable time impressive on my mind, to make a visit in the love of the gospel, to Southern and Concord quarterly meetings, in the yearly meeting of Philadelphia. I accordingly set out in the 11th month, with Jesse Merritt as my companion. In passing through Philadelphia, we attended Mulberry-street meeting in the forenoon, and Green-street in the afternoon. They were both very large meetings, many more coming together than the houses could contain. Truth was powerfully raised into dominion, and at the close of each meeting, many Friends manifested, in an affectionate manner, their unity and satisfaction with my labours amongst them. We then proceeded on the further service on which we nad set out, taking several meetings on the way, which were large and solemn opportunities, and favoured with the overshadowing wing of divine kindness; and having accomplished the prospects in view, we turned our faces homewards, having thankfully to acknowledge that best help had been near, enabling me to discharge myself faithfully in the various meetings, to the comfort and peace of my own mind.

In the early part of 1827, with the unity of my friends, I entered into the engagement of making a religious visit to the families of Friends within our own and Westbury monthly meeting, and I was favoured to go through this arduous service to the satisfaction and peace of my own mind.

Having felt an exercise and travail of spirit in the course of last year, to make a religious visit in the love of the gospel, to Friends and others in some parts of our own yearly meeting, and in the compass of the yearly meetings of Philadelphia, Baltimore, Ohio, Indiana, and a few meetings in Virginia; and apprehending the time had come to move therein, I spread the concern before my friends at Jericho monthly meeting, held the 20th of 3d month, 1828, and obtained their unity and concurrence therein. This concern, with the certificate from our monthly meeting, I laid before our quarterly meeting held at Westbury, the 24th of 4th month following; and obtained their unity and concurrence, with an endorsement thereof on my certificate from the monthly meeting.

I left home the 28th of 4th month, the week after our quarterly meeting, in order to accomplish the service above alluded to; and attended the three quarterly meetings of Purchase, Nine Partners, and Stanford, as they came in their usual course. On my way home, I attended Oblong monthly meeting, also four particular meetings, three of which were appointed at my request. In all these meetings the Lord, our gracious helper, manifested himself to be near for our support, making way for us at times where there seemed to be no way, to our humbling admiration. I was from home in the prosecution of this little tour of duty, two weeks and two days. After this I tarried at and about home until after our yearly meeting.

Soon after this I again left home, on the 14th of 6th month, and rode to New-York. The day following being the first of the week, we attended the morning and afternoon meetings of Friends in the city, which, through the gracious extendings of heavenly help, proved to be comfortable edifying seasons. My esteemed friend Jesse Merritt, an elder of our monthly meeting, accompanied me in this journey. We left New-York on second day, after taking a sympathetic farewell of our friends in the city, and proceeded on our journey to Rahway in New Jersey, and lodged with our kind friend William Shotwell, and the next day had an appointed meeting in that village. It was truly a comfortable edifying opportunity ; many truths of the gospel were clearly opened to the audience, humbling and contriting many who were present ; a sense of which inspired our minds with gratitude and thanksgiving to the blessed Author of all our mercies.

The next day being the fourth of the week, we attended Friends' monthly meeting held at Plainfield, for Rahway and Plainfield. The meeting for worship was large, many of the neighbouring people of other societies coming in, to whom the gospel was freely preached in the demonstration of the spirit, solemnizing the assembly, and truth was raised into victory over all. My mind was also comforted in the meeting for discipline, in observing the harmony and brotherly condescension of Friends, in the orderly conducting the affairs of the Church.

The next day we proceeded on our journey to Kingwood, and put up with our kind friend Henry Clifton. We had an appointed meeting here the day after at the tenth hour, and although the number of Friends was small that constituted this meeting, yet Friends being careful to give their neighbours of other societies information thereof, we had a very full meeting; and it proved a very solemn impressive opportunity in which truth reigned, comforting and contriting many minds.

After this we passed on to Solebury in Pennsylvania, and lodged with our kind friend Watson Fell, who met us at Kingwood and kindly took us to his house. The next day we had an appointed meeting here at the fourth hour in the afternoon

It was a solemn opportunity, and I parted with them under a thankful sense of the unmerited favour. We then rode home with our kind friend Moses Eastburn; and the next day being first day, and the 22d of 6th month, we attended Buckingham meeting in the morning, and had an appointed meeting at Plumbstead at four o'clock in the afternoon. After this we rode home with our worthy friend Israel Lancaster, and on second day had a meeting at Wrightstown; on third day in the forenoon, we attended Newtown meeting; and at the fourth hour in the afternoon had an appointed meeting at Makefield. These were all large favoured meetings, in which the gospel was preached in the demonstration of the spirit, and many hearts were humbled and contrited, and a precious solemnity spread over the meetings, comforting and rejoicing the honest-hearted, and to the praise of Him, who is calling us to glory and virtue.

On fourth day, the 25th, we attended a meeting at the Falls; on fifth day were at Middletown; on sixth day at Byberry; and on seventh day at Abington. These meetings were all large and very solemn, and the canopy of love, in a very comforting manner, was felt to spread over the assemblies; and much kindness and friendly regard were manifested towards us, not only by our friends, but by the people in general of other societies, who attended the meetings.

We attended Horsham meeting in the morning, on first day, the 29th, and had an appointed meeting at Upper Dublin at the fourth hour in the afternoon. They were very large; more attended than the houses could contain. As the last meeting was assembling there came on a heavy shower of rain, accompanied with an uncommon time of lightning, and very heavy peals of thunder: many flashes of the lightning appeared to strike down to the earth within a very small distance of the meeting-house, which brought a great solemnity over the meeting, and I was thankful in observing the stillness and quiet which prevailed generally among the people. These meetings were very solemn seasons, in which truth reigned, and I parted with them in peace of mind, and the fresh feelings of gospel love.

Our kind friend Joseph Foulke met us at Horsham; and after the latter meeting conducted us to his house, where we met a very cordial welcome, and were favoured with the company and conversation of his ancient and very worthy father Hugh Foulke. The two following days we attended meetings at North Wales and Plymouth. These were large favoured meetings, in which many truths of the gospel were largely opened to the edification, comfort, and apparent satisfaction, of those large assemblies, and to the peace of my own mind. It was the Lord's doing, and to him belongs all the praise, nothing due to man.

From thence we proceeded to Charlestown, and lodged with our kind friend James Wood; and the next day, being the fourth day of the week, we attended their meeting. After this we rode to Pikeland, where we were very kindly entertained by our friends Emmor Kimber and wife, and had an appointed meeting there the next day. We tarried here until the next morning; and then proceeded on to Uwchlan, where we had a meeting, by previous appointment, at the eleventh hour; and although it was in the midst of their harvest, and the care necessary for getting it in, very urgent, as many of their fields of grain appeared to be over-ripe, yet to our own and our friends' admiration, the meetings were unusually large, frequently many more assembled than the houses could contain. The people were generally very solid and quiet, and very attentive to hear what was communicated; and many minds were humbled and contrited, and truth's testimonies exalted, to the mutual comfort and encouragement of the honest-hearted, and to the general satisfaction of the assembled multitudes; and my mind was deeply humbled and made thankful for the continuance of those unmerited favours.

On seventh day, the 5th of 7th month, we attended a meeting at Downing's Town, held in an orchard, under the shade of the apple trees; which was a large, solemn, satisfactory meeting. A division having taken place in the Society of Friends, and the meeting-house in this place being in possession of the party termed Orthodox, they refused to permit Friends to occupy it on this occasion. There were, however, more attended the meeting, than could have got into the house, if we had been permitted to use it. The next day we attended Friends' meeting at East Caln ; and notice having been given of our intention of attending it, the house, although very large, did not contain more than three quarters of the people that assembled. It was a season to be remembered with gratitude, in which the Lord's presence was felt to preside, humbling and contriting many hearts, and truth was raised into victory over all.

On second day we attended a meeting, by appointment, at Sadsbury; and on third day their monthly meeting. On fourth day we had an appointed meeting at Lampeter. These were all favoured opportunities, wherein the Lord's power was manifested for our help, rejoicing and encouraging the honest-hearted, and settling and confirming the wavering, who were halting between two opinions, but were now satisfied, and openly declared themselves on the side of Friends, some of whom had previously gone with our opposers, but were now convinced of the impropriety of their conduct, and cheerfully united with Friends.

After the latter meeting, we dined with our friend Thomas Peart. We then took leave of our friends in near unity, and proceeded on our journey to Columbia, and lodged with our kind friend William Wright, who, with his worthy and affectionate wife, entertained us with great hospitality. We had an appointed meeting at this place the next day. The two following days we attended meetings at Little York and Newbury. All of these were favoured opportunities, in which truth was raised into dominion, and many hearts were humbled and contrited, and the faithful comforted and made to rejoice together in the unity of the one spirit, *Christ*, the only sure foundation, on which the true Church has been built in all the varied ages of mankind, from the beginning down to the present time; and on which all future generations must build, or their building must and will fall.

On first day, the 13th of 7th month, we attended Friends' meeting at Warrington, and the two following days the meetings of Huntington and Monallin. These were all favoured opportunities, in which ability was vouchsafed, by the blessed Author of all our sure mercies, to preach the gospel to the people in the simplicity, plainness, and demonstration of the spirit, which brought a precious solemnity over the assemblies; and I parted with them with the satisfactory evidence of having faithfully discharged myself among them, feeling that true peace of mind, which the world, with all its fading enjoyments, cannot give nor take away. The next day, the 16th, we proceeded on our journey through the mountains to Redstone, about one hundred and sixty-one miles; and arrived there on first day, the 20th, about eight o'clock in the morning, at the house of our kind friend Jesse Townsend. We attended their meeting at the eleventh hour, which was large and favoured. We lodged with our aforesaid friend, during the time we spent in this place.

On second day we rested. On third and fourth days we attended meetings at Providence and Centre. On fifth day we attended Westland monthly meeting; and the neighbourhood being informed of our coming, there were more people assembled than the house could contain; and I had a full opportunity to discharge myself among them in a large effective testimony, which brought a precious solemnity over the meeting, and many minds were humbled and contrited.

A Friend from abroad attended this meeting, and after I sat down he rose and made opposition, which greatly disturbed the meeting.

On sixth day we attended an appointed meeting at Pike Run. It was held in the side of a wood, the meeting-house having been burnt. There being but few Friends in this place, they met in a small private room: this induced them to make seats out of doors, as the house would not have held half the people that met. It was an unusually favoured season. In the silent part of the meeting, the divine presence was felt to spread over the assembly, producing such a sweet and precious solemnity, as I scarcely ever before witnessed in the same fullness, and which continued through the course of my communication. Surely it was the Lord's doing, and it was marvellous in our eyes.

After this meeting we dined with our kind friend John Grave, and then proceeded on our way about three miles towards Brownsville, and lodged with our friend Isaac Walker. On seventh day night we lodged at the house of our friend Solomon Philips, near Brownsville; and the next morning crossed the river Monongahela into the town. Here we put up again with our kind friends Jesse and Edith Townsend, where we had the company of many Friends, and many of the inhabitants of the town not members of our society, also came in to see us; as the unfounded reports of those who style themselves Orthodox, having been generally spread over the country, it created such a great excitement in the minds of the people at large, that multitudes flocked to the meetings where we were, to hear for themselves; and many came to see us, and acknowledged their satisfaction.

At this place we again fell in with the Friend from abroad, who attended the meeting with us; he rose in the early part of the meeting, and continued his communication so long, that a number left the meeting, by which it became very much unsettled: however, when he sat down I felt an opening to stand up; and the people returned and crowded into the house, and those that could not get in stood about the doors and windows, and a precious solemnity soon spread over the meeting, which has been the case in every meeting, where our opposers did not make disturbance by their disorderly conduct. The meeting closed in a quiet and orderly manner, and I was very thankful for the favour.

On second day we rested and wrote to our friends. On third day we attended their preparative meeting for Ministers and Elders, and on fourth day their monthly meeting. Here the Friend who had before made opposition opposed me publicly and personally in the meeting for worship; but I nevertheless had a favoured opportunity, to the general satisfaction of the meeting, and to the peace of my own mind.

We attended Westland meeting again on fifth day as it came in course. It was pretty large, many of the neighbouring inhabitants coming in. We had a very favoured meeting; Friends were comforted together, and the people went away satisfied; and my mind was fully relieved, and inspired with thankfulness and gratitude.

On sixth day we attended the quarterly meeting of Ministers and Elders held at Westland, where we met with but little opposition; and the next day we attended the quarterly meeting of discipline. I had good service in the meeting for worship, which preceded that for discipline. It was very large, a great number of those not in membership with Friends came in, and behaved very orderly. Here we met with some opposition, more particularly in the meeting for discipline from the Friend above mentioned. And Friends were so disturbed with the conduct of this Friend and his companion, that they proposed that the Elders and Overseers should take an opportunity with them, and see if they could not put a stop to such disorderly conduct; accordingly they had an interview with them, in which Friends relieved their minds pretty fully; but the few termed Orthodox, used their influence in their favour, which greatly prevented their being benefited by the opportunity.

Public notice was given at the close of the meeting on seventh day, that my companion and myself intended to be at their meeting the next day. A great number more assembled than the house could contain; and although the Friend above alluded to, had so fully discovered that not only Friends, but the people generally, had no unity with him, yet soon after the meeting was settled, he rose and stood a considerable time. After he sat down, I was favoured to clear myself among them in a large impressive testimony, that soon brought a precious solemnity over the meeting; and many hearts were broken and contrited, and I took an affectionate farewell of the assembly in the fresh feelings of gospel love. As I was about to close the meeting, the same individual again rose, and began to oppose what had been said by me; this so offended the people, Friends and others, that they rose up and went out in great numbers, he at the same time begging them to stay; but they refused and continued going out until he was discouraged and sat down.

Soon after I closed the meeting, feeling very sorry for the people to see them so imposed upon.

After this meeting we proceeded that afternoon about seven miles, on our way to Pittsburg. On second day we rode to Pittsburg, and lodged with Robert Townsend; who, although not in membership with Friends, entertained us with much kindness and hospitality. The day following at evening, we had a large satisfactory meeting in their court-house, Friends having no meeting in that town. On fourth day we proceeded on our journey, crossing the Alleghany river at Pittsburg, and arrived that evening at a village, at the great falls of the river Beaver. The next day we had an appointed meeting there, held in a field under some trees, which made a comfortable shade, the weather being very warm, and Friends meeting-house much too small to contain the people who assembled. It was a very solemn opportunity, in which truth was raised into victory over all, and the people appeared thankful for the favour; and I witnessed the consoling evidence of true peace, in faithfully discharging my duty among them.

After this favoured meeting, we went forward that afternoon towards Salem, in order to attend the quarterly meeting at that place, which opened the next day at the eleventh hour, with a meeting of Ministers and Elders. Friends met in a school-house which one of them had built on his own premises, with which, and a temporary shed that Friends put up adjoining to it, the meeting was pretty well accommodated. They conducted the business of the quarterly meeting in much unity and concord, and the Lord's presence was evidently felt to cover the assembly. The next day being first day, and as notice was spread of our being there, the meeting was very large. It was judged by Friends that upwards of two thousand people attended. It was a highly favoured season, in which I was enabled by Him, who when he opens none can shut, and when he shuts none can open, to declare the truth to the people in the demonstration of the spirit, and with a power attending which brought a precious solemnity over the meeting, and many hearts were humbled and contrited.

The next day we had a meeting by appointment at Fairfield. This was also a very large meeting, many more assembled than the house could contain. I had a favoured time among them, and was made thankful for the opportunity, and had cause to believe my labour was not in vain.

The day following we attended New Garden quarterly meeting. Here Friends had a trying time, as those called Orthodox, although they were but a small part of the meeting, had undertaken to disown a number of Friends; but Friends did not acknowledge their authority, nor consider their disownments of any effect, and they all came together as usual in the quarterly meeting. The Orthodox strove hard to get Friends to withdraw, but they refused, and proceeded with the business of the meeting, which those called Orthodox interrupted for a time; but finding that Friends would not give way, they finally left the meeting, and retired to a school-house, and Friends had a comfortable season together, and conducted their business in much harmony and condescension, and were evidently owned by the Head of the Church.

I appointed a meeting on fourth day for the public at large, Friends, and others. A large number assembled; many more than the house could contain. We had a precious meeting : the Lord's power prevailed in an eminent manner. It was a season thankfully to be remembered, and was truly an humbling time among the people.

After this we proceeded to New Lisbon, to attend a meeting there the next day, which we had previously appointed. It was held out of doors, there being no house in the town sufficient to hold the people that Friends apprehended would assemble. Being aware of this, they erected a booth or shed, by setting up posts, on which they laid long poles, and covered them with branches of trees to make a shade, as the weather was very warm. Under this we had a very large favoured meeting, to the general satisfaction of the people, and peace of my own mind.

The two following days we attended meetings, by appointment, at Springfield and Goshen. Those called Orthodox had possession of the meeting-houses at those places, and refused to admit us; but although they could shut us out of the meeting-houses, yet they could not shut us out from the divine presence, for this was felt eminently to preside in both these highly favoured meetings.

The next day, being first day and 17th of 8th month, we attended Marlborough meeting. It was very large, notice having been previously given of our intention to be there, so that hundreds assembled who could not get into the house. I had an open opportunity among them, to proclaim the everlasting gospel in the demonstration of the spirit, to the comfort and satisfaction of this large assembly, except those called Orthodox, who, when I sat down, made great opposition, which greatly offended the people.

We then proceeded to Canton, a pretty large country town, and attended a meeting at the fourth hour in the afternoon, and notice was publicly given that we were to be there. As there were no members of our society in the town, the meeting was held in their court-house. Many of the respectable inhabitants attended, and information being given to Friends of Kendal, a small meeting about seven miles distant, most of them attended, and many other inhabitants of that place came also to the meeting. We had a favoured opportunity with them, and left them with peace.

After this we returned to New Garden, and put up with our kind friend Nathan Galbreath. The next day being the fourth of the week, we rode to Salem, and attended Friends' monthly meeting, in which I was led to stir up Friends to faithfulness, in support of our religious testimonies, as the eyes of the people were upon us, watching our movements in this time of trial, Friends separating from each other, and setting up separate meetings, which caused a great breach of unity and confusion in most of our meetings, which a few years previous thereto had been united together in the bonds of Christian fellowship; but a few individuals who had gained some influence in society, letting in the spirit of jealousy, began to accuse some of their friends of promulgating unsound doctrines, without any just cause for so doing, by which they greatly disturbed the peace and quiet of society;

and being encouraged therein by several Friends from England, who as ministers, had obtained liberty from their friends at home, to come over on a visit to Friends in this country, they blew up the fire of discord, until they brought about a division in our once peaceful society; a small minority of which, in many places, separated themselves from the body, and set up separate meetings, assuming the names of the yearly, quarterly, and monthly meetings; and these, in their presumption, have taken upon them to deal with and disown the great body of the society.

The next day we returned to New Garden and attended Friends' monthly meeting there; and the neighbouring inhabitants being apprized of our return, a great number came in, and greatly enlarged the meeting; and He that openeth, and none can shut, graciously condescended to open my mouth among them, in a large effective testimony to the truths of the gospel; and many hearts were humbled and contrited. It appeared as a renewed visitation of the heavenly Father's love to Friends and others; and it was a season gratefully to be remembered by all present; for surely it was the Lord's doing, and marvellous in our eyes.

The day following we had an appointed meeting at Sandy Spring, at the fourth hour in the afternoon. The meeting was very large, and favoured with the overshadowing wing of divine kindness; and a precious solemnity pervaded the assembly, and my mind was opened to declare the truth to them, to the apparent satisfaction and comfort of the assembled multitude; and I took leave of them with thankfulness and peace of mind. · We remained here until the next morning and then proceeded on our journey to Richmond, about thirty five miles, where we took up our lodging at an inn. The next day being first day, and 24th of 8th month, we had an appointed meeting in the town. The inhabitants were mostly Presbyterians and Methodists. It was held in their school-house, a large convenient room. The people came in freely, and behaved with great propriety and order, and appeared to go away satisfied; and I felt true peace in having faithfully, in gospel love, discharged myself among them.

After this we proceeded about five miles on our way to Smith-field, and the next morning rode to that place; but being some-what unwell, we rested there through the day, and the next day had an appointed meeting there, at the fourth hour in the afternoon. Those called Orthodox, shut the meeting-house against us; but Friends provided seats under the shade of trees, in an adjacent wood, where we had a very solemn, favoured meeting, in which the Lord's power prevailed over all in an eminent degree, and broke down all opposition, and many hearts were broken and contrited; and we parted with them under a grateful sense of the Lord's mercy for the unmerited favour.

CHAPTER XVIII.

Continuation of his visit to Friends in some parts of Ohio, Indiana, Maryland, Pennsylvania and New Jersey in 1828.—Decease of his wife in 1829.—Visit to Friends in the yearly meeting of New-York in 1829.—Letter to Hugh Judge in 1830.—His decease in 1830.—Memorial of the monthly meeting of Jericho in 1830.

On the 27th of 8th month, 1828, we proceeded on our journey to Mount Pleasant, and attended on that day, their meeting in the middle of the week; it was large, by the attendance of many of the inhabitants who were not members of our society, and was, in the forepart, a solemn, quiet meeting; but the latter part of it was disturbed and its usefulness marred, by a long, tedious communication from a minister among those called Orthodox, who, after I sat down, publicly opposed and endeavoured to lay waste what I had said.

The next day we attended Short Creek meeting. Here also the meeting in the forepart, was truly a solemn season, in which I was favoured to open and declare many important truths of the gospel to the people, which brought a precious solemnity over the assembly, and many minds were contrited; but an opposition from the same person who caused the disturbance the day before, again took place, much to the dissatisfaction of the principal part of those assembled.

The next day being the sixth of the week, we attended an appointed meeting at Harrisville. Here we met with no interruption. This was a large crowded meeting, and very solemn and quiet. I had an open time among the people to declare many things, both old and new; setting forth the great declension of the professed Christian Churches, from the simplicity and integrity of the primitive disciples; and showing that it was all brought about by a departure from the only sure foundation of true and real Christianity, the *light within,* or *spirit of truth, the immediate revelation of the spirit of God,* in the immortal souls of men and women; the only and alone true teacher of the things of God under the gospel. And as a departure from this only sure guide, and turning back to the letter and external evidence, and building up, from these outward materials, many diverse systems of religion, in their own creaturely wisdom, brought confusion and anarchy into the Church, which enveloped it in a state of midnight darkness and death, as to the life and spirit of real Christianity; by which the worst of persecution, and the most cruel and sanguinary wars were introduced among Christians: so nothing short of a full and entire return to this only sure foundation and first principle, and placing an entire dependance thereon for our salvation, can ever produce a real restoration from the apostate state in which Christendom is at present involved. I was also led to lay before the people the inconsistency and hurtful tendency of Bible and Missionary societies; as believing them all to be set up and associated together in the will and wisdom of man, which never did, nor ever can, produce the righteousness of God, but tend to lead the mind down to a state of darkness and death, as a dependance on the letter and external evidence ever has, and ever will kill, as to the real spiritual life, agreeably to Paul's doctrine: "The letter killeth, but the spirit giveth life."

The next day we had an appointed meeting at Westgrove. The day following being the first of the week, and 31st of 8th month, we attended Concord meeting; and the three following days attended meetings at St. Clairsville, Plainfield, and Wrightstown. These were all large satisfactory meetings, in which the gospel was preached to the people, and by the power attending, many hearts were broken and contrited; and a precious sense of the divine presence was felt to preside, to the comfort and encouragement of the honest-hearted; a sense of which inspired my mind with thanksgiving and gratitude, to the blessed Author of all our sure mercies.

On fifth day, the 4th of 9th month, we had an appointed meeting at a place called Stillwater. It was a very large comfortable meeting, and I had a full opportunity in an effective testimony, to ease my exercised mind among them, to the comfort and apparent satisfaction of the people, both Friends and others. The next day we rode back to Mount Pleasant, and the day following being the seventh day of the week, and 6th of 9th month, the yearly meeting opened with a meeting of Ministers and Elders. When the time came for meeting, Friends gathered to the gate which led into the yard where the meeting-house stood, and found it guarded by a number of men of the opposing party, who refused to let us in; and Friends had to hold their meeting in the open air, outside of the yard; but after the first sitting, adjourned to a school-house near by, and afterwards held the remaining sittings in a private room, in Israel French's house.

The next day and first of the week, we attended Mount Pleasant meeting in the morning, and that held at Short Creek in the afternoon. In the morning meeting Elisha Bates and Anna Braithwaite made great opposition, endeavouring by long and tedious communications to lay waste what I had previously communicated, which very much disturbed many present. But the afternoon meeting was not interrupted, as none of those opposers attended.

On second day morning, the yearly meeting for discipline opened at the tenth hour. Not being present at this sitting, I was informed that great confusion and disorder took place; both Friends and those called Orthodox wished to retain possession of the meeting-house, and both parties went on with their business with separate clerks, for some little time, when the Orthodox adjourned their meeting to ten o'clock the next day, and left the house in the possession of Friends, who then proceeded quietly on with the business of the meeting until some time in the afternoon, and then adjourned to nine o'clock the next day; when they again met, and near the tenth hour a deputation from our opposing Friends came and demanded the use of the house, in the name of the yearly meeting of Ohio. Friends informed them that the yearly meeting was now sitting, and the doors were open, and they might come in; and after some further requisition for Friends to withdraw, and give them the entire use of the house, which Friends could not think right to do, as being entirely unreasonable, they then went away and did not give Friends any more interruption in that way. But they had recourse to the law and prosecuted a number of Friends, some in an action for a pretended trespass, for going into their own meeting-house, and some as rioters; and compelled them to leave their meeting and go before the magistrates, to answer for crimes they, without a just cause, had accused them of having committed. And a considerable number, it was said about thirty of their own principal members, such as Ministers and Elders, and other active members, left the sittings of their yearly meeting, and went to a town twenty miles distant, where they had compelled a number of Friends to attend, to be tried by the court then sitting, and were two days absent from the sittings of their meeting. After this they interrupted Friends no further, and Friends quietly proceeded with their business, and closed on sixth day.

We proceeded on our journey next day to Flushing, and the day after being the first of the week, we attended Friends' meeting there; and as notice had been given of our intention to be there, the meeting was very large, more than the house could contain. At this meeting those styled Orthodox made great opposition; for as soon as I came near the meeting-house several of them met me, and desired I would not interrupt the meeting: and soon after the meeting was gathered, before it became fully settled, Charles Osborn, an Orthodox minister, kneeled in supplication and continued on his knees, I believe, more than an hour. It was truly a distressing scene, and it greatly disturbed the meeting; and very soon after he took his seat, he rose and began to preach, and continued for more than an hour. However, when he sat down, although the meeting was much wearied with his long and tedious communications, I felt the necessity of standing up and addressing the people, which brought a precious solemnity over the meeting; but as soon as

I sat down, he rose again to contradict, and tried to lay waste my communication, by asserting that I had not the unity of my friends at home; which being untrue, I therefore informed the meeting that I had certificates with me to prove the incorrectness of his assertions, which I then produced, but he and his party would not stay to hear them, but in a disorderly manner arose and left the meeting; but the people generally stayed and heard them read, to their general satisfaction.

The next day we went to Cambridge, about thirty-seven miles; and the day following rode to Zanesville, twenty-four miles, and had an appointed meeting there in the evening, held in their court-house, a large room, but not sufficient to contain all the people who assembled. It was a very solemn instructive opportunity, and I parted with them under a thankful sense of the favour, and with peace of mind. The two following days we rode to Wilmington, and put up with our friend Warren Sabin, where we lodged the two next nights.

On seventh day the 20th of 9th month, we rode to Centre, and attended Friends' monthly meeting, composed of the preparative meetings of Centre and Wilmington. It was the first monthly meeting they had held since the separation; and notice being given of our attendance, the meeting for worship was very large, more than the house could contain; and the Lord, our never-failing helper manifested his presence, solemnizing the assembly and opening the minds of the people to receive the word preached; breaking down all opposition, and humbling and contriting the assembly in a very general manner; and we parted from each other with grateful hearts, from an humbling sense of the unmerited favour.

We returned that evening to Wilmington, and the next day attended Friends' meeting in that town; and as their meeting-house was small, Friends procured the court-house in that place to hold the meeting in. The meeting was very large, and we had a very favoured opportunity to declare the truth among them, to their general satisfaction; and the honest-hearted were comforted and edified, and Friends were made to rejoice for the unmerited favour. At the fourth hour in the afternoon, we had an appointed meeting at a place called Lital's Creek, a short distance from Wilmington.   Here we had a favoured opportunity with the people, greatly to their satisfaction.

The next day being the second of the week, and 22d of the month, we proceeded on to Springfield.   Here those called Orthodox shut the meeting-house and set guards at the doors to keep us out, and we held our meeting under some trees near by.   It was a precious season, wherein the Lord's power and love were exalted over all opposition, and many minds were humbled and contrited ;   and thanksgiving and praise were ascribed to His great and adorable name, who is over all, blessed for ever.

We had a favoured meeting the day after, at a place called the Grove.   Friends' meeting-house there being small, we had to hold the meeting out of doors to accommodate the people.   It was a very satisfactory opportunity.   The following day we had an appointed meeting at Lebanon, a pretty large country town, where there were no members of our society, but many sober people.   It was held in the court-house, but it was not sufficient to contain the people ; about one third of those who assembled had to stand out of doors.   It was an instructive opportunity; many gospel truths were opened to the people, and they appeared to go away well satisfied; and I parted from them with true peace of mind.

On seventh day, the 27th of the month, we attended the opening of Indiana yearly meeting, with the first sitting of the meeting of Ministers and Elders ; and although small, it was a favoured encouraging opportunity to the few who assembled. The next day, being first day, a large concourse assembled with Friends.   A great number had to stand without, although the house was very large.   And he that openeth and none can shut, and when he shutteth none can open, opened my mouth among them in a large effective testimony to the truths of the gospel ; in which, through adorable condescension, I was enabled to bring forth, out of the Lord's treasury, things new and old ; and truth was raised into dominion over all, to the comfort and rejoicing of the honest-hearted, and to the apparent satisfaction and edification of the people in general. Surely it was the Lord's doing, and it was marvellous in our eyes. The next day the meeting for discipline opened, and continued by adjournments until sixth day evening; and Friends were favoured, through the several sittings, to conduct the business in much harmony and brotherly condescension.

The day after, we proceeded on our journey towards Richmond, in Indiana; attending meetings on our way, at Springborough, Elk, Westfield, and Eaton. All these were seasons of favour, the Lord graciously manifesting his presence for our help. Blessed be his great and excellent name, for his mercy endureth for ever.

From Eaton we rode home with our kind friends John and Elizabeth Barnes, and lodged. The next day, being the fourth of the week, and 8th of 10th month, we rode to Richmond, where those called Orthodox were holding their yearly meeting; and as this day was the time for holding a meeting for worship, notice was given of our intention of being there. It was very large, and proved, through adorable condescension, a solemn heart-tendering season, in which truth reigned over all.

The three following days we attended meetings by our appointment, at Centreville, West Union and Milford. After this we returned again to Richmond, in order, agreeably to appointment, to attend their first day meeting. It was large like the former; a multitude of people assembled; and was a precious meeting, in which truth was triumphant, and ran as oil over the assembly, breaking down all opposition, and melting a great portion of the assembly into tears of contrition. Surely it was the Lord's doing, and marvellous in our eyes; and to him belongeth all the praise, who is over all, blessed for ever.

We parted from them with solid satisfaction, and peace of mind; and after dinner took a solemn and very affectionate leave of our friends, and rode on our journey about four miles, and spent the evening at the house of our esteemed friend Benjamin Stokes. We returned and lodged with our kind friend John Barnes; and the following day attended a meeting, by our appointment, at a place called the Ridge; it was a comfortable opportunity. The next day we attended a meeting at Orange. Here those called Orthodox made great disturbance, and hurt the meeting very considerably. The day after, we had a meeting at a place called Silver Creek. This was a precious meeting, in which truth reigned over all.

We then proceeded on our journey towards Cincinnati, and arrived there on seventh day, the 18th of 10th month. The next day being first day, we attended Friends' meeting at that place, at the usual time, which was very large, many more attending than the house could contain : and at three o'clock in the afternoon, we appointed a meeting to be held in the court-house. Both these meetings were highly favoured seasons, in which truth was raised into dominion over all opposition, to the praise of Him, who is calling us to glory and to virtue.

On second day morning we proceeded on our journey, towards home ; and attending meetings in our way, in the course of the week, at Salt Creek, Salem, alias Rochester, Newberry, and Clear Creek. All these meetings were composed of people of varied professions, to whom the gospel was preached in the demonstration of the spirit, attended with a power which silenced all opposition, humbling and contriting many hearts, without respect of persons or sects ; and Friends were comforted together, and made to rejoice for the unmerited favour ; and we parted from them under a thankful sense of the Lord's mercy, and with peace of mind.

The next day being first day, and 26th of 10th month, we attended Fairfield meeting ; and notice being given of our intention of attending it, the meeting was very large. Here those called Orthodox made public opposition in the early part of the meeting ; one of them informing the assembly that I was travelling without having the unity of my Friends, and other incorrect declarations, which I passed over without notice at the time. The meeting was soon gathered into a solemn quiet, and I had a favoured opportunity to declare the truth among them, which was raised into dominion, and many hearts were humbled and contrited. Before, however, I had concluded my communication, those called Orthodox, to manifest further disunity, rose and left the meeting; but Friends and others kept their seats, and we had a very solemn close, and great brokenness and contrition were manifest among the people; and to do away the false reports spread by the Orthodox, I had my certificates read, which gave full satisfaction to the assembly; an we took an affectionate farewell of our friends and others present

We then proceeded on our journey to Wheeling in Virginia, a town situated on the east side of Ohio river. We arrived here on sixth day, the 31st, a little before noon, and had an appointed meeting in the evening. As Friends have no meeting-house in this place, it was held in the Methodist meeting-house, which they kindly offered of their own accord. It was a pretty large collection of people, mostly made up of other societies, the number of Friends there being very small, insomuch that they have no steady meeting in the place. It was a comfortable, favoured opportunity.

We left them with peace of mind, and proceeded on our journey to Westland, in the limits of Redstone quarterly meeting, where we arrived on first day, the 2d of 11th month, in time to attend their meeting. It was a very solemn edifying opportunity, in which the power of truth was exalted over all opposition. After this we proceeded on to Redstone, about seven miles, crossing the Monongahela river in the way; and the next day had an appointed meeting in that town, at two o'clock in the afternoon.

The day after we passed on towards Waterford, alias Fairfax, in Virginia, where we arrived on first day the 9th of 11th month, and attended their meeting at the usual hour. At two o'clock n the afternoon, we had an appointed meeting for the inhabitants of the town in general; and the two following days attended meetings, by appointment, at Goose Creek and Southwest Fork. These were all large favoured meetings, particularly the two last, wherein I was led to expose the great evil of oppression, especially that enormous sin of holding our fellow creatures in slavery. Although in my communication I was led to lay judgment to the line, and justice to the plumb line; yet the slave-holders, divers of whom were present, were so brought down and humbled with the force and correctness of the testimony, that they frankly acknowledged the truth and propriety of it; and we parted from them with true peace of mind, and the honest-hearted were made to rejoice for the favour dispensed from the hand of the gracious Benefactor of every blessing.

The next day we rode to Alexandria, forty-three miles, and lodged with our kind friend Phineas Janney, and the day after attended their meeting as it came in course, and in the evening had another meeting for the inhabitants of the town in general. These were opportunities of favour: many truths of the gospel were set forth before the people, in the demonstration of the spirit, which brought a solemnity over the assembly, to the comfort and edification of the upright in heart. The next day we rode to Washington, and attended a meeting there in the evening. This was rather a trying season in the forepart, but, I trust, it ended well.

We then proceeded to Sandy Spring, in Maryland, and on first day, the 16th of 11th month, attended Friends' meeting there; and notice being given of our expectation of attending it, the meeting was large; and through condescending goodness, it proved to be a very favoured instructive season, and I parted with them with a thankful heart, and true peace of mind. The next day we proceeded on our journey to Elk Ridge, and lodged with our kind friend George Ellicot; and the day following being third day, we had, by appointment, a very comfortable, favoured meeting with Friends: many of the neighbouring inhabitants likewise attended, and appeared well satisfied with the opportunity. Many minds were humbled and contrited, and a precious solemnity prevailed over the meeting.

After this meeting we dined at our lodgings, and that afternoon proceeded in company with our kind friend John Marsh, who met us at this meeting, six miles on our way to Baltimore, and lodged at his house. In the morning we rode into the city, and on that and the following day attended Friends' meeting. held in the middle of the week, at the upper and lower houses; and not feeling fully clear, on sixth day evening, we had an appointed meeting for the inhabitants of the town in general, at the upper house. This was a very large meeting, made up of almost every class of the people, among whom, as to religious profession, were Romanists, Episcopalians, Presbyterians, Baptists, Methodists, Unitarians, and others of divers descriptions, and some slave-holders. These meetings were seasons of favour, particularly the last, in which truth in a very extraordinary manner was raised into victory over all, bowing and breaking down all under its baptizing influence, so that it appeared as though the whole assembly were baptized into one body; and when the meeting closed, all seemed desirous to take me by the hand. Surely it was the Lord's doing, and marvellous in mine eyes; and I parted with them with gratitude and thankfulness of heart.

The day following we rode to Gunpowder Falls; and the next day being first day, and 23d of the 11th month, we attended Friends' meeting there; and information being given of our intention of attending it, the meeting was large, and through the condescending goodness of Israel's unslumbering Shepherd, whose mercy is over all his works, it proved a precious favoured opportunity, in which many hearts were humbled and contrited, and truth was raised into dominion. The day following we went to the Little Falls, and on third day, the 25th, attended Friends' meeting in that place, and the day after attended Deer Creek meeting. These were very large favoured opportunities. After this we proceeded on our journey, crossing the river Susquehannah on our way to Little Britain; and on the three following days we attended meetings at Little Britain, West and East Nottingham. These were seasons to be remembered, in which the Lord's power was eminently manifested by its solemnizing influence. Surely it was the Lord's doing.

On second day, the 1st of 12th month, we proceeded to West Grove, in Chester county. Here our opposing brethren shut the meeting-house against us, and the care-taker of it refused to open it. However, when the people assembled, which they did in great numbers, many more than the house could contain, it was opened; and we had a very favoured, solemn opportunity with them, in which truth reigned over all. The three following days we attended the monthly meetings of London Grove.

New Garden, and Fallowfield, as they came in their usual course; and notice being given, of our attending them, to the neighbouring inhabitants, great numbers of the varied classes of the people assembled with Friends; insomuch that none of the houses were large enough to contain the multitude, and in some instances there were nearly as many standing without as the houses contained. These were all highly favoured seasons, the Lord's power evidently presiding over these large assemblies, solemnizing and humbling with its overshadowing influence, and causing a profound silence to prevail over all, to the praise of him who is over all, God blessed for ever.

On the two following days we attended meetings at Marlborough and West Chester. The first was by our appointment, the latter on first day. These meetings were like the former; great numbers attended more than the houses could contain: nevertheless, order and stillness prevailed in a remarkable manner in and without the houses, in every place, to the comfort and rejoicing of Friends, and to the instruction and edification, I trust, of the assembled multitudes. We took leave of them under an humbling sense of the unmerited favour, and with true peace of mind.

On second day, the 8th of the month, we attended Kennet meeting, and on third and fourth days we had meetings at Kennet Square and Centre. These were all crowded meetings, and in them all the divine presence was felt to preside, solemnizing the assemblies, and comforting and rejoicing the honest-hearted.

On fifth and sixth days we attended meetings at Hockesson and Stanton. Both were crowded, solemn meetings, and, I trust, instructive and profitable to many who were present. After the latter, we rode that afternoon to Wilmington, and rested on seventh day with our friend William Poole, who was in a weak state from bodily indisposition, but was so far recovered as to walk about. On first day, the 14th, we attended Friends' meetings in Wilmington, both forenoon and afternoon. They were both very large. In the forenoon meeting I had good service, but in the afternoon I was mostly silent, as the people appeared to be too much hungering for words, and too indifferent and careless in putting in practice what they had already heard and knew to be their duty. Hence I was led to set them an example of silence.

We left Wilmington on second day morning, and proceeded to Concord, and attended a meeting there by previous appoint ment. The four following days we attended meetings at Middle-town, Providence, Chester, and Darby. These were all very large favoured opportunities, in which the Lord's power was felt to preside, causing a precious solemnity to spread over the assemblies, and humbling and contriting many minds. To the Lord be the praise and glory of his own work; nothing due to man.

Leaving Darby, we proceeded on to Philadelphia; and on first day, the 21st of 12th month, we attended Friends' meetings in the city, that at Cherry-street in the morning, and at Green-street in the afternoon. At both these meetings hundreds more assembled than the houses could contain. On second day we left the city, and attended meetings, in the course of the week, at Haverford, Radnor, Newtown, Willistown, and the Valley. All these meetings were unusually large; the houses were generally too small to contain the people; many had to stand out of doors for want of room; nevertheless, the people behaved orderly, and the Lord's presence was felt to preside, solemnizing those crowded assemblies, in all of which my mind was opened, and ability afforded, to preach the gospel to the people in the demonstration of the spirit and with power, and many hearts were broken and contrited, and went away rejoicing, under a hankful sense of the unmerited favour.

After this we returned to the city, and on first day, the 28th of the month, we again attended Friends' meetings there, in the same order as before. On second day we attended Frankfort meeting by appointment. These were all large favoured meet-ings; many had to leave those in the city for want of room. My opposing brethren had, by their public opposition and erro-neous reports, created such excitement in the minds of the people generally of every profession, that it induced multitudes to assemble to hear for themselves; and they generally went away satisfied and comforted.

On third day we took leave of our friends in Philadelphia, and passed over into New Jersey; and the four following days attended meetings at Mullica Hill, Piles Grove, Salem, and Woodbury. These were very large favoured meetings; and I felt true peace of mind as a rich reward for my labour and exercise among them.

We attended Haddonfield meeting on first day, the 4th of 1st month, 1829. Here Friends, and those who styled themselves Orthodox, met together in the same house. As notice was given of my attendance, the people assembled in great numbers; and as soon as the meeting was fully gathered, a precious solemnity was felt to spread over the assembly; and the Lord, our gracious helper, was near for our support and strength, and the truth was raised triumphantly over all opposition.

The four following days we attended meetings at Moore's Town, Evesham, Cropwell, Mount Holly, and Upper Evesham. These were very large meetings, in which the Lord our gracious helper made bare his arm for our support, enabling to hand forth out of the treasury things new and old, to the comfort and edification of the honest-hearted, and solid peace of my own mind; to Him be all the praise, nothing due to man.

On first day the 11th, we attended Friends' meeting at Rancocus. This was said to be the largest meeting ever known in that place; in which the Lord's presence was felt to preside, humbling and contriting many minds, and baptizing the whole assembly into a very precious solemnity; and causing the upright in heart to rejoice, under a thankful sense of the unmerited favour.

In the course of this week we attended meetings at Old Springfield on second day, Mansfield on third day, Upper Springfield on fourth day, Arney's Town on fifth day, Crosswicks, alias Chesterfield on sixth day, Bordentown on seventh day, and Trenton on first day. All these were favoured opportunities, and in them all, although under considerable indisposition of body, I was favoured with strength, and way opened to labour in the Lord's cause in which I was engaged, and which produced that true peace of mind, that the world with all its perishing enjoyments cannot give, nor all its frowns and opposition take away.

On second day we proceeded on our journey towards New-York, being desirous of reaching our quarterly meeting to be held there on the following fifth day. We arrived in the city on third day afternoon, where I met my beloved wife and daughter Elizabeth, and several other branches of my family, and a number more of my near and intimate friends. It was truly a season of mutual rejoicing, and my spirit was deeply humbled under a thankful sense of the Lord's preserving power and adorable mercy, in carrying me through and over all opposition, both within and without. He caused all to work together for good, and the promotion of his own glorious cause of truth and righteousness in the earth, and landed me safe in the bosom of my dear family and friends at home, and clothed my spirit with the reward of sweet peace for all my labour and travail. Praises, everlasting high praises, be ascribed unto our God, for his mercy endureth for ever.

On seventh day, after the quarterly meeting we returned home, having been out on this journey seven months and ten days, and travelled nearly twenty-four hundred miles.

Soon after my return from the aforesaid journey, I had to experience a very severe trial and affliction in the removal of my dearly beloved wife. She was taken down with a cold, and although, for a number of days, we had no anticipation of danger from her complaint, yet about five days after she was taken, the disorder appeared to settle on her lungs, and it brought o an inflammation which terminated in a dissolution of her pre cious life, on the ninth day from the time she was taken ill. She had but little bodily pain, yet as she became weaker, she suffered from shortness of breathing; but before her close, she became perfectly tranquil and easy, and passed away like a lamb, as though entering into a sweet sleep, without sigh or groan, or the least bodily pain, on the 17th of 3d month, 1829 : And her precious spirit, I trust and believe, has landed safely on the angelic shore, "where the wicked cease from troubling, and the weary are at rest." To myself, to whom she was a truly affectionate wife, and to our children, whom she endeavoured, by precept and example, to train up in the paths of virtue, and to guard and keep them out of harm's way, her removal is a great and irreparable loss: and nothing is left to us in that behalf, but a confident belief, and an unshaken hope, that our great loss is her still greater gain; and although the loss and trial, as to all my external blessings, are the greatest I have ever met with, or ever expect to have to endure, yet I have a hope, that, through divine aid, I may be preserved from murmuring or complaining; and that I may continually keep in view the unmerited favour dispensed to us, by being preserved together fifty-eight years in one unbroken bond of endeared affection, which seemed if possible to increase with time to the last moment of her life; and which neither time nor distance can lessen or dissolve; but in the spiritual relation I trust it will endure for ever, where all the Lord's redeemed children are one in him, who is God over all, in all, and through all, blessed for ever. She was buried on the 19th, and on this solemn occasion, the Lord, who is strength in weakness, enabled me to bear a public, and I trust a profitable testimony, to the virtues and excellences of her long and consistent life.

On the 24th of 6th month, 1829, I again left home with Cornwell Willis for my companion, to complete the visit to Friends and others in the compass of our yearly meeting, agreeably to a certificate I received from our monthly and quarterly meetings, expressive of their unity with me therein. This certificate I received in the spring of the year 1828, expressive of my concern to pay a religious visit to Friends and others, in parts of the yearly meetings of Philadelphia, Baltimore, Virginia, Ohio, Indiana, and New-York. I accomplished my visit to the first four last season; that is, I visited parts of them, but found my mind released without going into the yearly meeting of Virginia.

Since I left home, we have attended meetings at Flushing, Newtown, Brooklyn, and two at New-York last first day. These

were favoured comforting opportunities, affording encouragement
to persevere in the path of duty.

We left New-York on second day the 29th, after taking an
affectionate farewell of our friends there, and proceeded to West
Chester, and attended a meeting at that place at the eleventh
hour ; and on the two following days, attended meetings at
Mamaroneck and Purchase. On fifth day we attended Friends'
meeting at Middlesex; and on sixth and seventh days, had
meetings appointed for us at a place called the Saw Pits, and at
Friends' meeting-house at North Castle. All these meetings
were seasons of favour, in which the divine presence was felt to
preside, solemnizing the assemblies, and affording ability to
minister to the people in gospel authority, and tendering and
contriting many hearts. To the Lord be all the praise, nothing
due to man.

On first day, the 5th of 7th month, we attended Shapaqua
meeting in the morning, and had an appointed meeting at
Croton Valley, at the fourth hour in the afternoon. The three
following days we attended meetings by appointment at Amawalk, Salem, and at the Valley, called Haviland's Hollow.
These were all unusually large meetings, in which truth reigned
over all, to the praise of His great name, who giveth us the
victory. From the latter meeting we proceeded to Oblong, and
put up with our kind friend Daniel Merritt, and the next day
attended their meeting. The two following days we had meetings by our appointment at the Branch, and Poughquague;
and on first day attended Nine Partners meeting. Those four
meetings were unusually large, and very solemn opportunities ;
n which truth's testimony went forth freely, tendering and
contriting many hearts, and rejoicing the faithful travellers
Zionward.

The two following days, we had meetings at Chestnut Ridge
and Oswego. These were likewise large satisfactory meetings.
We then proceeded by the way of Poughkeepsie, to Marlborough,
in order to attend Cornwall quarterly meeting, held at Marlborough at this time. It opened on fourth day, the 15th of 7th
month, with a meeting of Ministers and Elders. The next day

the meeting for discipline was held. Both were very favoured seasons. As I did not feel easy to leave the place without having a public opportunity with the people at large in that neighbourhood, a meeting was appointed the next day. This was likewise a large favoured opportunity. The following day being seventh day, we returned to Poughkeepsie, in order to attend Friends' meeting on first day; and having also appointed a meeting to be held there, at the fifth hour in the afternoon, for the inhabitants of the town at large. These meetings were largely attended, in which the power of truth was exalted over all.

The four following days we attended meetings at West Branch, Pleasant Valley, Creek, and Crumelbow. Although it was in the midst of harvest, such was the excitement produced amongst the people by the opposition made by those of our members who had gone off from us, and set up separate meetings, that the people at large of other societies flocked to those meetings in such numbers, that our meeting-houses were seldom large enough to contain the assembled multitude ; and we had abundant cause for thanksgiving and gratitude to the blessed Author of all our mercies, in condescending to manifest his holy presence, and causing it so to preside as to produce a general solemnity, tendering and contriting many minds, and comforting and rejoicing the upright in heart.

After the last mentioned meeting we proceeded on our journey, attending meetings at Stanford, Milan, and on first day the 26th of 7th month, the forenoon and afternoon meetings at Hudson. On second day we rested, on third day attended a meeting at Athens, on fourth day at Ghent, on fifth day ar Chatham, on sixth day at Nassau, and on seventh day evening we had a large meeting in Albany, held in their state-house, generally composed of people of other professions and inhabitants of the town, who behaved themselves very soberly, becoming the occasion. It was a solemn, and, I trust, a profitable opportunity, in which truth was raised into dominion ; and which in like manner was witnessed in all the foregoing meetings, the people coming together very freely and in great numbers, and a general solemnity prevailed over the assemblies from meeting to meeting. Surely it was the Lord's doing, and it was marvellous in our eyes ; witnessing that he had not left himself without an evidence of the truth in each mind, by which their understandings were opened to receive, and many of them to bear testimony to the doctrines delivered in those large solemn meetings.

From Albany we proceeded on first day morning, the 2d of 8th month, to Troy, and attended their forenoon and afternoon meetings. These were very large meetings. The first was held in Friends' meeting-house, but great numbers collected more than the house could contain : this induced Friends to accept the offer of a house belonging to the Episcopalians, which was not occupied, for the accommodation of the afternoon meeting. They gave the citizens an invitation to attend ; and although it was a very large building, yet it did not contain the people who assembled, many had to go away for want of room. This was likewise a highly favoured opportunity, in which truth reigned to the comfort and edification of the upright in heart, and to the general satisfaction of the assembled multitude. It was, in the estimation of Friends, the largest meeting which had ever been assembled on any occasion before in that city.

On second day we had an appointed meeting at Greenbush, a village on the east side of the river, opposite Albany. After this we proceeded on our journey about eleven miles to the town of Bethlehem, southwesterly from Albany. Here we lodged with our kind friend Thomas Rushmore, and attended a meeting in his house by appointment, on third day ; the few Friends of that place were privileged with holding a meeting for worship in this Friends' house. On fourth day we attended Friends' meeting at Stanton Hill ; and the three following days attended meetings at New Baltimore, Rensselaerville, and Oak Hill. These were all large satisfactory meetings.

On first day we were at Bern meeting in the morning ; and at the fourth hour in the afternoon had an appointed meeting at a village called Rensselaerville City, which was held in a large meeting-house belonging to the Methodist society. These were very large favoured meetings, in which the truths of the gospel went forth freely to the people, and appeared to be gladly and satisfactorily received by them; and I took leave of them with true peace of mind. On second day we had an appointed meeting at Middleburgh, much to our satisfaction. It was a very solemn instructive opportunity, and the people appeared to receive the word preached with much readiness of mind, and we left them with thankful hearts.

We proceeded on third day to Duanesburgh, in order to attend their quarterly meeting, which opened there the next day with a meeting of Ministers and Elders, and was a favoured opportunity. The meeting for discipline was large, and the business conducted in much harmony and condescension; and the public meeting the next day was very large; hundreds had to stand out of doors for want of room; and it was a highly favoured season, worthy of grateful remembrance.

From thence we proceeded to Charleston, and attended Friends' meeting there on first day, the 16th of 8th month. This was likewise a very large meeting, the largest, Friends said, that had ever been known there before. It was judged, that as many stood without for want of room, as the house contained; and it was a very solemn time, both within and without the doors. The divine canopy was felt to spread over the whole assembly, and we took leave of them with true peace of mind and thankfulness of heart, under a grateful sense of the unmerited favour.

On second day we rode to Utica; and the next day had an appointed meeting there at the eleventh hour. After this we proceeded to Bridgewater, and attended their fourth day meeting. These were not so large as in some other places, neither was there as much openness to receive our testimony as had generally been the case elsewhere. Our opposing Friends had filled their heads with so many strange reports, to which they had given credit without examination, by which their minds were so strongly prejudiced against me, that many in the compass of these two last meetings, were not willing to see me, nor hear any reasons given to show them their mistakes, and that the reports they had heard were altogether unfounded: however,

I was favoured to communicate the truth to those who attended, so that they generally went away fully satisfied, and I left them with peace of mind.

From this place we proceeded to Deruyter, having a meeting at Smyrna, on sixth day, in our way. On first day we attended Friends' meeting at Deruyter in the morning, and at the fifth hour in the afternoon had an appointed meeting in Deruyter village for the inhabitants generally, which was held in the Baptist meeting-house. These two meetings were very large, and they were highly favoured opportunities, in which truth was raised into dominion over all opposition; and we parted from them with true peace of mind, a rich reward for a faithful discharge of duty.

The next day, the 24th of 8th month, we proceeded to Sempronius, having a meeting by previous appointment on our way, in the town of Homer, at the eleventh hour. It was held in a large meeting-house belonging to the Methodist society, which they freely offered for the accommodation of the people, there being no Friends in the place. A very considerable number of the inhabitants attended, and behaved soberly, giving good attention to what was communicated, and went away apparently satisfied; and we parted with them under an humbling sense that the appointment, and our labour and service in this meeting, were owned by the Head of the Church. We arrived at Sempronius about sunset, and had an appointed meeting there the next day, held in Friends' meeting-house at the third hour in the afternoon. This was likewise a favoured opportunity, in which the power of truth went forth freely, humbling and contriting many minds.

After this we proceeded to Skeneateles, and put up with our kind friend William Willets, and rested here the next day. On fifth day we attended Friends' meeting at this place, as it came in course; and notice being given of our intention of attending it, the meeting was large. This was a very comforting satisfactory opportunity, apparently so to all present, although composed of many of the members of the varied societies of professed Christians common in our land, and divers of their ministers.

On sixth day we had an appointed meeting in the town of Auburn, at the third hour in the afternoon; and on seventh day, an appointed meeting at North-street, in Scipio. These meetings were largely attended, and, I trust, instructive profitable opportunities to many who were there. After the latter meeting, we visited several families of Friends, and took lodgings with our kind friend John Merritt.

The next day being the first of the week, and 30th of 8th month, we attended the meeting at South-street. The three following days we had meetings, by appointment, at Salmon Creek, Aurora, and Union Springs. These were all very large favoured meetings, in which the power of truth went forth freely, and appeared to have a ready entrance into the minds of the people in a very general manner, bringing a very comfortable solemnity over these large assemblies; and we took leave of them with thankful hearts and in true peace of mind.

We then proceeded on our journey to Junius, crossing Cayuga lake on the way. Here we had a meeting the next day, the fifth of the week, and 3d of 9th month; and the day following had an appointed meeting at Galen. These were highly favoured opportunities, in which the Lord's presence was felt to preside, reducing the assemblies into a very solemn state, and truth was raised into dominion over all, to the comfort and establishment of Friends on the ancient foundation, *the light within;* by the power and efficacy of which, our primitive worthies were gathered to be a people, from among the varied societies of professed Christians. For they were settled on that unshaken rock, which Jesus told his disciples he would build his Church upon, viz: the revelation of his heavenly Father, against which the gates of hell should never be able to prevail; and although the powers of the earth rose up against them, and used all their power and policy, both priests and people, to overthrow them, yet they were never permitted to prevail; for the Lord Jehovah, on whose almighty arm they had placed their entire trust and confidence for support and defence, delivered them from all their tribulations, and set them above their persecutors, and caused them to rejoice on the banks of deliverance. And he is the same God of power that he ever was, and a present helper in every needful time; and although many in the present day, who have left their first love, are rising up, and charging their fellow-professors with holding unsound doctrines, and are endeavouring, by unfounded and reproachful epithets, to destroy and undermine their religious and moral character among men, and have separated from their brethren, and set up separate meetings, giving them the names of the meetings of Friends; and in their usurped authority undertake to disown their fellow-members, who could not submit to their usurpation: yet all their formal disownments being altogether out of the order of the gospel, our meetings consider them of no effect.

From Galen we proceeded to South Farmington, and attended a meeting there on seventh day, at the third hour in the afternoon; and the next day being first day, we attended North Farmington meeting. The three following days we had meetings at Macedon, Palmyra, and Williamson. These were likewise large favoured meetings, in which truth was exalted over all, and we parted with them in true peace of mind, and proceeded on our journey to Rochester, and had a meeting on sixth day, by appointment: we also staid and attended their meeting on first day.

After this we proceeded to Wheatland, and had an appointed meeting there on second day, the 14th of 9th month; on third day we were at Henrietta, and on fourth day at Mendon. These were all favoured opportunities; the people's minds seemed to be open to receive us and our testimony with gladness. From this place we turned back through Farmington and Scipio, to Skeneateles, and attended a meeting by our appointment at a village about five miles from the village of Skeneateles, on the east side of the lake. On first day we attended Friends' meeting at Skeneateles; on second day we proceeded to Verona; and the next day had a meeting there, held in a meeting-house occupied by the Baptists, Friends' meeting-house being too small to contain the people who assembled.

The next day being fourth day, we proceeded to Utica, and had an appointed meeting in the evening. Here we remained over the next day, and attended Friends' meeting as it came in course. From this place we proceeded to Charleston, and attended their meeting on first day. These meetings, in like manner, were all solemn seasons; and, I trust, profitable and comfortable to many; and I left them with peace of mind. After the last meeting, we rode about thirteen miles, and lodged with our kind friend Zacheus Mead. The following day we proceeded on our journey to Newtown; and the next day attended Friends' meeting there. After this we proceeded to Saratoga, and attended Friends' preparative meeting at that place; and not feeling clear to leave it, we had an appointed meeting there the day after, of which public notice was given. It was very large; and it proved a highly favoured season; the Lord's presence was manifested for our help, and truth was raised into dominion, and ran like oil over the assembly. Many hearts were broken and contrited, and the upright in heart were made to rejoice for the unmerited favour.

The following day we had an appointed meeting at Milton. After this we proceeded to Galway, and lodged with our ancient friend Philip Macomber, who was in the ninety-first year of his age. Here we had a meeting on seventh day. The next day, the 4th of 10th month, we attended Providence meeting, which was very large. On second day we had an appointed meeting at Mayfield. These were all seasons of favour, particularly that at Providence, in which truth was exalted over all opposition, and many hearts were contrited; from a sense of which, our minds were bowed in reverence and humiliation before Him, who is the author of all our sure mercies.

We proceeded from Mayfield to Greenfield, and on fourth day attended Friends' monthly meeting at that place, which was composed of that and Milton preparative meetings. We had good satisfaction in sitting with our Friends, and in observing their commendable order, and the harmony and condescension manifest in conducting the affairs of the Church.

From thence we proceeded to Easton, and had an appointed meeting there on sixth day. On seventh day we were at Cambridge, on first day at White Creek, and on second day we rode to Danby, and the next day had a meeting there. These were all large and very solemn seasons, in which the great Head of the Church manifested his gracious presence, convicting and contriting many minds, and the upright in heart were edified. From Danby we proceeded to Granville, and had an appointed meeting there the next day, which was a large solemn opportunity. The day after we proceeded on our journey to Shoram, a town on the eastern shore of Lake Champlain. Here we had a meeting the next day with the few Friends of that place, and some of the neighbouring inhabitants. It was a comfortable opportunity, and we left them with peace of mind. We then rode to Ferrisburgh, and on first day, the 18th of 10th month, had a very large favoured meeting at that place. On second day we had an appointed meeting at Monkton. This was likewise a large favoured opportunity, in which truth reigned over all opposition, to the praise of his own excellent name, who is over all, God blessed for ever.

As I was somewhat unwell, we rested on third day with our kind friends Thomas and Rowland T. Robinson; and feeling my mind now clear from any further service in these parts, on fourth day we turned our faces homewards, and proceeded back to Shoram. On fifth day we had an appointed meeting in that village, principally for those not members of our society. Although the people came together in a negligent manner as respected the appointed time, yet they generally behaved orderly, and appeared to give good attention to what they heard; and my mouth was opened by Him who opens and none can shut, in a large effective testimony to the truths of the gospel; which brought a precious solemnity over the assembly, and they appeared to go away satisfied, and we left them with the answer of peace in our own minds.

The next day we proceeded on our journey to Granville, and from thence the following day to Queensbury. On first day, the 25th of 10th month, we attended Friends' meeting there;

and notice being given to the neighbouring inhabitants of our attendance, they came in until the house was filled, and a number had to stand without for want of room; and a blessed meeting we had, in which the power of truth ran as oil over the assembly, tendering and contriting many minds, and to the comfort and rejoicing of the upright in heart.

We had an appointed meeting on the following day at Moreau, which was a large favoured meeting. From thence we proceeded to Saratoga, and lodged with our kind friend Thomas Wilbur, and the next day Thomas accompanied us to Pittstown, where we had an appointed meeting on fourth day. This was truly an humbling season, in which truth was exalted over all; great brokenness and contrition of spirit were manifested among the people, and we were edified together in love, which inspired our minds with thanksgiving and gratitude for the unmerited favour.

From this place we proceeded to Troy, and as I was somewhat unwell, we rested the following day with our kind friend Isaac Merritt. On sixth day we proceeded on our journey to the neighbourhood of Hudson, and put up with our kind friend Thomas Wright; and seventh day being very rainy and inclement we continued here, and attended Hudson meeting on first day, which was a large satisfactory meeting.

On second day we proceeded on our journey to Stanford, and lodged with our kind friend John Hull. The two following days we attended the quarterly meeting at Nine Partners. At this place there is a very large body of Friends united together in gospel fellowship, and they were favoured to conduct the business of the quarterly meeting in harmony and condescension. The public meeting was very large. It was attended by a great number who were not in membership with us, and who behaved orderly, and it was indeed a very solemn edifying season.

After the close of this meeting, we returned that evening to Stanford, in order to attend the quarterly meeting at that place, which opened the next day with a meeting of Ministers and Elders. I attended this, and the following day, the meeting for discipline. A large number of the neighbouring inhabitants attended this meeting, and sat with Friends, until the partition between the men and women was closed. They behaved very orderly, and a precious solemnity spread over the assembly, and many essential doctrines of the gospel were opened to the people in the demonstration of the spirit, truth was raised into victory over all, and the upright in heart were edified and comforted. The meeting of Ministers and Elders was likewise a precious opportunity, in which comfort and encouragement were freely administered to them.

From Stanford we proceeded on our journey to Cornwall, crossing the Hudson river on our way. We arrived here on seventh day evening, and attended their meeting on first day, the 8th of 11th month. This meeting was large, and a truly baptizing season, in which many hearts were humbled and contrited, and truth reigned over all; thanks be to God, who giveth us the victory, nothing due to man.

The two following days we had meetings appointed at the Lower and Upper Clove. These were well attended, and, I trust, profitable edifying seasons to many present. They were composed of people of various professions, conditions, and states; yet all appeared to be brought down and subjected by the solemnizing influence and power of truth, that reigned victoriously over all. Surely it was the Lord's doing, and it was marvellous in our eyes. These meetings closed my labour and exercise in the gospel, to Friends and others in the yearly meetings of Philadelphia, Baltimore, Ohio, Indiana, and New-York, as expressed in a certificate of unity and concurrence, given me by the monthly meeting of Jericho, and quarterly meeting of Westbury.

From the latter meeting we proceeded the next day directly to New-York, where we arrived on fourth day evening. The day after we attended Friends' meeting at Hester-street, it being their usual meeting day; and a marriage being accomplished at the close of it, it was larger than usual, as many of the neighbouring inhabitants attended. Way opened for me to declare the truth among them, to the peace of my own mind, and to the mutual comfort and encouragement of the upright in heart.

I rested here until first day, and attended Friends' meeting at Rose-street in the morning, and that held at Hester-street in the afternoon. They were both very large solemn meetings. On second day evening I had an appointed meeting at Brooklyn, likewise a large and very favoured season. In all of these meetings the word preached had free course, and I had, in the openings of truth, to declare to these large mixed assemblages many things concerning the kingdom of God; and the only sure way by which an admittance into his kingdom of peace and joy may be obtained by the children of men.

The foregoing meetings were times of favour, and as a seal from the hand of our gracious and never-failing Helper, to the labour and travail which he has led me into, and enabled me to perform, for the promotion of his great and noble cause of truth and righteousness in the earth, as set forth in the foregoing account, and not suffering any weapon formed against me to prosper. "This is the heritage of the servants of the Lord, and their righteousness is of me, saith the Lord." For all these unmerited favours and mercies, in deep humiliation my soul doth magnify the Lord, and return thanksgiving and glory to his great and excellent name; for his mercy endureth for ever.

On third day we proceeded homeward, and attended Westbury monthly meeting on fourth day, on our way. After this I rode home, and found my family well, to our mutual rejoicing; and we greeted each other with thankful hearts for the unmerited favour.

We travelled in this journey nearly fifteen hundred miles.

ELIAS HICKS.

E. H. here closed his Journal, and signed his name; after which he lived a little more than two months.

APPENDIX.

LETTER TO HUGH JUDGE, OF OHIO.

Jericho, 2d mo. 14*th*, 1830.

DEAR HUGH,

THY very acceptable letter of the 21st ultimo, was duly received, and read with interest, tending to excite renewed sympathetic, and mutual fellow-feeling; and brought to my remembrance the cheering salutation of the blessed Jesus, our holy and perfect pattern and example, to his disciples, viz: " Be of good cheer, I have overcome the world." By which he assured his disciples that, by walking in the same pathway of self-denial and the cross which he trod to blessedness, they might also overcome the world; as nothing has ever enabled any rational being, in any age of the world, to overcome the spirit of the world, which lieth in wickedness, but the cross of Christ.

Some may query, what is the cross of Christ? To these I answer, it is the perfect law of God written on the tablet of the heart, and in the heart of every rational creature, in such indeli ble characters that all the power of mortals cannot erase nor obliterate. Neither is there any power or means given or dispensed to the children of men, but this inward law and light by which the true and saving knowledge of God can be obtained. And by this inward law and light, all will be either justified or condemned, and all be made to know God for themselves, and be left without excuse, agreeably to the prophecy of Jeremiah, and the corroborating testimony of Jesus in his last counsel and command to his disciples, not to depart from Jerusalem until they should receive power from on high; assuring them that they should receive power, when they had received the pouring forth of the spirit upon them, which would qualify them to bear witness of him in Judea, Jerusalem, Samaria, and to the uttermost parts of the earth; which was verified in a marvellous manner on the day of Pentecost, when thousands were converted to the Christian faith in one day. By which it is evident, that nothing but this inward light and law, as it is heeded and obeyed, ever did, or ever can make a true and real Christian and child of God. And until the professors of Christianity agree to lay aside all their non-essentials in religion, and rally to this unchangeable foundation and standard of truth, wars and fightings, confusion and error will prevail, and the angelic song cannot be heard in our land, that of "glory to God in the highest, and on earth peace and good will to men." But when all nations are made willing to make this inward law and light, the rule and standard of all their faith and works, then we shall be brought to know and believe alike, that there is but one Lord, one faith, and but one baptism; one God and Father, that is above all, through all, and in all; and then will all those glorious and consoling prophecies, recorded in the scriptures of truth be fulfilled. Isaiah ii. 4, " He," the Lord, " shall judge among the nations, and rebuke many people: and they shall beat their swords into ploughshares and their spears into pruning hooks: nation shall not lift up sword against nation; neither shall they learn war any more." Isaiah xi. " The wolf also shall dwell with the lamb, and the leopard shall lie down with the kid; and the calf, and the young lion, and the fatling together; and a little child shall lead them. And the cow and the bear shall feed; their young ones shall lie down together; and the lion shall eat straw like the ox. And the sucking child shall play on the hole of the asp, and the weaned child put his hand on the cockatrice's den. They shall not hurt nor destroy in all my holy mountain: for the earth," that is our earthly tabernacles, "shall be full of the knowledge of the Lord, as the waters cover the sea."

These scripture testimonies give a true and correct description of the gospel state, and no rational being can be a real Christian and true disciple of Christ, until he comes to know all these things verified in his own experience, as every man and woman has more or less of all those different animal propensities and passions in their nature; and they predominate and bear rule, and are the source and fountain from whence all wars, and every evil work proceed, and will continue as long as man remains in his first nature, and is governed by his animal spirit and propensities which constitute the natural man, which Paul tells us " receiveth not the things of the spirit of God, for they are foolishness unto him, neither can he know them, because they are spiritually discerned." This corroborates the declaration of Jesus to Nicodemus, " that, except a man be born again, he cannot see the kingdom of God;" for " that which is born of the flesh is flesh, and that which is born of the spirit is spirit." Here Jesus assures us, beyond all doubt, that nothing but spirit can either see or enter into the kingdom of God; and this confirms Paul's doctrine, that " as many as are led by the spirit of God are the sons of God," and "joint heirs with Christ." And Jesus assures us, by his declaration to his disciples, John xiv. 16, 17, " If ye love me, keep my commandments; and I will pray the Father, and he shall give you another comforter, that he may abide with you for ever, even the spirit of truth, whom the world cannot receive;" that is, men and women in their natural state, who have not given up to be led by this spirit of truth, that leads and guides into all truth ; " because they see him not, neither do they know him, but ye know him, for he dwelleth with you, and shall be in you." And as these give up to be wholly led and guided by him, the new birth is brought forth in them, and they witness the truth of another testimony of Paul's, even that of being created anew in Christ Jesus unto good works, which God had fore ordained that all his new-born children should walk in them and thereby show forth by their fruits and good works, that they were truly the children of God, born of his spirit, and taught of him; agreeably to the testimony of the prophet, that "the children of the Lord are all taught of the Lord, and in righteousness they are established, and great is the peace of his children." And nothing can make them afraid that man can do unto them ; as saith the prophet in his appeal to Jehovah, " Thou wilt keep him

56

in perfect peace, whose mind is staid on thee, because he trusteth in thee." Therefore, let every one that loves the truth, for God is truth,"trust in the Lord for ever, for in the Lord Jehovah there is everlasting strength."

I write these things to thee, not as though thou didst not know them, but as a witness to thy experience, as " two are better than one, and a threefold cord is not quickly broken."

I will now draw to a close, with just adding, for thy encouragement, be of good cheer, for no new thing has happened to us ; for it has ever been the lot of the righteous to pass through many trials and tribulations, in their passage to that glorious, everlasting, peaceful, and happy abode, where all sorrow and sighing come to an end—the value of which is above all price ; for when we have given all that we have and can give, and suffered all that we can suffer, it is still infinitely below its real value.   And if we are favoured to gain an inheritance in that blissful and peaceful abode, " where the wicked cease from troubling, and the weary are at rest," we must ascribe it all to the unmerited mercy and loving-kindness of our heavenly Father, who remains to be God over all, blessed for ever.

I will now conclude ; and in the fulness of brotherly love to thee and thine, in which my family unite, subscribe thy affectionate friend,

ELIAS HICKS.

To HUGH JUDGE.

Please present my love to all my friends, as way opens.

The writing of the preceding letter was the last act in the life of this eminent individual, and the attentive reader will not fail to regard it as an act of peculiar interest.   It was as a seal to the labours of a long life, and evinced the abiding and lively efficacy of that internal principle which he had uniformly sought as his director and preserver.   But the work of this faithful servant was now accomplished ; " the silver cord was loosed," and that spirit which had been so diligently active in the service of its Divine Master, was now to rest from its labours, and to reap its reward. Just when he had finished the letter alluded to, he was attacked with a paralytic affection, under the effects of which he became gradually weaker; but his mind remained established in great peace and serenity, and on the 27th of 2d month, 1830, he calmly expired, aged nearly eighty-two years.

Of the character of this extraordinary man, it is not necessary now to speak. The preceding pages describe the nature of his engagements; and an estimate may thence be formed, of the fervency of his spirit, and the brightness of his example. In his general deportment, and in the expression of his countenance, there was a remarkable union of gentleness and dignity, indicating the habitual benevolence and solemnity of his feelings; and his public communications were accompanied with a power and an authority which demonstrated the purity of the source from whence they were derived. The promotion of spiritual holiness and practical righteousness in the earth, were the objects of his constant solicitude ; and he endeavoured, through divine assistance, to exemplify in his own daily experience, the comprehensive command of the prophet, " To do justly, to love mercy, and to walk humbly with thy God."

THE MEMORIAL OF JERICHO MONTHLY MEETING OF
FRIENDS CONCERNING OUR ANCIENT FRIEND ELIAS
HICKS.

We believe the example exhibited in the life and religious
exercise of this our beloved Friend, is eminently calculated to
set forth the efficacy and sufficiency of that divine grace, which,
when believed in and obeyed, bringeth salvation.

He was born in the town of Hempstead, Queens county,
Long Island, state of New-York, the 19th day of the 3d month,
1748. His parents' names were John and Martha Hicks. At
the age of seventeen he was placed as an apprentice to learn the
trade of a carpenter ; on the expiration of his term, he returned
to his father, with whom he lived until the time of his marriage,
which took place about the twenty-third year of his age, to Jemima, daughter of Jonathan and Elizabeth Seaman, of Jericho, in
said county, where he resided the remainder of his life.

From his own account we learn, that when very young, he
was favoured with clear and powerful impressions of divine
grace operating on his mind as a reprover for evil, which not
duly regarding, and being naturally of a lively and active disposition, he associated with those who indulged in the vanities
and amusements too common in the world, though mostly in
things deemed innocent by the generality of mankind. But the
gift of divine grace, which was so early manifested, did not forsake him, though he often strove to stifle its convictions, but
followed him in judgment and in mercy, until a willingness
was wrought in him to give up all to follow Christ, in the
regeneration. On one occasion, when preparing to join in the
dance, and surrounded by his jovial companions, the pure witness
rose so powerfully in his mind, and so clearly set before him the
evil tendency of the course he was pursuing, that he reasoned
not with flesh and blood, but gave up to the heavenly vision,
and in deep contrition and prostration of soul, entered into cove

nant with the God of his life, that if he would be pleased to furnish him with strength, he would endeavour not to be again found in the like disobedience; which covenant, through mercy, he was favoured to keep inviolate. Thus, submitting to the purifying operation of the Holy Ghost and fire, he was, in due time, qualified and called to declare to others what God had done for his soul; under the divine anointing, he was enabled to unfold the truths of the gospel, in the demonstration of the spirit and with power. And, through a faithful obedience to that which had begun the good work in him, he became an eminent instrument in the Lord's hand, for the promotion of truth and righteousness in the earth.

He first appeared in the ministry, about the twenty-seventh year of his age, and from this period, his time and talents were devoted to the cause of his Divine Master, labouring diligently for its advancement, not only at home, and in his own neighbourhood, but in most parts of this continent where there are settlements of Friends, and also, in many places amongst those not of our society. In declaring what he believed to be the counsel of God, he was bold and fearless, and his ministry, though unadorned with the embellishments of human learning, was clear and powerful. In argument he was strong and convincing, and his appeals to the experience and convictions of his hearers, were striking and appropriate. He saw, and deeply lamented the great departure of many in the society of Friends, from that plainness and simplicity, and that godly sincerity, which characterized it in the beginning. Hence he felt himself called upon, under the influence of the love of the gospel, to admonish his brethren in religious profession, to rally to the ancient standard, the light of truth manifested in the heart, and to follow no man any further, than he should be found a follower of Christ. He assailed the strong holds of superstition and bigotry with great boldness, which sometimes alarmed the timid, and roused the prejudices of others. Yet to the candid inquirer and sincere seeker after truth, he breathed the language of encouragement, of consolation and of comfort. His great and primary concern was to draw the minds of the people to practical righteousness—from all outward dependance to the sure foundation, the rock of ages, the spirit of truth, the comforter, "Christ within, the hope of glory." He generally corroborated the doctrines which he preached, by appropriate references to the testimonies and experience of those who have gone before us, as recorded in the scriptures of truth. Through the efficacy of that power which enabled him to say, "By the grace of God, I am what I am," many were convinced of the truth, through his ministry.

So full and pointed was his testimony against a hireling ministry, which he held to be, not only in direct violation of the great gospel precept "Freely ye have received, freely give," but fraught with incalculable injury to the best interests of mankind, that he sometimes gave offence to those, whose minds were strongly biased in its favour. Yet such was the general kindness and benevolence of his character, that he did not willingly give offence to any. While he condemned the practice, he was kind and charitable to those, who, through the influence of education and early prejudice, differed from him on this subject. Such was his concern that his examples should comport with his testimony, that he was scrupulously careful to defray his own expenses when travelling as a minister.

When his meetings were attended by a large concourse of persons of various denominations, the solemnity and stillness that prevailed, were often very remarkable, reminding us of the testimony of primitive Friends, that the power accompanying their gospel labours so overshadowed the assemblies, that truth reigned over all. Being deeply sensible of his own inability to promote the cause of truth and righteousness, without divine aid, he was engaged to dwell near the fountain of light and life, and to minister as this opened and gave ability. He was indeb' an example of Christian humility, and eminently preserved from being elated by the applause of men, or depressed by their censure. Many were the exercises which he felt on account of the evils which abound in the world, and the oppressed condition of the African race excited his tenderest sympathy. Their cause engaged his earnest solicitude for the greater part of his life, and he was often led feelingly and powerfully to advocate it. We believe that many were convinced, through his labours, of the cruelty and injustice of holding them in bondage. He bore for many years a faithful testimony against slavery, by carefully abstaining from the use of articles which he believed to be produced by the labour of slaves. When at home, and not engaged in services more strictly of a religious character, he laboured diligently with his own hands, believing it the duty of all to be usefully employed in obtaining the necessaries of life; and when acquired, he acted as a steward under the direction of the bountiful Giver, being restrained from using them for selfish gratification. In the various relations of life he was a bright example, worthy of imitation: he was an affectionate husband; and as a father and guardian, his concern for the religious and moral education of his children, and those placed under his care, was very great, that they might be brought up in the fear and admonition of the Lord. For these ends he exercised the authority of a parent with firmness, but in much tenderness and love. His tender sympathy was excited for the poor, to whom he was a kind and liberal friend, often supplying their necessities. It may be truly said of him, that he was a man fearing God and hating covetousness. He was a peace-maker, endeavouring, both by precept and example, to promote harmony in his neighbourhood; and in this respect he was very useful, his Christian deportment having gained the confidence and affection of his neighbours. He was very diligent in the attendance of religious meetings, and often led to encourage others, assuring them, from his own experience, that none could expect to increase in the divine life, until they considered that important duty paramount to temporal concerns: he was also conspicuously useful in supporting the discipline of the society.

At a very advanced age he continued to labour in the Lord's vineyard, with the same fervent zeal, the same dedication of heart, for which he had been so eminently distinguished in the earlier stages of his life; and in the exercise of his gift in the ministry, he was as lively, clear, and cogent, as at any former period. Having been long taught in the school of Christ, and being deeply experienced in the things which concern our eternal well-being, he was well qualified to administer counsel and encouragement to others; and was frequently led, feelingly and forcibly, to impress upon the minds of the rising generation, the importance and necessity of early attention to the inward discoveries of divine light; cautioning them not to rest in the tradition of their fathers, but to walk by the same rule, and to mind the same thing, which has led the righteous in all ages safely through time; nor to depend upon the teachings of men, for that knowledge which brings life and immortality to light in the soul; declaring that faithfulness and obedience to the influence of divine grace in their own hearts, could only qualify them to advance the standard of truth and righteousness in the earth. His dedication to the law of the spirit of life in Christ Jesus, his firmness in the support of those testimonies which he felt himself called upon to maintain, and his plainness in reproving unfaithfulness in others, and bearing testimony against every appearance of evil, gave offence to some; yet none of these things moved him, neither counted he his life dear to himself, so that he might finish his course with joy, and the ministry he had received, to testify the gospel of the grace of God; and we are persuaded that his feet were established upon that rock, against which the powers of darkness shall never be able to prevail. He was favoured, in times of the greatest trial, to experience the truth of the prophetic declaration, "Thou wilt keep him in perfect peace, whose mind is stayed on thee, because he trusteth in thee."

He was favoured with a good constitution, and in the decline of life, was still actively engaged in the concerns of society, and industriously employed in his temporal avocations.

His mental powers continued strong and vigorous to the end of his labours. His comprehensive and energetic mind was apparently but very little impaired by the revolution of more than fourscore years. Within the last two years of his life, he travelled extensively in the work of the ministry.

When he was eighty years of age, he opened in this monthly meeting a concern to pay a religious visit to Friends and others in some parts of the yearly meetings of New-York, Philadelphia,

Baltimore, Virginia, Ohio, and Indiana. He obtained a certificate of unity and concurrence from this monthly meeting, endorsed by Westbury quarterly meeting. In this visit he experienced many deep probations on account of the unsettled state of society. "For the divisions of Reuben, there were great searchings of heart." Yet he was enabled to accomplish his visit to the southern and western yearly meetings, agreeably to his prospect. Shortly after his return from this journey, he met with a severe affliction in the loss of his beloved companion, with whom he had lived in near union and affection for fifty-eight years.

In the summer of 1829, in pursuance of his prospect as before mentioned, he visited most of the meetings of Friends in the northern and western parts of our yearly meeting. His gospel labours, during these arduous and extensive visits, were productive of satisfaction and peace to his own mind, and were peculiarly seasonable and acceptable to his friends, as appears by numerous certificates of near unity, which he produced to this meeting on his return home; after which, he attended all the meetings of Friends in the city of New-York, and on this island, very much to their satisfaction. In these last visits, as heretofore, his gospel labours were remarkably clear and powerful, and we trust are profitably remembered by many. He seemed renewedly concerned on account of the deviations from that plainness and simplicity into which the truth would lead; and expressed the comfort it would be to him to see a reformation in these respects.

On first day morning, the 14th of 2d month last, he was engaged in his room, writing to a friend, until a little after ten o'clock, when he returned to that occupied by the family, apparently just attacked by a paralytic affection, which nearly deprived him of the use of his right side, and of the power of speech. Being assisted to a chair near the fire, he manifested by signs, that the letter which he had just finished, and which had been dropped by the way, should be taken care of; and on its being brought to him, appeared satisfied, and manifested a desire that all should sit down and be still, seemingly sensible that his labours were brought to a close, and only desirous of quietly waiting the final change. The solemn composure at this time manifest in his countenance, was very impressive, indicating that he was sensible the time of his departure was at hand, and that the prospect of death brought no terrors with it.   During his last illness, his mental faculties were occasionally obscured, yet he was at times enabled to give satisfactory evidence to those around him, that all was well, and that he felt nothing in his way.

His dependance had long been upon that arm of power alone, which supported him under every probation, and near the conclusion of the letter above alluded to, he thus expressed himself: "And if we are favoured to gain an inheritance in that blissful and peaceful abode, where the wicked cease from troubling, and the weary are at rest, we must ascribe it all to the unmerited mercy and loving kindness of our heavenly Father, who remains to be God over all, blessed for ever."   He continued gradually to decline until the evening of the 27th, when he quietly passed from the trials of time, we doubt not, to receive the reward of the righteous.

His funeral took place on fourth day, the 3d of 3d month.   It was attended by a large concourse of Friends and others, and a solid meeting was held on the occasion; after which, his remains were interred in Friends' burial ground at this place.

Signed by direction and on behalf of Jericho Monthly Meeting, held 4th month, 15th, 1830.

> WILLET ROBBINS, } *Clerks.*
> ABIGAIL HICKS,   }

At Westbury Quarterly Meeting, held at Westbury, the 22d of 4th month, 1830,

A memorial of Jericho Monthly Meeting, concerning our late beloved friend Elias Hicks, was produced and read, and being satisfactory to the meeting, was approved, directed to be endorsed, and forwarded to the Meeting for Sufferings.

Signed on behalf of the meeting by

> STEPHEN UNDERHILL, } *Clerks.*
> SARAH COCK,   }

At a Meeting for Sufferings held in New-York, 5th month, 26th, 1830,

The memorial from Jericho Monthly Meeting, endorsed by 'he Quarterly Meeting of Westbury, concerning our beloved friend Elias Hicks, deceased, being deliberately attended to, was approved and directed to the Yearly Meeting.

Extract from minutes of said meeting.

JOHN BARROW, Clerk.

At the Yearly Meeting of New-York, held by adjournments, from the 24th of the 5th month, to the 28th of the same inclusive, 1830,

A testimony of Jericho Monthly Meeting, endorsed by West bury Quarterly Meeting, and approved by the Meeting for Sufferings, concerning our ancient beloved friend Elias Hicks, was read and approved. Much solicitude was felt and expressed that it may, with the remembrance of his exemplary life, encourage us to walk by the same rule, and to mind the same thing, which enabled him to become so eminently useful in his day and generation.

SAMUEL MOTT,   } Clerks.
ANN M. COMSTOCK, }